Bill Clinton

Bill Clinton

New Gilded Age President

Patrick J. Maney

UNIVERSITY PRESS OF KANSAS

Published by the University Press of Kansas (Lawrence, Kansas 66045), which was organized by the Kansas Board of Regents and is operated and funded by Emporia State University, Fort Hays State University, Kansas State University, Pittsburg State University, the University of Kansas, and Wichita State University

Library of Congress Cataloging-in-Publication Data

Maney, Patrick J., 1946– author.

Bill Clinton : New Gilded Age president / Patrick J. Maney.

pages cm

Includes bibliographical references and index.

ISBN 978-0-7006-2194-1 (cloth : alk. paper) — ISBN 978-0-7006-2199-6 (ebook)

1. Clinton, Bill, 1946– 2. Presidents—United States—Biography. 3. United States—Politics and government—1993–2001. I. Title.

E886.M27 2016

973.929092—dc23

[B]

2015035636

British Library Cataloguing-in-Publication Data is available.

Printed in the United States of America

10 9 8 7 6 5 4 3 2 1

The paper used in this publication is recycled and contains 30 percent postconsumer waste. It is acid free and meets the minimum requirements of the American National Standard for Permanence of Paper for Printed Library Materials Z39.48-1992.

In memory of Bob and Gay Zieger

CONTENTS

Photo gallery follows page 140.

ACKNOWLEDGMENTS

This study would not have been possible without the help and encouragement of many. My greatest debt is to Lawrence Powell of Tulane University—friend, colleague, and sounding board for thirty-five years. He reads just about everything I write and always makes it better. Everybody should be so lucky.

I am grateful to Fred Woodward for inviting me to write about Clinton. He has an inexhaustible store of patience as well as an unerring knack for knowing when to prod and when to reassure. In a transformative era in publishing, his leadership at the press has been nothing short of remarkable. Insofar as the press is concerned at least, nothing's the matter with Kansas. Thanks are also due to the press's managing editor, Kelly Chrisman Jacques, and to copyeditor Martha Whitt. Herbert Reagan at the Clinton Library in Little Rock was enormously helpful in the selection of photographs.

Kent Germany of the University of South Carolina read an early draft of the manuscript and improved it immeasurably, as did Burton I. Kaufman, whose meticulous scholarship I have long admired. My Boston College colleague Seth Jacobs read the chapters on foreign policy and saved me from numerous errors of fact and judgment. I can't thank them enough for their help.

Longtime friends and former colleagues Clarence Mohr, Robert Hunter, Dan Carter, Patricia Sullivan, and Bill and Bobbie Malone have been steady providers of useful ideas and timely encouragement. In addition, Clarence Mohr gave me an opportunity to try out some of my ideas by inviting me to speak at the University of South Alabama, where he is history department chair extraordinaire.

Here at Boston College a smart and dedicated group of undergraduates provided invaluable research assistance: David Quinn, Gregory Manne, Brady Conley, Matthew Wagner, Alexandra Laham, and Giancarlo Ambrogio. They proved particularly adept at tracking down and analyzing sources that had eluded me.

I am grateful to economists Laura D'Andrea Tyson, Alicia Munnell, and Robert Murphy for helping me to understand "Clintonomics" as well as many other aspects of the administration in which they served. Sidney Blumenthal, whose *Clinton Wars* remains a major work to be reckoned with, generously offered encouragement and advice. A conversation with the late John Hope Franklin, who spearheaded President Clinton's Initiative on Race, deepened my understanding of an underappreciated and misunderstood episode of the Clinton presidency.

Two years ago, Robert and Gay Zieger died just months apart from one another. Bob was my academic adviser and first history teacher in college. I became a historian because of him. For my wife, Elaine (also a Bob student), and me, the Ziegers were dear friends, mentors, and role models for over forty years. Hardly a day goes by that we don't think about them. It is to their memory that we dedicate this book.

I owe my deepest appreciation to family. Sons Kevin, John, and Thomas, and Kevin's wife, Alli, are constant sources of joy and inspiration. As with everything I've ever done, Elaine has brought a sharp eye and keen intelligence to bear on this project. She is the anchor of our family—an inexhaustible source of love, optimism, and common sense.

Bill Clinton

INTRODUCTION: BILL CLINTON AND
THE NEW GILDED AGE

Bill Clinton's quest for the presidency coincided with America's re-discovery of the Gilded Age, that late-nineteenth-century era unforgettably christened by Mark Twain and Charles Dudley Warner. It was a nation glittery on the outside but cheap and tawdry beneath the surface.[1] Before the 1990s, the Gilded Age was largely of interest to history buffs and devotees of writers like Twain, Edith Wharton, and O. Henry. For four dollars visitors could take a guided tour of "Millionaires' Row," the stretch of Fifth Avenue between 78th and 91st Streets in New York City that was once the habitat of the Vanderbilts, Whitneys, and Mellons. Or they could visit "The Breakers," the Vanderbilt's seventy-room Italian villa in Newport, Rhode Island, where Gilded Age reenactors rode the grounds in ornate, horse-drawn coaches.[2]

But just as Clinton was embarking on his presidential campaign in the early nineties, interest in those gilded decades took a more serious turn. Commentators began noting disturbing similarities with their own times: unsettling change, growing income inequality, conspicuous consumption, racial and ethnic tensions, government largesse for the rich and well born. And in politics: scandals—real and trumped up—and partisan warfare out of proportion to the actual differences between the parties. If the roaring nineties had Millionaires' Row with its ornate mansions, the 1990s had McMansions inside gated communities. It was enough to constitute a new Gilded Age. "Too many stretch limousines in Manhattan, too many yacht jams off Newport Beach and too many fur coats in Aspen," onetime conservative activist Kevin Phillips complained in 1990, noting that during the 1980s alone the number of millionaires had tripled, while median family income had budged hardly at all.[3]

In both ages, economic forces were in the driver's seat, presidents and politicians along for the ride. "There is no other period in the nation's history," historian Richard Hofstadter wrote of the original Gilded Age, "when politics seems so completely dwarfed by economic changes, none in which the life of the country rests so completely in the hands of the industrial entrepreneur. The industrialists of the Gilded Age [here he's thinking of the Carnegies, Rockefellers, and J. P. Morgans] were . . . men of heroic audacity and magnificent exploitative talents—shrewd, energetic, aggressive, rapacious, domineering, insatiable. . . . From them the era took its tone and color."[4] "Change the industrial references to high tech," wrote columnist E. J. Dionne, Jr., "and Hofstadter's description of the late 19th century sounds like a brilliant evocation of our own 1980s and '90s."[5] Any number of commentators have since extended the Gilded Age analogy well into the twenty-first century to the point that it's almost become a cliché.[6]

The parallels between the two eras were not lost on Bill Clinton. He returned to the first Gilded Age time after time, as well as to the Progressive Era that followed. He believed those times were most like his own, with useful lessons for the present.

To Clinton, the defining characteristic of both ages was change—change so vast and far-reaching, it happened only a few times in American history. But when it did happen, the way people lived and worked was changed forever. Clinton employed the argot of social science to capture the change he had in mind: it was, he said, nothing less than a "paradigm shift." The Gilded Age was when agrarian America morphed into an urban industrial behemoth. A century later Clinton observed: "We're going from the industrial age to an information-technology age, from the Cold War to a global society." The results were uncannily similar. He spotlighted the "enormous changes in the way people work and live." There has been, he said, "a large increase in immigration and an increasing diversity in America, with all the tensions that that brings. There are vast fortunes being made—people are having opportunities they never dreamed of. But a lot of people have been dislocated." Clinton had a more nuanced view of the Gilded Age than many. There was more to it than robber barons and huddled masses. It was an age of grand inventions like the electric light, telephone, phonograph, automobile, and motion picture; of medical and scientific breakthroughs; of new and interesting ways of understanding human behavior. Clinton also acknowledged important differences between the two ages. The middle class of his time was both larger and protected by a social safety net that had been practically nonexistent a century earlier. On the other hand, Americans were less inclined to look to Washington for a solution to their problems than their counterparts in the late nineteenth and early twentieth centuries.[7]

What did Clinton learn from the past that might be of use to the present? Mainly, that the Industrial Revolution had been worth it, but not at the cost of children working sixty hours a week, women being exploited in the workplace, or small businesses being crushed by monopolies. Eventually government had to step in to ameliorate hardships and level the playing field. In his own time, it needed to upgrade education and job training so that American workers could compete in a global economy. It needed to reform health care so that Americans wouldn't be hamstrung by spiraling medical costs. And it needed to help the country surmount racial disparities so that it might be unburdened by the divisions of the past.

At the same time, Clinton was convinced that there was no holding back change. A fundamental transformation was under way, and the sooner Americans accepted it and adapted to it, the sooner they would enjoy its benefits.

Interviewed by the editors of the *Atlantic* midway through his presidency, Clinton expressed hope the United States could get through the current transformation "more quickly" and with "less disruption" than a century earlier. His *Atlantic* interviewers weren't quite so sure. "He was reassuring and upbeat," they observed, "but beneath his action plan seemed to be a fatalistic awareness that this transition would be wrenching, like the one a century ago that accompanied the rise of unions and mass production."[8]

Historians now take the presidents of the first Gilded Age more seriously than they once did. No longer are the White House occupants from Rutherford B. Hayes to William McKinley treated as interchangeable nonentities. Some Gilded Age presidents, it's clear, were abler and more influential than others. Even so, most historians would agree that none left an indelible mark on his time and place or significantly altered the course of American history. None exerted the influence of a Washington or a Jefferson, a Jackson or a Lincoln. They "are largely forgotten men," writes one historian, "because so little was expected of them."[9]

The presidents of the new Gilded Age—from Gerald Ford through Bill Clinton to Barack Obama—are a different breed. They've been far more engaged and certainly haven't suffered from low expectations.

Indeed, since Franklin Roosevelt, they've been expected to perform miracles. Still, they have much in common with their late-nineteenth-century counterparts. Modern presidents have been more market-oriented than most of their immediate predecessors—more supportive of deregulation and more inclined to elevate supply over demand as the engine of economic growth. Economically speaking, Bill Clinton was closer to Jimmy Carter, Ronald Reagan, and the Bushes—father and son—than to Harry Truman, John F. Kennedy, Lyndon Johnson, or even Richard Nixon. Of Clinton's deregulatory policies, a lobbyist representing small banks said, "Teddy Roosevelt is turning over in his grave."[10] "Ever since Bill Clinton came to office," wrote *New York Times* reporter David Sanger, "he has done more for the Fortune 500 than virtually any other President in this century." Sanger was talking only about the first term. There was more to come.[11]

So far, none of the presidents of Clinton's cohort has achieved the distinction or exerted the influence of a half-dozen or so of their predecessors. There were no Roosevelts—Theodore or Franklin—Woodrow Wilsons, Harry Trumans, or Lyndon Johnsons in their ranks. It's not their fault. Despite the public's fixation on the White House—and fixation it was—the flywheel of contemporary history was powered in the private, not public, realm. Clinton wanted to be a Theodore Roosevelt or a Woodrow Wilson. But the new Gilded Age lasted too long, and he came too early to fulfill his wish.

As his presidency neared an end, Clinton appeared to reconcile himself to a less exalted place in history than he had hoped. He began to express a certain kinship with his Gilded Age brethren. He extolled their forgotten virtues. According to one reporter, Clinton told aides that Grover Cleveland and Rutherford B. Hayes "were underappreciated as progressive reformers who tried to limit the power of big business and undercut the nativism and class hatreds of their age—stances he obviously considers parallel to his own." (The reporter also noted that Clinton stopped talking about Cleveland openly after he learned that his portly predecessor's nickname was "Big Jumbo.")[12]

Given the odds against him—sweeping forces largely beyond his control, no mandate, a weak political base, perhaps the most relentless opposition faced by any president since FDR, and no great crisis around which to mobilize public opinion—Bill Clinton racked up notable successes. Anyone even vaguely familiar with the history of health care could have predicted the long odds facing the Clintons' proposed reform. But who could have predicted his success in refashioning the Democratic Party along centrist lines? Or his ability to neutralize hot-button issues like crime and welfare with which Republicans had been bludgeoning Democrats for decades? And who, in the aftermath of the 1994 Republican Party takeover of Congress, could have imagined that Clinton would not only win reelection but also finish out his second term with the highest performance ratings of any modern president? A vigorous deployment of executive power and rule-making authority allowed Clinton to put on the books an array of measures, from health-care expansion to gun control, that stood no chance of getting through Congress after the Republicans seized control in 1994. Clinton could also boast prudent stewardship of the economy, although the lion's share of the credit for the economic boom of the nineties would have to go to the emergence of the computer and telecommunications industries and of the Internet.

Clinton opened the presidency to American popular culture in ways that made it more relevant to most people's lives. As *New York Times* reporter Todd Purdum put it, "Clinton made the modern presidency more understandable and approachable, and eliminated a substantial measure of the distance that had insulated the office and its occupants."[13] That he did so in the face of persistent antigovernment sentiment is even more remarkable.

The first baby boomer to occupy the White House, almost no matter who it was, was bound to alter public perceptions of the office. Yet it would be hard to imagine others of Clinton's generation connecting with popular culture as effectively as he did. It's hard to imagine Al Gore, George W. Bush, or Newt Gingrich playing a saxophone rendition of "Heartbreak Hotel" on Arsenio Hall's talk show; doing an Elvis impersonation on *Imus in the Morning*; wolfing down Big Macs on the way back from jogging; identifying his underwear preferences on MTV (briefs); or inspiring a best-selling novel, *Primary Colors*, a film of the same name, and the enormously popular television series *The West Wing*.

Every so often a president has to refurbish the image of the presidency to keep it relevant. Roosevelt did it in the 1930s; Kennedy did it in the sixties; Reagan, with his star quality and image consciousness, did it in the eighties. And Clinton did it in the nineties. But there is a world of difference between refurbishing an office's image and guiding the economic destinies of a great nation.

Maybe that is why Clinton unexpectedly chose to concentrate as much as he did on foreign policy during his presidency. After a stumbling start, the administration devised a plausible strategic substitute for the containment policy that had guided the United States throughout the Cold War. Formulated by Clinton's national security adviser Anthony Lake, the new strategy called for the enlargement of the world's free-market democracies. The administration also devised a checklist of sorts to determine when, and under what circumstances, the United States would participate in international peacekeeping operations. Although much derided at the time, the checklist, had it existed and been taken seriously in the sixties, might have avoided disaster in Vietnam.

More controversially, Clinton expanded the president's war-making authority over Congress; anticipated some of his successor's tactics in the post-9/11 War on Terror; and, by accusing Saddam Hussein of concealing weapons of mass destruction, helped lay the groundwork for the US invasion of Iraq in 2003. The crisis that erupted in the spring of 2014 in Crimea and Ukraine was at least partly related to Clinton's decision to extend NATO membership to some former Soviet satellites. Yet, despite the long reach of his foreign policy, Clinton was never able to put his personal stamp on it, with the result that few people today think of foreign policy when they think of Clinton.

Clinton's biggest challenge was translating into concrete and compelling terms his vision of a nation moving from one era to another. "If you look at some of our most difficult times," he told one audience, "they're the times of transition when we're moving from one era to another and people can't give you a clear map." He recalled his grandfather telling him that as poor as people were in the Great Depression, "there was a certain happiness of spirit people felt after Roosevelt got in, and everybody knew that they were working together and they were going somewhere."[14] FDR's goals, though daunting, were clear: end the depression and win the war. Similarly, during the Cold War the goal was equally clear: contain, and ultimately defeat, the Soviet Union. Presidents might argue over means but ends were never in doubt. But how to describe the journey out of the new Gilded Age and to impale it on a memorable catch phrase or slogan? Clinton tried out a number of phrases—"the third way," "the vital center," "the New Covenant"—but none caught on. Finally, he hit upon the metaphor of a bridge, a bridge to the twenty-first century. Accepting the nomination of his party in 1996, he said: "Tonight let us resolve to build that bridge to the 21st century, to meet our challenges, protect our basic values and prepare our people for the future." Four years later it was mission accomplished. At the 2000 convention that nominated Al Gore, Clinton said, perhaps a little prematurely, "My fellow Americans, tonight we can say with gratitude and humility: We built our bridge to the 21st century. We crossed that bridge together. And we're not going back."

Margaret Sullivan, the public editor of the *New York Times*, captured something of Clinton's dilemma in a speech to college newspaper editors in 2014. "Because we are in the midst of such radical change," she said, "we can't see clearly what's going on. . . . No one can say what the new landscape will be, even five years from now."[15] Sullivan was talking about the "monumental" changes reshaping the communications industry. She could just as easily have been talking about the transformative changes being wrought by a Second Gilded Age. The biggest problem with the bridge metaphor was the inability of Clinton, or anyone else for that matter, to describe what was on the other side. Or how you would know when you got there.

Clinton's quandary is also the historian's. The first chroniclers of Franklin Roosevelt's presidency could bring closure to their stories. The depression was over, the war won. The transformative era over which Clinton presided continues to unfold, with no end in sight. The legislative accomplishments of his presidency—free trade, welfare reform, deregulation—remain works in progress. Even admiring coworkers cannot agree on his legacy. Janet Yellen, chair of the Federal Reserve Board, chaired Clinton's Council of Economic Advisers. So did Noble Laureate Joseph Stiglitz. Both were admirers of the president. Yellen coauthored, with another of Clinton's economic advisers, a book entitled *The Fabulous Decade*, extolling the accomplishments of the administration. Stiglitz's book, *The Roaring Nineties*, compares the Clinton nineties with the 1920s, a period of excess, misplaced priorities, and missed opportunities.

It's not clear what those missed opportunities were in an era when presidential power is forced to take a backseat to economic forces beyond its control.

1

Making of a President, 1946–1992

The American South where Bill Clinton was born and raised provided a fertile training ground for an aspiring young politician with national ambitions. It was also a treacherous training ground that claimed more than its share of casualties. To succeed during those years when the Jim Crow system of racial segregation was being dismantled, one had to adapt—often at a moment's notice—to the fast-changing realities of southern politics. Clinton's training, especially as a five-term governor of Arkansas, equipped him with the political survival skills and coalition-building techniques that served him well in the 1990s, by which time national politics had taken on many of the characteristics of southern politics.

Clinton's childhood and adolescence equipped him with survival skills of another sort, skills that enabled him to survive a multitude of personal crises that would imperil his ascent to the presidency and his presidency itself. Christened William Jefferson Blythe III, after a father he would never know, he was born on August 19, 1946, in Hope, a town of 7,500 in southwest Arkansas. Three months earlier, the elder Blythe was driving back to Arkansas from Chicago, where he had a job selling heavy equipment and planned to move his wife. Outside of Sikeston, Missouri, his Buick blew a tire, flipped over, and apparently pitched Blythe headfirst into a drainage ditch filled with water. He was twenty-eight years old. Growing up, Clinton knew almost nothing about his father except that he had married his mother after a whirlwind courtship, had almost immediately gone off to war, had earned his living as a salesman, and had a winning personality. Not until Clinton became president and reporters began to dig into his past, did he (or his mother) learn that Blythe had probably been married three times before meeting his mother and that he had at least two other children.[1]

Clinton's mother, Virginia, twenty-four years old when he was born, became the center of his life, and he of hers. A larger-than-life figure with painted-on eyebrows and black hair with a dramatic white streak in the front, she was smart, lively, fun-loving, optimistic, and resilient. She loved to dance and play the horses. She smoked two packs of Pall Malls a day and enjoyed Scotch and water. "I'm friendly, I'm outgoing, and I like men," she wrote in her memoir. "Always have, always will." She added: "Ever since I was a girl, when I showed up someplace, I've wanted people to know I'm there." She need not have worried. At the nightclubs she frequented, she would invite herself onstage to sing with featured performers like Frankie Laine and Teresa Brewer.[2] But there was another side to her as well. She was an accomplished nurse who specialized in administering anesthesia during surgery. She worked a grueling schedule and was often on call twenty-four hours a day. Her struggle to forge a career within a profession dominated by men and medical doctors was a story in itself—one that rivaled in drama and intrigue some chapters of her son's political career.

Virginia trained as a nurse anesthetist at Charity Hospital in New Orleans. While there, she left Bill, who was two, in the care of her parents in Hope. Although his grandparents lavished him with attention and kindness, living in the household could not have been altogether pleasant. His grandfather, who ran a small grocery store, was a kindly man of generous sympathies. He served black and white customers alike, hardly a common practice in the late 1940s and early 1950s, when the rigid barriers of segregation were only beginning to be breached. He frequently forgave the debts owed him by poor customers, black and white. Clinton credited his grandfather's example with his own liberal views on race. "I could see that black people looked different," Clinton recalled, but because his grandfather "treated them like he did everybody else, asking after their children and about their work, I thought they were just like me."[3] But Clinton's grandmother, despite sharing her husband's racial tolerance, may have been mentally unstable. She had a violent temper. In fits of rage she would scream and throw things at her husband and even at Clinton's mother during her visits home from New Orleans.

One time she threatened to go to court to gain custody of Bill. But life with his grandparents was only a prelude to the domestic turbulence that was to come. Soon after completing her training in New Orleans, Virginia returned to Hope and married car dealer Roger Clinton (whose name Bill eventually took). Roger moved his new family to Hot Springs, a rowdy gambling and resort mecca of 50,000 in northwest Arkansas, where he ran the parts department in his brother's Buick dealership. At first everything seemed fine. The Clintons lived in a comfortable five-bedroom, four-bathroom house in a pleasant, middle-class neighborhood. Even after stepbrother Roger Jr. was born, Bill had his own room, and later a Buick convertible. It soon became clear, however, that the elder Clinton was an alcoholic whose idea of a good time, as Bill Clinton later put it, "was to gamble, get drunk, and do crazy, reckless things in cars or airplanes or on motorcycles."[4] During drunken sprees, he would sometimes beat his wife and threaten the boys. When Bill was five, Roger fired a handgun inside the house, barely missing Virginia. The police hauled him off to jail in handcuffs. Another time he held a pair of scissors to Virginia's neck. By his early teens, Bill, now six feet tall, had been thrust into the role of family defender. He "was father, brother, and son in the family," his mother said. During one altercation, Bill broke into his parents' bedroom and forced a drunken Roger to stand. "Hear me," he said. "Never . . . ever . . . touch my mother again."[5] The Clintons divorced but remarried six months later after Roger pleaded for a second chance. Roger soon picked up where he had left off. Roger Jr., who was ten years younger than Bill, recalled how bad it was: "I'd pray he wouldn't get drunk—he'd go get drunk. I'd pray he wouldn't hit us—he'd come home and hit us. I'd pray we would have a happy household—we wouldn't." Then, when the elder Clinton was dying of cancer, Roger Jr. remembered praying "for him to die, and he wouldn't die. That's when I got tired of praying."[6] But he did die, when Roger Jr. was eleven and Bill was away at college. Virginia married two more times.

The most striking thing about Bill Clinton's turbulent homelife is that almost no one outside the family knew about it. "I came to accept the secrets of our house as a normal part of my life," he wrote in his memoir. "I never talked to anyone about them—not to a friend, a neighbor, a teacher, a pastor." Noted one of his biographers: "He decided to pretend it didn't exist. To pretend that everything was all right. To go to church . . . with his bible under his arm and be sunny and energetic, and positive, and simply not to accept it."[7]

Still, it would be a mistake to view Clinton's early life as Southern Gothic, a tale out of William Faulkner or Flannery O'Connor. Even during the worst of times, he was the adored son, the adored stepson, and the adored stepbrother. Clinton's mother devoted an entire wall in their home, dubbed "the shrine" by Clinton's friends, to his photographs, medals, and ribbons.

He was also the center of attention at Hot Springs High School, where he excelled in academic and extracurricular activities. "He just took over the school," a classmate recalled. "He didn't mean to, but he just took the place over." Recalled another: "Bill was the kind of person who would come up to everyone new in high school and say: 'Hi. How are you? My name's Bill Clinton, and I'm running for something,' whatever it was." He was president of the Key Club and the Beta Club. He played tenor saxophone in the band and helped form a jazz group named The Three Blind Mice. On Sundays, he sang in the choir of the Baptist Church. A member of the National Honor Society and a National Merit Scholarship semi-finalist, he graduated fourth in his class, out of 363.[8]

The high point of high school came the summer between his junior and senior years when he represented Arkansas at the national convention of Boys Nation in Washington, DC. There, in the Rose Garden at the White House, he got a chance to shake hands with his boyhood hero, President Kennedy, a moment fortuitously captured on film. Clinton greatly admired Kennedy. Not all white southerners did. By the summer of 1963, many considered Kennedy a traitor to his race for his support of civil rights. Six months later, when word came of President Kennedy's assassination in Dallas, applause erupted in some white classrooms in the South.

In the fall of 1964, Clinton was back in Washington, this time as a freshman at Georgetown University. Once again, he quickly made his presence felt. As students moved into their dorms, Clinton went from room to room, introducing himself to them and to their parents. To some, the six-foot-two, bushy-haired, garrulous, self-confident Clinton with a southern drawl must have seemed an oddity. And as one of the few southerners in his class, he was. But most liked him, and before long "the amiable farm boy," as the student newspaper described him, was elected president of the freshman class.[9]

If classmates assumed the Arkansas farm boy was more amiable than bright, he quickly surprised them. In a famously demanding first-semester survey of Western Civilization, he was one of two students out of 230 to earn an A. He may have made it look easy, but he was also ambitious, competitive, and hardworking. After a lecture, he would be one of the students to go up front to ask the professor to clarify this point or that. He developed a knack for "reading" his professors, for anticipating from the professor's interests what was likely to be on the test, even when it was not obvious to other students. A voracious reader, he always had two or three books unrelated to class going at any one time. When one of his history professors noted that great leaders required less sleep than ordinary mortals, Clinton began setting his alarm to awaken him after five hours of sleep. He would then refresh himself with an occasional catnap during the day.[10]

By his third year, Clinton was devoting as much or more time to outside activities as to the classroom. That's because he was working part-time in the office of his home state senator, J. William Fulbright. Former president of the University of Arkansas, a Rhodes Scholar, and chair of the powerful Senate Committee on Foreign Relations, the urbane Fulbright was a role model for Clinton in part, perhaps, because he defied the "farm boy" image that Clinton probably had to combat. By the time Clinton went to work for Fulbright, the senator was a leading critic of the war in Vietnam. Otherwise, Fulbright voted with his conservative southern colleagues on most other matters, including civil rights. Clinton, more liberal on domestic issues than Fulbright but less inclined to criticize the war, eventually came to oppose the war probably because of Fulbright's influence. While he was at Georgetown, the first major demonstrations against the war occurred in Washington, including the legendary March on the Pentagon in 1967, chronicled by Norman Mailer in his *Armies of the Night*. But Clinton took no part in this or other demonstrations. At this stage, he remained more observer than participant in the antiwar movement.[11]

Even with all of his outside activities and less-than-stellar attendance record, Clinton graduated Phi Beta Kappa and with a 3.7 grade point average. The biggest honor was yet to come. In 1968, he joined the elite company of thirty-two young men from across the country who were chosen to study at Oxford University as Rhodes Scholars. The two years Clinton spent at Oxford allowed him to shed the parochialism he shared with most of his countrymen. Before he returned to the United States he visited the British Isles, France, Germany, Austria, and Eastern Europe, including brief visits to Czechoslovakia and the Soviet Union. Even among a high-powered cohort of fellow scholars, Clinton stood out. Recalled Strobe Talbott, who shared a house with Clinton for a year: "You just knew that Bill Clinton was going to be a politician and that he was going to probably be President."[12]

The Oxford years counted most for Clinton's political future, however, because of the decisions he made regarding the draft. Upon turning eighteen, Clinton, like all young men, became eligible for two years of military service, including service in Vietnam. At Georgetown, student deferments had kept him out of the draft. But those deferments ended upon graduation, so Clinton could be drafted at any time by his hometown draft board in Hot Springs. The details of Clinton's encounter with the draft did not come to light until twenty years later, when he was running for president. Even then they were so complicated it was difficult to make sense of them. But three things about Clinton and the draft were clear. First, he pulled strings to avoid being called up, and he did so in ways that, although not illegal, raised questions about his honesty and ethical standards. Second, among members of his generation, he was hardly alone. Millions of young men contrived to avoid service, many of them successfully. But a third thing about the episode was also clear: Clinton agonized over his actions to an extent that later generations, coming of age after the draft ended in 1974, would have difficulty comprehending. He agonized over the possible impact of service—or nonservice—upon the political career he hoped to pursue. He also spent many late nights talking with friends about the morality of the draft and of the war itself and whether one was obligated to serve in a war considered immoral. And then there was the agonizing question whether it was fair for privileged individuals to avoid service while others could not.[13]

Clinton returned to the United States in 1970 to begin law school at Yale University. He applied to Yale because it was one of the two or three most prestigious law schools in the country, but also because it would give him the time to pursue his political ambitions. Operating on the assumption that if you were smart enough to get in, you were smart enough to graduate, Yale required neither regular class attendance nor formal grades beyond honors, pass, or fail. "This is a tough country club to get into," one professor told his class. "But once you're in, you're in."[14] Clinton spent his first two months in New Haven canvassing Irish and Italian working-class neighborhoods on behalf of Joseph Duffey, a Democrat running unsuccessfully for the US Senate on a pro–civil rights, anti–Vietnam War platform. When the campaign ended, Clinton had to ask a classmate if he could borrow her class notes. "For what?" she asked. "For everything," he answered. In another class, he showed up half an hour late for the final because it was open book, and he hadn't yet gotten himself a copy.[15]

In 1972, while still a full-time student, Clinton greatly advanced his political education. Upon the recommendation of Rick Stearns, a fellow Rhodes Scholar, he was hired to work on South Dakota senator George McGovern's presidential campaign. A leading opponent of the war, McGovern was challenging the incumbent, Richard Nixon. Clinton worked the convention floor for McGovern at the Democratic conclave in Miami and then, in the fall, comanaged the senator's campaign in Texas. Although McGovern was crushed in a landslide, the experience was nothing but a plus for Clinton. At the age of twenty-six, he had been part of electoral politics at the highest level. While in Texas, he expanded his already formidable circle of friends and acquaintances; indeed, many of the persons he met, including, most importantly, Betsey Wright, would play recurring roles throughout Clinton's own career.[16]

But the real importance of the McGovern campaign for Clinton was to prepare him for challenges awaiting anyone aspiring to a career in Democratic politics, particularly from a southern base. Among the biggest challenges was making one's way in a party that was slowly and painfully unraveling. The modern Democratic Party had originally taken form during the Great Depression of the 1930s when a shared sense of economic need, coupled with the leadership of Franklin D. Roosevelt, forged a broad electoral coalition. The party of Roosevelt had never been the invincible powerhouse of legend. What with its potentially volatile mix of southern whites, northern blacks, working-class ethnics, union members, big-city bosses, good-government progressives, rural Protestants and urban Catholics and Jews, the timeworn line—"I'm not a member of any organized party, I'm a Democrat"—actually held more than a grain of truth. But Vietnam, civil rights, and all the other divisive issues of the sixties and early seventies strained the Democratic coalition to the breaking point. In 1964, Republican presidential candidate Barry Goldwater, though crushed by Lyndon Johnson in the election, garnered votes from millions of white southerners opposed to the Civil Rights Act. "Hunting where the ducks are," Goldwater said of his efforts to pluck off disaffected Democratic voters. In 1968, Alabama governor George C. Wallace, running for the presidency on a third-party ticket, demonstrated how divisions among Democrats could be both exacerbated and exploited for political advantage in the South and elsewhere. The segregationist governor, without directly mentioning race, convinced many white working-class and middle-class voters that the Democrats had abandoned them for blacks, feminists, welfare cheats, and antiwar protesters. In 1972, the Nixon campaign employed a variant of Wallace's approach to bury McGovern in a landslide.[17]

The Democrats unwittingly played into the hands of their opponents. McGovern, for example, had compiled a consistently prolabor record— no small feat for a senator from a predominantly rural state. But not until the final stages in the campaign did he focus on the pressing economic needs and social anxieties of blue-collar workers. By then, it was too late. To make matters worse, some of his followers were openly contemptuous of "hardhats," dismissing them as bigots and warmongers.[18] For Clinton, the lesson of the McGovern campaign was clear, if daunting: make room in the party for those too long excluded from the centers of power—blacks, feminists, opponents of the war—but without further alienating the predominantly white working- and middle-class voters who had sustained the Democratic Party since the New Deal.

Unquestionably the most important thing that happened to Clinton at Yale Law School was meeting Hillary Rodham. If he cut a big figure on campus, so did she. She had grown up in Park Ridge, Illinois, an affluent white suburb north of Chicago where her father ran a small manufacturing firm and her mother worked at home raising Hillary and her two brothers. In some accounts, the Rodham household, though lacking the turbulence of the Clinton's, was far from placid, with a gruff, authoritarian father setting the tone.[19] Hillary's father encouraged her interest in politics but demanded that the television be turned off during the Democratic National Convention. "My dad was a rock-ribbed, up-by-your-bootstraps, conservative Republican and proud of it," she recalled. Her mother "was basically a Democrat, although she kept it quiet in Republican Park Ridge."[20] Like Bill, Hillary was a joiner. She joined the Brownies and Girl Scouts, played softball in high school, and was active in the student council, school newspaper, Young Republicans, and a Methodist youth group. Her parents encouraged her to excel, and excel she did. Voted "most likely to succeed" by the senior class, she went on to Wellesley College, an elite women's school outside of Boston. Like many of her contemporaries she underwent a political epiphany of sorts during college. By her senior year she was tutoring black children in an inner-city neighborhood in Boston, going door-to-door for antiwar presidential candidate Eugene McCarthy, and switching party allegiance from Republican to Democratic. At commencement, she delivered an address that brought graduates to their feet and earned her national attention. *Life* magazine featured Rodham, along with graduates of three other universities, in an article entitled, "The Class of 69: With Eloquent Defiance Top Students Protest Right through Commencement."[21]

Almost from the first Bill and Hillary were inseparable. During their last year in law school, they shared an apartment in downtown New Haven. Upon graduation, however, they went their separate ways, at least for the time being. Until the opportunity to run for office presented itself, Clinton taught at the University of Arkansas Law School. He was a popular teacher perhaps in part because he was an easy grader. "Bill doesn't give D's and F's, because he might someday need those votes," said a colleague.[22] But students also enjoyed his informal approach and his genuine interest in their lives. He was especially popular among African American students, who dubbed him "Wonder Boy," because he was so much more comfortable in their presence than other white faculty members. Hillary, meanwhile, worked on the staff of Marian Wright Edelman's Fund for Children, the precursor of the Children's Defense Fund. In 1974, she secured a position that put her at the center of one of the most dramatic and exciting events in American political history. In the summer of 1974, she joined the staff of the House Judiciary Committee that eventually recommended President Nixon's impeachment. Clinton had been offered a staff position, too, but recommended Hillary instead. Rodham's work on the impeachment committee, which impressed superiors and colleagues alike, opened even more opportunities for her. When Nixon resigned to avoid certain impeachment and removal from office, Hillary probably could have had her pick of jobs: a position in a prestigious Washington law firm or in the federal government, perhaps. Or, given all the contacts she had made on the impeachment committee, perhaps she could have explored the possibility of running for office herself. She did none of these things. To the chagrin of admiring friends, one of whom told her she was "crazy," Rodham moved to Arkansas, first to teach law and then to practice law as a member of the Rose Law Firm in Little Rock. Why, friends wondered, was she willing to give up so much for so little. The most obvious answer was also the most likely. "She was absolutely, totally crazy about Bill Clinton," recalled one of her colleagues on the staff of the impeachment committee. "'Besotted' is not a word I would normally apply to Hillary, but I think she was besotted." There was also the promise of what he might accomplish in the future—and what they might accomplish together. To another of her incredulous colleagues she repeatedly insisted, "You know . . . Bill Clinton is going to be President of the United States someday!"[23] Bill and Hillary married a year after her arrival in Arkansas. The morning of the ceremony, Clinton warned his mother that Hillary was keeping her own name. Virginia, who had not yet fully warmed up to her daughter-in-law-to-be, burst into tears.[24]

Clinton launched his career in 1974 when he took on the longtime Republican incumbent congressman John Paul Hammerschmidt. In the year of Watergate, Clinton sensed that Hammerschmidt, a staunch defender of Richard Nixon, was vulnerable. With the Duffey and McGovern campaigns fresh in mind, Clinton avoided contentious social issues like abortion and race and concentrated on the economic needs of middle- and working-class voters. He adopted a populist tone, calling for a crackdown on corporate subsidies, selective wage and price controls, greater congressional oversight of the Federal Reserve, and restrictions on imports that were squeezing out small farmers. One veteran Arkansas reporter recalled being astonished "to hear this 28-year-old law-school teacher addressing conservative Rotary Clubs on the dangers of corporate abuse of power."[25] He so impressed state labor leaders during what was meant to be a perfunctory courtesy call that they switched their endorsement, practically on the spot, from another candidate to

Clinton. Clinton easily bested three opponents in the primary but lost to Hammerschmidt by only two percentage points in the general election. Clinton won by losing. Because he came closer to pulling off an upset than anyone expected, he instantly became a young man with a future. The next morning Clinton was in downtown Fayetteville thanking voters. As one of his biographers put it, "The next race had already begun."[26]

The next race came two years later when Clinton won an overwhelming victory for attorney general, affording him a platform from which to speak out on behalf of consumers, utility-rate payers, and crime victims. Clinton performed his duties conscientiously, and in the process gained statewide recognition; it is doubtful, however, that he ever regarded the attorney generalship as anything more than a stepping stone to higher office, although what that higher office would be was not immediately clear to him. To help him decide where to go next, he employed for the first time the services of Richard "Dick" Morris, the controversial political consultant who would play a pivotal role at critical times in Clinton's long career. With his loud suits and brash personality, Morris was the stereotypical New Yorker of every white southerner's imagination, and at one time or another, he offended just about everyone on Clinton's staff. Clinton aide Betsey Wright once described Morris as "one of the smartest little sons of bitches" she'd ever met. "Mean. But God he was good."[27] Yet, Morris quickly proved his value. He helped Clinton position himself for a successful run for the governorship while at the same time adroitly sidestepping two other rising stars in the state's Democratic Party, Dale Bumpers and David Pryor, both of whom harbored national aspirations of their own. In 1978, at the age of thirty-two, Bill Clinton became the youngest chief executive in the nation.[28]

At first glance, Clinton's new position seemed an unlikely launching pad for a major national career, much less a career that would lead to the White House. Arkansas was the fifth-smallest state in the country. It had only one city, Little Rock, with more than 100,000 residents. It ranked at or near the bottom in almost every quality-of-life indicator, including household income, lifespan, and education. For many Americans, the mention of the state's capital and largest city still conjured up memories of one of the most infamous episodes in the civil rights era. Arkansas had produced its share of influential statesmen, including Senator J. William Fulbright, Clinton's mentor, and Representative Wilbur

Mills, powerful chairman of the House Committee on Ways and Means. But given its size and relative backwardness, it was not surprising that Arkansas had not produced a national leader of the first rank. Political scientist William Galston, who would serve as a domestic policy advisor in the Clinton White House, went so far as to say that being governor of a small state was "the worst" preparation for being president. "You do it by yourself. . . . You're personally involved in every detail of the policy process. You are the sun, and everybody rotates around you." That may be what happens in Little Rock or Atlanta, Galston believed, but not in the constellation that is the nation's capital.[29]

Yet there were advantages to starting out in a state like Arkansas, especially in the seventies and eighties, and Clinton would make the most of them. For one, no matter what office Clinton secured, he would be forced to grapple with problems that were no longer confined to Arkansas or to the South in general but were increasingly national in scope—a fragile economy, a crumbling infrastructure, industrial down- sizing and outsourcing, and a citizenry increasingly skeptical of gov- ernment and unwilling or unable to pay higher taxes. Then there was race. To get elected as a progressive Democrat, he would have to patch together a biracial coalition, and that meant satisfying the aspirations of newly enfranchised African Americans without alienating white vot- ers. With blacks constituting only 15 percent of the population—the lowest percentage in the Deep South—and with a third of white voters still supporting segregation, coalition building was no easy task.[30] But if Clinton could pull it off, and survive politically, as a number of southern governors, including Jimmy Carter, were already doing, he could make a name for himself well beyond Arkansas. Even the state's remoteness from the national spotlight might be an advantage. It could allow Clin- ton to experiment with different approaches to problems and even to make mistakes from time to time without being subjected to the make- or-break scrutiny of the national media.

The biggest advantage Arkansas had to offer was an advanced educa- tion in the dying art of "retail politics," that intimate practice of interact- ing with voters on an individual basis. And in Clinton, Arkansas never had a more eager or adept student of the art. The Baby Boom generation of politicians who began to occupy positions of power in the seventies and after were, like Clinton, often better educated in a formal sense than their political elders. Products of the television age, they were more adept than their forebears at using the electronic media and more likely, too, to employ polling and focus groups to develop their positions. But unlike their elders, who had come up through the ranks, perhaps by serving on a county board or city council or in some voluntary capacity, the new breed entered politics almost immediately out of college or law school. Their leap-frog approach left a conspicuous gap in their education. Accustomed to communicating with voters primarily through intermediators like pollsters, focus-group moderators, and lobbyists, they hadn't undergone the seasoning process that came from regular one-on-one contact with constituents.

But in Arkansas, as in much of the South, politics was still practiced as it had been for decades. A candidate might conduct polls and run television and radio ads. But he had almost no chance of getting elected, or staying elected, without going one-on-one with voters. In Arkansas, incumbents and challengers alike were expected to attend the annual Coon Supper in Gillett, the Chicken Fry in Mount Nebo, the Pink Tomato Festival in Warren, and the Watermelon Festival in Clinton's birthplace, Hope. They were expected to visit small-town coffee shops and stop in at barbershops and beauty parlors. "No crowd was too small, no organization too far from his home base, for a Clinton appearance," recalled Arkansas reporter Meredith L. Oakley. "Rarely the first to arrive—even then he found it impossible to keep a schedule—he usually was the last to depart, hanging around to chew the fat until the last straggler was all talked out."[31]

This friends-and-neighbors retail politics gave officials a feel for public opinion they could get in no other way. As Clinton later explained it, "It's easy for a politician in this mass-media culture to reduce electioneering to fund-raisers, rallies, advertisements, and a debate or two." But in so doing, "candidates miss out on a lot, including the struggles of people who have their hands full just getting through the day and doing the best they can for their kids."[32] Clinton recalled greeting workers outside a factory gate when a man, accompanied by three children, dropped off his wife. The man told Clinton that every morning they had to awaken the kids by a quarter to four, get his wife to work by five, and drop the kids off at the babysitter's so he could get to work by seven. But if one-to-one politics helped Clinton sympathize with the struggles of ordinary people, it also exposed him to the unpredictable mixture of ignorance and wisdom, prejudice and nobility that inhabit the citizenry in a democratic society. Over the years, Clinton met people who believed Arkansas was overrun with "Commies," the moon landing was a hoax, and civil rights was the root of all evil. He met a prosperous businessman who kept his wife's glass-encased casket in his house because God had told him he was going to raise her from the dead. Clinton met the Democratic chairman of a conservative rural county who drove a pickup truck with a gun rack and a bumper sticker reading, "Don't Blame Me, I Voted for McGovern." On the road with Senator Fulbright, when Alabama's segregationist governor, George Wallace, was at the height of his popularity, Clinton heard an influential white citizen in a small town say that black sharecroppers were getting a raw deal and that poverty was the country's biggest problem.[33] The cumulative effect of sitting down with people such as these, listening to their stories, and asking for their support probably helped make Clinton a political realist who viewed the public neither cynically nor idealistically.

For scores of friends, wrote biographer David Maraniss, Clinton's inauguration as governor in January 1979 "had the aura of a generational rite. From all sections of the country they made the pilgrimage to gray, freezing Little Rock. They were there to witness the coming of age of one of their own, the first in their class to reach such prominence on the political stage." Those attending the inauguration represented nearly every stage of Clinton's life. They included friends from high school, dorm mates from Georgetown, and law school colleagues from Yale. Two attendees from Louisiana had been with him in the White House Rose Garden when he shook hands with President Kennedy. From Texas came Betsey Wright, who had worked with Clinton on the McGovern campaign in 1972.[34]

What was there about Clinton that attracted this loyal assemblage? For one, it attested to his knack for forging lasting friendships. A veteran Arkansas newsman described how it might begin: "He gets close to you, he touches, he establishes a physical connection—arm on a shoulder, a handshake. He looks you in your eye, and for a short period of time makes you think you're the only person in the room. And he quickly finds the common foundation—hometown, knows your cousin, knows somebody who went to the school you went to, knows your boss."[35]

Clinton made it look easy. But he worked at it, too. After meeting people, he would jot down relevant information on scraps of paper or index cards: "Names, addresses, phone numbers, and birthdays, weddings, and children, updated with new jobs and latest publications, new meetings, and family bereavements, they were cross-referenced, with a note of any campaign contributions they had made." In time the index cards filled shoebox upon shoebox. By one count, he had accumulated 10,000 individual files by the time he became governor. So the natural also possessed the instincts of a master organizer.[36] Then Clinton stayed in touch. Recalled fellow Arkansan David Pryor: "You'd hear from people, 'Oh, I just heard from Bill Clinton. He dropped me a post card,' or 'He called me up on my birthday,' or 'My mother broke her ankle and Bill Clinton called her.'"[37]

There was more to Clinton's attraction than assiduous cultivation. For many who had come of age in the sixties and seventies, he seemed to exemplify shared values, even if on occasion, as with the aspiring Georgetown Jesuit who was certain Clinton was Catholic, admirers projected their own values onto Clinton.[38] Projection worked the other way as well. At every stage of his life there were those who thought him "a little too slick," as one Georgetown classmate put it.[39] But over the years admirers vastly outnumbered detractors.

Clinton's ever-widening circle of friends and acquaintances, unofficially convening for the first time at his inauguration, played a critical role in his rise to prominence. Later dubbed "Friends of Bill" (FOB), it gave him a national network of supporters, many of whom would achieve distinction in journalism, academia, and business. Just as they were willing to make the pilgrimage to Little Rock in 1979, so they and their counterparts would be willing to drop what they were doing, almost at a moment's notice, to assist Clinton when the need arose. And it wasn't just Bill; Hillary, too, was building an influential following of her own.

Clinton's first term as governor began with soaring hopes and ended in bitter disappointment. Almost from the beginning, things got off track. Interpreting his huge victory as a mandate for sweeping change, he proposed an ambitious agenda. During his first state of the state message, he reeled off some seventy initiatives, including economic and educational reforms. The office Clinton inherited did not match his ambitions. A simple majority of the state legislature could overturn a gubernatorial veto. All that was required to block a request for an income tax hike was 25 percent of the legislature. And before 1986, Arkansas governors had to run for reelection every two years, meaning they had little time to settle in before having once again to face the voters. Clinton's laundry list of proposals received almost unanimous approval in the abstract, but when he tried to implement them, he was met by fierce resistance, especially from powerful business interests. His plan to finance needed road construction by raising annual automobile registration fees angered just about everyone. In addition to an institutionally weak governorship, Clinton encountered other factors beyond his control, including a shrinking economy, a prolonged drought, and several devastating tornadoes. President Jimmy Carter, for whom Clinton had campaigned in 1976, didn't help either. In 1980, the president sent 18,000 Cuban refugees, some of whom had been released from Cuban prisons and mental hospitals, to an internment center at Fort Chafee, Arkansas. When hundreds of the detainees rioted over bad conditions, Clinton got the blame even though the president had dispatched many of the refugees to Fort Chafee over Clinton's objections. In any case, voters had had enough. In 1980, Clinton went down to defeat at the hands of businessman Frank White, who depicted Clinton as arrogant and out of touch. In just two years, Clinton noted sardonically, he had gone from being the youngest governor in the nation to being the youngest ex-governor.[40]

Having prepared a lifetime for a career in politics, Clinton described the defeat as a "near death experience."[41] He did not grieve for long. With every intention of making a comeback, he interrogated friends and acquaintances about what had gone wrong. "They just thought you were an arrogant son of a bitch," one friend told him. Others, even among his own age group, said Hillary's decision to keep her own name hurt. One member of the Arkansas House put it this way: "Hillary's gonna have to change her name, and shave her legs."[42] Once again, Clinton brought in Dick Morris for advice. Morris's surveys revealed that voters still liked Clinton personally but had wanted to send him a message to listen to them more. On Morris's advice, Clinton took the unusual step of buying time on state television stations and apologizing to Arkansans for "leading without listening." Clinton also began cutting his hair shorter and regularly attending Sunday morning services at Immanuel Baptist Church. Hillary formally became Hillary Rodham Clinton.[43]

In 1982, Clinton regained the State House, this time for good. Once in power, he replaced the bearded young outsiders who had dominated—at least visibly—his first administration with longtime veterans of Arkansas politics. And he took to heart the old adage that if you've got more than two or three priorities you don't have any priorities. Education and economic development now dominated Clinton's agenda for the remainder of his years in Arkansas. Never seriously challenged again, Clinton won election three more times. In the process, he constructed a reliable biracial coalition that differed from the coalitions he had put together for earlier campaigns. No longer was he the populist champion of the working class, denouncing corporate arrogance and greed. Now he assiduously courted business and industry, including Tyson Foods, one of the world's largest processors of meat, and Wal-Mart, the nation's largest retailer, on whose board Hillary would eventually sit. Following his reelection, Clinton's white supporters became more urban and more middle class than earlier. Upwards of 95 percent of African Americans, who accounted for about 14 percent of the state's population and 4 percent of the electorate, consistently voted for Clinton. Clinton appointed more blacks to high office than any previous governor. One became the director of finance and administration, "arguably the most important job in state government after the governorship," Clinton later wrote.[44] Otherwise he avoided explicitly race-related issues that might scare off white voters. The Legal Defense Fund, claiming racial discrimination in voting, filed three lawsuits against the state's Democratic Party and one against Governor Clinton. In an unusual turn, the Legal Defense Fund lawyer who filed the suits, Lani Guinier, was a Yale Law School classmate and friend of the Clintons. (The relationship between Guinier and the Clintons would take an even stranger turn early in Clinton's presidency.) Although Clinton and his fellow Democrats prevailed in the courtroom, political scientist Hanes Walton, Jr., later concluded that "in the final analysis, a southern governor who saw himself as a progressive, and whom many called a new progressive, acted much less than progressively on the matter of racial participation in his state."[45] Above all, Clinton focused on the economy and education, which united voters across racial lines.

For decades Arkansas, like its southern neighbors, had attracted business to the state with the promise of low wages, low taxes, weak unions, and other enticements. But no longer. By the seventies and eighties, southern businesses, like their northern counterparts, were downsizing, outsourcing, or simply closing down and moving out of the country. Clinton identified education as the state's Achilles' heel and argued that the best hope of retaining business was to produce a better-educated, more competitive workforce.

As it was, Arkansas ranked last among states in spending per pupil, last in teacher salaries, and last in the number of residents who had graduated from high school. By one estimate, a quarter of the adult population was functionally illiterate. Only about half of the state's public high schools offered courses in physics and advanced biology, and many offered no courses in chemistry, advanced mathematics, or foreign languages. An outside consultant concluded that the average student in Arkansas would be better off in almost any other state in the country. Clinton had scored some successes during his first term. He had raised teacher pay, instituted standardized tests to measure student progress, and required new teachers to pass competency tests as a condition of employment. Upon regaining the state house, Clinton redoubled his efforts, with Hillary Clinton now playing a central role. She headed a commission that held hearings throughout the state and then recommended a series of school reforms. The commission's most controversial proposal, which Clinton adopted, required all teachers to take standardized competency tests as a condition of keeping their jobs. Compulsory testing set the governor at odds with the state's teachers' organization and even the National Education Association, which accused him of making scapegoats out of teachers. Some charged the governor of deliberately picking a fight with the teachers' union to burnish his national image as a new kind of Democrat willing to take issue with a traditional Democratic Party interest group. On the issue of teacher competency, however, Clinton probably had the better of the argument. At almost every stop on Hillary's state tour, parents handed her letters their children's teachers had written that were replete with grammatical and spelling errors. Parents told her about one teacher, apparently unfamiliar with roman numerals, who spent several weeks covering World War Eleven. If anything, Clinton's supporters argued, the tests teachers would have to take were too easy because they only required competency at the eighth-grade level. Clinton eventually prevailed, but only after prolonged struggle. Tests were instituted, pay raises provided, and the curriculum expanded.[46]

In addition to educational reforms, Clinton did everything in his power to revive the state's economy. When he heard about an innovative "micro-credit" program that was successfully funneling loans into poor areas of Bangladesh, he sat down with the program's Bangladeshi designer and then implemented a trial program in Arkansas. He tried to tap into the economic research and development potential of the state's universities as North Carolina was doing with its famous Research Triangle. When the Japanese electronics giant Sanyo announced its intention to shut down its assembly plant in Arkansas, Clinton convinced Wal-Mart to market the firm's television sets nationally in exchange for keeping the plant open. A few years later, he brokered a similar deal between Wal-Mart and a shirt factory once owned by Van Heusen.[47]

By the mid-eighties, Clinton was earning a reputation as one of the nation's best governors. In an influential study, journalist David Osborne identified him as one of a half-dozen governors (and the only southerner) who were transforming their states into modern-day "laboratories of democracy." "More than perhaps any other governor of the 1980s," Osborne wrote, "Clinton has demonstrated how to talk about issues such as education and economic development in ways that not only make sense to voters but move them." But even Osborne conceded that Clinton had been unable to perform an Arkansas miracle. He had made "an impressive beginning," Osborne concluded, but "overall, Clinton's programs are not yet of sufficient scale to deal with the huge challenges Arkansas faces." This was not the governor's fault, he noted. The state was starting from so far back in the pack with so few resources that "it must run hard just to stay in the same place."[48]

But even at the height of his popularity, Clinton was never in the driver's seat. Business and industry were. Then and later, critics complained that Clinton pandered to the state's economic interests. When Tyson Foods was found to be dumping animal waste into the state's rivers and streams, Clinton appointed an investigatory panel weighted with industry representatives. Labor leaders complained that he would not even consider rescinding the open shop for fear of offending Wal-Mart and other nonunion employers.[49] "Bill Clinton is the kind of man who'll pat you on the back and piss on your leg," said one disgruntled laborite.[50] Clinton's critics probably underestimated prevailing power arrangements. He doubtless feared that if he pressed Tyson or Wal-Mart too hard he would only end up driving two of the state's largest employers out of the state. He later recalled helping to persuade Wal-Mart "to buy more products made in America and to advertise this practice as a way to increase sales." In response, the company launched a popular "Buy American" campaign, which boosted the sale of domestic products, including products made in Arkansas. A few years later, however, Wal-Mart abandoned the practice, and there was nothing Clinton could do about it.[51]

Though hardly a household name, Clinton was increasingly generating national attention. His colleagues in the National Governor's Conference elected him chair, and national reporters touted him as a potential presidential candidate. Clinton came close to running in 1988 but withdrew himself from consideration at the last moment, even as friends and supporters gathered in Little Rock for the expected announcement. A national campaign, which would require him to be on the road for much of the next sixteen months, would take too heavy a toll on his family, especially seven-year-old daughter Chelsea, he explained. The last straw, he wrote in his memoir, came when Chelsea asked him where they were going for their summer vacation. "When I said I might not be able to take one if I ran for president, Chelsea replied, 'Then Mom and I will go without you.' That did it."[52] Some political insiders suspected that a more compelling reason for his last-minute decision was fear that alleged extramarital affairs, long rumored in Little Rock, would bring embarrassing scrutiny. One version of events had Clinton's chief of staff, Betsey Wright, confronting Clinton with names of women with whom he had allegedly been involved. "Now I want you to tell me the truth about every one," she reputedly said. When Clinton finished, Wright went over the names again, asking him which, if any, of the women were likely to reveal their stories to reporters. When they concluded, Wright urged Clinton to stay out of the race.[53]

In an earlier era, none of this probably would have mattered. The prevailing rule-of-thumb, honored by most of the press, had once maintained that the private lives of public officials were nobody's business unless they adversely affected their performance in office. But by Clinton's time, the rules had changed. The turning point probably came in 1969, when a young woman in the company of Senator Edward Kennedy had drowned under mysterious circumstances in a car accident in Chappa-quiddick, Massachusetts. The incident not only prompted lurid speculation but also concerns about Kennedy's character and fitness to occupy high office. The Watergate scandals further blurred the line between the public and private behavior of politicians. Then, in 1987, even as Clinton was pondering a run for the presidency, Senator Gary Hart of Colorado, married and the father of two, dropped out of contention for the Democratic presidential nomination when a tabloid ran a front-page photograph of him with another woman sitting on his lap aboard a yacht bearing the name *Monkey Business*.

Even though Clinton was not in the running for president in 1988, he faced an unexpected threat to his future prospects. The Democratic nominee that year, Massachusetts governor Michael Dukakis, asked Clinton to deliver one of the nominating speeches. It was a disaster. Before his largest national audience thus far, he delivered a long and boring speech. As he went on for thirty-two minutes, twice the allotted time, cameras caught delegates at first talking among themselves and then drawing their hands across their throats as the speech wore on and shouting, "Get the hook." When Clinton said "in conclusion," the audience broke into raucous applause. It wasn't all, or even mostly, Clinton's fault. Dukakis's aides, not Clinton, had written the speech, and convention organizers had failed to dim the houselights for his appearance. Still, because ridicule can be more poisonous to a career than defeat, the episode was a bad blow. The next night, *Tonight Show* host Johnny Carson announced in his opening monologue that Clinton had just been approved as an over-the-counter sleeping aid by the surgeon general. Recalled Clinton's Arkansas colleague David Pryor: "After that speech was the lowest point I've ever seen him—he'd been laughed at, booed, hissed at, the national press were ridiculing him—jokes, editorial cartoons."[54] But then Clinton's survival instincts kicked in, and that, plus a stroke of good luck, salvaged the situation. It so happened that the Clintons had befriended Hollywood television producers Harry and Linda Bloodworth-Thomason. What followed was a dramatic example of the Friends of Bill (and Hillary) in action. The Thomasons managed to get Clinton a spot on the *Tonight Show* not long after Johnny Carson's devastating putdown. Clinton's self-deprecating humor, on-camera poise, and brief saxophone solo won the day. Far more people saw his winning performance than his speech at the convention.[55] From then on, the television talk show became the first stop for politicians in trouble.

The defeat of Michael Dukakis in 1988—the third in a row for the Democrats—sent a deep chill through party ranks. Among those most concerned were members of the Democratic Leadership Council (DLC), an organization founded after Ronald Reagan's reelection in 1984 by moderate to conservative party members, many of them vulnerable southerners.[56] DLC members, including Clinton, feared their party was destined to minority status unless it regained the support of white middle-class and working-class voters who had been drifting to the GOP in ever-increasing numbers since 1968. For years Republicans had been bludgeoning Democrats with charges of being profligate spenders, soft on crime, weak on national defense, and beholden to special-interest groups. When voters in 1984 were asked by pollsters who comprised the Democratic Party, they frequently responded with a list that included black militants, women's liberationists, welfare recipients, gays and lesbians, and union members. By 1988, those identifying themselves as Republicans had pulled almost even with those identifying themselves as Democrats. More ominous still, 53 percent of all eighteen-to-twenty-nine-year-olds identified themselves as Republicans.[57]

Face up to it, DLC members told fellow Democrats, the party's problems ran far deeper than a succession of dull candidates, flawed strategies, or the failure to turn more Democratic-leaning minorities out at the polls. True, Republican depictions of the party were often unfair and overdrawn. After all, it was not a Democrat but Republican icon Ronald Reagan who had run up the biggest deficits since World War II. Still, there was no denying the party was in trouble. The most influential case documenting the party's plight was a paper published in 1989 by the DLC's think tank, the Progressive Policy Institute. Entitled "The Politics of Evasion" and written by political scientists and party activists William Galston and Elaine Kamarck, the paper marshaled sobering polling data to bolster its conclusion that "the national Democratic Party is losing touch with the middle class, without whose solid support it cannot hope to rebuild a presidential majority."[58] Meeting the following year in New Orleans, DLC members issued a declaration of "enduring principles" affirming, among other things, that "the Democratic

Party's fundamental mission is to expand opportunity, not government"; that "the U.S. must maintain a strong and capable defense"; that "the free market, regulated in the public interest, is the best engine of general prosperity"; and that "the purpose of social welfare is to bring the poor into the nation's economic mainstream, not to maintain them in dependence." Members also affirmed their belief "in preventing crime and punishing criminals, not in explaining away their behavior," and in expanding trade, not restricting it.[59]

The DLC spurred a sharp backlash. Black civil rights activist Jesse Jackson, who attended the New Orleans conference but was not invited back thereafter, dismissed the DLC as the "Southern White Boys Club" and the "Democrats for the Leisure Class." Organized labor looked askance at the organization because of its support for free trade and close ties to the corporate interests that bankrolled its operations.[60] To liberal historian Arthur M. Schlesinger, Jr., the DLC's agenda smacked of "Me-Too Reaganism" and was a recipe for disaster.[61] To counter the DLC's influence, Senator Howard Metzenbaum of Ohio and three dozen of his congressional colleagues created the Coalition for Democratic Values (CDV). "The future of the Democratic Party does not lie in the fine-tuning of Reaganism," CDV leaders proclaimed.[62] As if to underscore their departure from party orthodoxy, DLC members seemed to welcome, even provoke, criticism from their liberal counterparts. Less welcome was the skepticism of nonpartisan observers who doubted the DLC could remake the Democratic Party in its own image. In the view of one reporter, council gatherings were like grownup versions of Boys Nation: "Officers are elected and issues are debated with great seriousness that amounts to naught." Give the DLC its due, said David Broder of the *Washington Post*: "For an outfit that was born out of pique, fear and frustration the Democratic Leadership Council has turned into a surprisingly healthy and intelligent 6-year-old. It is contributing positive and practical policy ideas to a party in desperate need of them." But the council had reached the end of the line, Broder believed. It "has done about all it can do for the Democrats. Someone or something else will have to take the next steps for the Democrats' revival."[63]

The "someone," as it turned out, was Bill Clinton. Following the 1988 election, council president Al From pressed Clinton to take on the chairmanship of the organization. Despite lingering memories of

Clinton's dismal performance at the Democratic National Convention and persistent rumors about his personal life, From regarded the Arkansas governor as "the most attractive political animal he had seen in his life."[64] Clinton's relative popularity among blacks in his home state was also a plus, for it promised to counter the DLC's image as the "Southern White Boys Club." And that he had been so active in McGovern's presidential campaign might make him more acceptable—or at least less objectionable—to the liberal wing of the party. There were other moderates to choose from, including Senator Al Gore of Tennessee, who had carried the DLC's banner in his abortive campaign for the Democratic nomination in 1988. But Clinton was the one From wanted. "Have I got a deal for you," he remembered telling Clinton. "If you take the DLC chairmanship, we will give you a national platform, and I think you will be President of the United States."[65]

Accepting the offer, Clinton promptly proved his worth. "This guy delivers our message better than any other politician," said From.[66] In return for his service as chairman, Clinton got the national platform he was promised plus a nascent campaign organization replete with a staff of advisers, a steady flow of detailed policy briefs from the council's newly created think tank, and access to the DLC's wealthy benefactors.[67]

The DLC also furnished the setting for the unofficial launching of Clinton's presidential campaign. In May 1991, at the council's national convention in Cleveland, he delivered a speech that all but erased memories of his dismal performance at the Democratic National Convention three years earlier. Speaking from a one-page list of handwritten prompts, he began by saying that although America's "magnificent victory" in the Gulf War had confirmed the nation's diplomatic and military pre-eminence, it was falling behind—often far behind—in other vital areas. Eighteen countries did a better job than the United States at preventing infant mortality, while children in a dozen countries did better on international math and science tests. Every major nation afforded their citizens greater access to health care, while two of the country's economic competitors, Germany and Japan, were running circles around the United States. Military might aside, the only category the United States led the world in was the percentage of its people in prison. Meanwhile, Clinton pointed out, middle-income Americans were working longer hours but earning less than they had just a decade earlier, even as

CEOs were awarding themselves pay raises four times as much as they gave their employees and three times as much as their corporate profits increased. That all of this coincided with Republican occupation of the White House would seem to be a bonanza for Democrats. But such was not the case. Voters were not turning to the Democrats, and in the most quoted line in his speech Clinton explained why: "Because too many of the people that used to vote for us, the very burdened middle class we are talking about, have not trusted us in national elections to defend our national interests abroad, to put their values into our social policy at home, or to take their tax money and spend it with discipline."[68]

Clinton's agenda for reconnecting with voters and with the country as a whole foreshadowed his presidential campaign platform and his presidency itself. He called for expanded world trade; government investments in technology, education, and job training; health-care and welfare reform; tax relief for middle- and lower-income workers; and bureaucratic downsizing. Government should do its part, Clinton said. But citizens needed to do theirs as well. The country had a right to expect those on welfare to find jobs, recipients of college loans to repay society with a year or two of national service, and students to stay in school or lose their driver's licenses. "Is what I just said to you liberal or conservative?" Clinton asked. "The truth is, it is both, and it is different. It rejects the Republicans' attacks and the Democrats' previous unwillingness to consider new alternatives." The speech brought the audience to its feet, and though it received little media coverage word of it quickly spread among those who counted most: party insiders, well-heeled donors, and influential journalists.[69]

With every retelling, Clinton's performance embellished his reputation as "phenom," a politician of extraordinarily raw talent, the likes of nobody had ever seen before. After all, how many people could bring a crowd to its feet with a speech "improvised from twenty-one single word cues . . . scrawled on a piece of paper," as journalist Joe Klein described it? But there was more to the story. Clinton's address wasn't a brilliant improvisation: it was a collaborative effort. "We worked a long time on that speech, and Bruce Reed in particular," recalled DLC founder From with reference to DLC policy director Reed. "I remember going over it, over and over again, in my office." Then, the night before his appearance, Clinton didn't go to bed but worked and reworked the speech until he made it his own. Like the Georgetown student resetting his alarm to squeeze more hours out of the day, Clinton worked hard to perfect his craft.[70]

Despite Clinton's triumph, doubts persisted about his and the DLC's ability to remake the Democratic Party. "The Cleveland convention did not look or feel like a Democratic gathering," observed journalist David Broder. "You looked around the floor and saw few teachers or union members, few blacks and even fewer Hispanics." Broder added: "In their place, you had dozens of corporate lobbyists who pay the DLC's bills in return for access to its influential congressional members and governors. Many of the lobbyist-delegates acknowledged being Republicans; one was a top staffer for Spiro Agnew. But they were in there voting on resolutions, just as if they really cared about the Democrats' winning."[71]

Nevertheless, the enthusiastic reception Clinton received in Cleveland removed any doubts he may have had about running for the presidency. Six months later, on October 3, 1991, in front of the Old State House in Little Rock, he made it official.

Reprising his DLC address, he set the tone for his campaign: "Middle-class people are spending more hours on the job, spending less time with their children, bringing home a smaller paycheck to pay more for health care and housing and education. . . . The country is headed in the wrong direction fast, slipping behind, losing our way, and all we have out of Washington is status quo paralysis. No vision, no action. Just neglect, selfishness and division."[72]

When Clinton made his announcement, the prospects of any Democrat capturing the White House seemed remote. With George H. W. Bush still riding high in the polls in the aftermath of the US victory over Iraq in the Gulf War, the party's most prominent Democrats, including New York Governor Mario Cuomo, declined to offer themselves up to a seemingly hopeless cause, thus opening the door to the party's B-list of lesser-knowns. Besides Clinton they included: Paul Tsongas, a fiscally conservative former senator from Massachusetts; Thomas Harkin, a liberal senator from Iowa; and Robert Kerrey, a Vietnam veteran who'd lost a leg in the war, Congressional Medal of Honor winner, and Nebraska senator whose centrist views mirrored Clinton's. Although commentators never tired of noting that heavyweights in the party, like Cuomo, remained on the sidelines, the declared candidates were each smart, serious, and issue-oriented. The remaining Democrat to enter the race, former California governor Edmund "Jerry" Brown, Jr., who was also smart and serious but had no chance of winning the nomination himself, remained dangerous because of the political mischief he could create for others, especially Clinton.[73]

Clinton's most formidable foe turned out to be his own past. A month before the primary season was to open in New Hampshire, Clinton led the pack. He had raised an impressive amount of money, had hired a talented staff, and was delivering a message that was resonating not only with mainstream Democrats but also with Democrats who had been voting Republican in recent elections. Then there was that raw political talent. Richard Cohen of the *Washington Post* christened him "The Natural," a political incarnation of Roy Hobbs, "the supremely gifted baseball player" of Bernard Malamud's famous novel. "There is not a pitch he cannot hit, no question he cannot answer," Cohen wrote of Clinton.[74] Moreover, it began to appear that the Democratic nomination might be worth having after all. Although President Bush still had a comfortable lead in the polls, the afterglow of the successful Gulf War was dimming, and people were increasingly expressing concerns about a lingering recession. But just when Clinton's prospects looked brightest, the trouble began. A supermarket tabloid reported that Clinton had carried on a longtime affair with Gennifer Flowers, a onetime television reporter and nightclub entertainer in Little Rock. According to the story, Clinton would regularly stop by Flowers's apartment on the pretext that he was visiting aides who lived in the same high-rise. Flowers herself soon appeared on the scene to confirm the story and to play tape-recorded excerpts from telephone conversations between herself and Clinton. At a raucous press conference someone asked Flowers if Clinton had used a condom. After an initial bout of hand-wringing, mainstream television and newspaper editors put the story into general circulation on the pretext that it raised profound questions about the propriety of discussing the private lives of public figures.[75]

With his candidacy suddenly in peril, Clinton once again went on national television. Accompanied by Hillary, he appeared on CBS's highly rated *60 Minutes* immediately following the network's broadcast of the Super Bowl. The program marked a milestone of sorts in the history of American politics. Never before had a major candidate for public office been asked in a national setting to disclose the intimate details of his personal life, including whether he had committed adultery. Clinton denied—falsely as it turned out—that he had had an affair with Flowers. About as close to the truth as he came was when, without providing details, he admitted to "wrongdoing" and to "causing pain in my marriage." But it was probably Hillary's steadfast support that left the stronger impression. "She saved his bacon," recalled the interviewer, Steve Kroft. In defending her husband, however, she sparked controversy of her own. When Kroft suggested, in a backhand way, that theirs was a marriage of convenience—an "understanding and arrangement," she reacted indignantly: "You know, I'm not sitting here—some little woman standing by my man like Tammy Wynette. I'm sitting here because I love him, and I respect him and I honor what he's been through and what we've been through together. And you know, if that's not enough for people, then heck, don't vote for him." The reference was to country music singer Wynette and her signature song, "Stand by Your Man." Wynette demanded an apology, and got it.[76]

It occurred to journalist Joe Klein that Clinton's alleged infidelities may have worked to his advantage among one segment of the population—"working-class white males, who figured that dating lounge singers, dining at McDonald's and being smart enough to be President was the coolest thing ever." (Why, Klein asked, "did Clinton once mention that he had a pickup truck with AstroTurf carpeting the bed?")[77]

More harmful were the new controversies that soon arose. The *Wall Street Journal* recounted how Clinton had avoided the draft twenty years earlier. Then, pressed to say if he had ever used drugs during his college years, Clinton admitted trying marijuana once or twice at Oxford. But he added that he "didn't like it, and didn't inhale, and never tried it again." The "didn't inhale" line, which became one of Clinton's six entries in *Bartlett's Familiar Quotations*, reinforced an impression of duplicitousness he would never shake. It was what aides called the "Slick Willie" problem, an image that he would do or say anything to get elected.[78] Clinton's artful—and sometimes not so artful—mincing of words exasperated even his most loyal advisers. "As time went on," recalled press aide Dee Dee Myers, "you'd always find out there was more to the story. It wasn't that what he told you wasn't true, it just wasn't the whole story." That, she concluded, "was hard for everybody."[79]

The rapid-fire controversies raised doubts about Clinton's honesty. But they also drew attention to a more attractive characteristic: a remarkable resiliency in the face of setbacks. Not that he remained impervious to events. Personal attacks could still trigger a ferocious temper followed by bouts of self-pity and depression. But somehow he always bounced back.

Everyone who knew him had a story to tell about his resiliency. For Wisconsin's veteran congressman, David Obey, it was about Clinton's visit to the Badger State a week before its primary. Clinton was flying in from New York, and Obey met him at the airport. "All day the headlines had pounded him mercilessly," Obey recalled. "When he stepped out of the plane and climbed into the waiting car for the drive to the Legion Hall in Stevens Point for a rally, he was in a subdued mood." "How are you doing?" Obey asked. "I know it's been a rough week." Looking straight ahead at the back of the driver's seat and slowly rubbing his hands together, Clinton replied in a hoarse, barely audible voice, "I'm all right. I'm all right." "We'll get through this. We'll get through this," he kept repeating. As they entered the Legion Hall Clinton paused, took a deep breath, and then plunged into the crowd as he made his way to the podium. Along the way he grasped every outstretched hand he could, taking time to look each person in the eye. "With every handshake, the crowd was warming him up and energizing him," Obey recalled. "By the time he spoke, he had been transformed from a physically pallid, preoccupied, million-miles-away figure to a funny, charming master of the crowd. The energy of that crowd had flowed into his body and spirit every bit as much as if he had been given a blood transfusion." Obey had never seen anything like it: "I remember thinking that I had never seen a human being who possessed such an ability to draw upon his own inner resources as he had shown in that car ride to Stevens Point. And I had never seen a politician with such an astonishing ability to soak up every bit of warmth and energy from a crowd and make it his own."[80]

In the end, Clinton outlasted his opponents. Jerry Brown and Paul Tsongas stayed in the longest, waiting for another disclosure that would deliver the knockout blow; it never came. Although Clinton had seemingly won enough delegates to ensure a first ballot victory at the Democratic Convention in New York City, the primaries had left him bloodied and bruised. Even those who had voted for him may have been experiencing "buyers' remorse," suspecting that the all-but-certain candidate of their party could never survive the general election. As the convention approached, some delegates pledged to Clinton were being rumored to be switching their support to another candidate, presumably Mario Cuomo, to salvage any hopes of victory in November.[81]

Clinton's biggest problem, his aides concluded, was not solely a result of the misdeeds he had been accused of. Internal polls and focus groups revealed that people believed not only that he had done bad things but also that he was the product of a privileged, out-of-touch upbringing. Clinton aide Paul Begala later summed up the campaign's findings: "This is what people knew: Yale, Georgetown, Oxford, dodged the draft, smoked pot, cheated on his wife. And because we reason by inference, they stitched all those things together and they came up with: rich, spoiled, never had a hard day in his life, driving his father's Alfa Romeo around Ivy League campus."[82] Many voters had no idea the Clintons had a daughter, perhaps assuming instead that Bill and Hillary were ambitious careerists too busy for such mundane matters as raising a family. When participants in focus groups were told details about Clinton's early life in Hope and Hot Springs—about his father dying in a car wreck, about his middle-class upbringing, about Chelsea—they immediately viewed him more favorably.

To dispel misconceptions about their candidate, aides redoubled efforts to book him on what they called "pop-culture" shows. And to anyone within the campaign who thought such appearances were unpresidential, staffers Mandy Grunwald and Frank Greer responded, "Bull. This is how people get information. These are forums for more personal and varied looks at Bill and Hillary and Chelsea."[83] Perhaps his most talked-about appearance was on the late-night talk show hosted by Arsenio Hall. Clinton walked out on stage wearing wrap-around sunglasses and a fluorescent tie and played "Heart Break Hotel" on his saxophone. He told Hall that he had wanted to "inhale" but just didn't know how.[84] On Don Imus's syndicated radio show, whose host had been scornfully referring to him as "Bubba," Clinton joked that where he came from to be called Bubba was a badge of honor.

The campaign, meanwhile, took an unexpected turn when Texas billionaire H. Ross Perot entered the race as an independent candidate. Perot, who had made his fortune in computer services, ran on the promise of restoring business principles and fiscal integrity to Washington. Even more than Clinton, Perot relied on television talk shows to communicate with the electorate. He announced his candidacy on Larry King's popular cable television program and rarely appeared in public. Perot was easy to parody. In a campaign retrospective, *Newsweek* reporters described the sixty-one-year-old Texan as "a banty rooster of a man with question-mark ears, a mangled nose, a barber-college haircut and an East Texas drawl as thin and sharp as wine gone to vinegar."[85] Perot ran one of the most unconventional campaigns in history. He not only refused to appear at rallies but also ignored the advice of the seasoned professionals he hired to run the campaign. Then, at the height of his popularity, he mysteriously suspended his campaign for several critical months only to later reenter the contest. Yet, so strong was anti-Washington sentiment and an enveloping sense of national unease that at the beginning of the summer Perot led both Bush and Clinton in the polls. Moreover, his promise to rein in runaway deficits set the tone for the campaign (and for Clinton's first months in office).[86]

The Democratic and Republican conventions played a larger role in the campaign than they had since the seventies. Not that the nominees for either party were ever in doubt. But for Clinton, the convention in Madison Square Garden in New York City gave him his last, best chance to reintroduce himself to the public as a champion of the middle class rather than a slick politician with a pampered past. He made the most of it. A brilliantly produced, fourteen-minute film, *The Man from Hope*, sought to dispel, once and for all, his silver-spoon image. The film was the handiwork of the very same Hollywood producer and Clinton friend Linda Bloodworth-Thomason, who, with her husband, had helped salvage Clinton's career four years earlier by getting him on the *Tonight Show*. Once again she came to the rescue. *The Man from Hope* depicted Clinton as the embodiment of small-town, middle-class America—a devoted son, husband, and father who had had his share of troubles in life but had surmounted them all. The convention as a whole went off without a hitch. Dissident voices, like Jesse Jackson and the anti-abortion governor of Pennsylvania, Robert Casey, were kept off center stage, while Clinton's mother, wife, and daughter were much in evidence. Clinton's most effective move, however, was the center-staging of vice presidential nominee Senator Al Gore of Tennessee, whose selection he had announced the week before. Casting aside the usual considerations of geography and ideological balance, Clinton tapped, in Gore, a fellow-southerner and self-described "New Democrat," supposedly not wedded to the liberal orthodoxies of the past. It helped, too, that Gore was a Vietnam veteran, although he had served well behind combat lines. "In a way that no one really anticipated," recalled Bruce Reed, who had worked at different times for both Clinton and Gore, "the sight of these two young men of the same generation, with young families, turned the election into a generational contest that we hadn't really expected." Insiders were also struck by the differences between the two. Reed again: "Gore had a computer-like approach. . . . He was more a scientist than a politician." Clinton "was more impressionistic," more improvisational. "He loved to riff." On the stump, Clinton never gave exactly the same speech more than once; Gore nearly always did. Everyone agreed Gore was the more structured and self-disciplined of the two.[87] Immediately following their convention triumph, the two candidates updated the legendary whistle-stop train trips of yore by leading a bus caravan through the tier of northern states—from New York to Illinois—the campaign considered a key to victory.[88]

The Republican convention, by contrast, did more harm than good to its candidate. Speaker after speaker assailed the Clintons as embodiments of the worst excesses of the 1960s. Columnist and former Nixon aide Patrick Buchanan, who earlier had challenged Bush for the GOP nomination, accused the Clintons of trying to impose on America "abortion on demand, a litmus test for the Supreme Court, homosexual rights, discrimination against religious schools, women in combat units." In the epic "struggle for the soul of America," which Buchanan compared in importance to the Cold War, the Clintons "are on the other side and George Bush is on our side."[89] Following their convention, Bush supporters continued the assault. In hopes that the public would imagine the worst, they called attention to the fact that Clinton had visited the Soviet Union twenty years earlier while a student at Oxford. What was he doing there, they asked with feigned innocence? And why couldn't he remember the details of his trip? But with the Cold War over, what Clinton may or may not have been doing in Moscow those many years before didn't resonate as it might have in times past. Frustrated by the apparent ingratitude of the public and by its seeming unconcern about the character of his opponent, Bush increasingly resorted to shrill attacks. By the end of the campaign, he was referring to Clinton and Gore as "bozos" and to Gore as "Ozone Man" because of his warnings about the depletion of the upper atmospheric ozone layer.[90]

In defeating Michael Dukakis four years earlier, President Bush had earned a reputation for being willing to unfairly besmirch the character of his opponents. Indeed, the mastermind of Bush's last campaign, Lee Atwater, had apologized for the campaign's tactics before his death in 1991. Bush's reputation probably helped blunt his attacks this time around. As two journalists later noted, "the public mind-set on Bush as a negative campaigner gave Clinton a freer hand to hit at him." Or as Clinton aide George Stephanopoulos put it, "There was nothing we could do to make people think we were more negative than Bush. There was just no way."[91]

Clinton entered the three presidential debates, all held in October, with commanding leads over Bush and Perot, who ended his hiatus from the campaign in time for the first debate. The most talked-about moments both occurred during the second debate in Richmond, Virginia. At the insistence of the Clinton campaign, the debate was conducted like a town meeting with members of the audience, rather than reporters, asking the questions. The key moment came when a woman asked the candidates how the national debt affected them personally. President Bush struggled to respond, asking the questioner for clarification. Here was a situation in which all those years of "friends and neighbors" campaigning in Arkansas would pay off for Clinton. When it came his turn, he stood up, took a couple of steps in the direction of the questioner, and, understanding that her awkward question about the national debt was really about economic hard times, asked her how the downturn had affected her. "You know people who've lost their jobs and lost their homes?" he asked. When she answered yes, Clinton began a brilliant two-minute colloquy saying that when somebody got laid off in Arkansas, he could feel for them because he probably knew them personally. While Clinton spoke, the camera caught a seemingly impatient President Bush checking his watch. His campaign aides said later that he was seeing if Clinton was exceeding the agreed-upon time limits for answering questions, but Clinton's response and Bush's reaction helped fix in the minds of many the image of Clinton as a man who could empathize with the struggles of ordinary people and of a president who was bored by the whole subject. Clinton's staff was ecstatic. For all intents and purposes, recalled campaign chair Mickey Kantor, "this was the end of the campaign." Perot may have benefited most from the trio of debates, more than doubling his poll numbers from the first to the last. But the biggest impact of the debates was to deny Bush a last chance to change the dynamics of the race, which had remained constant since the conventions.[92]

Back on the stump, Clinton continued to burnish his image as a New Democrat, willing to break with Democratic orthodoxies of the past. He vowed "to end welfare as we know it" and "put more policemen on the street and more criminals behind bars." Four years earlier, Michael Dukakis had been tripped up by his opposition to the death penalty. Clinton was for it. As if to drive home the point, he had returned to Arkansas in January to preside over the execution of Ricky Ray Rector, a brain-damaged black man convicted of murdering a white police officer. He also had seemed to go out of his way to distance himself from controversial black leaders like Jesse Jackson. In June, at a meeting of Jackson's Rainbow Coalition, Clinton had compared another guest, black rap singer Sister Souljah, to Louisiana white racist David Duke. A month before, in the aftermath of race riots in Los Angeles, Souljah had told the *Washington Post:* "If black people kill black people every day, why not have a week and kill white people? So if you're a gang member and you would normally be killing somebody, why not kill a white person." The comments were outrageous, to be sure. But that Clinton remained silent about them until he appeared on the program with Souljah struck Jackson as a stunt to attract white votes.[93]

Given his effort to jettison the stereotypical "racial liberal" image, Clinton surprised at least one of his aides by reworking his schedule so he could spend the final weekend of the campaign visiting African American churches. To pollster Stan Greenberg, who believed the greatest challenge of the Democrats was to regain the support of disaffected white working- and middle-class voters, Clinton's last-minute decision made no sense. Why would Clinton devote the precious, closing hours of the campaign wooing voters who were already his? Had somebody gotten to him, "his Arkansas supporters, maybe his liberal Hollywood friends?" Only years later did Greenberg think he had made sense of the episode. Clinton's quest for the presidency, the pollster came to believe, involved both a "political project" and a "personal mission." The political project, which was key to getting elected, was to champion the middle-class, without appeals to race. But it was a means to an end. The end—Clinton's personal mission—was "to take the South and the country beyond the deep racial divisions and the racial thinking and to make our diversity a national strength." Only later would Clinton's intentions fully manifest themselves, Greenberg believed, although the signs of those intentions were apparent throughout Clinton's early life if one looked closely enough.[94]

On Election Day, November 3, Clinton received just fewer than 45 million votes or 43 percent to 39 million or 37 percent for Bush and 18 million or 19 percent for Perot. Perot's share was the largest for a third-party candidate since Theodore Roosevelt in 1912. Clinton earned a more comfortable margin in the Electoral College with 370 to 168 for Bush and a single vote for Perot. Then and later Bush partisans insisted Perot had cost the incumbent the election.[95] Subsequent analysis suggested, however, that Clinton would have prevailed even if Perot had remained on the sidelines. Some projections had Clinton amassing seven more percentage points in a head-to-head with Bush. In exit polls, 38 percent of Perot voters said they would have voted for Clinton if Perot had not been in the race, 38 percent said they would have voted for Bush, and 24 percent said they would have stayed home.[96]

Clinton could take satisfaction in being the first Democrat to win the presidency since 1976. Had Bush won, an entire generation of voters would have come of age without a first-hand memory of a Democrat in the White House, a situation that, barring a depression or some other major crisis, might have immunized younger voters from supporting a Democrat for the foreseeable future. Clinton could take pride, too, in having run an almost flawless campaign after the primaries concluded. The campaign's nerve center in Little Rock, dubbed the "war room" by Hillary Clinton, set a new standard for coordinating rapid-fire attacks and counterattacks against their foes. The brainchild of James Carville, the war room became the prototype for future campaigns, Democratic and Republican.[97]

There were disappointments. Falling short of a majority meant Clinton would have difficulty claiming a mandate. Nor, as a self-described "new" Democrat, did he succeed in winning back many of the Democrats who had been voting Republican at least since 1980. The so-called Reagan Democrats deserted Bush in droves, but most of them voted for Perot and not for Clinton. Clinton may also have been disappointed that his share of the black vote, though large at 83 percent, was less than the previous two Democratic candidates.[98]

In the final accounting, the election turned more on the incumbent than on his challengers. In the largest turnout since 1968, two-thirds of the electorate had voted against President Bush. Fully a month before the election, Bush campaign aides privately concluded the race was over, and had been since a week after the conventions. "People are sick of the president. They don't dislike him but they want him gone, and we're powerless to do anything about it."[99] As for Clinton, as one analyst put it, "He won not a personal mandate but a chance to prove himself."[100]

Taking Office, 1993

Of the problems Clinton faced upon taking office, the economy was most pressing. He had won the election on a promise to create good jobs, and now he had to deliver. This meant grappling with America's role in an increasingly global economy. Globalization, to use the catchword, was hardly a new phenomenon; the integration of national economies had been going on for centuries. But the end of the Cold War accelerated the process by opening up vast new areas of the world to economic development. For the United States, globalization offered both opportunities and pitfalls. On the plus side, it held out the promise of expanded markets for American goods and services. Having to compete in a global marketplace might spur American businesses to become more innovative, productive, and efficient. On the negative side, globalization could lead to plant closings and job losses, as American corporations, unable to compete with their foreign counterparts, either went out of business or moved their operations to countries where labor costs were cheap and health, safety, and environmental regulations practically nonexistent. For American workers, globalization was producing winners and losers. Well-educated workers with strong conceptual and problem-solving skills—from software designers to investment bankers—were prospering as never before. The rest of the population, some 80 percent, were either stuck in neutral or falling behind.[1] Clinton had witnessed both sides of globalization in his home state. Now he would confront them on a national scale.

Globalization was inextricably linked with Clinton's second great challenge: the need to redefine America's role in the world in the aftermath of the Cold War. At first glance, he appeared to be in an enviable position. As Clinton critic William Hyland put it, "The nation was at peace. Its principal enemy had collapsed. The United States was the world's only genuine superpower." "The new President," Hyland concluded, "was free to reconstruct America's role in the world."[2] But appearances were deceiving. The Soviet Union had collapsed all right, but it had left in its wake large stockpiles of nuclear weapons and smoldering ethnic, religious, and nationalistic conflicts, any one of which could disrupt international stability. Moreover, there existed starkly different visions of the emerging post–Cold War world. Were democracy and capitalism destined to take root throughout the world, as scholar Francis Fukuyama predicted in his much-discussed book, *The End of History and the Last Man*? Or would the world fragment along ethnic, religious, and cultural lines, as political scientist Samuel P. Huntington argued in *The Clash of Civilizations and the Remaking of the World Order*?[3] And what could the United States do to steer the world in the desired direction? As Clinton cast about for an answer, he found, as President Bush had before him, that the policy of containment, which had guided the thinking of every president from Truman to Reagan, was suddenly obsolete. Clinton now had to reassess America's strategic interests, square them with his campaign pledge to promote democracy and human rights, formulate a coherent policy, and sell it to an American public largely indifferent to events abroad. In some ways, he faced the toughest challenge of any president since Harry Truman, whose administration had set the United States on its nearly half-century course of containment.

Closer to home, any hope Clinton had of advancing his agenda depended upon his ability to expand his political base beyond the 43 percent of the electorate that had voted for him in 1992. Success would also require breathing new life into a Democratic Party that, while momentarily buoyed by his election, remained deeply divided and still burdened with the heavy baggage of having lost four out of the last six presidential contests.

"Governing in the modern era," reporter John Harris noted, "is above all a task of communication."[4] Therein lay a fourth problem for Clinton, for by the time he became president, recent changes in the way the media covered politics had made the task of communicating with the public more challenging than ever. There was the twenty-four-hour news cycle, with its insatiable demand for sound bites and vivid images and its ability to magnify many times over—and replay endlessly—the slightest presidential misstep. There was the proliferation of talk radio and tabloid television programs, which gave almost unlimited airtime to Clinton's foes like Rush Limbaugh and a host of less-talented imitators. And there was the emerging Internet, which even in its infancy had the potential to instantly circulate throughout the globe the most outlandish rumor. Clinton's toughest challenge was simply to be heard above the clatter.[5]

The nation was in a sour mood when the new administration took office, the public dispirited, skeptical, and apprehensive. The economy was mostly to blame, and not just the recession. By 1993, almost all economic indicators were headed upward. Yet a pervasive uncertainty about the future remained, what with almost daily headlines about factory closings, "outsourcing," and corporate mergers. Most Americans had never heard the word "globalization," much less grasped its implications. They were, nevertheless, worried about the economic future.

Racial and ethnic tensions, never far from the center of American life, contributed to the unease. In April 1992, in the middle of presidential primary season, the acquittal of three white policemen who had been accused of using excessive force in the arrest of Rodney King, an African American, touched off one of the deadliest riots in American history. Before it was over, 55 persons were killed, 2,300 injured. As the King verdict and its aftermath demonstrated—and as the infamous O. J. Simpson murder trial would soon underscore—racial polarization remained an unsettling reality in American life.

Just as disquieting was the surge of immigration, three-quarters of it from Latin America and Asia, just then washing over the country. The wave had been set off by the repeal of the exclusionary quota system that had restricted entry into the United States from the 1920s to its repeal in 1965. During ensuing decades the United States experienced the largest influx of immigrants since the first decades of the twentieth century. By the time Clinton became president, nearly one in five Americans could point to one parent born in Latin America or Asia. In addition to familiar complaints that immigrants competed for scarce jobs, depressed wages, and strained local and state social services, some critics feared that the nation was becoming Balkanized along ethnic and racial lines. Historian

Arthur M. Schlesinger, Jr., no foe of immigration, decried the "cult of ethnicity" that threatened the cherished ideal of America as melting pot.[6]

Before and after Clinton became president, there was much talk about America's fall from grace as a great nation. In 1941, publisher Henry Luce had famously proclaimed the twentieth as the American century. Now, as the century neared an end, some wondered if the United States would retain its dominance. With the Soviet Union no longer a danger, some believed the nation's chief threat came from within—from an un-raveling of its moral fiber. As historian James T. Patterson noted, many such complaints "emanated from conservatives who were feeling mar-ginalized by liberalizing cultural changes and who were outraged by what they perceived as ever expanding evils: sexual immorality, violent crime, vulgarity and sensationalism in the media, schools without stan-dards, trash that passes as 'art,' and just plain bad taste." But concerns about the moral health of the nation arose from other quarters as well. Iconoclastic Senator Daniel Patrick Moynihan of New York deplored the growing tendency "of defining deviancy down" by accepting as nor-mal behavior once considered aberrant, such as out-of-wedlock births. Others bemoaned the decline of civic engagement and volunteerism.[7]

To even a casual student of history, most of these laments had a fa-miliar ring. Americans, for all of their vaunted optimism, even hubris, had always been given to periodic bouts of self-doubt. It was, after all, the widespread belief that the United States had allowed itself to be-come militarily and morally flabby in the face of the Soviet threat that helped propel Clinton's hero, John F. Kennedy, to the White House. But if handwringing about the state of the nation was not new, an acute pes-simism about America's ability to solve what ailed it—at least through government—may have been. One of the most talked about books of the early nineties—and a Clinton favorite—was journalist E. J. Dionne's *Why Americans Hate Politics.* Dionne argued that since the 1960s liber-als and conservatives had increasingly offered the public a series of false, either/or choices when in fact most Americans were somewhere in the middle. Dionne pointed out, for example, that most people felt sharply conflicted on the issue of abortion. But politics allowed no ambivalence: Abortion was either murder or a fundamental right. Nowhere was the polarization Dionne talked of more evident than in Congress where sev-eral key insiders feared extreme partisanship was undermining efforts to solve common problems.[8] By the mid-nineties, two-thirds of all votes fell along party lines as compared to a third in the late sixties and early seventies. During one four-year stretch, the Democratic and Republican leaders in the House personally spoke to each other only eight times. For this state of affairs, Republicans singled out the rancorous Senate hearings over Republican Supreme Court nominees Robert Bork and Clarence Thomas in the late eighties and early nineties as the point of no return. Democrats, at least in the House of Representatives, dated the flashpoint to the rise of Georgia Republican Newt Gingrich. Political scientists told a more complicated story involving long-term political realignments in the South and elsewhere.[9] But whatever the origins of discord, much of Clinton's appeal as a self-proclaimed new Democrat was his promise to inaugurate a new era of bipartisan collaboration on Capitol Hill.

For all the daunting challenges Clinton faced, there were also welcome opportunities. The end of the Cold War required fundamental rethinking of American foreign policy, a process that American policy makers had not confronted since the 1940s. But the collapse of the Soviet Union also potentially freed up a substantial portion of the federal budget for addressing long-neglected domestic needs. It offered the possibility of refreshing the intellectually stale, but politically potent, argument about which party offered a more effective bulwark against the Russian threat. And despite a prevailing mood of public pessimism, the fact that the election had drawn a larger percentage of voters to the polls than at any time since 1968 suggested that the public continued to believe that Washington still mattered in their lives.

Between the election and the inauguration, Clinton devoted most of his time—too much time, he later conceded—fulfilling a campaign pledge to choose a cabinet that "looks like America." The final assembly, in certain respects the most diverse in history, included three African Americans, three women, two Hispanics, and a disabled Vietnam War veteran. Otherwise most picks were surprisingly conventional, especially from one who was promising dramatic change. For secretary of state, Clinton chose sixty-seven-year-old Warren Christopher, a prominent lawyer whose long career had included service in the Johnson and Carter administrations. Best known for negotiating the release of the

American hostages in Iran during the Carter presidency, Christopher had cochaired Clinton's transition team along with Clinton intimate and civil rights icon Vernon Jordan. Defense went to iconoclastic Wisconsin congressman and chair of the House Armed Services Committee, Les Aspin.

More formidable was Treasury Secretary Lloyd Bentsen, a key appointee in view of Clinton's outsider status and the importance he attached to the economy. Seventy-two years old, Bentsen was a conservative Democrat from Texas who had served in both houses of Congress. He was best known as the Democratic vice presidential candidate in 1988 who, during a televised debate, had devastated his Republican counterpart, Dan Quayle, with his withering, "You're no Jack Kennedy" put-down. Clinton chose Bentsen because of his legislative experience but also to reassure business and financial interests that the economy would be in safe hands. Dubbed "Loop-hole Lloyd" by liberal detractors for his business-friendly tax views, Bentsen had made millions in the financial services industry and had close ties to the oil and gas and banking sectors in his home state.[10] Impeccably dressed, Bentsen projected a courtly but intimidating presence. Upon assuming his new position, Bentsen invited his colleagues to call him by his first name. One high-ranking Treasury official tried and tried but could never get "Lloyd" out; it was always "Senator" or "Mr. Secretary."[11] Bentsen even intimidated cabinet colleagues. At one of their first meetings, Clinton went around the room asking each secretary for ideas on how to eliminate wasteful spending. Labor Secretary Robert Reich suggested that henceforth cabinet members fly coach rather than first class. "Coach?" asked Bentsen. "I don't believe that would be appropriate."[12] Another time, Bentsen, with no thought that he might have to clear it with the president, made a major announcement on tax policy on *Meet the Press*. Yet, as one of the few experienced Washington insiders in the new administration, the new Treasury secretary was a stabilizing force during Clinton's hectic first year.

Other cabinet appointments of particular note were Bruce Babbitt, the smart and able former governor of Arizona, at Interior; Henry Cisneros, the accomplished former mayor of San Antonio, at Housing and Urban Development; and University of Wisconsin chancellor Donna Shalala at Health and Human Services. The task of filling the Justice

Department post stoked the only major controversy. Because Justice was considered to be one of the four most prestigious cabinet positions along with State, Treasury, and Defense, Clinton very much wanted a woman for the post to offset the men he had placed in the other three positions. His first two choices were forced to withdraw when it came to light that they had failed to pay social security taxes for household employees. Clinton finally settled on Janet Reno, a state attorney general from Dade County, Florida, whose independence from the White House would nettle Clinton loyalists and eventually have an unexpectedly major impact on Clinton's presidency.

If one had had to predict at the outset which cabinet member would exert the most influence, Labor Secretary Robert Reich would have been a good bet. He had known Clinton since their years in Oxford together as Rhodes Scholars, and his ideas, spelled out most fully in his book *The Work of Nations*, helped shape Clinton's views as a New Democrat. "We are living through a transformation that will rearrange the politics and economics of the coming century," Reich wrote. "There will be no national products or technologies, no national corporations, no national industries." There was a time, Reich explained, when General Motors hired American workers to make cars with American parts for American consumers. No longer. GM's popular Pontiac Le Mans was designed in Germany and assembled in South Korea with components made in Taiwan, Singapore, and Japan. British firms formulated advertising and marketing strategies for GM, while workers in Ireland and Barbados provided data processing services. The internationalization of production was transforming not only the auto industry but also the manufacturers of everything from ice-hockey equipment to jet airplanes to space satellites. There was no turning back the clock, Reich argued. Neither restrictions on foreign imports nor bailouts of faltering American industries could long stem the tide of globalization. But the United States still had two major assets over which it did have control: its workforce and its infrastructure. Government needed to enhance both. It needed to equip its citizens with the conceptual and problem-solving skills to better enable them to thrive in the new international economy, and it needed to upgrade its public highways, bridges, trains, and schools.[13]

Reich's ideas resonated with Clinton. They helped put in perspective his experiences as governor. Capital might come and go, but the state's people and infrastructure remained. And what Clinton had tried to do, especially with education reform, was what Reich was recommending for the nation as a whole. Clinton's campaign booklet, *Putting People First*, drew heavily from Reich's ideas, and Clinton put him in charge of the economic team during the transition. By any measure then, Reich should have been one of Clinton's most trusted advisers. He was not. Though remaining personally close to the president, he never became part of Clinton's inner circle. On occasion Reich even had to funnel memos through Hillary Clinton to make sure the president, his friend of twenty-five years, would read them.[14]

As it turned out, Clinton's economic team had his ear more often than Reich or most other cabinet members. There was Lloyd Bentsen at Treasury, of course, but also Bentsen deputy Lawrence Summers, chief economist at the World Bank and a rising star in the economics profession. By his own estimation and that of everyone who knew him, the thirty-eight-year-old Summers was brash and brilliant. The nephew of two Nobel laureates in economics, Summers had a sterling academic resume: a BS from MIT, a PhD from Harvard, and the youngest Harvard professor in modern times to earn tenure. He had published dozens of path-breaking articles and was the recipient of his profession's most prestigious award, the John Clark Bates Medal. Summers prided himself on being a hardheaded realist who eschewed untested dogma. Indeed, the citation for the Bates Medal credited him with restoring "the primacy of actual economies over abstract models in much of economic thinking."[15] Nor, like Clinton, did he consider himself to be a political ideologue. He had advised Michael Dukakis in 1988 and Bill Clinton in 1992. But he had also served as chief economist on Reagan's Council of Economic Advisers. And while he eventually became critical of the Reagan administration's fixation on supply-side economics, he espoused positions that defied liberal orthodoxy such as lowering corporate and capital gains tax rates. Summers alarmed environmentalists by suggesting that the United States and other developed nations should encourage polluting industries to relocate in Third World countries, where, presumably, they could take advantage of a pollution deficit. The suggestion, contained in a paper Summers had written at the World Bank, outraged environmentalists (reportedly including Al Gore) when it leaked to the press and probably cost him a more prestigious position than undersecretary at Treasury. But Summers's misstep only temporarily slowed his ascent to power.[16]

An even more important cadre of economic advisers was lodged in the White House. Here the key person was Robert E. Rubin, a prominent investment banker whom Clinton selected to head the newly created National Economic Council (NEC). Historically, responsibility for formulating economic policy had been divided among a half-dozen or more cabinet departments and executive agencies. At least since Franklin Roosevelt's time, presidents had been trying to centralize economic planning and make it more systematic and orderly. But the growth of the federal government, coupled with the increasing complexity of economic management, outpaced all efforts at reform. Now it was Clinton's turn. His solution was to create by executive order the National Economic Council, which was loosely modeled on an informal setup in the Reagan White House. Clinton envisioned the NEC as an economic version of the National Security Council (NSC), which served as a clearinghouse for almost all matters relating to national security and foreign affairs and reported directly to the president. Like the NSC, the NEC was to gather and evaluate information from all relevant departments and agencies, debate the issues, and recommend specific policies to the president. If the president adopted these policies, the NEC would monitor their implementation. In an age of globalization, with the boundaries between domestic and foreign policy often overlapping, the new sixteen-member agency was also charged with responsibility for coordinating domestic and international economic policies.[17]

Like most of Clinton's high-level appointees, the head of the NEC, fifty-five-year-old Rubin, had an academic and professional background reminiscent of John F. Kennedy's foreign policy advisers—"the best and the brightest," in journalist David Halberstam's famous (and ironic) formulation. Born in New York City and raised there and in Miami, Rubin was the son of a successful real estate lawyer. A graduate of the Miami public schools, Rubin liked to tell about his harrowing first years as an undergraduate at Harvard where most of his classmates had attended elite preparatory schools like Groton or Andover or top-flight public schools. At the beginning of the class on English literature, the professor, wanting to assign books the students had not already read, asked for a show of hands as he went through a long list of classics. As the other students repeatedly put up their hands, Rubin's remained in his lap. "It wasn't only that I hadn't read these books," he recalled. "I had never even heard of most of them."[18] But by the time he graduated, he had acquired enough self-confidence that he wrote the dean of admissions at Princeton, where he had been turned down four years earlier. "I thought you might be interested to know what happened to one of the people you rejected. I just wanted to tell you that I graduated from Harvard summa cum laude and Phi Beta Kappa." (The Princeton dean got the last word, however. "Thank you for your note," he wrote Rubin. "Every year, we at Princeton feel it is our duty to reject a certain number of highly qualified people so that Harvard can have some good students too.")[19] From Harvard, Rubin went to the London School of Economics and then to Yale Law School, where he graduated in 1964, a decade before the Clintons. But it was the stock market, not the law, that ultimately captured Rubin's interest. By the 1980s he was cochairman of the investment firm of Goldman Sachs and a Wall Street star. Rubin made his name—and his fortune—by mastering arbitrage, the nerve-wracking, high-stakes game of simultaneously buying securities in one market and selling them in another in hopes of profiting from price differences. In the late seventies, Rubin began raising money for Democratic candidates, including Jimmy Carter. Although he considered himself more of a Democrat than a Republican, he believed the Democrats needed to rein in their spending habits. Listening to a stirring speech by Senator Edward Kennedy calling for a host of new government programs, he recalled thinking that as much as he agreed with Kennedy's goals, he wondered, *How are we going to pay for this?*[20] He was no less skeptical of what he considered the counterproductive habit of some liberals to demonize business and corporate interests. Before one big speech, Rubin told Clinton it was all right to vilify opponents of his budget proposals and free trade policies. But he cautioned the president to "avoid anything that can be interpreted as critical of economic success or anti-business."[21]

Although shy and self-effacing, even awkward in some situations, Rubin was a shrewd inside player who prevailed more often than not over more polished colleagues. His background helped, too. The professional economists in the administration were a distinguished lot. But they studied Wall Street from the outside; Rubin had been on the inside and presumably understood its innermost workings. On close calls, Clinton deferred to Rubin because of his superior experience.

Filling out the president's economic team were Budget Director Leon Panetta, a Democratic congressman from California known for his passion for civil rights and deep aversion to deficits; Panetta's deputy, Alice M. Rivlin, an early recipient of a "genius" grant from the MacArthur Foundation, first director of the Congressional Budget Office, and, like Rubin and Panetta, a "deficit hawk" who had criticized Clinton during the campaign for failing to be more specific about how he would curtail spending; and Berkeley economist Laura D'Andrea Tyson, chair of the Council of Economic Advisers (CEA). Tyson's appointment stirred the most controversy. Conservatives thought her insufficiently committed to free trade, while some of her professional colleagues, including MIT's Paul Krugman, himself a candidate for the position, believed that the MIT-trained Tyson simply lacked the qualifications to be the nation's chief economist. Some even argued that Clinton's creation of the National Economic Council made the forty-seven-year-old CEA obsolete. Tyson's defenders, noting that she was the first woman to be nominated for council chair, believed the outcry against her said more about a male-dominated economics profession than about her qualifications.[22] Tyson, who had the strong backing of Robert Reich, won the position in part, she recalled, because "the people who were really vying for it were too busy knocking each other out to really think of me." Knowing that economists like Krugman would say "I told you so" if the CEA lost ground to Robert Rubin's NEC, Tyson was determined to create "the best possible CEA imaginable."[23]

Once confirmed, Tyson held her own. She recruited to the three-member council two of the nation's leading academic economists, Alan Blinder of Princeton and future Nobel Laureate Joseph Stiglitz of Stanford. And she reached an understanding with Rubin that the two councils would try to complement one another rather than compete for influence. In Washington, Tyson recalled, influence is measured by "face time" with the president and vice president and by being included in meetings where the important decisions are made. Vice President Gore helped with the face time. He told Tyson that he and the president had plenty of briefings on national security but not enough on economic matters. Why not brief the president and vice president every day just as the chair of the National Security Council did? That, Tyson decided, was too much face time. With only a fraction of the personnel available to the huge national security apparatus, having to prepare a daily briefing would stretch CEA resources beyond the limit. So she and the vice president decided on weekly briefings. Perhaps even more important than face time with the president, Tyson believed, was gaining access to the key meetings. If she learned of a meeting to which she or her colleagues had not been invited, she would make her case to the president's chief of staff. In that way she became the first CEA chair to have a seat at the chief of staff's morning meeting, where, she recalled, "a lot of decisions get made about what the administration should be working on or what should be done."[24] Still, try as she might, Tyson could not prevent the NEC from eventually gaining the upper hand. In 1995, she herself left the CEA to head the NEC.[25]

The nomination that unexpectedly caused Clinton the most personal and political anguish was that of University of Pennsylvania law professor Lani Guinier to head the Justice Department's Civil Rights Division. A graduate of Radcliffe College and Yale Law School, the forty-three-year-old Guinier was the daughter of a black professor at Harvard and a white Jewish mother. Before teaching law, she had served in the Civil Rights Division she now hoped to head and on the staff of the NAACP's Legal Defense and Education Fund. Guinier first met the Clintons in law school. They had been friends ever since. The Clintons had attended her wedding. Three days after the inauguration, she and two friends had the new president and first lady to dinner. "In his moment of public triumph," she remembered thinking at the time, "Bill Clinton had simply left his grand House to celebrate in the modest home of an honest-to-goodness black friend. We were impressed. We knew that Bill Clinton was probably the very first president of the United States to have enough black friends to hold a party, not just convene a photo opportunity."[26] Before the president put her name forward she was chiefly known as a successful civil rights litigator and critic of the Reagan administration for its lax enforcement of the Voting Rights Act. As if to underscore his commitment to racial justice, Clinton liked to boast that when he was governor of Arkansas, Guinier had sued him over a voter registration provision. "Not only that, she didn't lose. And I nominated her anyway."

The trouble began when critics scoured her law review articles and occasional op-ed pieces. In these writings, Guinier argued that even with the Voting Rights Act, African Americans were often unable to influence politics to an extent anywhere close to their numbers in the population. That was because the nation's winner-take-all electoral system allowed whites, voting as a bloc, to negate minority influence. Guinier was hardly the first to recognize this downside to the American system. A century-and-a-half earlier, Alexis de Tocqueville coined the phrase "tyranny of the majority" in his classic *Democracy in America.* Guinier's remedies included requiring supermajorities—not just 51 percent—to pass legislation in certain circumstances and a process called "cumulative voting." As she later described cumulative voting, "instead of dividing a city with seven elected officials into seven wards or districts, all city voters [regardless of race] get seven votes. Voters can use their seven votes in any combination to support candidates of their choice. They could vote all seven for one candidate or divide their votes, putting three on one candidate and four on another." In practice, cumulative voting had the potential to give minorities a greater say in the outcome than they might otherwise have had. None of Guinier's proposals was without precedent. Corporate shareholders commonly employed cumulative voting to select their boards of directors. Some states, including Illinois and Alabama, had used the practice from time to time in certain localities. As for super majorities, the filibuster rule in the US Senate, requiring sixty votes to pass legislation, was a conspicuous example. Variants of Guinier's proposed practices were fixtures in Israel and most European countries.[27] Still, Guinier's proposals, written in the abstruse language of law review articles, defied easy comprehension. One writer resorted to algebraic formulas in an attempt to explain how cumulative voting would work in a hypothetical situation: "In this situation any vote share above $1/(1 + s)$ where s equals the number of seats guarantees a seat—in this case, group [x] has $1/10$ of the votes and only needs $1/11$ to make sure of winning a representative."[28] More to the point, the very suggestion that the persistence of racism required tinkering with the electoral system was sure to unsettle many, especially many whites, who believed discrimination was largely a thing of the past.

The first anti-Guinier salvos came from the Right. In an op-ed piece in the *Wall Street Journal* entitled "Clinton's Quota Queens," Clint Bolick, a former member of the Reagan administration, accused the nominee of setting "the standard for innovative radicalism." She was, he said, in favor of "racial quotas in judicial appointments" and "abandonment . . . of majority rule itself."[29] *Journal* columnist Paul Gigot characterized her ideas as "a racial apartheid system." GOP Minority Leader Robert Dole, who had once praised Guinier, accused her of advocating "vote-rigging schemes that make quotas look mild." The "Quota Queen" sobriquet—and worse—quickly spread. A *Philadelphia Inquirer* editor called her a "mad woman" with "cockamamie ideas." To *US News and World Report*, she was a woman with "a strange name, strange hair, strange ideas." Abigail Thernstrom, a longtime opponent of affirmative action, called her a "racial separatist."[30] Many of the attacks were so patently ill-informed and polemical they could be easily dismissed or even turned to Guinier's advantage.

Not so with the second round of salvos that came not from the Right but from the heart of Clinton's fragile political coalition: the center and center-right. An editorial in *The New Republic*, entitled "Withdraw Guinier," summed up the centrist case: "We do not doubt Guinier's competence; but we do not share her convictions. . . . Her intellectual response to racial polarization is to polarize it further; to assume that racism is so endemic that electoral gerrymandering has to be supplemented with legislative gerrymandering; to hold that a colorblind equality of opportunity has to give way to a race-saturated equality of outcomes."[31] Members of the Democratic Leadership Council, Clinton's springboard to the presidency, were particularly upset. Will Marshall, director of the DLC's Progressive Policy Institute, said Guinier's views had "nothing to do with civil rights as most people understand them and everything to do with the new agenda of racial preferences and entitlements being pushed by some activists and academicians."[32] Clinton's domestic policy adviser, William Galston, who had co-authored the DLC's call to arms, probably sealed Guinier's fate with a private memo urging the president in no uncertain terms to withdraw the nomination. "The perspective she would bring to the Justice Department," Galston wrote, "would ill serve the interests of our country and your administration." She was possessed of "a startling worldview that would be rejected by most of her fellow citizens as well as most of your party and administration."[33] Clinton confidant Vernon Jordan, who knew Guinier's family, also weighed in against the nominee, telling the president "that Guinier was 'just like her dad,' and would take offense under pressure. She would behave regally, as though the nomination were hers by birthright."[34] Senate Judiciary Committee Chair Joseph Biden privately let the administration know that the committee would not vote to confirm.[35]

Guinier's defenders, including members of the Congressional Black Caucus and the leadership of the NAACP, accused foes of twisting her ideas beyond recognition, adding that her proposed remedies were not etched in stone but meant to prompt debate. Four hundred law school professors, including the deans of a half-dozen prestigious law schools, signed a letter in Guinier's support. But to no avail. The death watch was on, punctuated by "no comments" from White House aides and predictions of her imminent demise leaked to the *New York Times* and *Washington Post.* Guinier knew she was in trouble when she passed Hillary Clinton in a West Wing hallway. "Hey kiddo!" Hillary said without breaking stride. A few steps later the first lady briefly stopped and looked back over her shoulder. "She was half an hour late for a luncheon, she said breezily. Then she raced off."[36]

President Clinton doubtless hoped Guinier would take the not-so-subtle hints and step aside. She refused. She'd been unfairly maligned and deserved a chance to defend herself before the Judiciary Committee, she told the president during a tense ninety-minute meeting in the Oval Office. Clinton recalled telling her that his administration was already "bleeding in the water" and couldn't afford another hit. If she wouldn't step aside, he would withdraw the nomination. "I'll be the asshole, and you can be the hero." Guinier didn't remember it quite the same way, but the upshot was the same.[37] At a hastily called press conference hours later, Clinton announced his decision. "At the time of the nomination I had not read her writings," he said, adding that "in retrospect, I wish I had. Today, as a matter of fairness to her, I read some of them again in good detail. They clearly lend themselves to interpretations that do not represent the views that I expressed on civil rights during my campaign and views that I hold very dearly, even though there is much in them with which I agree. I have to tell you that had I read them before I nominated her, I would not have done so." Pressed by a reporter, Clinton said he found some of her ideas "antidemocratic."[38]

The episode was over but not forgotten. For a president who viewed racial reconciliation as his mission in life, it was setback before he'd even gotten started. In the starkest personal terms it spoke volumes about the persistence of the racial divide in the country—a divide both Clinton and Guinier believed, at least between the two of them, had been bridged. Here after all were friends of twenty years, both persons of good will, who thought they knew one another. They didn't. Clinton didn't know, or hadn't taken the time to find out, how Guinier felt about race. Nor was Clinton the man Guinier thought she knew, the man who had come to dinner three days after becoming president. "This was not simply about due process or fundamental fairness," Guinier bitterly recalled in a memoir. "This was a test of presidential leadership, a window on the presidential soul. The manner in which the president of the United States would treat a friend was an insight into his character as a human being, but it was even more than that. It would become an unexpected peek into his character as a leader."[39]

Clinton later admitted he'd spent too much time assembling his cabinet and subcabinet and not enough time choosing his White House staff. For chief of staff, he tapped Thomas "Mac" McLarty, whom he had known since kindergarten in Hope. Head of a Fortune 500 natural gas company, Clinton's childhood friend was no political neophyte. He was elected to the Arkansas legislature at age twenty-three, when Clinton was still at Oxford. If you had asked anybody back then which one was more likely to reach the governor's office, a friend of both recalled, "by far the heavy betting" would have been on McLarty. Over the years, the two Arkansans developed a symbiotic relationship. As two reporters described it, "McLarty built a family fortune in part on marketing savvy and shrewd political connections with people such as Clinton; Clinton built a political machine in part on the right ties with business people such as McLarty."[40] In addition to his experience in business and politics, McLarty's ties to members of both parties undoubtedly made him an attractive choice for chief of staff. President Bush had appointed him to the Federal Reserve Board in St. Louis and to the National Petroleum Council; with Henry Kissinger, secretary of state under presidents Nixon and Ford, he had cofounded a consulting firm in the nation's capital. Before moving into his West Wing office, McLarty contacted high-ranking officials who had served in every administration since Lyndon Johnson's, asking them how he might be

most effective. The consensus, McLarty recalled, was that he should be
an honest broker, conveying to the president information from cabinet
members and others without distorting it with his own views. In this
regard, his antimodels may have been Donald Regan and John Sununu,
who had served presidents Reagan and Bush, respectively, and whose
unhappy tenures had riled members of both the Cabinet and Congress.[41]
Some suspected that McLarty—described in one profile as "all wrinkle-
free Southern graciousness"—lacked the toughness needed for a tough
job, and, almost from the beginning, many faulted him for running too
loose a ship.[42] Before long White House staffers were referring to him
as "Mack the Nice."[43] It's unlikely, however, that Clinton, upon assuming office, would have tolerated a tough-minded approach. It was not in
his nature. In McLarty he got what he wanted—or what he thought he
wanted. Not until later did Clinton realize he needed a more structured
and disciplined setup, something neither he nor McLarty could provide.

More problematic was the influx into the administration of a large
number of persons who had performed with skill and loyalty in the
campaign but who lacked White House, or even Washington, experience. "When it came to the White House staff," recalled Office of Management and Budget Director Leon Panetta, "it was almost like, 'My
goodness, we're at inauguration day, we better bring in a lot of people
who worked on the campaign!'" "You can not do that," he added. "You
have got to have people . . . who know how the White House operates,"
people "that have experience, that have been around, that bring a level of
stability and management to the operation, so that you have a disciplined
operation." Panetta's deputy, Alice Rivlin, echoed his complaint: "So
many White House staff were kids right out of college who'd worked
on the campaign and had never had a job before. This was their first
job, and they were doing important stuff in the White House throwing their weight around." Besides the "kids" from the campaign, William Galston identified two other "tribes" that comprised a fractured
White House staff: "the Little Rock tribe" and "the friends of Bill and/
or Hillary tribe." "If you weren't a member of one of those tribes," he
recalled, "the best you could be was an anthropologist trying to study
the customs."[44] But as with his selection of McLarty, for Clinton to have
hired otherwise would have been out of character. It would have been
in his eyes the height of ingratitude to have sidelined the talented cadre

of aides who had bonded with him and with each other in the cauldron of political warfare. And it might have cost him more in support than it would have gained him in experience.

The roles that would be played by the vice president and first lady were, at the outset, the source of endless speculation. For most of American history the vice president, having helped the president get elected, played little role in shaping policy. They might occasionally help maneuver measures through Congress, as John Nance Garner did for FDR; or they might serve as a political "attack dog," as Spiro Agnew did for Richard Nixon before being forced out of office on corruption charges. But Jimmy Carter's vice president, Walter Mondale, broke the mold. He was the first to have regular access to the president and the first to help shape and execute the administration's agenda. Gore picked up where Mondale had left off. "You cannot overestimate the importance of the vice president," at least during the first term, said Laura Tyson, who, because of her own struggle for influence, was keenly sensitive to the pecking order in the White House. Galston considered the vice president Clinton's "single best advisor." He gave the president "the clearest, the crispest, and the frankest advice he got." In dealing with the president, Gore was not confrontational or argumentative. "His style," recalled Leon Panetta, "was to discern the president's views on the issue and then help inform and guide them, but he did so against the backdrop of his own deeply held beliefs formed as a representative from Tennessee."[45] A staff member on the CEA recounted a small but telling example of how Gore sought to remain in the presidential loop. Before completing their weekly economic report to the president, CEA staffers would, at the request of the vice president, run it by one of his advisers. Sometimes, the Gore adviser would say, "You can't run that piece because it's going to interfere with something the vice president wants to make a splash with," perhaps relating to energy or climate control. Then, upon completion of the report, the CEA would deliver the first copy to the vice president's residence on the grounds of the US Naval Observatory.[46]

Hillary Clinton's role was unprecedented. Many of her predecessors had wielded significant influence, including her role model, Eleanor Roosevelt, and more recently, Nancy Reagan. But none played the precise role she did. That she would be her husband's closest adviser—that everyone assumed. But both Clintons envisioned a more formal role. Elect Bill Clinton, the candidate had said during the campaign, and you will get "two for the price of one." At first they considered the attorney generalship. But antinepotism laws enacted after Robert Kennedy had occupied that same position in his brother's administration precluded a cabinet appointment. The Clintons decided instead that she should reprise the role that had brought her glowing notices in Arkansas: spearheading the drive for education reform. Only now, instead of overhauling public education in one state, she would be charged with reforming the nation's health-care system. She had an office in the West Wing and a large staff that occupied spacious quarters, soon known to all as "Hillaryland," in the Old Executive Office Building across the street from the White House.

Clinton brought to the White House a management style that reflected his own personality. On the personal side, he valued openness and informality. He had little use for chains of command or bureaucratic lines of authority. If he had a question about foreign policy he was as likely to call an assistant secretary of state as he was the secretary of state himself. He "wanted to hear, feel, touch and have interchange with various members of the administration and, in some cases, members from outside the administration" said McLarty.[47] He might spontaneously solicit advice from someone he met at a fundraiser or a reception or during a visit to Martha's Vineyard, then ask his staff to check into the matter. "This was the most eclectic President we've had in many, many years," said adviser Samuel Berger. "He didn't stay inside the box." In this he resembled Franklin Roosevelt and Lyndon Johnson. The only problem National Security Adviser Anthony Lake had with the president's out-of-the-box style was that Lake's staff had to spend too much time responding to "half-assed ideas" Clinton brought in from the outside.[48]

He was not a micromanager like Jimmy Carter, who reputedly monitored the signup sheet for the White House tennis court. But he wanted to be on top of everything that was of interest to him. And his attention to detail did keep staff members on their toes. The weekly reports he received from the CEA—the same ones Vice President Gore was screening in advance—were often technical in nature. It was not unusual for him to fill the margins with comments and questions written in his often in-decipherable left-handed scrawl; there were even times when he detected mathematical errors that had escaped the notice of the council's stellar staff of economists.[49]

Critics deplored Clinton's management style as amateurish and un-disciplined. In truth, it resembled a management technique then sweep-ing corporate America during this business-in-the-saddle era. Dubbed "adhocracy," the technique was being embraced by established corpora-tions like Ford Motors and General Electric and by upstarts like Micro-soft and Apple. Practitioners of adhocracy eschewed formal, top-down, bureaucratic structures in favor of flexible, teamwork approaches to problem solving. The hallmark of adhocracy was the work team. Cre-ated on an ad hoc basis—hence the name—the work team (or task force) empowered persons with different backgrounds and specializations to examine a specific problem from all sides and then to recommend a solu-tion. Within the group, members were more or less equal; it was not their rank that mattered, but their ideas. Once the problem was solved the group disbanded, its members moving on to new groups and different problems. Adhocracy advocates, like Tom Peters, author of *Liberation Management: Necessary Disorganization for the Nanosecond Nineties*, liked to think of themselves as the antithesis of the "organization man" or "the man in the gray flannel suit" of fifties renown. "Putting on a tie makes me want to puke," Peters would tell business leaders who paid $1,400 a piece to attend his popular seminars. "Putting on a black suit makes me want to puke even more."[50]

Adhocracy diminished even further the formal role of the cabinet, which, as a collective body, had been falling into disuse since at least the Eisenhower administration. Clinton convened the cabinet fewer times than any president since Kennedy. On those rare occasions when he did call a meeting, he probably did so because he feared someone would criticize him for ignoring the body altogether.[51] From the point of view of the White House, Robert Reich recalled, "cabinet officials are pro-vincial governors, presiding over alien, primitive territories. Anything of any importance occurs in the imperial palace, within the capital city."[52]

Paradoxically, although the cabinet as a whole was a relic of a bygone age, its members had probably never been more important. By the 1990s, each secretary presided over a huge bureaucracy that probably touched more lives than the entire federal government had before the New Deal. Reich's Labor Department, to take but one example, employed 14,000 persons and oversaw enforcement of health and safety regulations in the nation's workplaces. Donna Shalala's Health and Human Services issued rules and regulations affecting thousands of hospitals and medical facilities and millions of their patients. Housing and Urban Development received scant public attention during Clinton's tenure but nevertheless waged a crusade to reduce discriminatory barriers to homeownership among minorities, a crusade that had far-reaching consequences.

Modern cabinet secretaries not only presided over vast bureaucratic empires but also, as Reich unhappily observed, represented well-organized interest groups. During one of the cabinet's rare meetings, Reich, pretending to listen as Clinton "droned on," looked around the room and made a list of the "real cabinet." The Secretary of the Interior, for example, was really the Secretary of the West, in charge of mediating the interests of mining and timber companies, cattle ranchers, and environmentalists. The Secretary of Commerce was Secretary of Corporate America, representing the interests of "Fortune 500 Companies, global conglomerates, top exporters and importers, large trade associations." The Secretary of the Treasury was Secretary of Wall Street, representing "bond traders, investment bankers, institutional investors, money managers, the very rich." Before he finished going around the table, Reich had identified just about every powerful interest in the country along with their cabinet sponsors. As for himself, he was Secretary of Blue Collar America, representing "industrial unions, service unions, building trades, unorganized low-wage workers, the shrinking middle class, the working poor."[53]

Whatever its merits, Clinton's version of adhocracy appeared messy in operation. Besides chief of staff "Mack" McLarty, a half-dozen or more aides could walk into the Oval Office without notice. Nebraska Senator Robert Kerrey never forgot his first visit to the Clinton White House. Throughout the meeting, George Stephanopoulos and others wandered in and out, whispered in Clinton's ear, and talked among themselves. "Show some respect for the president," Kerrey thought to himself. The Nebraska senator was not alone in complaining about the looseness of the White House operation. Clinton's inability to stay on schedule, a lifelong problem, annoyed even those who had been with him since Arkansas days. Long before Clinton's affair with intern Monica Lewinsky, White House interns and other low-level employees were instructed by their supervisors to avoid making eye contact with the president if they passed him in the hallway. This unusual directive arose not out of concern the president might make unwanted advances but in an attempt to keep on schedule a president who had an irresistible desire to stop and talk with everyone he saw.

And then there were the meetings themselves. "The most meetingest fellow I've ever met," said Lloyd Bentsen of Clinton. "Sometimes it felt more like a college bull session than Presidential policy making," remembered Stephanopoulos about a lengthy budget session, a session replete with a late-night pizza delivery.[54] The image of college sophomores talking the night away quickly caught on with the press. The presidential operation, wrote *New York Times* reporter Maureen Dowd, "has the smell of a dormitory about it, with everyone cramming for exams." Pollster Stanley Greenberg recalled the nerve-wracking process that went into a major speech: "Early drafts discarded, multiple drafts, multiple points of entry, competing and unresolved views in the room, issues closed and reopened, all-night sessions entering edits and merging drafts, long hand-written pages for Clinton, practice sessions just hours before the event, and further edits just minutes before delivery."[55] On Inauguration Day the Clintons were late picking up the Bushes for the trip to the Capitol because the president-elect was still revising his inaugural address.

Clinton's work habits not only kept aides on edge but also rankled members of the staff assigned to the White House living quarters. The Reagans and Bushes had kept regular hours, or at least as regular as a president and his family could. Ronald Reagan was famous for returning from the Oval Office precisely at five and then having dinner with wife Nancy in front of the television set. If last-minute changes to their schedules arose, the Reagans and Bushes made sure the staff was notified as soon as possible so that they could make the proper arrangements. The Clintons, and especially Bill, were different. He often did not go to bed until two or three. Then he might get up at six-thirty and go for a jog. Or he might get up at six-thirty, go down to the Oval Office, and then go for a jog. Members of the household staff and security detail, meanwhile, had to remain on standby almost twenty-four hours a day, ready to act at a moment's notice. Unlike the Reagans and the Bushes, the Clintons were unaccustomed to having people wait on them—and of a generation and class that probably made them a little self-conscious about it, too.[56] Their very first morning in the White House, the Clintons were startled when someone opened the door to their bedroom without knocking. "What are you doing in my bedroom," Clinton shouted. It was the White House usher with their breakfast tray.[57] As a result of their discomfort, the Clintons could be unintentionally insensitive to the needs of their attendants, some of whom made their displeasure known. One of the White House ushers never removed the "Re-elect Bush" sticker from his car. Others began to tell Clinton stories to friends and family, some of which, embellished with each telling, found their way into print. The most famous account had Hillary capping a late-night shouting match by throwing a lamp at her husband. In other versions it was a bible or a vase. One account had a Secret Service agent, concerned about the president's safety, entering the room to break up a fight.[58]

Clinton, for his part, resented all the new restraints on his activities and intrusions into his privacy that living in the White House entailed: Secret Service agents posted outside of the bedroom; having to be escorted by four agents—two in front and two in back—just to go from the living quarters to the Oval Office; being told he could not decide on the spur of the moment to attend a friend's book-signing party a mile from the White House; having to have practically everything he ate examined in advance by security personnel. In Little Rock he'd been able to walk Chelsea to school while Hillary drove herself to work in her Olds. "Why can't I do what I want?" he shouted on one occasion. Only partly in jest, he referred to the White House as "a penitentiary."[59]

The Clintons had barely settled in before stories appeared not only about lamp-throwing in the living quarters but also about amateur hour in the Oval Office. Three weeks after the inauguration, a front-page article in the *Washington Post* described a weekend retreat at Camp David attended by the president, vice president, the cabinet, and top staffers. Entitled "A Bonding Experience at Camp David," it conjured up images of sixties-era consciousness-raising and sensitivity-training sessions. The article failed to note that bonding sessions, like adhocracy, were commonplace in modern corporate culture. The first books to be published about the new administration, including ones by venerable journalists Bob Woodward and Elizabeth Drew, left the impression of internal discord and disarray. But it was reporter Dowd who created the unforgettable image. Referring to a slovenly character in a popular comic strip, *Peanuts*, she wrote: "Each White House reflects the personality of its leader, and this President, immune to punctuality and discipline, will always have a Pigpen cloud of chaos around him."[60] It didn't help that accounts of White House operations were replete with colorful quotes from eager-to-talk, but anonymous inside sources. During his first months, Clinton recalled, "the White House leaked worse than a tar-paper shack with holes in the roof and gaps in the walls."[61]

Clinton's defenders argued that there was a method to his apparent administrative madness. Yes, meetings ran long and involved much give-and-take. But that was because Clinton wanted to consider all options before making a decision. "If you don't tell me what you really think, I'm dead," he told Robert Rubin. CEA chair Laura Tyson said Clinton wanted his staff to have every opportunity to speak out in private so that they would not feel compelled to speak out in public to make their views heard. Defenders might also have pointed out that some of Clinton's most successful predecessors earned uniformly low grades from their contemporaries for breaches of management orthodoxy. "The worst administrator I've ever seen," complained Franklin Roosevelt's Secretary of War Henry L. Stimson.[62]

But if critics exaggerated Clinton's managerial lapses, even loyalists sensed before long that something was wrong. Political operative Paul Begala believed that policy meetings may have appeared to be frank and open but that participants often played to the audience rather than providing the president with frank opinions. And for all the talk about diversity—a White House that looked like America—some complained that some were more equal than others. "It's kind of a guy thing around here," Press Secretary Dee Dee Myers complained to friends. The first woman to hold the title of presidential press secretary, Myers never felt that she was taken as seriously as her male counterparts. She lacked the access to the president (and the office space) of men she supposedly outranked. Nor was she alone. Myers recalled one incident that occurred during an important meeting of Clinton's economic advisers. All the men, including the president, sat around a table. The only women present were seated against the wall. When a subject involving Laura Tyson's expertise came up, Tyson repeatedly tried to speak but the men just kept talking. She practically had to shout before Clinton brought her into the conversation.[63] Tyson herself recalled asking someone in the White House chief of staff's office why she hadn't been invited to a particular meeting. "Because you didn't ask," a staffer replied, adding that Tyson's male counterparts asked all of the time. "Well thank you," Tyson said. "I'm asking now." "It was a boy's club," remembered Alicia Munnell, who served in the Clinton Treasury Department and on the CEA. "There were women there but you felt that the real power rested with the boys."[64] The president prided himself on hiring women, his personal secretary, Betty Currie, noted. "But to hire them and to use them are two different things." African American staffers also felt left out of the inner circle, added Currie, who was herself African American. "I had thought from the campaign that there would be no circles. There would just be us, everybody." Such turned out not to be the case. Still, Currie was willing to give Clinton the benefit of the doubt: if he had been aware of the problem he might have done something about it. Women staffers may have raised the issue with him, Currie concedes, but in a "joking fashion" that he didn't take seriously. "The women may have said it, and he may have gone, 'Ha, ha, ha, not true.'" Clinton's Health and Human Services secretary, Donna Shalala, who had served in the Carter administration, remembered it a little differently. At the first Cabinet meeting, she said, "We looked around. There were all these women in the Cabinet. It was like there was a revolution. We just giggled. It was just—the guys were feminists too." Yet, Shalala conceded, there was still "an old boys' club, and even Clinton himself is a kind of macho guy." But she gained admittance to the boys' club because she liked sports, played golf, and had overseen a football team as chancellor of the University of Wisconsin. The president even invited her to the White House to watch the Super Bowl. After leaving the White House, Joan N. Baggett, who had headed the president's political affairs office, would run into others who had left. "The guys all wanted to go back, and the women didn't miss it at all."[65]

Of all the aspects of Clinton's initial administrative set-up, none proved more troublesome—or seemingly insoluble—than media relations. The tone was set on Inauguration Day, and it did not change much thereafter. "What are you trying to hide," reporter Helen Thomas shouted at Dee Dee Myers, who had just announced that a small area outside the press secretary's office would no longer be open to reporters. Thomas, a pressroom gadfly, had been asking barbed and embarrassing questions of press secretaries since the Kennedy administration, and many of her colleagues did not take her seriously. But this time she was voicing what many reporters felt: that Clinton and his aides did have something to hide and were, moreover, contemptuous of the press. In one respect, the Clintonites were victims of their own success. The astonishing effectiveness of the Clinton campaign's war room earned the grudging admiration of reporters but also fueled suspicions that the Clintonites viewed them simply as pawns to be manipulated.[66]

During ensuing weeks and months, things went from bad to worse. Complaints from the White House press corps multiplied: legitimate questions were going unanswered; phone calls were returned late or not at all; when the administration did have news it bypassed White House reporters in favor of local—and less challenging—media outlets around the country.

For their part, both Clintons, still reeling over the unfair coverage they thought they had received during the campaign, came into office with a huge antimedia chip on their shoulders. Both believed that reporters were more interested in dwelling on nonexistent misdeeds, such as their investment in the failed Whitewater development during the 1980s, than in reporting the news. Nothing aroused Clinton's explosive fury more than the press. In private he would shake with anger and curse and shout at the unfair treatment he believed he was receiving. When the subject came up in a conversation with his friend Taylor Branch, he shook with rage, got beet red, and had to stop talking and walk around before regaining his composure. Even the most outrageous attack from a political foe did not enrage him as much as a critical story in the *New York Times* or *Washington Post*. One time he asked Senator Alan Simpson, a Republican from Wyoming, if Simpson and his colleagues really believed all the bad things they were saying about the Clintons. "Oh, hell no," Simpson replied. They were just trying to repay the Democrats for all the bad things they'd said about Ronald Reagan a decade earlier. Telling Taylor Branch about Simpson's response, Clinton just laughed, as if to say that political paybacks were just part of the game. But let the press join in—that was a different matter.[67] From time to time, Clinton tried to charm journalists into submission, only to be disappointed when they continued to depict him critically, or at least critically as he saw it. Michael McCurry, who later became his press secretary, sensed that Clinton "equated hospitality and socializing with opening up" but did not realize that the way to generate good will was to help journalists "do their job, day in and day out."[68] Not since the Nixon administration had relations between the White House and the press been so tense.

"On the Edge," 1993

Few presidents have experienced a shorter honeymoon than Bill Clinton. No sooner had he taken office than he was swamped by controversy. "His presidency," noted veteran journalist Elizabeth Drew, "was constantly on the edge—because of his past and what came to be called his 'character,' and because of the legislative gambles he took."[1] Within months his public approval ratings had plummeted and pundits were talking about his "failed presidency." *Time* magazine entitled a cover story "The Incredible Shrinking President," while *Newsweek* asked simply: "What's Wrong?"[2] Clinton did achieve two of the most significant legislative victories of his presidency—a budget bill, the centerpiece of which was deficit reduction, and the first, and most controversial, in a series of free-trade bills. Combined they would form the basis of Clinton's disputed legacy. At the time, however, they were overshadowed by the chaotic events of Clinton's first year in office.

His cabinet and staff in place, Clinton turned to the ambitious agenda he hoped to push through Congress during his first 100 days in office, just as he imagined FDR had done. It was a tall order.

During the campaign and its aftermath, Clinton had promised health care for all, an overhaul of the welfare system, a 10 percent tax cut for the middle class, measures to lift the working poor out of poverty, and ratification of a free trade agreement with Mexico and Canada. He had also pledged to cut the deficit in half by the end of his first term. The centerpiece of his agenda, rhetorically at least, was a package of expenditures—investments he called them—to jumpstart a still sluggish economy and lay the groundwork for long-term economic growth. Reflecting the influence of Robert Reich, Clinton promised to rebuild the nation's infrastructure of roads, bridges, and airports; to expand scientific research and development; and to bolster the nation's educational system. For both Clinton and Reich, education was the key. The nation's elementary and secondary schools needed an infusion of funds. But programs also had to be created to allow older workers in dying industries to upgrade their job skills in order to compete in the emerging global economy.[3]

To pay for his initiatives and still reduce the deficit, Clinton proposed a combination of spending cuts, including the elimination of 125,000 federal jobs, and tax increases on those with annual incomes over $250,000. Businesses of a certain size would be required to set aside a percentage of their profits every year to help finance worker retraining programs.

Clinton's proposals, detailed in a campaign booklet with the deceptively sloganish title *Putting People First*, were more coherent than anything issued by the Bush or Perot campaigns or by most previous presidential campaigns, for that matter. For one thing, the numbers more or less added up. The bottom line did not depend on promises of billions to be recouped by eliminating "waste and fraud."[4] For another, Clinton's emphasis on public investment was supported by findings that for decades American industries had been focusing on short-term payoffs rather than long-term growth. During the late forties, fifties, and sixties, the federal government had taken up the slack with the GI Bill of Rights, the Federal Highway Act, federal aid to education, the National Science Foundation, and an array of other agencies and programs that created the world's most elaborate infrastructure. The result was a flourishing economy and the emergence of the computer and other new industries. By the eighties, however, the country had allowed its infrastructure to deteriorate. It was living off the past. It was slipping behind global competitors like Japan and Germany. It was time, Clinton argued, for a new round of investments that would spark future innovation and growth. In truth, his specific proposal—$200 billion spread out over four years—was modest in a multi-trillion-dollar economy. But at least it would begin to make up for recent neglect.[5]

Even before he took office, new realities forced Clinton to reevaluate his priorities. The economy appeared to be on the rebound. The bad news was what he and his advisers had already suspected: the deficit was larger—one-third larger—than initially thought, thus jeopardizing some of his spending initiatives. Moreover, many of his top economic advisers—Bentsen, Rubin, Panetta, Rivlin, Summers—insisted that deficit reduction needed to take precedence or dire consequences would ensue. Alan Greenspan, the conservative chairman of the Federal Reserve Board who had been advising Republican presidents since Richard Nixon, made the same point in a three-hour meeting with Clinton. In Clinton, he found a surprisingly receptive audience. "To my delight," recalled Greenspan, "Clinton seemed fully engaged. He seemed to pick up on my sense of urgency about the deficit, and asked a lot of smart questions that politicians usually don't ask." Greenspan also liked the "fiscally conservative centrists" who comprised most of Clinton's economic team. "Choosing them made Bill Clinton seem about as far from the classic tax-and-spend liberal as you could get and still be a Democrat."[6]

The argument Greenspan and Clinton's advisers made was that the deficit had gotten so large it threatened economic recovery in the short run and doomed growth prospects in the future.[7] As they explained it, the amount of money the government had to borrow each year simply to finance interest on the national debt removed money from the economy that might otherwise be available to businesses and consumers. Deficit spending at current levels also threatened to unleash a surge of inflation such as had happened in the seventies and early eighties. Inflation concerns were already leading to unusually high interest rates on 10-year, 20-year, and 30-year bonds. The concerns roiled Wall Street bond traders, who feared deficit-induced inflation would occur before their bonds matured and reduce the value of accrued interest. More ominous still, according to self-described deficit hawks, were rising interest rates on long-term bonds, which foreshadowed higher interest rates on home mortgages and business loans. But just as big deficits caused bad things, lowering them might produce big payoffs. Convince bond traders, as well as Greenspan and his Federal Reserve Board colleagues, that the government was serious about curbing deficits, and watch interest rates on bonds drift downward, along with the borrowing costs of buying homes and contracting loans. A surge in economic growth was likely to follow, a surge greater than the government could produce through traditional spending and taxation policies. But from a president's perspective there were two problems with this rosy scenario. First, both the Federal Reserve and bondholders had to be convinced that the president not only wanted to slash the deficit but also could pull it off. Second, even if the deficit were lowered and bond rates fell, it might take years for the positive effects to manifest themselves, and in politics even a few years was a lifetime. Exasperated that his fate was not in his own hands, a red-faced Clinton complained to aides: "You mean to tell me that the success of the program and my reelection hinges on the Federal Reserve and a bunch of fucking bond traders?" Well, yes, they had to admit.[8]

All of Clinton's advisers, along with Democratic leaders in Congress, favored attacking the deficit. But not all agreed it should be the top priority, especially if it jeopardized other initiatives. If spending had to be slashed, wondered Robert Reich, what was to be the fate of all the investments in education and infrastructure that were critical not only to long-term growth and prosperity but also to America's economic leadership in the world? Laura Tyson and her colleagues at the CEA feared that too drastic a cut in federal spending would jeopardize the economic recovery then under way. Moreover, not all of the CEA's statistical models supported the optimistic projections of the deficit hawks. But the loudest complaints came from political consultants who had played a central role in the campaign. Paul Begala, Mandy Grunwald, James Carville, and Stanley Greenberg forcefully reminded Clinton that he had been elected, first and foremost, on a promise to create jobs, not cut the deficit (although he had promised that too). Pollster Greenberg cited figures showing that while half of the voters ranked jobs as their top priority, only a third cited the deficit. Some of Clinton's aides thought the emphasis on the deficit was a cruel hoax. Where, they asked, were the warnings of gloom and doom when the Reagan administration was running up the huge deficits? Even proponents of deficit reduction knew it entailed big risks. Economist Blinder called it "root canal politics." Everyone's in favor of reducing the deficit until it affects them. "After all," Blinder said later, "deficit reduction is about cutting somebody's program or raising somebody's taxes. You don't have to have studied political science a lot to know that's probably not a winning formula, and Clinton was very much aware of that."[9]

Laura Tyson, although skeptical of the scenario projected by the deficit hawks, believed that a budget with an investment centerpiece never had a chance. There was the inconvenient reality of Ross Perot's 19 percent of the 1992 vote. Deficit reduction had formed the centerpiece of his platform. There was the fact that all or most congressional Republicans were likely to oppose the president's budget regardless of its provisions, requiring the administration to secure the support of just about every Democrat in both houses, including conservative Democrats, who would never vote for a liberal investment agenda. Those who argued for additional infrastructure spending, like Robert Reich and CEA member Joseph Stiglitz, Tyson maintained, overestimated the president's ability to maneuver. In a multi-trillion-dollar economy, there was no politically feasible way of pushing through Congress a spending program big enough to jumpstart the economy. In her view, the die was cast by the time Clinton moved into the Oval Office. Or as William Galston put it, "By the time Bill Clinton took office, it was pretty clear that Rubin had won the big game, and Reich and company had lost it."[10]

And so it was. Even before Clinton's political advisers weighed in, he had decided deficit reduction was to be the cornerstone of his first budget. For the first time, but not for the last, his decision offered a corrective to the popular belief about the influence of political consultants in his administration. "The role of the consultants in the Clinton administration was without precedent," wrote Elizabeth Drew, adding that they were "omnipresent, involved in everything from personnel to policymaking to the president's schedule."[11] It was even said that in advance of the first family's summer vacations, the president's pollsters ran surveys to determine which spots would appeal most to swing voters (Martha's Vineyard? Jackson Hole, Wyoming? The Rockies?). It was certainly true that political consultants had never been more visible to the public than they were during Clinton's presidency. James Carville and Paul Begala may not have been household names, but they were well known to all serious political observers. Before long, Dick Morris would join their ranks. But the notoriety of Clinton's political team probably owed as much to their colorful personalities and their penchant for self-promotion as to their impact on public policy. The release in 1993 of *The War Room*, the acclaimed documentary about the presidential campaign, added to the team's celebrity, as did the odd-couple marriage the same year between James Carville and his counterpart in the Bush campaign, Mary Matalin. But the real story of Clinton's early tenure in office was the extent to which he rejected the advice of the political operatives in framing his first, and most important, budget proposal. And in the end, it would be his proposal. No provision was too small to escape his interest. "As far as I know," recalled Leon Panetta, "no other modern President has ever taken the time to examine every line of the federal budget."[12]

The president's proposal aimed to halve the deficit over five years. It would achieve this goal through a combination of spending cuts and tax increases—roughly $191 billion in cuts and $281 billion in tax increases. Of particular importance were reductions in the growth of entitlement programs like Medicare and Social Security. Although more symbolic than substantive in terms of dollar amounts, these reductions would supposedly send a message to the Federal Reserve Board and to bond traders that Clinton was so intent upon reducing the deficit that he was willing to take on sacrosanct entitlement programs and their Democratic defenders.[13]

Even so, the five-year plan Clinton presented to Congress did include some progressive features. Most notably, it expanded the nation's largest but least-known antipoverty program, the Earned Income Tax Credit (EITC). Created as a temporary provision in 1975 during the Ford administration and made permanent and expanded under presidents Carter, Reagan, and Bush, the EITC provided a refundable tax credit over and above the tax liability of low-income workers. Under Clinton's proposal, which eventually became law, some 18 million taxpayers earned an average of $1,480 additional income per year. Because its benefits went to the working (and presumably deserving) poor and operated through the tax system, the EITC aroused less opposition than traditional welfare programs.[14] By countering some of the income tax cuts given to upper-income groups in the Reagan years, Clinton's proposed budget restored a measure of progressivity to the structure. Only families with annual earnings over a $100,000 would see their income taxes go up. Perhaps the bill's most far-reaching provision proposed to tax producers of oil, coal, natural gas, and nuclear energy according to the heat content of their products. Called the Btu tax, after the British thermal unit, it was the brainchild of the vice president and of prominent environmentalists. It was intended to raise $72 billion in revenue over five years but also discourage the use of fossil fuels and encourage the use of nonpolluting energies like wind and solar power. The administration estimated that the average American family would have to pay only

$17 per month in Btu taxes. It was the most important environmental proposal since the passage in 1971 of the Environmental Protection Act.[15]

Finally, as a concession to those who feared that deficit reduction would decrease aggregate demand and plunge the nation back into recession, the budget proposal contained a $30 billion stimulus package of short-term expenditures.

Clinton's plan was just as notable for what it excluded. Gone were the middle-class tax cuts. Gone, too, or at least significantly reduced, were the investments in education and training and in infrastructure. In an almost $10 trillion economy, the plan's stimulus package fell far short of what some of Clinton's advisers wanted. But Clinton's budget was also memorable for what it heralded: a fundamental policy shift begun by Jimmy Carter from the policies that had guided Democratic administrations from the late thirties through the sixties.

By the late thirties, key figures in the Roosevelt administration had abandoned any plans they may have had to fundamentally reform capitalism by dismantling oligopolies or introducing central economic planning. The regulatory measures of the early New Deal—creation of the Securities Exchange Commission, restrictions on holding companies, and the separation of commercial and investment banking—were thought sufficient to ameliorate the excesses of capitalism. Going forward, the government could ease, if not prevent, economic downturns by implementing the recommendations of British economist John Maynard Keynes. In times of economic decline, Keynes argued that central governments should stimulate the demand for goods and services by borrowing, spending, and cutting taxes.[16] Neither Roosevelt nor his successors entered office as Keynesians. They became Keynesians, often without acknowledging the fact, because Keynesian economics worked. It ended the depression and kept the economy humming for two-and-a-half decades. Between 1945 and 1969, recessions were short-lived; employment was high, inflation low; the Gross National Product doubled; median family income more than tripled; and the gap between rich and poor narrowed. Little wonder that President Nixon would unabashedly admit to being "a Keynesian in economics."

Then came the 1970s, and with it the confluence of high unemployment, double-digit inflation, and soaring interest rates. "Stagflation" baffled economists and politicians alike—prices weren't supposed to rise when the economy was sluggish and unemployment was on the rise—and dimmed the hopes of Keynesians, who thought they'd found the magic formula for sustaining economic growth. President Carter, who ultimately bore the political brunt of stagflation, reexamined the Keynesian legacy bequeathed to him by his Democratic predecessors and modified it significantly. He hinted at what was to come in his second annual message to Congress. "Government cannot solve our problems," he said. "It can't set the goals. It cannot define our vision. Government cannot eliminate poverty, or provide a bountiful economy, or reduce inflation, or save our cities, or cure illiteracy, or provide energy."[17] After a period of dispirited soul-searching, Carter set the nation on a course that relied on market forces more than government intervention to boost the economy; that elevated inflation over unemployment as a central concern; that identified deficits as the source of the nation's current ills; and that focused on enhancing the supply of capital instead of consumer demand for goods and services.[18] Carter paid a steep price for his apostasy. Senator Edward M. Kennedy (D-MA) challenged him for the Democratic nomination, and liberal critics compared him to Warren G. Harding and Herbert Hoover. Historian Arthur M. Schlesinger, Jr., said that the Democrats had not seen his ilk since Grover Cleveland. "To take Carter's view of government is to deny the heritage of the modern Democratic party," Schlesinger wrote.[19] Given Carter's fate, it was not surprising that Clinton put as much distance as he could between himself and his one-term predecessor. Yet, as the historian Iwan Morgan noted, "Far from being the 'Jimmy Hoover' of liberal obloquy, Carter was really 'Jimmy Clinton' because in seeking solutions for stagflation his administration laid the foundations of a new political economy that the next Democrat President would build upon."[20]

In selling his budget, Clinton had to compete with a multitude of other controversies that erupted during the first year of his presidency. None proved more damaging than the unexpected, and probably unavoidable, furor over gays and lesbians in the military. During the campaign, Clinton had pledged to lift the ban on gays and lesbians in the armed services.

With the Cold War over and the United States facing no imminent threat, the time seemed right to lift the ban. Moreover, no one could honestly deny that gay men and women had been serving honorably forever and that lifting the ban would simply acknowledge a fact of military life. Proponents noted, too, that gays served openly in the armed services of other countries without any apparent harm. But Clinton faced a revolt on the part of his already-suspicious military commanders, including Colin Powell, the popular chair of the Joint Chiefs of Staff, who warned that allowing gays to serve openly would erode morale and weaken national defense. Influential members of Congress, including Senator Sam Nunn, chair of the Armed Services Committee, publicly sided with the military. Veteran Democratic Senator Robert Byrd of West Virginia, who prided himself on his knowledge of ancient history, declared that homosexuality had led to the decline and fall of the Roman Empire and that it would do the same for the United States. Opposition to lifting the ban wasn't confined to Pentagon officials or members of Congress. When the courts ordered the navy to reinstate Keith Meinhold, a twelve-year veteran who had been discharged for revealing he was gay, a staff member on Clinton's National Security Council complained that returning Meinhold to active duty was "a terrible idea" and would destroy "the morale and cohesion of whatever sub he is put on."[21]

During the transition, Clinton advisers had devised a plan to give the new president some breathing room to deal with the issue: Upon taking office, he would appoint a committee to study the matter and report its findings in six months. "The committee would come back with recommendations," recalled one aide, "and we'd sort of kick the ball down the road a bit so we had time to talk to the military." Neither the press nor the Republicans cooperated. During the campaign Clinton had vowed support for a family and medical leave act requiring employers to grant workers up to three months of unpaid leave when a baby was born or a family member got sick. When the bill was introduced, Senate Minority Leader Robert Dole (R-KS) promptly proposed an amendment requiring congressional approval before the ban on gays in the military could be lifted. Clinton's supporters managed to quash the amendment, but it had roiled already rough waters.[22]

In the end, Clinton settled for a clumsy compromise. Called "Don't Ask, Don't Tell," it maintained the ban on gays but prohibited military authorities from directly asking military personnel about their sexual orientation. It pleased no one. "The military resented the intrusion," recalled George Stephanopoulos, "Democrats were furious, the public was confused, and the gay community felt betrayed."[23]

Other controversies dominated the news at the expense of Clinton's attempt to focus on the economy. On April 19, FBI agents ended a standoff with a fringe religious sect led by David Koresh in Waco, Texas, by storming a building in which Koresh and his followers lived. The siege ended in tragedy when Koresh and ninety-four of his followers, including several children, perished in a fire of uncertain origin. Critics wondered if other tactics might have averted the deaths and also complained that by allowing Attorney General Janet Reno to take responsibility for the incident, Clinton had shirked his own responsibility for it. Weeks later a much less serious incident proved almost as damaging to Clinton's image. Concluding a visit to Los Angeles, Clinton reportedly brought air traffic to a standstill while he received a $200 haircut aboard Air Force One from Hollywood hairdresser Cristophe. The incident was greatly exaggerated. Air delays were minor. But the defensive responses of Clinton and his staff ("Everyone needs a haircut," said communications director George Stephanopoulos) made it worse. More surprising still was the inability of the reigning master of politics to anticipate how such an incident would play out in the media. Within days, another incident, this one involving the White House Travel Office, which handled arrangements for reporters when they travelled with the president, was topping the news. At the request of Hillary Clinton, who had learned of fiscal malfeasance in the office, the staff was fired. The incident, replete with missteps and misunderstandings, eventually prompted full-scale investigations by the FBI, committees in both houses of Congress, and two special prosecutors. This and other early controversies not only tarnished Clinton's image as a "New Democrat" but also made it almost impossible for him to maintain his focus on the budget bill then making its way through Congress. "Instead of a President fighting to change America for the better," Clinton wrote in his memoir, "I was being portrayed as a man who had abandoned down-home for uptown, a knee-jerk liberal whose mask of moderation had been removed."[24]

Clinton's budget proposal, meanwhile, encountered new dangers every day. Any hopes of bipartisanship quickly evaporated as Republicans in both houses denounced the president's proposal as a typical Democratic "tax and spend" scheme. Even moderate Republicans like New Mexico's Pete Domenici, burned by conservatives in their own party for having supported tax increases in the waning days of the Bush administration, declined to offer assistance.[25] The first casualty was the already modest stimulus package, which fell to a Republican filibuster in the Senate. The president's "investments" in education, job training, and infrastructure met the same fate. Republicans weren't the only problem. A small but influential group of Democrats, led by Oklahoma senator David Boren, also took aim at Clinton's budget, deeming its spending cuts insufficient. At the very least, Boren argued, the government needed to further restrict the growth of Social Security, Medicare, and Medicaid. But the chief target of the Boren group, most of whom hailed from oil-producing states, was the Btu energy tax. The innovative proposal had actually gotten off to a promising start. Clinton had described it as a win-win-win tax, one that would cut the deficit, curtail pollution, and lessen the nation's dependence on foreign oil. All this, he said, and the average family would only have to pay an extra $17 a month. The Sierra Club and other environmental groups quickly signed on in support as did a couple of oil company executives, relieved that oil wouldn't be singled out alone for tax increases. But just when it appeared that the Btu tax might become a reality, energy producers and their spokesmen in Congress went on the attack, jeopardizing not only the tax itself but Clinton's entire budget proposal. Joined by heavy consumers of energy, like the aluminum and airline industries, foes predicted massive job losses and a skyrocketing cost of living if the tax went into effect. Clinton's attempt to appease critics made matters worse. When he exempted ethanol producers and the aluminum and airline industries from coverage, others pleaded that they, too, should be exempt.[26] By the time the proposal reached the Senate for consideration, a reporter described it as "one of the most exemption-loaded, head-scratchingly complicated, brow-furrowing revenue raisers in history."[27] So watered down had it become that environmentalists withdrew their support. In the end, Clinton scrapped the proposal altogether in favor of a less controversial gas tax, angering congressional proponents who had gone out on a limb to support the Btu tax in the first place.[28]

If Clinton could have done more to build support for his proposals is anybody's guess. He probably had more contact with legislators than any president since Lyndon Johnson, though as one journalist noted, he was more of a listener than a lapel-grabber like LBJ.[29] Clinton shared Johnson's passion for working the phones, especially late at night. The wife of one congressman, picking up the phone after they'd gone to bed, leaned over to her husband: "It's HIM again."[30] There was no one Clinton couldn't draw out in conversation, including fierce critics like North Carolina senator Jesse Helms, whose racially tinged views made him anathema to many liberals. Legislators from whom the president wanted something or whose company he simply enjoyed could expect an invitation to play golf. Clinton also fielded an experienced and able legislative team: Majority Leaders George Mitchell in the Senate and Richard Gephardt in the House, House Speaker Thomas Foley, and director of legislative operations, Howard Paster. Still, some believed Clinton could have done even more to curry favor on Capitol Hill, especially given his extraordinary ability to connect with people. Mickey Kantor, chair of Clinton's campaign in 1992 and US trade representative during the first term, faulted him for failing to use the White House: "It was one thing to have fifty people at the White House every night and doing what he does brilliantly, touching everybody," he said. But that's not the same as inviting someone like Dick Gephardt to the family quarters—"alone two or three times, with his family, without family, sitting down, having dinner, talking things through." That's how you instill loyalty, Kantor believed, how you got someone to "run through brick walls" for you. But Clinton couldn't bring himself to make the extra effort. Maybe it was because, like Jimmy Carter, he harbored "a lingering resentment" from the campaign that no matter what he did the Washington establishment would never accept him.[31]

Still, it probably wasn't Sunday supper at the White House that earned Franklin Roosevelt, Lyndon Johnson, and Ronald Reagan their loyal followers. It was coattails. They had them, Clinton didn't. Most Democrats had won their districts or states by larger margins than Clinton had. "Nobody felt particularly indebted to Bill Clinton for getting there," recalled one of his legislative leaders.[32] Democrats often had more to fear from opponents in the next election than from defying the president of their own party. Clinton was also paying the price for Democrats having been out of the White House for so long. Powerful figures like Senator

Boren, Sam Nunn, and others had grown accustomed to acting as independent agents—men above parties and partisanship. They were not about to change now, even with one of their own in the White House.[33]

With Republicans united in opposition and Democrats divided, Clinton got a needed boost from Federal Reserve Chairman Alan Greenspan, whom Clinton showcased sitting next to Hillary in the House gallery during the State of the Union address. Later, in testimony before Congress, Greenspan, in his Delphic way, also called the president's plan credible.

As the final vote loomed in August, it was clear that defeat was a real possibility and victory, if it came, would be razor thin. In the end, the bill passed the House by two votes. Its fate in the Senate hinged on the vote of one senator, Robert Kerrey of Nebraska, Clinton's rival for the presidential nomination. Days before the vote, Kerrey informed Clinton he would join six other Democratic senators in opposing the bill. At the last minute, he voted in favor, producing a tie in the upper house. In his capacity as president of the Senate, Vice President Gore promptly cast the deciding vote in the administration's favor. Clinton had lost his stimulus package and many of his proposed investments. But the heart of the budget—deficit reduction—had survived, if only by the narrowest of margins.[34]

Now it was a matter of waiting and watching. Would the bond markets respond by lowering interest rates, freeing up capital, and jumpstarting the economy, as the deficit hawks predicted? Or, as the Keynesians feared, would the budget's combination of spending cuts and tax increases reduce aggregate demand for goods and services and stall an already sluggish recovery? The first signs, though hardly decisive, were encouraging. Clinton's deficit reduction plan was apparently "large, genuine, and credible" enough to bring down long-term interest rates even before final passage of the budget. As a consequence, those segments of the economy particularly sensitive to fluctuations in interest rates, such as housing and the manufacture and sales of durable goods and plant machinery, grew significantly.[35] Although it would be several years before the full effects of the budget could be assessed, Clinton had at least bought himself some breathing space before he entered into his next bruising battle, this one over the adoption of the North Atlantic Free Trade Agreement (NAFTA).

The Bush administration had negotiated an agreement with Canada and Mexico to create the largest "free trade" zone in the world.[36] It was now up to Clinton, who had endorsed the pact during the campaign, to push it through Congress. NAFTA, he said, would provide a huge shot in the arm for a still sluggish economy. By reducing tariff barriers, it would expand markets for American goods and services. In the auto industry alone, car sales in Mexico would increase from 1,000 cars per year to 50,000. By 1995, Clinton predicted, NAFTA would create 200,000 new jobs in the United States. The Mexican economy would also benefit, meaning that there would be fewer impoverished Mexicans illegally entering the United States in search of a better life. Yes, Clinton conceded, some Americans would lose their jobs because of enhanced competition north and south of the border. But these displaced workers could be retrained to take even better-paying jobs than the ones they had lost. Failure to ratify NAFTA, Clinton warned, would lead to dire consequences. Japan or Europe might move in to capture the lucrative Mexican market for themselves, thus leaving the United States out in the cold. America's global economic leadership would also suffer a serious setback.[37]

In pushing for enactment of the pact, Clinton encountered a different political calculus than he had faced during the budget fight. Because NAFTA had originated in the Bush administration and had strong business support behind it, Clinton could count on Republican approval. Democrats were another matter. Organized labor and its representatives in Congress denounced the agreement. "This NAFTA is nothing but a job-stealing, tax-raising, community-destroying agreement," said Democratic House whip David Bonior of Michigan. As for job retraining, laborites were scornful. What was some fifty-year-old who'd worked his or her whole life on an assembly line in Detroit to do? Uproot the family and go back to school? Then uproot the family again to search for some elusive job? When AFL-CIO President Lane Kirkland heard Robert Reich saying that modern workers could expect to change jobs six or seven times in a lifetime, he offered the labor secretary some frank advice: "Stop it. . . . Talk instead about job security. Do you get me? Security. My people are losing their fucking jobs. . . . And you're babbling about career changes. . . . We need security. We don't need goddamn retraining."[38] Environmentalists were equally skeptical of the trade deal.

The United States, they predicted, would be forced to lower its environmental standards to compete with Mexico, where standards were lax. US trade ambassador Mickey Kantor did gain some concessions from Mexican and Canadian negotiators, but not enough to appease the pact's critics, who included almost the entire Democratic leadership of the House of Representatives.

Vice President Gore helped turn the tide in the administration's favor when he debated the merits of NAFTA with one of its most strident opponents, H. Ross Perot, who, during the presidential campaign, had famously predicted that the trade pact would create "a giant sucking sound" of jobs draining to Mexico. Gore and Perot appeared on CNN's *Larry King Show* before one of the largest audiences in cable television history. The event, which had received almost as much notice as a presidential debate, was more a clash of personalities than of reasoned debating points. Gore came off as levelheaded and reasonable, Perot as cranky and unstable. An op-ed headline captured viewer reaction: "Gore Flattens Perot." It was an indication of how cable television was shaping politics that the debate produced a decisive shift in public opinion. Among viewers, some 60 percent said they were now inclined to support NAFTA. Clinton also weighed in by skillfully lobbying legislators in whose districts and states he had run strongly in the election. Between them, the president and vice president saw or phoned 200 legislators, while cabinet members made 900 calls. The effort paid off when Clinton prevailed by a vote of 234 to 200 in the House and 61 to 38 in the Senate. Although a majority of Democrats in both houses opposed the measure, Clinton persuaded just enough of them to join a majority of Republicans to put NAFTA over the top.[39] All those phone calls helped, but the president dispensed more tangible favors as well. In the final days, the administration picked up critical support in the Florida and Louisiana delegations by retaining import restrictions on Mexican citrus fruits, vegetables, and sugar beets. NAFTA foe Ernest "Fritz" Hollings, a Democratic senator from South Carolina, claimed Clinton bought off one Texas congressman with a federal culture center in his district and another with a lucrative defense contract. "He knew how to work votes, and he beat us," Hollings recalled. "He beat us."[40]

Ratification did nothing to quell the debate over NAFTA. As the agreement went into effect, critics, including organized labor, argued that the pact gave corporations a green light to move their operations to Mexico, wiped out millions of jobs in the United States, and swelled the trade deficit. The only winners, critics argued, were big corporations and their stockholders. Defenders conceded that some jobs were lost but argued that they were offset by the lower prices consumers had to pay on a host of products and by the boost to the economy that came from a doubling of trade between the United States and its partners. Through it all, public opinion remained ambivalent, with a plurality of Americans generally in favor of NAFTA but with large numbers undecided about its merits.[41]

Clinton displayed no such ambivalence. He followed NAFTA with over 300 other agreements, some dealing with esoteric subjects like banking and investment services, access to cyberspace, and the protection of intellectual property rights.[42] In addition to formal trade pacts, Commerce Secretary Ronald Brown—a one-time aide to Jesse Jackson, the first African American chair of the Democratic National Committee, and perhaps the most underrated member of the cabinet—became the unofficial ambassador for US corporations seeking footholds abroad. Brown's first trip to China produced a dozen commercial agreements and $5 billion in contracts for American businesses. To reporters who covered the trip, the commerce secretary denied that he had elevated economic concerns over human rights. But internal State Department accounts indicated that he did just that. Meeting with Chinese Premier Li Peng, Brown raised the issue of human rights but also made it clear that the purpose of the trip "was to strengthen the two countries' economic, trade, and investment ties" and gain support for US contract bids.[43] Months earlier, Secretary of State Warren Christopher had angered Chinese leaders by making expanded trade with the United States contingent upon an improvement in human rights. Christopher returned to Washington only to learn that the two issues had become uncoupled in his absence.[44] "President Clinton," a reporter noted early on, "is compiling a more ambitious record of trade liberalization than any President since at least Harry S. Truman."[45]

Besides NAFTA, Clinton achieved two other late-year legislative victories. The first created AmeriCorps, a public service program Clinton likened to FDR's Civilian Conservation Corps and JFK's Peace Corps. In exchange for two years of community service—teaching inner-city pre-schoolers to read, building houses for the poor, caring for the elderly in their homes, helping patrol city streets—volunteers could receive up to $10,000 toward college tuition or vocational training. Dismissed by critics like Pennsylvania congressman Rick Santorum as a program "for hippie kids to stand around a campfire holding hands and singing Kumbaya at taxpayers' expense," AmeriCorps passed mostly along party lines. Although the program neither acquired the iconic status of the Peace Corps nor fulfilled Clinton's goal of guaranteeing "every American who wants a college education the means to obtain one," it eventually was embraced by Democrats and Republicans alike.[46] Clinton also achieved passage of the Brady Handgun Violence Prevention Act. Named after Ronald Reagan's press secretary James Brady, who had sustained a brain injury during an assassination attempt on Reagan in 1981, the Brady bill required a five-day waiting period and a background check on handgun purchases. Under pressure from the National Rifle Association, President Bush had vetoed an earlier version of the bill. Clinton prevailed by marshaling support from law enforcement officers and skillfully making the debate about crime and public safety rather than about the Second Amendment. The Brady bill was the first significant gun control measure since 1968, in the aftermath of the Martin Luther King and Robert Kennedy assassinations.

Allegations of scandal continued to swirl. But Clinton's late-year legislative victories, coupled with the highest public approval ratings since his first months in office, suggested he had finally found his footing.

4

Defeat, 1993–1994

The prolonged debates over budget and trade legislation, while fending off recurrent allegations of wrongdoing, delayed Clinton's coming to grips with the most ambitious initiative of his presidency: overhauling the health-care system. Although the quest for comprehensive reform had bedeviled presidents since Franklin Roosevelt, there was reason to think its time had finally come. By the early nineties, even longtime foes of reform were alarmed by the skyrocketing costs of health care and the insecurities inherent in the system. The administration's task force on reform, chaired by Hillary Clinton, devised what seemed like an ingenious plan—one that addressed real deficiencies in the system but also took into account the prevailing skepticism of government activism. It was not to be. In the end, the administration's plan died aborning. Not since FDR lost his battle over court packing had a president suffered so devastating a legislative defeat, and it contributed, in short order, to Clinton's loss of both houses of Congress in the 1994 elections. The failed reform effort and its electoral aftermath appeared to doom any prospects of a second term. Some observers even worried that the two episodes, taken together, rendered the American political system incapable of meeting the most basic needs of its citizens.[1]

When Bill Clinton decided to run for the presidency, he probably never imagined that health care would play so central a role in his administration. Not that he didn't recognize the need for reform. As governor of a poor rural state where medical facilities were expensive and few and far between, he appreciated the inadequacies of the current system. And when the situation required, he could reel off as well as anyone the statistics documenting the inadequacies of that system not only in Arkansas but across the nation: medical bills rising at twice the rate of inflation; nearly 40 million persons, many of them children, without medical insurance; Americans spending one-third more on health care than citizens of other nations but still trailing them in lifespan, prevention of infant mortality, and other indicators of physical well-being. Even so, embracing the cause of reform appeared to be a fool's errand, especially for a self-styled "New Democrat." Except for Lyndon Johnson, whose Medicare and Medicaid programs were among the crown jewels of his Great Society, every president who had sought to overhaul the system had hit a brick wall.[2] Piecemeal reforms had sometimes produced unwanted consequences. In 1986, bipartisan majorities in both houses of Congress passed, and President Reagan signed, the Emergency Medical Treatment and Active Labor Act, which required hospitals to provide emergency treatment to anyone who needed it, regardless of their ability to pay. To cover the additional costs of this unfunded mandate, hospitals hiked prices on everything from rubber gloves to open-heart surgery. Insurance companies, in turn, passed these increased costs on to their policyholders. Meanwhile, the knowledge that they could not be denied care in an emergency lessened the incentive for many, including many young and healthy citizens, to buy insurance.[3] But dare anyone propose fixing the system, shrill cries of "socialized medicine" were sure to ring out.

Then, in November 1991, almost exactly a month to the day after Clinton announced for the presidency, a special election in Pennsylvania suddenly changed his and everyone else's calculus. The election, to fill a vacant seat in the US Senate, pitted Harris Wofford, a distinguished but little-known Democrat, against Richard Thornburgh, a popular former state governor then serving as attorney general in the Bush administration. Trailing by fifty points and with nothing to lose, Wofford broke the taboo against talking about health care. "If criminals have the right to a lawyer," he said, "I think working Americans should have the right to a doctor." Wofford won by ten points.[4]

Suddenly politicians in both parties, having dodged the issue for ages, scrambled to devise health-care plans of their own.[5] President Bush proposed giving uninsured Americans tax cuts to enable them to purchase coverage. Among Democrats, three plans generated the most attention: a single-payer system, modeled on Canada's, requiring the federal government to reimburse doctors and hospitals for the basic medical services they provided every American; the gradual expansion of Medicare to cover all Americans; and a so-called play or pay system requiring employers either to provide medical benefits to their workers or pay into a national pool that would finance coverage for the uninsured and jobless.[6]

Clinton not only embraced reform but drove home the point by enlisting in his campaign the architects of Harris Wofford's victory, a pair of then-unknown political operatives, James Carville and Paul Begala. At first, Clinton hesitated to commit himself to a specific plan. But under pressure from his opponents in the primaries and then from President Bush in the general election, he came out in favor of an approach different from single-payer, play or pay, or Bush's tax rebate proposal. Called "managed competition," it had been a hot topic of debate for more than a decade within a small circle of health-care experts and industry representatives; it had also stirred interest among a few, mostly conservative Democratic members of Congress. But until Clinton started talking about it on the campaign trail, few had ever heard of it.

The intellectual godfather of managed competition was Alain Enthoven, an economist at the Stanford University School of Business. Enthoven was best known as one of the "whiz kids" or "defense intellectuals" recruited by Defense Secretary Robert McNamara to modernize the operations of the Pentagon during the Kennedy and Johnson administrations.[7] Shortly after leaving Washington, Enthoven turned his attention to the nation's health-care system, which he concluded was as cumbersome, inefficient, and wasteful as the military bureaucracy he had spent a decade trying to reform. The system's fatal flaw, he concluded, was the absence of competition. Because health-care providers didn't have to compete for business, they had few incentives to cut unnecessary expenses and deliver high-quality care to their patients. The system was rigged in favor of doctors, hospitals, and insurance companies who got paid—and paid well—regardless of the prices they charged or the quality of service they provided. Enthoven had seen enough of government, he later recalled, to know that it was not the answer to what ailed the health industry. So, over the course of two decades and in consultation with others, he devised managed competition, a system that relied heavily on market forces to control the costs and quality of health care.

In his proposed system, most Americans would continue to get health insurance through their workplaces. Only now their workplace might join others in the area to create an alliance for the purpose of purchasing insurance. With the power of numbers behind them, workplace alliances would have more bargaining power than an individual or a single business when it came to securing health benefits for their members. Enthoven imagined that as the purchasing alliances came into existence, many doctors and hospitals would, with the help of insurance companies, form organizations of their own in order to compete for the business of the alliances. A set of rules would govern the system—hence the "managed" component of managed competition. All health-care providers would be required to offer basic services, and they could no longer deny coverage to persons with preexisting illnesses. The system would not be completely privatized; government would organize and certify regional alliances, specify the minimum services all providers must offer, and require employers to participate in the plan. It would also help the unemployed secure and pay for health care. Still, the market, not government, was the motor of the proposed setup.

Nothing on the scale envisioned by Enthoven had ever been done. Several states, corporations, and universities had experimented with smaller versions of managed competition, and the results had been promising.[8] Enthoven conceded that his proposal wasn't perfect. It would be difficult to organize workplace alliances in rural and sparsely populated areas, and 5 or even 10 percent of the population might still find themselves without coverage. And while it seemed reasonable to assume competition would bring down costs, Enthoven conceded there was no guarantee. In the unlikely event costs got out of hand, federal officials might have to propose (though not impose) price guidelines to rein in costs. Enthoven might also have noted another potential problem: the plan's complexity. The basic principles behind managed competition were straightforward enough. But when Enthoven began talking about the "capitation rates of integrated financial and delivery organizations" or adjusted risk indexes, eyes glazed over.[9]

For all its drawbacks, the politics of managed competition held promise. Here was a plan that might actually get through Congress. True, many liberals, including Hillary Clinton, preferred a single-payer approach. One month after the inauguration, Hillary's close friend from

Arkansas, political science professor Diane Blair, was having dinner with the Clintons when the subject came up. The first lady, Blair noted in her journal, "thinks managed competition a crock; single-payer necessary; maybe add to Medicare."[10] But the first lady undoubtedly also understood that a single-payer plan had no chance of surviving in the prevailing conservative climate—Harris Wofford's Pennsylvania miracle not withstanding. As for moderates and conservatives, a market-oriented approach should prove a welcome departure from previous government-centered reforms. The real genius of managed competition, or so it must have seemed to Clinton, was its potential for co-opting longtime foes of national health insurance. Private insurance companies would presumably like managed competition because it allowed them to sell health plans to the regional alliances. Reformers should warm to the idea of having insurers on the inside rather than fighting reform from the outside as they had in the past.[11] The nation's doctors should rally around it as well: they stood to gain nearly 40 million previously uninsured patients. Even big corporations would have cause to lend support—or at least not go to the wall in opposition as they had done in the past—for if managed competition succeeded in containing soaring health-care costs, corporate America would be in a better position to compete in a global market. So, despite its uninspiring name, which Clinton rarely used, managed competition was a godsend, a plan that offered the new administration a chance to break the logjam that had blocked comprehensive health reform for the better part of a century.

Early on, Clinton made three fateful decisions that shaped health-care deliberations. First, he decided to create a White House task force—the president's Task Force on National Health Reform—to write a bill and present it to Congress. Like every president since Franklin Roosevelt, Clinton was captive to the enduring legend of the president as legislator-in-chief, a legend that had FDR and his brain trust of advisers creating a full-blown legislative agenda and driving it through a pliant Congress. But he was misreading history. The New Deal was the product of a richly collaborative process involving not just the president and his advisers but members of Congress, representatives of well-organized interest groups, and government bureaucrats. Of the participants in the New Deal, Congress played the most important role. Indeed, all but two or three of the fifteen major pieces of legislation that passed during Roosevelt's storied first 100 days originated in the legislative branch and many had long legislative histories. By Clinton's time, this complicated history had gotten papered over by commentators long accustomed to making unexamined claims that Roosevelt "gave" the nation Social Security or the FDIC. That glib reading of the past encouraged facile expectations of the future. Pass health care, AFL-CIO president Lane Kirkland told Clinton, and future generations would thank him as they thanked FDR for Social Security.[12] Even professional historians, who should have known better, kept the legend of Roosevelt's legislative prowess alive, embellishing it with each telling. Clinton was hardly alone in deciding to originate health care in the White House. His congressional leaders—Speaker Tom Foley and Majority Leader Richard Gephardt in the House and Majority Leader George Mitchell in the Senate—were just as deeply in thrall of the Roosevelt legend as Clinton, and they seemed eager for him to take the initiative. It was a misreading of history that would prove fatal.[13]

So it was with another Roosevelt legacy that inspired Clinton's second fateful decision: the notion that new presidents must achieve great things during their first months in office or forever be adjudged failures. In the case of health care, speedy action probably made sense. Why not seize upon the momentum of Harris Wofford's election before it dissipated? As adviser James Carville warned, "The more time we allow for the defenders of the status quo to organize, the more they will be able to marshal opposition to your plan, and the better their chances of killing it."[14] Influential congressman David Obey agreed: "the best chance of doing it right was to get it done before the 1994 congressional campaign season hit us."[15] Members of the Democratic Leadership Conference didn't object to speedy action, but they thought the president should shore up his image as a New Democrat by leading off with welfare reform rather than with a new entitlement program. Powerful Senate Finance Committee Chair Daniel Patrick Moynihan also made it known that he considered welfare reform the more urgent problem.[16] The health care–first strategy prevailed.

To ensure prompt consideration, the administration's congressional lieutenants recommended attaching health care to the president's first budget bill. Under a process adopted by the Senate in 1974, known as "reconciliation," budget bills were not subject to filibusters. That meant that a simple majority of fifty-one votes was all that was required for passage, whereas breaking a filibuster required sixty votes. With a fifty-seven to forty-three margin in the Senate, Democrats appeared to be in a strong position to carry the day in the upper house. Reconciliation would further expedite deliberations by limiting floor debate to twenty hours. It was, counseled the administration's congressional liaison on health care, Christopher "Chris" Jennings, "the best (and probably the only) option to pursue if there is a desire to pass health reform this year in the Senate."[17] Not everyone agreed. Clinton's economic advisers worried that strapping health care onto an already controversial budget bill would jeopardize the budget bill's chances of passage. The Senate's senior Democrat, Robert Byrd, opposed reconciliation, but for a different reason. A stickler for tradition, he was the one who predicted the United States would go the way of Greece and Rome if it allowed gays into the military. He also had a near-biblical reverence for the Senate rules, including the rule that required attachments to the budget (and other measures) to be germane to the subject. For him, health care was too great a stretch. He also believed—and here he stood on firm ground—that health care deserved more time for debate than the twenty hours allowed under the reconciliation process. Senators Edward Kennedy and George Mitchell and the president himself tried to change Byrd's mind, but he would not budge. Colleagues might sometimes roll their eyes at Byrd's stentorian pronouncements; but they respected him because of his encyclopedic knowledge of Senate rules and his unwavering dedication to the Senate as an institution. Given his opposition, the Clintons decided they had no choice but to reject the reconciliation option.[18]

It was Clinton's third major decision, to appoint Hillary to head the task force, that caused the biggest stir. Many believed she had cleverly maneuvered to secure the position. Economic adviser Laura Tyson was probably closer to the truth when she recalled that "Hillary didn't object to being chair, but it was Bill's idea. He wanted her to do for health care what she had done for education in Arkansas."[19] The appointment became controversial only when health-care reform became controversial. At the time there seemed no logical reason why this smart and talented woman, her husband's equal in every way, should have continued the charade in which, as reporter Maureen Dowd later put it, "presidential wives pretended to know less than they did and to be advising less than they were."[20]

Hillary Clinton would serve as the public face and principal spokesperson for health-care reform. To organize the task force and manage its day-to-day operations, President Clinton turned to Ira Magaziner, yet another fellow Rhodes Scholar (and charter member of the Friends of Bill), to join the administration. The son of a New York City bookkeeper, Magaziner was something of a wunderkind who had already made a name for himself by the time he met Clinton at Oxford. At the age of nineteen, while a student at Brown University, he coauthored a 400-page proposal to overhaul Brown's curriculum. The proposal was eventually adopted and remains in place today. At graduation, his valedictory address was featured in *Life* magazine along with Hillary Rodham's speech at Wellesley's commencement. Magaziner achieved his greatest prominence during the seventies and eighties as a consultant hired to improve the global competitiveness of General Electric, Volvo, Wang, and other big corporations. Great Britain, Ireland, and Sweden also enlisted his services. As a consultant, Magaziner's trademark was the massive, 1,000-plus-page study he would compile before advising clients on a course of action. He was of the view, the dean of his alma mater recalled, that if a problem existed, you "don't tweak it here or tweak it there." You "revamp the system."[21] Magaziner was also a proponent of what economists dubbed "industrial policy," the practice of central governments steering public and private investments away from dying industries and toward more promising enterprises. In Magaziner's view, high-tech enterprises were especially promising. He was not without his critics. In 1982, he had coauthored with Robert Reich a book espousing industrial policy. MIT economist Paul Krugman savaged the effort: "It was a stunningly ignorant book—a willfully ignorant book. You can be an industrial policy advocate and get facts right. What's really interesting is that he showed no inclination whatsoever to kick the tires of his idea."[22] Others, though acknowledging his impressive resume, wondered if the two years he had spent studying Rhode Island's health-care system in the early nineties was sufficient background for taking on the most ambitious project of the Clinton presidency.

But the Clintons liked him, and that's what mattered. Though brusque and impatient, gangly and untailored—"a cross between Ichabod Crane and Svengali," said one acquaintance—he shared with the president a passion for policy and for eighteen-hour workdays. Most important, he had worked in both private and public sectors and shared with the Clintons a belief that lay at the heart of managed competition—that market forces and government activism could be combined to restructure health care.[23]

From the beginning, almost nothing went according to plan. The debate over the budget bill proved far more contentious and time consuming than anyone had expected. To hasten the budget's adoption, the president delayed health care—a decision not totally unwelcomed by members of the task force, for they were finding the job of formulating a bill more complicated than they had imagined. And for good reason. They were trying to duplicate within the confines of the White House a process— from hearings to bill markups—that usually took place in congressional committees under the guidance of legislative experts. Then there was Magaziner's tendency—reminiscent of Civil War general George McClellan—to prepare for every contingency before heading into battle. "He's a smart person, not a dummy by any means," CEA economist Alan Blinder said of Magaziner. "But if there's a simple way and a complex way to do it, he always wants the complex way."[24] Even before things got underway, Magaziner warned the president that people were telling him, "we're gonna get killed." To avoid the worst, Magaziner said, "We'll need at least four to five years to put together a package that will pass Congress."[25] The army of health-care experts Magaziner assembled eventually numbered between 500 and 600. As one journalist described the process, "experts met in almost continuous secret session for the first five months of 1993. They gathered in 'clusters' and 'working groups,' sometimes until 2 a.m. on Sunday mornings. They subjected each other to papers, presentations and slide shows. Finally, their work was offered up for criticism by 'contrarians' and 'auditors.'" The end result, this same journalist concluded, was "probably the most ambitious policy study in the history of the federal government."[26]

But as with Lincoln's first general, delay proved costly. It meant that the 100-day deadline came and went and with it the aura of inevitability that had once enveloped reform. And as James Carville had predicted, delay gave opponents time to mobilize. The closed-door proceedings of the task force further complicated the situation. Although Hillary Clinton and Ira Magaziner began their deliberations with a series of public hearings, the critical discussions took place in private, doubtless in the not unreasonable belief that privacy would discourage the grandstanding and playing-to-the-cameras that normally accompany public forums. Opponents of reform immediately took the administration to court, arguing that Hillary Clinton, technically a private citizen and not a government employee, had no right to hold private meetings. The courts ruled in Clinton's favor, but only after costly and distracting litigation. Paranoia festered the longer the task force deliberated, feeding rumors that Hillary Clinton was plotting a government takeover of the health-care system.

Congress proved to be the administration's most formidable challenge. Congressional liaison Chris Jennings, an Ohio native with ten years of experience on Capitol Hill, presciently outlined the nature of the challenge in an early memorandum to Magaziner. "In the recent history of the U.S. Congress," Jennings wrote, "it has been virtually impossible to pass any large and potentially controversial initiative without identifying, getting to know, educating, stroking, and responding to an ideologically diverse and ego sensitive Congress that, individually and collectively, has become more and more independent." "This is," he added, "a time consuming, redundant process that can seem to be (and frequently is) frustrating. But it is essential to increase the likelihood of a positive reception to the eventual Clinton health reform proposal."[27] If anything, Jennings underestimated the difficulty of attracting congressional support for a proposal drafted outside normal legislative channels.

The lobbying effort eventually fell short, but it was not for want of effort. Just weeks after the inauguration, Hillary Clinton began the arduous task of meeting with legislators and their staffs. The meetings stretched on for over a year, even as controversies over the budget, NAFTA, Whitewater, Travelgate, and all the rest swirled about. Individual sessions, often presided over by Mrs. Clinton alone, required deep knowledge of the issues and personalities she was dealing with—as well as an almost unlimited supply of patience. One day she would be reassuring congressmen that military veterans would be well served by reform, the next day promising to take into account the needs of small business owners and rural constituents. Always there were personal issues to work around. She met with Democratic Senator Patrick Leahy of Vermont, though he was not a major player on health care, because he complained that his Republican counterpart was getting more attention than he in home-state newspapers. Why was she neglecting the Pacific/ Asian contingent in Congress, California congressman Norman Mineta complained. Efforts to mollify the group quickly followed. One congressman, considered a grandstander by colleagues, received the same respectful hearing as others.[28]

Chris Jennings and his congressional liaison staff devised personalized strategies to attract the support of Democratic senators. For some, like Richard Bryan of Nevada, the plan was to get influential constituents to apply the pressure: "Needs to Hear from Seniors . . . Running for reelection and needs political and financial support . . . Call on financial donors who are advocates of health reform to weigh in . . . Labor may also have an effect." For others, like John Breaux of Louisiana, it was thought that personal appeals would do the trick: "Breaux wants most of all to facilitate the final deal on health care. Regular cabinet contact to make him feel a part of the action and a meeting with the president to solidify his role are suggested." For still others, like Dianne Feinstein of California, the plan combined the two approaches: "Needs to hear from as many supportive groups as possible. Labor, in particular, needs to weigh in. Senator Feinstein is in a potentially tight race for reelection. Grassroots efforts are most important here. This should be combined with a meeting with the first lady to make the substantive case."[29] In some cases, the administration planned to encourage influential constituents in the senator's home state to lobby the member. In other cases a meeting with the president, first lady, or other high-ranking official was recommended.

Critics later complained that Hillary Clinton and other members of the task force ignored Republicans. That wasn't true. From the beginning, the first lady and her advisers knew they needed Republican votes. "Obviously," Chris Jennings wrote in April 1993, "if we have any chance of passing health care reform this year, we will have to have Republicans on board." The first lady met numerous times with GOP moderates like Senators Nancy Kassenbaum of Kansas, John Chafee of Rhode Island, and David Durenberger of Minnesota, as well as Senate Republican leader Bob Dole. As often as not, it was they, not Clinton, who kept their distance for fear of appearing to be co-opted. One Republican senator, discreetly leaving the punch line to the imagination, told his colleagues they "would get more than a good night's sleep" if they went "to bed with the Administration on health care."[30]

Despite the efforts of Clinton and her colleagues, the drive for health-care reform slowly lost momentum. By the spring of 1993, the sense of inevitability had been lost. The delay in unveiling legislation caused legislators to wonder if health care remained a top priority. To regain the momentum, Chris Jennings urged the Clintons to summon congressional leaders to the White House and make it clear that the president not only wanted legislation but also wanted it before year's end. The meetings didn't go as planned. At one, recalled White House aide Harold Ickes, son of FDR's legendary Secretary of the Interior, "Hillary gave an impassioned plea to the legislative leaders that this had to be done, the people wanted it, America needed it." She went on to say that the White House would arouse such strong support for reform that "when members of Congress got back home on recess and they hear from their constituents, they will come back and this health care bill will pass." If only it were that easy, thought Senate Majority Leader Mitchell. "The fact is," he confided to Ickes, as Ickes remembered it, "when we go back, we meet such a . . . tiny group of people, most of them are people that we know, a lot of them are our contributors. Yes, we have our town halls and all that, but Hillary's just really missing the mark on how much public pressure is going to be brought to bear on us as we go back to our states." At a gathering of Democratic senators in late April, Magaziner elicited an equally skeptical response. Congress, he insisted, needed to pass a bill by July 4 and certainly no later than the August recess. Senator Bill Bradley of New Jersey, a fourteen-year veteran in the upper house, had never seen a major bill clear the necessary legislative hurdles in such a short time. And here Magaziner was talking about the imminent passage of sweeping legislation still in the drafting stage. What would happen if Congress missed the deadline? Bradley asked. "You don't understand," Magaziner replied. "Those people who oppose us, we'll demonize them, and it'll pass."[31] Bradley probably didn't understand that Clinton and Magaziner were primarily trying to reassure him and others that they wouldn't be going into battle alone. Still, this morale-boosting message was lost on legislators like Bradley who believed the task-force leaders had lost touch with political reality.

The most frequent complaint was that Clinton and Magaziner were running a closed-door operation. To help her counter the complaint, Chris Jennings prepared talking points for the first lady: "The truth and irony is that our process may well be the most open in the history of the Federal Government. How can anyone seriously argue that 500 people, made up of over 100 Congressional staff members, well over 50 physicians, numerous other health care professionals (including nurses, social workers, pharmacists, and many others), and representatives from virtually every Department within the Administration is a closed process?"[32] Still, as long as the command center was situated in the White House and not on Capitol Hill, there was no convincing skeptical lawmakers. The administration's "big mistake," recalled Louisiana Senator John Breaux, "was doing it all in the White House." Legislators, he said, resented "that we weren't involved in it, and they were cutting Congress out and it was going to be sent over as a fait accompli: here take it and pass it." House Majority Leader Richard Gephardt, neglecting to mention that he had originally urged the Clintons to take the lead in preparing legislation, agreed with Breaux. "This was a case where the White House kind of wrote a bill and handed it to the leaders in Congress and said, 'This is what we want.'" Gephardt's chief of staff, Thomas J. O'Donnell, was even more blunt: "We had all these people who had worked on this issue for years, and then we have a new administration come in and they want to write [it], they won, he's the executive. But we ended up being handed a health care bill and we were supposed to pass it, and it just didn't work that way."[33] These retrospective judgments weren't entirely fair. But it was the perception that mattered, and the perception at the time and later was that the White House had shunted aside Congress.

Members of Congress weren't alone in feeling marginalized. Managed competition "at its core" was "a very good plan," recalled CEA member Blinder. It was the add-ons that were the problem. "They took this basically good structure, sort of a nice-looking Douglas fir tree," he said, "and then they hung on it all kinds of baubles and bells and whistles that weighted the branches down till they cracked." But when he and his CEA colleagues offered suggestions, as they did in a twenty-five-page critique of the emerging plan, their suggestions were not taken seriously. Hillary Clinton thanked them profusely for their report and then, according to Blinder, went on to ignore it. It was the difference between listening and hearing, Blinder thought. Clinton and Magaziner listened to their concerns but didn't hear them. "So basically," he said, "zero of the many, many suggestions we made for changes in the healthcare plan got into the healthcare plan."[34]

Still, all was not lost. On September 22, 1993, President Clinton delivered a stirring address to a joint session of Congress that almost single-handedly revived the reform cause. With telling statistics and vivid anecdotes, he made a compelling case for change. How, he asked, would Americans be able to master the formidable challenges of the future if they had to live in constant fear of being "just a pink slip away from losing their health insurance, and one serious illness away from losing all their savings?" Under his plan, Clinton explained, a number of private health-care alliances would be established in every state. These alliances would compete for business by offering their own health insurance plans. Employers, in turn, would be required to offer their workers at least three insurance plans from which to choose. Employers would pick up 80 percent of the cost, employees 20 percent. No one could be denied coverage even if they had a preexisting medical condition or changed jobs. Even the jobless would be covered under separate provisions. In the short run, Clinton conceded, some would see their insurance premiums increase. The vast majority of Americans, however, would pay the same or less for coverage that was at least as good as what they already had. The administration later estimated that the average two-adult family with children would pay an annual premium of $872, with the employer picking up the rest.[35]

Clinton delivered some moving addresses during his presidency—in the aftermath of the bombing of the Murrah Building in Oklahoma City, at the funeral of assassinated Israeli Prime Minister Yitzhak Rabin, and during peace negotiations in Belfast, Northern Ireland. But measured by the public reaction, his health-care address was probably his most effective. In truth, he usually performed better in less structured situations than he did on big formal occasions. Although astonishingly well read, he lacked the "ear" for speechifying possessed by a Lincoln or a Franklin

Roosevelt, or even a Kennedy or a Reagan. His Inaugural and State of the Union addresses, although engagingly delivered, had the written-by-committee quality that rendered them almost instantly forgettable. "He was less an orator than a Baptist preacher with highly responsive parishioners," said foreign policy advisor Strobe Talbott. His speeches were easy to listen to but hard to sum up in a few memorable phrases."[36] The few memorable phrases Clinton did utter during his presidency came during the scandals that plagued his later years in the White House, and they were memorable for the wrong reasons. Clinton was aware of the problem. Preparing for one of his State of the Unions, he complained that the draft was "too damn long" and that people wouldn't listen "because you've got to push every damn little button." "Somebody ought to give a five minute State of the Union," he said, prompting laughter from his aides. The famous evangelist Billy Graham, he added, "never talked more than twenty minutes. He's more effective than I am."[37]

Among his formal addresses, the health-care speech was an exception, not in brevity but in effectiveness. "Once in a rare while we hear passion in a President's speech," wrote columnist Anthony J. Lewis, who was reminded of Kennedy's Oval Office address in 1963 calling for adoption of the civil rights act.[38] It was notable for another reason as well. As veteran reporters Haynes Johnson and David Broder told it: "In the most important speech of his life, the moment that would launch a titanic battle affecting the lives of every citizen and a seventh of the U.S. economy, that could define his presidency, restore badly eroded public faith in the political system's ability to serve the people, and redeem a promise more than sixty years in the making to provide universal health care, the president found the wrong speech displayed on the teleprompter." Worse, Clinton couldn't make out the printed version in front of him because he'd forgotten his reading glasses. Ten or fifteen minutes passed before the right text showed up on the screen. But Clinton carried it off with aplomb. Almost no one in the chamber or among the millions of television viewers realized that anything was amiss. A minor legend was born.[39] In the days ahead, support for health-care reform reached its high-water mark of 60 percent, while Clinton's overall approval rating climbed above 50 percent for the first time since his first weeks in office.[40]

Hillary Clinton followed up her husband's address with winning appearances on Capitol Hill. "The most impressive testimony on a complex program anyone could remember," wrote one reporter. "If this had been a three-day, 12-hour oral exam for a Ph.D. on healthcare," said another, "she would have gone directly to tenure." Some commentators complained that the questioning—from Republicans as well as Democrats—was patronizing and obsequious but most believed she had refashioned her own image and perhaps even redefined the role of first lady.[41]

Having quickly regained the momentum, the Clintons just as quickly let it slip away. In the critical months following his speech to Congress, the president had turned his attention to the still unfinished business of NAFTA and to unexpected crises in Somalia and Haiti. Critics, meanwhile, began to raise questions about the ambiguous and incomplete parts of the health-care proposal. Before long a furious and well-financed opposition arose, the centerpiece of which was a thirty-second television ad that became a classic. Financed by the Health Insurance Association of America (HIAA), the ad featured a fictional middle-class couple, Harry and Louise, looking over their insurance policies at the kitchen table:

> ANNOUNCER: "The government may force us to pick from a few health care plans designed by government bureaucrats."
> LOUISE: "Having choices we don't like is no choice at all."
> HARRY: "They choose."
> LOUISE: "We lose."[42]

Harry and Louise were only the beginning. The HIAA launched a $20 million campaign against the plan, dispatching operatives to the home states of key legislators and producing "more than four hundred fifty thousand contacts with Congress—phone calls, visits, or letters—almost a thousand to every member of the House and Senate."[43]

As in the budget fight, many of those whose support the Clintons had been counting on turned against the plan, often with unexpected vengeance. Everyone wanted reform, it seemed, but only on their own terms. Small business owners, acting through the National Federation of Independent Business, objected to being required to offer insurance to their workers, even though workers would share premium costs and the government would help businesses pick up the tab. The most objectionable provision of the bill imposed a cap on annual insurance premiums. The Clintons and Magaziner remained hopeful that market forces alone would curb soaring health-care costs. But just in case competition didn't prove sufficient—as even Alain Enthoven had conceded was a possibility—they included a backstop provision limiting annual premium increases to the rate of inflation. Almost to a person Clinton's economic advisers opposed the provision as unworkable. But the president, after listening to the two sides debate the issue for over two hours, sided with Hillary and Magaziner. That did it for most insurance companies. They now flocked to the opposition en masse. That did it, too, for Enthoven, who denounced the premium caps as a betrayal of the free-market principles that lay at the heart of managed competition. "The first thing Congress should do," he said, "is delete pages 1 through 1,342 of Clinton's 1,342-page bill."[44]

Not even the weighty public-interest groups from which the Clintons were expecting critical support could save the day. The American Association of Retired Persons (AARP), the Kaiser Foundation, and the League of Women Voters supported the administration's proposal but declined to endorse it by name for fear of jeopardizing their nonpartisan tax-exempt status. In an ironic twist, the American Medical Association (AMA), which had almost single-handedly killed previous reforms, endorsed major parts of the Clinton plan, although not the plan itself. By the 1990s, however, the AMA was no longer the powerhouse it had once been; nor did it any longer speak for a majority of the nation's physicians.[45]

Despite the enthusiastic reception both Clintons had received during their appearances on Capitol Hill, efforts to rally congressional support encountered unexpected difficulties. Some legislators insisted upon pushing their own versions of reform to the exclusion of all others. Dan Rostenkowski of Illinois, White House ally and chair of the all-important House Committee on Ways and Means, was hobbled by a federal indictment on corruption charges that would soon put him in prison. Then there was Rostenkowski's unpredictable counterpart in the Senate, Daniel Patrick Moynihan, chair of the Finance Committee, who withheld support because he was annoyed with Clinton for taking on health care before welfare reform. "Boob bait for bubbas," the

New York senator called the health care plan. Asked on *Meet the Press* to clarify his remarks, Moynihan said, "We don't have a health care crisis in this country. We do have a welfare crisis."[46] Nor did Clinton attract the expected backing of kindred spirits in his own party, southern moderates like Senators John Breaux of Louisiana and David Boren of Oklahoma. Most of them did not directly oppose the reform plan. But for reasons that were never quite clear—perhaps their pride in seeing one of their own in the White House was tinged by envy—they didn't do all they might have to help the cause. Falling short as well were many of the Democratic committee and subcommittee chairs with jurisdiction over health care. Some got cold feet when various interest groups threatened reprisal. But most simply had difficulty understanding the intricacies of managed competition and even more difficulty explaining those intricacies to their constituents.

Even as the Clinton proposal struggled to survive, some GOP leaders believed Republicans needed to do more than oppose reform. They needed to offer an alternative. To that end, Rhode Island Senator John Chafee offered a proposal of his own. Requiring employers to foot most of the bill for insurance premiums as Clinton wanted to do, Chafee argued, would endanger the economy in two ways: It would discourage employers from making new hires, thus increasing unemployment; and employers would simply pass on to consumers the extra costs of doing business, thus sparking inflation. Far better, Chafee maintained, to require individuals to buy insurance. Moreover, because individuals would be assuming the full cost of premiums, they would be more prudent in their use of the health-care system. They would, in other words, think twice about seeking unnecessary care. Proponents of the individual mandate, including the conservative Washington think tank, the Heritage Foundation, likened it to commonsense requirements that automobile passengers wear seatbelts. Other than replacing the employer mandate with an individual mandate and offering less comprehensive coverage, Chafee's plan had much in common with the Clintons'. Employers would be required to offer employees insurance policies (though not pay for them); health-care alliances would compete for business; and the government would help offset the costs of insurance premiums by offering vouchers to the unemployed and tax breaks to just about everyone else. Nineteen Republican senators, including Minority Leader

Dole, and two Democrats, Senators Boren and Kerrey, signed on as cosponsors.[47]

Hopes that the Chafee bill might lead to a compromise were short-lived. A number of the administration's economic advisers, including Alan Blinder, were open to Chafee's individual mandate. In fact, they preferred it to the employer mandate, which they considered unworkable. Task-force leaders, however, including Hillary Clinton and Ira Magaziner, stuck with the employer mandate. And they did so, in Blinder's view, not on the merits but because the Heritage Foundation supported the individual option, and the Heritage Foundation was "right wing."[48] An explosive two-day Republican retreat in Annapolis in May 1994 made it official. "Republicans have to make it clear we are not signing on to any of this government control and mandate stuff," said Senator Trent Lott of Mississippi. House members in attendance not only opposed the Chafee bill but health-care reform of any kind. Representative Phil Gramm of Texas, taking aim at Senator Dole's front-runner status for the GOP presidential nomination in 1996, declared that health-care reform of any type would pass "only over my cold dead politician's body."[49] Here Gramm was echoing the advice congressional Republicans had earlier received from William "Bill" Kristol, former chief of staff to Vice President Dan Quayle and son of neoconservative icons, Irving Kristol and Gertrude Himmelfarb. Health-care reform should go down on its own merits, Kristol wrote, but also because of the mortal danger it posed to the Republican Party. If the Democrats succeeded, they would reestablish themselves as "the generous protector of middle-class interests." And, he warned, it would "strike a punishing blow against Republican claims to defend the middle class by restraining government." It would, in other words, do for the party of Bill Clinton what Social Security had done for the party of Franklin Roosevelt. Kristol did not rule out some future "principled" incremental reform, but only after the Clinton bill—or anything like it—was safely interred.[50]

By the spring of 1994, public support was hemorrhaging, down forty points from six months earlier. It was little consolation for the Clintons that when queried about the specific provisions of the Health Security Bill, people registered strong support; when Clinton's name was affixed to the title, they turned thumbs down.[51] Democratic legislators up for reelection were especially skittish about identifying with the measure.

California Senator Dianne Feinstein went so far as to withdraw her name as a cosponsor.[52] Senate Majority Leader George Mitchell launched an intensive rescue mission. But to no avail. A last-ditch effort by Hillary Clinton to avert defeat proved disastrous. In late July she travelled to the West Coast to mobilize support. Menacing crowds greeted her at every stop, prompting her Secret Service detail to insist she don a bulletproof vest. Upon her return to Washington she urged her husband to make one final appeal from the Oval Office. He declined, and in September 1994, all efforts at compromise having failed, Mitchell withdrew the Health Security Bill from consideration.

The first wave of second-guessing that followed the demise of healthcare reform predictably stressed the personal element: The Clintons had moved too fast or not fast enough, depending on the commentator's point of view; having won only 43 percent of the vote, the president was foolish to have attempted a monumental task that had stymied all of his predecessors; the president should have known better than to put his wife and his old Oxford friend in charge of the task force. Or as Ira Magaziner put it to the president: "Right now, as you know, the first lady and I and to some extent you, are blamed for the so called 'health care debacle' by the Washington conventional wisdom. We allowed a group of policy wonks meeting in secret to produce a complicated, big government, unrealistic plan which overreached and was dead on arrival. You were influenced by your ultra liberal wife and 'wonky' old college friend to accept this unwise venture over the objections of most of your advisers."[53] Even administration officials who later claimed to have known from the beginning that the Hillary-Magaziner approach would never work said they had no choice but to go along with it. "It was screwy," recalled Health and Human Services Secretary Donna Shalala, who was largely left out of the process. "But when the president and First Lady decide they want to do something first on, unless it's illegal you support it." Far better, Shalala believed, to have given the states the leeway to experiment with their own health-care reforms as they were already doing with welfare. That way the administration could have learned what worked and what didn't work before trying to overhaul the system on its own.[54] Congress came in for its share of criticism. The Democratic leadership wasn't what it had been in its glory days: Senate leader George Mitchell was no Lyndon Johnson, House Speaker Tom Foley no Sam Rayburn. Complained Magaziner, "We depended on the old Democratic leadership structure in congress to push through a bill for us and they were too weak and their power too diffuse to do so."[55] For some, the public was to blame. The 83 percent of Americans who had coverage through their employers or through Medicare or Medicaid didn't care enough about their fellow countrymen and women who lacked insurance. For Clinton partisans the explanation was clear: the opposition was too well financed and too skilled in the art of misinformation.[56] In an appearance before a convention of pediatricians in Washington, DC, Hillary Clinton singled out leaders of the insurance companies: "They like being able to exclude people from coverage, because the more they can exclude, the more money they can make." Worse, she said, those same companies had "the gall to run TV ads that there is a better way, the very industry that has brought us to the brink of bankruptcy because of the way they have financed health care."[57] Once the dust settled, both Clintons conceded they probably had tried to do too much too fast, though the president also blamed Senate Minority Leader Robert Dole for supposedly reneging on a pledge to support a compromise.[58]

Most explanations, offered with the full, but unacknowledged, benefit of hindsight, contained a grain of truth. But only a grain, as two examples may illustrate. For one, the contention that Clinton's slim margin of victory in 1992 doomed health care from the start ignored the bipartisan consensus that had formed after Harris Wofford's election in Pennsylvania that health-care reform was an idea whose time had come. "Although few are willing to admit it now," political scientist Jacob Hacker observed after the bill's demise, "there was a near-universal perception in early 1993 that some type of health reform plan would pass the 103rd Congress."[59] Indeed, Clinton would have been irresponsible to allow a historic opportunity to slip away. For another, Clinton partisans were correct in pointing out that the opposition spent more to defeat reform—an estimated $300 million—than almost any previous lobbying effort aimed at bringing down a single bill. And it was true as well that reform foes misrepresented central elements of the Clinton plan and muscled wavering legislators into opposition. Still, the heavy-handed tactics of the opposition can't explain why someone like Alain Enthoven, who inspired Clinton's plan in the first place, ended up so firmly in the opposition camp.

The plan's baffling complexity was a more compelling explanation for the reform's demise. There had been early warning signs. CEA Chair Laura Tyson confessed that she had a hard time making sense of the plan when it was first unveiled. Labor Secretary Robert Reich, writing years later, said that he still didn't understand the plan. "I've been to dozens of meetings on it, defended it on countless radio and TV programs, debated its merits publically and privately, but I still don't comprehend the whole." "It was too complicated for me to explain and I'm used to explaining complicated things," said Health and Human Services Secretary Donna Shalala.[60] If Tyson, with a doctorate in economics from MIT, Reich, a Rhodes Scholar and Yale Law graduate, and Shalala, a former university chancellor, had trouble comprehending the whole, it's hardly surprising others did as well.

Clinton might have helped his cause by following up his congressional call to arms with a series of less stirring speeches explaining some of the thornier parts of his plan. In doing so he would have been emulating not the FDR of myth but the FDR of reality, whose first fireside chat explained a complex banking crisis so clearly that even the bankers understood it, as humorist Will Rogers quipped. Clinton might also have been wise to frankly admit some of managed competition's limitations. And limitations there were. Even loyal supporters had a hard time believing that nearly 40 million uninsured Americans could be brought into the system without raising taxes, reducing benefits, or limiting anyone's freedom of choice.[61] But Clinton had promised all that and more: his plan would both slow soaring medical costs and reduce the national deficit. Perhaps so, but more explanation was required. The president and his allies skipped over the hard parts, apparently in the belief that they might further confuse an already confused public.

Then there was the fact that from gestation to birth the plan had developed almost entirely outside the regular legislative process. As political scientist Jacob Hacker observed, managed competition, which lay at the plan's core, may have had much to recommend it. But it took shape within an insular world of economists and health-care specialists.[62] And it assumed its final form in the almost equally insular world of the president's Task Force on National Health Reform. Or, to put it another way, unlike Social Security, Medicare, or most other successful reforms of the twentieth century, it had shallow legislative roots. By contrast, by the time the Social Security Act reached the floor of Congress in 1935, many of its elements, such as unemployment insurance and old-age pensions, had been discussed for years at both the national and state levels. Legislators had a stake in its provisions.[63] The same was true for Medicare in the 1960s, and indeed for almost every other major reform of the twentieth century.

Maybe, when all is said and done, it was the post–New Deal mythology of the president as legislator-in-chief that doomed health-care reform. Ironically, there was a New Deal precedent for what Clinton had done, though probably not the one he had in mind. In 1937, Roosevelt made one of his rare forays outside the normal legislative process. The result was his court-packing proposal, and it led to the biggest legislative defeat of his presidency.

But these were matters of errant strategies and tactics and misleading historical models. For some, the failed reform signaled something more troubling. To journalists Haynes Johnson and David Broder, who wrote a seminal account of the health-care debate, it symbolized "the inability of the U.S. system of government and politics to deal with critical issues that affect the lives of all citizens." Foes of reform, like Newt Gingrich, saw it differently. "I look back on the negative achievement of not imposing an obsolete health model as one of the crowning glories of The System," he said. "It worked. The country didn't want it. It wasn't the right thing to do, and despite all the efforts of the president of the United States, it failed."[64]

As the midterm elections of 1994 approached, President Clinton knew his party was in for a drubbing. Even in the best of times, new presidents lose seats in Congress their first time out, Franklin Roosevelt being the only twentieth-century exception. And these were not the best of times. Health care remained a debilitating issue, but so, too, did the economy in general. Although some improvement had taken place, growth remained sluggish, and the incomes for most American families remained stagnant. Ironically, rising medical costs were offsetting what increases in family incomes there were. Clinton's public approval ratings sank to the lowest level of any president after two years since the advent of polling. Two-thirds of the public believed the country was headed in the wrong direction.

Sensing the possibility of a big, perhaps even historic, victory, Republicans set out to turn the election into a referendum on the Clinton presidency, thus defying Thomas "Tip" O'Neill's tiresome but wise maxim that all politics is local. The chief architect of the GOP's strategy was none other than the man Democrats blamed for the decline of bipartisanship in Washington, House minority whip, Newt Gingrich. An "army brat" who had grown up on military bases in the United States and abroad, Gingrich earned a doctorate in European history from Tulane University and taught at a small Georgia college before winning a seat in Congress in 1978. Brash and confrontational, he quickly rose to prominence within his party. In the late eighties, he was instrumental in forcing Democratic House Speaker James Wright out of office on conflict-of-interest charges. Having wreaked havoc on the Democrats, Gingrich in the early nineties turned his sights on a member of his own party, House Minority Leader Robert Michel of Illinois, whom Gingrich considered too willing to consort with members of the opposition. When Gingrich let it be known that he intended to challenge Michel for the leadership position, Michel, a thirty-eight-year House veteran, announced his intention to retire. Throughout his life Clinton had been adding to his stable of admirers—the famous FOB or Friends of Bill. At almost every stage of his life, Gingrich had left people by the wayside as he moved on to his next big thing.

Gingrich's broadsides against the Democrats were often outrageous. They were, he said, "the enemy of normal Americans" who had "no concept of family." They were the "party of total hedonism, total exhibitionism, total bizarreness, total weirdness." One time he tried to link Democrats to a deranged South Carolina woman who drowned her two young children; another time to comedian Woody Allen who allegedly had an incestuous relationship with an adopted daughter. When Republicans spread unfounded rumors that Democratic House Speaker Tom Foley was gay, a Gingrich aide was quoted as saying, "We hear it's little boys."[65] Preparing Republicans for the election, Gingrich encouraged them to use incendiary words when talking about the Democrats—words like betrayal, bizarre, decay, antiflag, antifamily, pathetic, radical, sick, and traitor.[66] "In political debate," wrote the *New Yorker*'s Hendrik Hertzberg, "Gingrich often displays the qualities of a clever, if slightly maladjusted, teenage boy. When he is in one of his combative moods, he is insolent, sarcastic, self-righteous, narcissistic, and allergic to understatement." Rabble-rouser that he was, however, Gingrich gave voice to a widespread feeling that the United States was in a state of moral decline. "It is impossible," he said, "to maintain a civilization with 12-year-olds having babies, 15-year-olds killing each other, 17-year-olds dying of AIDS, and 18-year-olds getting diplomas they can't read."[67] His most important contribution to the campaign was a ten-point "Contract with America," which he and his colleagues promised to pass during the first 100 days of a Republican-controlled Congress. Proposals included tax cuts, congressional term limits, welfare reform, and a constitutional amendment requiring the federal government to balance the budget. Although polls showed that most Americans remained unfamiliar with the GOP manifesto, it energized Republican candidates and probably helped increase Republican turnout in the election.[68]

Clinton, meanwhile, played into the hands of Republicans hoping to make the election a referendum about his leadership by campaigning on behalf of beleaguered Democrats across the country. Some of his advisers urged him to maintain a low profile as Harry Truman had done in 1946, another bad year for Democrats. But that wasn't Clinton's style. He couldn't resist going on the stump.

The election was a rout of historic proportions. Republicans picked up fifty-two seats in the House and nine in the Senate, more than enough to take control of both houses of Congress for the first time since 1953. House Speaker Tom Foley became the first incumbent Speaker since the Civil War to lose reelection. Most poignant of all for Democrats was the defeat of Harris Wofford in Pennsylvania, whose election in 1991 on the promise of health-care reform had probably done more to shape national politics during the previous two years than anything except for Clinton's ascension to the presidency. Democratic losses were not confined to Washington. Republicans picked up fourteen governorships and eighteen state houses. New York Governor Mario Cuomo was the most prominent Democratic governor to go down to defeat, but many others fell as well.

A combination of short- and long-term factors shaped the outcome.

The GOP succeeded in nationalizing the election and in taking advantage of public dissatisfaction with Clinton, whose average approval rating over two years was the lowest in recorded history for a new president. "Hillarycare," as critics dubbed health-care reform, hurt Democrats, but so, too, in some races did support for gun control and the stillborn Btu energy tax. Still, the election wasn't just about Clinton and his policies. Only 21 percent of those who turned out at the polls said they were voting against Clinton.[69] Among long-term factors, none was more important than ever-increasing skepticism about the role of government in American life. As any number of public opinion experts noted, it would have been inaccurate to describe the public as "antigovernment." The vast majority of Americans supported Social Security, Medicare, public education, national defense, and government efforts to control crime. Americans were, however, wary of expanding government's reach into existing or new areas. In one 1994 poll, 68 percent of respondents agreed with the statement that "government is doing too many things better left to business and individuals." In the early sixties, 75 percent of the public trusted government to do what was "right" always or most of the time. By 1994, 78 percent of the public trusted government none or only some of the time. Other long-term trends shaping the outcome included the continuing exodus from the Democratic Party of white southerners, white Protestants, and Catholics. On the other hand, Democratic support among women, blacks, Hispanics, and Asian Americans remained firm.[70]

Pundits groped for words to convey the magnitude of the outcome, describing it variously as a revolution, an earthquake, a tidal wave, or a tsunami.[71] Even political scientists and historians, who tend to take a longer view, believed at first they were witnessing something of epic significance. "Very probably the most consequential off-year election" in a century, wrote the dean of American political scientists, Walter Dean Burnham. "The shape of American politics will very probably never be the same again." Burnham believed 1994 was one of those rare "critical elections" during which one party or voting coalition gains dominance for years, perhaps even for generations, to come.[72]

In retrospect, 1994 was the critical election that *didn't* happen. Rather than reshaping politics for generations to come, the election was one of those recurring party shifts somewhat reminiscent of the shifts that occurred during the first Gilded Age. Only this time, voter allegiances were increasingly becoming unmoored from the two major parties, prompting political scientist Everett Carll Ladd to write that it was "by no means certain that the United States will ever again have a majority party in the complete sense that the Republicans were a majority for the 1890s through the 1920s and the Democrats for the 1930s through the early 1960s."[73]

But that's not how it looked at the time. At the time, it looked like a political earthquake, with Gingrich-led Republicans poised to obliterate Clinton-led Democrats. Following the election, Gingrich began receiving the kind of attention usually reserved for newly elected presidents. On a four-day trip to New Hampshire, ostensibly to observe moose in their natural habitat, the newly elected Speaker of the House attracted two busloads of reporters and two helicopter crews.[74] The president, meanwhile, was thrust into the role of powerless lame duck. During a postelection press conference a reporter asked the president if he worried about being able to have his voice heard in coming months. As if to reassure himself as much as anyone, Clinton responded: "The constitution gives me relevance. The power of our ideas gives me relevance. The record we have built up over the last two years and the things we're trying to do to implement it, give it relevance. The president is relevant here, especially an activist President."[75]

With a sense of urgency, Secretary of State Warren Christopher carried the same message abroad. The president, he reassured nervous foreign leaders, was still in charge. There would be no sudden change in foreign policy, no backing away from previous commitments. "Over and over again," Christopher recalled, "we had to emphasize that our powers remained, if somewhat singed a little bit, nevertheless in full force and effect."[76]

5

In Search of Three Syllables: Foreign Policy, 1993–1996

Don't even try, George F. Kennan, the most influential American diplomat of the twentieth century, told Clinton's advisers. The president had been pressing his staff to come up with a compelling word or phrase that would convey the thrust of the administration's post–Cold War foreign policy. And who better to consult than the architect of containment, the strategy that had guided American foreign policy for nearly a half-century? When the opportunity presented itself, Clinton's secretary of state, Warren Christopher, mentioned to the ninety-year-old diplomat that the president had assigned to his staff "the job of replicating what Kennan had done with 'containment'—reducing a big, complicated task to a single word." That's when Kennan told Christopher and deputy secretary of state Strobe Talbott they were on a fool's errand. As Talbott tells the story, Kennan "was sorry he had tried to pack so much diagnosis and prescription into three syllables. He certainly regretted the consequences, since containment had led to 'great and misleading oversimplification of analysis and policy.'" Clinton's advisers would be better off producing a "'thoughtful paragraph or more, rather than trying to come up with a bumper sticker.'" Told about the exchange, Clinton laughed and said, "Well, that's why Kennan's a great diplomat and scholar and not a politician."[1]

President George H. W. Bush had also struggled to find an alternative to "containment" before finally settling on "new world order." He abandoned the phrase when conservative Republicans accused him of advocating a "one-world government."[2] During the 1992 campaign, Clinton had taken Bush to task for invoking a new world order without offering "a compelling rationale for America's continued engagement in the world." In so doing, the administration had "invited a new birth of isolationism on the left and the right." Bush's foreign policy was "reactive, rudderless, and erratic." Clinton faulted the president for ignoring strife in the Balkans, for giving Haitian refugees the back of his hand, and for kowtowing to the Chinese over human rights abuses.[3] Clinton's attacks were glancing blows on the incumbent's stewardship of international affairs. A headline in the *Christian Science Monitor* captured the essence of his approach: "Clinton Hits Bush on Foreign Policy, but Not Too Hard."[4]

The fact is, one could have imagined the members of Clinton's foreign policy team serving comfortably under George Bush or even Ronald Reagan if the circumstances had been right. There was Warren Christopher at State, an across-the-table diplomat of the old school who was cautious, carefully spoken, and so fastidious that Clinton once said he ate his M&Ms with a knife and fork. The most important member of the team, though, was National Security Adviser Anthony Lake, who had served under Presidents Kennedy, Johnson, Nixon, and Carter. A top aide to Henry Kissinger, Nixon's national security adviser, Lake became disillusioned by the administration's secret bombing of Cambodia. In 1970, he resigned in protest. By the time he began advising candidate Clinton in 1992, he was teaching international relations at Mount Holyoke College and had long since put his protesting days behind him. A self-described "pragmatic neo-Wilsonian," he once told a reporter he thought Mother Teresa and Ronald Reagan were both trying to do the same thing—"one helping the helpless, one fighting the Evil Empire."[5] Unlike his old boss, Henry Kissinger, the fifty-four-year-old Lake shunned the limelight. Standing next to the president in a *New York Times* photograph, the caption identified him only as "unidentified man." Reporters invariably described him as soft-spoken and low-key. "The tweedy Tony Lake looks like an unassuming paper-pusher," wrote one.[6] During the first year or year-and-a-half, Lake conformed to image. He was more coordinator than adviser, the honest broker who presented the president with an array of options without showing his own hand. Perhaps sensing that Lake's reticence was leaving the administration unfocused and adrift, Colin Powell, chairman of the Joint Chiefs, told him, in essence, "You have to change the way you're doing your job and become more aggressive and more assertive."[7] That apparently was all

Lake, a self-described "Type A competitor," needed to hear. Although he continued to avoid the front pages and Sunday talk shows, he began to display the "temperament of a Beltway warrior," as one reporter put it. The reporter wasn't just using a figure of speech. At one meeting, convinced that Clinton aide John Podesta had deliberately embarrassed him in front of others, Lake caught up with Podesta in the hallway and shoved him up against a wall. Lake had his critics. One staffer called him a "backstabber" and others described him as the administration's resident Machiavellian. CEA chair Laura Tyson thought him overly protective of his council's turf. The president would occasionally tell him he was pushing his colleagues too hard or that his elbows were "a little sharp." One time, when Lake strongly disagreed with Clinton's friend and adviser on Russia, Strobe Talbott, Clinton became angry with Lake because he felt Lake had "dissed Strobe."[8] The National Security Adviser's personality and style were controversial, but no one doubted his influence. "There are very few times that Tony ultimately is reversed or changed or modified," said Clinton's second chief of staff, Leon Panetta.[9]

At Defense was longtime Wisconsin congressman Les Aspin. An MIT-trained economist, he had been one of Robert McNamara's "whiz kids" at the Pentagon. He supported Lyndon Johnson's reelection campaign in 1968 right up to the day LBJ took himself out of the running. As chair of the House Committee on Military Affairs in the eighties and early nineties, he broke party ranks to support President Reagan's decisions to deploy MX missiles and to supply arms to the Contras trying to overthrow Nicaragua's leftist government. He supported the first Gulf War even more strongly than Clinton. Aspin had a reputation of being a gadfly and iconoclast, but he was smart and unconventional in outlook. Since the collapse of the Soviet Union, he had been thinking about ways to reconfigure the nation's military forces in the face of the decentralized challenges of the new era. Unlike Lake, however, he showed little talent for bureaucratic infighting. He was out before the year ended.

Other key advisers included the vice president; Talbott at State; Samuel "Sandy" Berger, Lake's deputy on the National Security Council; and ambassador to the United Nations Madeleine Albright. Richard Holbrooke, ambassador to Germany and later assistant secretary of state for Canadian and European affairs, would play a pivotal role in

US policy toward the Balkans. Colin Powell, a holdover from the Bush administration as chairman of the Joint Chiefs of Staff, exerted influence far beyond his position and length of tenure. The first African American to head the Joint Chiefs, he had already butted heads with his commander in chief over the issue of gays in the military. Powell had served two tours of duty in Vietnam, and he argued passionately that the nation must never again go to war without an invincible force, attainable goals, and a clear exit strategy. Powell left the administration after only nine months, but the so-called Powell Doctrine remained enshrined in the thinking of the military high command long thereafter. "Powell simply overwhelmed the administration," recalled Richard Holbrooke. "He regarded the new team as children. And they regarded him with awe."[10]

Clinton had entered the White House with the intention of staying focused on the economy. The day-to-day conduct of foreign policy he would leave to trusted subordinates. It was not an unreasonable expectation. The Cold War was over, the Gulf War successfully concluded, and no major threat loomed on the horizon. Moreover, the United States stood at the apex of its power. By any measure—economic, political, or military—it reigned supreme. Not that an immersion in foreign policy was unwelcome. After all, he understood better than most that in an era of globalization the line between domestic and foreign policy was rapidly disappearing. And when the circumstances required, he was a quick study—"the quickest study I've ever seen," said Anthony Lake, "more than Henry Kissinger, more than anyone I've ever worked with." Clinton once told Madeleine Albright that the US ambassadorship to the United Nations was second only to the presidency as the job he most coveted.[11] Still, he was undoubtedly surprised to find himself being drawn into diplomatic and military affairs so soon after taking office. Russia was the reason.

For over forty years, the Cold War had dominated American life. It shaped everything, even developments seemingly removed from international affairs. There would have been a civil rights movement during the fifties and sixties under any circumstances. But the nation's need to present itself in a more favorable light among the peoples of Africa, Latin America, and Asia, where the competition between the United States and the Soviet Union was keen, made even more urgent the quest for racial justice. The Cold War also produced countervailing tendencies. In the case of civil rights, fear of Communist subversion handed foes of civil rights a blunt instrument with which to bludgeon the movement. For those who came of age during the Cold War, including Bill Clinton, its end in their lifetimes seemed unimaginable. Then suddenly the unimaginable happened. The Cold War was over. Just as suddenly, in an act of willful amnesia, the conflict became old news. Or was it? The Soviet Union had splintered into fifteen states. But the largest, Russia, remained a formidable—and now unstable—presence. As Clinton's chief adviser on Russian affairs, later explained, "Even shorn of empire, Russia was still by far the largest country on earth, almost twice the size of the U.S. It sprawled 5,200 miles across Eurasia. Moscow still had an army of 2.8 million and an arsenal of over 20,000 nuclear weapons. No country on earth had as many immediate neighbors, and all thirteen of Russia's were nervous."[12]

In 1990, in the aftermath of the sudden breakup of the Soviet Union, Boris Yeltsin had replaced Mikhail Gorbachev as the head of Russia. The Bush administration had backed Yeltsin. By 1992, however, the Russian leader had come under intense pressure from hard-liners who believed he was moving too fast to dismantle centralized economic controls. With inflation soaring and food in short supply, Russia was on the brink of rebellion. As Yeltsin's peril increased, the Bush administration held him at arm's length for fear he might soon be out of power.

For advice on Russian affairs, Clinton turned to fellow Rhodes Scholar and former Oxford housemate Strobe Talbott, who had spent much of his career reporting on the Soviet Union for *Time* magazine. Talbott urged all-out support for Yeltsin. He disabused Clinton of any notion he could delegate Russia to subordinates; it would require the president's sustained personal attention. Talbott acknowledged the risks of backing Yeltsin. The Russian leader could be exceedingly difficult to deal with. He shamelessly bullied subordinates, had an epic weakness for vodka, and often acted erratically. Still, he was better than the likely alternatives. And although his survival by no means guaranteed stability in Russia or in the other former Soviet states, his downfall would almost certainly doom prospects for a peaceful transition from communism in Eastern Europe. As Talbott explained it, whereas Russian strength had once been the chief threat to America's national security, now it was

Russian weakness. Estonian President Lennart Meri described Russia as a "malignancy in remission" but one that could relapse at any moment.[13]

Former president Richard Nixon also weighed in on Yeltsin's behalf, telling Talbott that Clinton's relationship with Russia would shape his *takes advice* historical reputation more than anything he did at home. The economy, the former president said, was largely beyond Clinton's control. But not so foreign policy. In a private meeting with Clinton at the White House that lasted until two in the morning, Nixon personally drove home the point.[14]

Clinton was persuaded. He directed aides to suggest ways the United States could help Yeltsin deal with his biggest threat to power, a faltering Russian economy. "Think big," Clinton said. Not everyone shared the president's determination to rescue Yeltsin from the brink, especially if it cost money. Worried about the larger-than-expected deficit the administration had inherited, George Stephanopoulos, for one, was wary of going out on a limb to help someone who might not survive. During one meeting, Stephanopoulos walked over to Talbott and whispered in his ear, "No new money! No new legislation!" Clinton, who saw the exchange out of the corner of his eye, later told Talbott: "I'll worry about George and our Congress—you worry about Yeltsin and his." In April, Clinton secured from Congress $1.6 billion in Russian aid. By that time, too, Talbott recalled, "Clinton had become the US government's principal Russia hand, and so he remained for the duration of his presidency." Before leaving office, Clinton would meet Yeltsin eighteen times, just shy of the number of times all of his predecessors, from Truman to Bush combined, had met with their Soviet counterparts.[15]

Complicating relations was the future of the North Atlantic Treaty Organization (NATO), the military alliance the United States had organized to deter Soviet expansion in Western Europe. After commissioning an internal study on the subject of NATO's future, Warren Christopher presented the president with three options: disband the alliance; maintain it in its present composition; or expand its membership by gradually admitting former Soviet bloc states. The last option, which Christopher recommended and Clinton adopted, offered the promise of a stabilizing presence in Europe as former socialist republics transitioned out of communism. Extending membership to new states also had the advantage of allowing the United States to make democratic reforms and respect for human rights requirements for admission. But the prospects of NATO enlargement also alarmed Yeltsin and other Russian leaders, rekindling ancient fears of western encirclement. Nor did Clinton's plans elicit overwhelming support within the United States. National Security Adviser Tony Lake was all for it, but Secretary of Defense Aspin opposed it, as did almost all of the military brass at the Pentagon. Talbott supported enlargement but worried about the timing, believing it might be better to wait until Yeltsin had achieved a more stable hold on power. No less a figure than George Kennan advocated scrapping the forty-four-year-old military alliance. "Expanding NATO would be the most fateful error of American policy in the post cold-war era. Such a decision may be expected . . . to impel Russian foreign policy in directions decidedly not to our liking."[16] The Cassandra-like warnings of Kennan and the others reverberated well into the next century.

Still, in the short run, the new relationship between the United States and Russia survived NATO expansion and other rough patches. Key to the survival of the relationship was the relationship Clinton forged with Yeltsin. At first, some of Clinton's aides wondered why Clinton would shrug off Yeltsin's erratic, frequently outrageous personal and diplomatic behavior. During his first visit to the United States, the Russian leader showed up drunk at a joint press conference. "What we found appalling in Yelsin's conduct Clinton found amusing," Strobe Talbott recalled. But in time, the president's Russian adviser figured it out. "The key, as I saw it," he recalled, "might be that Yeltsin combined prodigious determination and fortitude with grotesque indiscipline and a kind of genius for self-abasement. He was both a very big man and a very bad boy, a natural leader and an incurable screw-up. All this Clinton recognized, found easy to forgive and wanted others to join him in forgiving." Clinton, it's likely, saw something of himself in Yeltsin. The politician in Clinton also understood, as some of his most trusted advisers did not, the political pressures the Russian leader faced at home. He was willing to put up with Yeltsin's bluster because he realized Yeltsin needed to play to a home audience to maintain his shaky hold on power. "I get the feeling he's up to his ass in alligators," Clinton told Talbott. "He especially needs friends abroad because he's got so many enemies at home."[17]

US-Russian cooperation produced significant dividends for both countries. None was more important than continuing to secure the stockpiles of nuclear weapons in the arsenals of Russia and its former satellites. The danger, of course, was that unsecured warheads—"loose nukes"—might fall into the hands of terrorists or rogue nations. Ukraine, with 170 intercontinental ballistic missiles, was of special concern because many experts feared it was "spiraling into chaos."[18] Critics faulted Clinton for failing to speed political and economic reform in Russia. But as had been the case in the declining years of the Soviet Union, events in Russia were more decisive than anything the United States did or didn't do. At considerable risk, Clinton had supported Yeltsin diplomatically, financially, and perhaps most important, personally. Beyond that there was little he could do.

Dealing with Russia was a challenge, but at least it was a known quantity. The State Department remained well stocked with area specialists, and the administration had at its disposal experts like Strobe Talbott who had devoted their careers to studying Russian history and politics. To only a slightly lesser extent, the same was true of China and of North Korea, with which the United States had a brief, but dangerous, standoff during Clinton's first term. The administration, like its predecessor, was less well equipped to deal with conflicts erupting with increasing frequency in East Africa, the Balkans, and elsewhere. Warren Christopher admitted as much during his confirmation hearings when he said that the United States could not afford "to careen from crisis to crisis" but "must have a new diplomacy that seeks to anticipate and prevent crises, like those in Iraq, Bosnia, and Somalia, rather than simply managing them."[19] Crafting a new diplomacy was a conceptual challenge. Containment was obsolete; a new strategic vision was needed. Redefining America's role in the world in the aftermath of the Cold War would not be easy.

The administration's strategic vision was enunciated by the normally media-shy national security adviser Anthony Lake on September 21, 1993. In an hour-long address before students and faculty at the Johns Hopkins University School of Advanced International Studies in Washington, DC, Lake denounced "calls from left and right to stay at home rather than engage abroad"—calls, he said, that were being "reinforced by the rhetoric of Neo-Know Nothings." But engagement was not enough; the United States needed to lead. Lake rejected the conflicting visions of both Francis Fukuyama and Samuel Huntington. "We have arrived at neither the end of history nor a clash of civilizations" but at "a moment of immense democratic and entrepreneurial opportunity." Democracy and market-based economies were on the ascent, and the fundamental goal of American foreign policy should be to broaden their scope. The catchphrase came next: "The successor to a doctrine of containment must be a strategy of enlargement—enlargement of the world's free community of market democracies." Importantly, Lake added, the United States would work to enlarge both democracy and market economies: "Democracy alone can produce justice, but not the material goods necessary for individuals to thrive; markets alone can expand wealth, but not that sense of justice without which civilized societies perish." Lake's formulation was a classic expression of the New Deal's vision of a mixed economy, though now projected on the world scene.[20]

Lake envisioned a four-step process for putting democratic enlargement into practice. First, the United States would give highest priority to shoring up its own economy and those of key democratic allies, such as Europe, Canada, and Japan. Expanded trade agreements would be crucial to this effort. Second, the United States would nurture the growth of market democracies in areas of strategic importance, including the former Soviet Union and the Asian Pacific. Third, it would isolate "backlash" states like North Korea, Iraq, and Iran that threatened the growing community of market-based economies, even deterring them by force if necessary. Finally, helping the victims of natural disasters and human rights violations would play "an important supporting role in our efforts to expand democracy and markets." Yet, in an age when demands for humanitarian missions might depend on "where CNN sends its camera crews," caution was in order. Before intervening, the United States would have to consider "cost; feasibility; the permanence of the improvement our assistance will bring; the willingness of regional and international bodies to do their part; and the likelihood that our actions will generate broader security benefits for the people and the region in question." The United States would have to be especially cautious about intervening militarily in "intra-national ethnic conflicts." Rejecting the open-ended, "pay any price, bear any burden" commitments of administrations during the Cold War, Lake cautioned that "we will have to pick and choose" where and when to intervene in the world increasingly wracked by "intra-national ethnic conflicts."[21] Bereft of stirring passages or memorable phrases, Lake's address was, nevertheless, the most detailed, straightforward, and thoughtful attempt since the collapse of the Soviet Union to redefine American foreign policy.

Six days later, in his first appearance before the General Assembly of the United Nations, President Clinton repeated Lake's call for democratic enlargement. "In a new era of peril and opportunity, our overriding purpose must be to expand and strengthen the world's community of market based democracies," he stated. "During the cold war we sought to contain a threat to the survival of free institutions. Now we seek to enlarge the circle of nations that live under those free institutions." During the campaign, Clinton had championed the UN as a peacekeeping force. He had even proposed creating a permanent UN "rapid deployment force" that would "stand at the borders of countries threatened by aggression, preventing mass violence against civilian populations, providing humanitarian relief and combatting terrorism."[22] Now, however, the president adopted a more cautious tone: "The United Nations simply cannot become engaged in every one of the world's conflicts. If the American people are to say yes to U.N. peacekeeping, the United Nations must know when to say no."

If Clinton and his national security adviser hoped that democratic enlargement would supplant containment in the diplomatic lexicon, they were to be disappointed. Historian Douglas Brinkley described the reaction. "The foreign policy community," he wrote, "greeted the Clinton and Lake speeches with indifference and even derision. Critics called enlargement uninspired, the predictable byproduct of Lake—a professor—perusing arcane geopolitical text books."[23] To some, including UN Ambassador Madeleine Albright, the word "enlargement" conjured up thoughts of late-night TV ads for sexual enhancement products.[24]

Beginning in the fall of 1993, a series of regional and ethnic conflicts put democratic enlargement to the test. The first test came in Somalia. In 1992, the Bush administration had dispatched a small contingent of American troops to the East African nation as part of a UN famine relief mission. During the transition, President Bush's National Security Adviser, Brent Scowcroft, told the incoming administration not to worry. The troops would be out by Inauguration Day.[25] When political instability imperiled the delivery of relief supplies, American forces found themselves in the middle of a civil war between a ruthless war-lord, Mohammed Aidid, and a barely functioning central government. In September 1993, just days before retiring as chairman of the Joint Chiefs of Staff, Colin Powell, in apparent contradiction to his own doctrine, convinced Clinton to authorize American forces to capture or kill warlord Aidid. A firefight ensued, resulting in the downing of two US Black Hawk helicopters and the deaths of eighteen Americans and 500 Somalis. Mobs dragged the bodies of two dead Americans through the streets of Mogadishu, the nation's capital. To make matters worse, Aidid escaped capture, and his supporters took one American hostage. Lost in the tumult was the fact that before its inglorious end, the US-UN mission saved 100,000 Somalis from starvation.[26]

On Capitol Hill confusion reigned. Some legislators urged the president to bolster American forces in the East African nation, others to immediately withdraw. "No more of this cops and robbers stuff," one senator said. "A Common Cry across the US: It's Time to Exit," read a *New York Times* headline. Criticism of the UN, a perennial target of conservative Republicans, intensified. Even though the American troops who had been caught in the fatal firefight in Somalia were under US command, Senate Minority Leader Robert Dole introduced legislation requiring congressional approval before American troops could serve under UN military leaders.[27] The parents of some of the dead soldiers asked Clinton to his face why their sons had died in vain. "You're not fit to be commander in chief," a father told the president at a ceremony awarding his son a posthumous medal of honor. The episode further estranged Clinton from much of the military, many of whom were already so contemptuous of their commander in chief that they did little to conceal their identities when mocking him. "Did you hear about the protestor who threw a beer at Clinton?" a sailor was quoted as saying. "Not to worry. It was a draft beer and Clinton dodged it."[28]

In May 1994, the administration issued detailed guidelines, known as Presidential Decision Directive 25 (PDD-25), governing where, and under what circumstances, the United States would engage in multilateral peacekeeping operations. The directive—actually a checklist to supplement Anthony Lake's enlargement speech—clearly showed the initial impact of Somalia on American foreign policy. Multilateral operations, PDD-25 maintained, could "serve as a cost-effective tool in many cases to advance such American interests as the maintenance of peace in key regions and the relief of suffering abroad." The lengthy document went on to list some twenty factors that would have to be considered before the United States would participate in such operations. Would the proposed operation advance American interests? Were its objectives clear and realistic? Was there an exit strategy? Did it have the potential to attract congressional and public support? The directive sought to allay fears that multilateral operations would jeopardize American sovereignty: American troops would ordinarily be led by American commanders, and no operation would be allowed to undermine the US Constitution, federal law, or the Uniform Code of Military Justice. To appease critics of the UN, PDD-25 proposed extensive structural and financial reforms of the UN.[29] Briefing reporters, Anthony Lake stressed the directive's underlying caution. "When I wake up every morning and look at the headlines and the stories and the images on television of these conflicts," Lake said, "I want to work to end every conflict, I want to work to save every child out there, and I know the president does and I know the American people do. But neither we nor the international community have the resources nor the mandate to do so."[30]

The administration's guidelines drew fire from all sides. Internationalists viewed them as an abdication of leadership and a checklist for inaction. "Mean spirited feebleness," said British journalist Martin Walker. Others found the guidelines too permissive. Newt Gingrich called the presidential directive "a profound mistake" that "continues to subordinate the United States to the United Nations, provides money to the UN when we cannot provide adequately for our own defense and places Americans in a UN chain of non-command." It was, he said, an expression of Clinton's "multinational fantasy."[31]

For a strategic vision, the Clinton administration would never improve upon the views expressed by Anthony Lake in his democratic enlargement address and its corollary, the inelegantly entitled Presidential Decision Directive 25. But as the president and his advisers were soon to learn, beginning with Rwanda, no strategic vision, no matter how thoughtful, could serve as a master plan for the crises that would become commonplace in a post–Cold War world.

In April 1994 a tribal war erupted in the East African nation of Rwanda between Hutus and Tutsis. In the space of 100 days, an estimated 800,000

men, women, and children, most of them Tutsis, were killed at the hands
of machete-wielding Hutus. Not even the Germans killed that many
Jews in so short a time, one commentator later noted.[32] A small UN
force was already on the ground, but without reinforcements it found
itself helpless to prevent the slaughter. Within the State Department, a
few African experts tried to drum up support for intervention, but they
aroused little interest in the upper reaches of their own department or
at the Pentagon. The same story played out in Congress. A handful of
legislators, most of them Democrats, tried to sound the alarm; but GOP
leader Dole expressed the prevailing view in both parties when he said,
"I don't think we have any national interest here. I hope we don't get involved."[33] Nor was there any appreciable support for intervention in the
media. On April 23, the *New York Times* editorialized that "the world
has little choice but to stand aside and hope for the best." Above all, neither the administration's enlargement strategy nor its recently released
presidential directive compelled US intervention. Were national security
or vital interests at stake? No. Would intervention end the bloodshed?
Perhaps. But wasn't it just as likely that fighting would resume as soon as
US forces left? And so on down the list, with few reasons to check items
in the affirmative. It wasn't that a gun-shy administration feared another
Somalia. Intervention was never seriously on the table.[34] Compounding
the problem, intelligence was particularly bad. Who was killing whom?
"Was it between the Hutus and the Tutsis or was it between various
elements of the Hutus?" Warren Christopher recalled wondering. The
United States had no one on the ground to clarify the situation.[35] It therefore came as no surprise that the administration declined to act on its
own. Somewhat surprising, however, was the extent to which it went to
prevent others from intervening. It opposed UN efforts to reinforce its
peacekeeping force in Rwanda, even though no American troops would
be involved. And the president and his aides bent over backward to
avoid labeling the systematic slaughter of Tutsis as "genocide," presumably because an official finding of genocide would require intervention
under international law. Nor would the administration even accede to
suggestions that Pentagon technicians be allowed to jam inflammatory
radiobroadcasts in Rwanda that were inciting the violence. In view of all
he did to avoid intervention, President Clinton sounded an unintentionally ironic note when he declared in July that "from the beginning of this

tragedy, the United States has been in the forefront of the international community's response."[36]

Nevertheless, Clinton himself later acknowledged that he had failed to comprehend the extent of the tragedy. "Never again must we be shy in the face of the evidence," he said. Later still, he described his failure to act as the biggest mistake of his administration.[37]

June 1994 brought a crisis that everyone in the administration believed far more serious than genocide in Rwanda. The crisis involved North Korea, and it began when the nation's aging, autocratic, and reclusive leader, Kim Il-sung, violated the terms of the Nuclear Non-Proliferation Treaty by denying international inspectors access to his nation's nuclear reactor at Yongbyon. Kim's actions immediately fueled suspicions that North Korea was planning to produce nuclear weapons. A nuclear-armed North Korea, the administration feared, might embolden it to attack South Korea, which the United States was committed to defend. At the very least, it would destabilize the entire region, and other regions as well if North Korea sold its weapons to the highest bidder. "I was determined to stop North Korea from developing a nuclear arsenal, even at the risk of war," Clinton recalled in his memoirs.[38] Accordingly, the Pentagon began to formulate war plans. It also came up with a plan to bomb North Korea's nuclear reactor with cruise missiles. Recalled Anthony Lake: "Some folks, normally sensible folks here in Washington, were saying that we should bomb the facility." An excellent idea, Lake noted wryly, except for the fact the nuclear fallout from the preemptive strike would kill large numbers of South Koreans and Americans stationed below the Demilitarized Zone. The State Department's North Korean expert, Robert Gallucci, believed a strike would have led to war—a war the Pentagon estimated might claim upwards of 1 million lives.[39]

Although not ruling out military intervention, the administration settled on a less risky option. It tried to persuade the United Nations Security Council to impose harsh economic sanctions on the impoverished nation. Even this was not risk free, for the North Korean diplomats warned Gallucci that they would regard sanctions as an act of war. Just as the crisis was coming to a head, Jimmy Carter unexpectedly entered the scene. He had been invited to Pyongyang by Kim Il-sung, the former president told the White House, and he would do what he could to end the standoff. Knowing Carter's reputation for unpredictability and fierce independence, many of Clinton's advisers doubted the ex-president's ability to stick to the script. But with Vice President Gore's encouragement, Clinton gave the mission his blessing. Four days after his arrival in the North Korean capital, Carter informed the White House that he had achieved a dramatic breakthrough. The North Korean leader, he said, was willing to allow inspectors back into his country so long as the United States was willing to engage in direct negotiation. Carter also said any plans for economic sanctions would have to be dropped. Even before the White House had a chance to react to the news, Carter went on CNN to announce an end to the crisis.[40] Publicly, President Clinton reacted cautiously to Carter's announcement. The United States, he said, would have to see the details of any agreement before declaring the crisis over. Privately, many of Clinton's aides were incensed, especially by Carter's television appearance. He was, they thought, "a pious show-boater." A week of not-so-private recriminations followed. "I wouldn't want to call him naïve or gullible," one administration member was quoted as saying of Carter. "But let's just say that we're a lot more skeptical than he is about whether the North Koreans mean what they say." The seventy-year-old ex-president, who undoubtedly had expected to come home to a hero's welcome, responded in kind. He still found it "inconceivable," he told reporters, that President Clinton hadn't sent a delegation of his own to try to resolve the crisis. As for the administration's sanctions, he added, they were "counterproductive." During the next several months, negotiations between the United States and North Korea did resolve the crisis. North Korea put its nuclear weapons program on hold, and the United States dropped its plans for economic sanctions. For the favorable outcome, Anthony Lake was willing to give both Clinton and Carter credit. The North Koreans would never have come to the negotiating table without the threat of sanctions, he felt certain. But nor would they have agreed to a settlement if Carter hadn't given them a way to save face. The odd-couple relationship between the two presidents was, Lake concluded, "an unpleasant but extremely useful collaboration."[41] Reporter John Harris later added a revealing footnote to the North Korean crisis. Few people, he wrote, would remember June 1994 "as the month when the United States stood on the edge of a war that, had it erupted, would almost certainly have killed hundreds of thousands of people." For that was "the month of O. J. Simpson's white Bronco chase and his arrest on murder charges."[42]

In Rwanda, Clinton followed his own policy directives and came to regret it. In Haiti, where trouble erupted just as it was ending in Rwanda, Clinton largely ignored those same directives and achieved better results. The Haitian crisis had its roots in 1990, when Jean-Bertrand Aristide, a Catholic priest, won Haiti's first democratic presidential election. His tenure was short-lived. Within a year, a three-man junta ousted him from power and sent him into exile in the United States. Almost immediately thousands of Haitians sought refuge from the repressive junta by crowding into rickety, makeshift boats for the hazardous 700-mile voyage to American shores. Worried about an unstoppable influx of refugees, the Bush administration began intercepting the overcrowded vessels and returning their passengers to Haiti or sending them to an encampment at the US naval base at Guantanamo Bay, Cuba. During the campaign, Clinton berated the administration for its callous actions and promised to welcome the refugees. Once in office, however, Clinton was told that upwards of 200,000 Haitians might flee to the United States and that some of them were already tearing off parts of their roofs to build makeshift boats for the perilous journey. He abruptly reversed course and resumed the Bush administration's practice of interception.[43]

Meanwhile, Clinton sought to persuade junta leaders to step aside and allow Aristide to return. In October 1993, thinking he had the junta's assent, the president, in collaboration with the UN, dispatched a team of army engineers and civilian advisers to the island nation to prepare the way for Aristide. The ship carrying the team, the USS *Harlan County*, no sooner entered the harbor at Port-au-Prince than it was met by a stone-throwing mob that forced it to turn around and head back to the United States. The humiliating retreat, just a week following the firefight in Mogadishu, conjured up in the minds of some Richard Nixon's fear of the United States becoming a "helpless pitiful giant."

Once again the administration had to confront the dilemmas of policymaking in a post–Cold War era. National security was not at stake, nor were any vital national issues. No foreign power threatened to use the island nation to menace the United States. Trade with Haiti was negligible.[44] But Haiti did raise humanitarian and moral issues. Didn't the United States have an obligation to help a struggling nation whose destiny had so often been intertwined with its own? The members of the congressional Black Caucus, who had been relatively quiet on the subject of Rwanda, thought so. So, too, did black activist Randall Robinson, who went on a highly publicized hunger strike to protest US inaction. Robinson and the Black Caucus also thought they detected a trace of racism in the reluctance to intervene in Haiti. After all, many of the same people now urging inaction had thrilled a decade earlier when the Reagan administration dispatched troops to Granada to protect a handful of white American medical students.[45]

Opponents of intervention outnumbered proponents. Sixty percent of the public opposed sending troops as did most members of Congress, save for the Black Caucus and a handful of liberal stalwarts. Few doubted that US forces could make short work of ousting the Haitian junta and restoring Aristide to power. "An easy day's work," Taylor Branch was told by the president. But then what? Before retiring, Colin Powell had warned the president that unless the United States more or less permanently occupied the country, its authoritarian tendencies would quickly reassert themselves. The last time the United States had sent troops to Haiti, Powell reminded the president, they had stayed for twenty years. Clinton told Taylor Branch "Nobody is for this. Nobody." A friend, he said, had called him "three turns short of loopy" for even considering intervention, especially during a midterm election year.[46]

It wasn't completely true that nobody supported intervention. Vice President Gore suggested telling the ruling junta either to step aside voluntarily or be forcibly ousted. Anthony Lake strongly agreed, while Sandy Berger, Strobe Talbott, and Warren Christopher were at least willing to go along with intervention. William Perry, who had replaced Les Aspin as defense secretary, sympathized with the political difficulty of defying public and congressional opinion but assured the president the military would do what was necessary to carry out the mission. On the other side, Hillary Clinton expressed skepticism. CIA Director Woolsey was known to oppose intervention, and some insiders suspected him of going behind the president's back to spread rumors that Aristide was mentally unstable.

Adding to the pressure on Clinton, a bipartisan group of senators planned to introduce a resolution requiring him to consult with the Senate before taking action. Dale Bumpers, fellow Arkansan and Clinton's best friend in the Senate, warned him he risked censure or even impeachment if he acted without congressional authorization. "I've never been in anything like this before," Clinton complained to Branch. "I keep telling you, nobody is for it." And if even one American soldier died, Clinton said, "I'm a dead duck."[47]

Beyond hostile domestic reaction to intervention, Clinton worried about being in the odd position, as Taylor Branch put it, "of going against the democratic will in his own country to enforce it in someone else's."[48] Then, too, US intervention might inadvertently rekindle fears in Haiti and elsewhere in Latin America of the "ugly American" and "Yankee imperialism."

In the end, Clinton decided to act, even though his decision was at odds not only with congressional and public opinion but also with most of the criteria for intervention he had approved in his presidential decision directive. Perhaps even then he was beginning to regret his hands-off stance in Rwanda. It was also likely that the pleas of Black Caucus members, who stressed the moral and racial reasons for intervention, weighed heavily on Clinton's mind. To pollster Stanley Greenberg, the president's decision to act was yet another example of the high value the president placed on racial reconciliation.

On September 15, 1994, hoping to rally public opinion behind him, Clinton delivered a forceful address to the nation from the Oval Office. His most important audience, however, was the military junta in Port-au-Prince and their "armed thugs," whom he accused of conducting "a reign of terror, executing children, raping women, killing priests." "Your time is up," he warned. "Leave now, or we will force you from power."

The president's address made few converts, although he did trim public opposition to an invasion from 73 to 60 percent. Aside from the Black Caucus, legislators remained unswayed. Senator Richard Lugar (R-IN), the ranking Republican on the Senate Committee on Foreign Relations, spoke for many when he said, "There is no physical threat from Haiti to the United States, no strategic interest whatsoever."[49]

Even as US forces were poised to invade, unexpected circumstances intervened. As the Haitian crisis reached its climax, Jimmy Carter once again appeared on the scene. Even as US planes were fueling up for the flight to Haiti, the former president suggested that he, Colin Powell, who had long since stepped down as chair of the Joint Chiefs, and Senator Sam Nunn, chairman of the Senate Armed Services Committee, travel to Port-au-Prince to confer with junta leader Raul Cedras. "Here we go again," many of Clinton's aides thought when Carter offered to mediate. But given the sour mood of the public and the resistance of Congress, any reasonable effort to restore Aristide to power without force was probably in Clinton's interests. Clinton approved the mission, along with firm orders to Carter to stick to the agreed-upon script. During the ensuing forty-eight hours a dramatic and sometimes farcical scenario played out in Port-au-Prince. In the end Carter and his cohorts achieved the desired transfer of power, though not without modifying Clinton's explicit instructions and upstaging him in the process. Still, had the invasion not been averted, some believed a permanent breech may have been created between the president and Congress. The Senate "would have exploded," said Daniel Patrick Moynihan. "The mood in the Senate was, son of a bitch!"[50] To the dismay of Clinton's political advisers, 70 percent of the public gave Carter, not Clinton, credit for having averted bloodshed. It wasn't just the political advisers who were upset. Warren Christopher thought the former president's intervention highly inappropriate, while Strobe Talbott, recalling the episode years later, just rolled his eyes. Once again, however, Anthony Lake was willing to give both presidents their due. "The truth is," he recalled, "it was both power and diplomacy." Without the threat of force, "Cedras never would have left; without Carter, it would have been a fight." Even if Clinton didn't get all the credit he deserved, the peaceful outcome temporarily slowed what had been the steady decline in his overall job rating.[51]

As for Haiti, the restoration of Aristide to power ended the junta's reign of terror but otherwise left conditions little changed. Six years after Aristide's return, journalist Amy Wilentz, an admirer of the Haitian president, offered a sober assessment: "Poverty is unrelenting, the environment remains degraded, infrastructure, where it exists at all, is crumbling." "Political assassinations," she added, "have become as much a feature of the terrain as they were under the military regimes."[52] Clinton had been willing to defy the Congress and the public over Haiti, and he never lost interest in it. Few others, however, seemed to care, and Haiti receded from public view as quickly as it had appeared.

Of the foreign policy crises Clinton confronted, none was more confounding than that which arose in the Balkans. The crisis played out in two acts: Bosnia during Clinton's first term, Kosovo during his second. Bosnia was one of the half-dozen republics on the Balkan Peninsula that had been part of the multireligious, multiethnic Communist nation of Yugoslavia. The collapse of the Soviet Union unleashed ethnic, religious, and nationality conflicts in Yugoslavia that had been suppressed during the years of Communist rule. In 1991, the republics of Slovenia and Croatia declared their independence from Yugoslavia. Bosnia followed suit the following year. Almost at once, however, Muslim, Serb, and Croatian inhabitants of Bosnia were at each other's throats. Supplied with money and arms by Slobodan Milosevic, president of neighboring Serbia, Bosnian Serbs, though outnumbered by Muslims, waged a genocidal war—"ethnic cleansing" was the euphemistic phrase of the time—to rid Bosnia of Croatians and especially of Muslims. Over the next four years, 250,000 persons, most of them Muslims, would die and upwards of 2 million would be forced to leave their homes. President Bush, who was still in office when the trouble began, deplored the violence but opposed American intervention, especially in the aftermath of the Gulf War. To most Americans and even to government officials, Bosnia was too remote and too complicated to be of concern. "Which ones are the Serbs?" President Bush once asked his national security adviser. "And which ones are the Croats?" Keeping the sides straight didn't seem to matter. "We don't have a dog in that fight," concluded Bush's secretary of state, James Baker. To the Pentagon brass, the whole region had Vietnam written all over it. Intervention would require at least a half-million troops, Colin Powell had warned. And that was just for starters, he added.[53]

During the campaign, Clinton criticized Bush's inaction. At the urging of future national security adviser Anthony Lake and diplomat Richard Holbrooke, he called for the lifting of a UN-supported arms embargo so that Bosnian Muslims might acquire weapons to defend themselves against the already well-armed Serbs. And if the Serbs continued to block the delivery of relief supplies to besieged civilians, Clinton said, the United States should join other nations in launching airstrikes against Serbian targets.[54]

Once he was in office, however, he failed to follow through on his promises. As had been the case with the Haitian refugee crisis, Clinton found that Bosnia looked more complicated from the Oval Office than it had from the campaign trail. And it was complicated. For one thing, with the exception of German Chancellor Helmut Kohl, European leaders, some of whom had fellow countrymen serving on UN peacekeeping teams in the region, opposed lifting the arms embargo and launching airstrikes. If European leaders were unwilling to address a crisis in their own backyard, why should the United States take the lead? A book Clinton was reading on the history of the Balkans may have given him second thoughts as well. The book, which he had picked up at the urging of Colin Powell, was journalist Robert D. Kaplan's *Balkan Ghosts.* It depicted the region as impervious to outside influence—"a hopeless case, a cauldron of mysterious squabbles and ancient animosities, murderous hatreds fueled by memories of persecutions and massacres." Kaplan denied having written a brief for nonintervention, but that was the unmistakable conclusion many readers, perhaps even the president, came away with.[55]

Clinton's change of heart did not go unnoticed. In April 1993, at the rain-soaked dedication of the Holocaust Museum in the nation's capital, Holocaust survivor and writer Elie Wiesel concluded his speech with a spontaneous plea to the president. "I have been in the former Yugoslavia last fall," he said. "I cannot sleep since for what I have seen. As a Jew I am saying that we must do something to stop the bloodshed in that country! People fight each other and children die. Why? Something must be done." Recalling the incident twenty years later, Clinton said Wiesel was telling him "in his polite way, I needed to get off my rear end and do something about Bosnia."[56]

At the time, however, Wiesel's admonition failed to stir Clinton to action. During the next two years, he more or less relegated Bosnia to his aides. During one critical stretch, Clinton, Gore, and Christopher were all on vacation while their assistants grappled with what Richard Holbrooke described as "some of the most important decisions" since Clinton took office. "As the hours and the days blurred into one continuous crisis session," Holbrooke recalled, "the deputies were in charge—so much so that they began teasing each other about it." Strobe Talbott, the acting secretary of state, joked that they felt like the eight-year-old boy in the film *Home Alone*, whose family inadvertently left him behind as they flew off to Paris for Christmas.[57]

Within the administration, the most persistent advocate of US involvement in the Balkans was Undersecretary of State for European and Canadian Affairs Richard Holbrooke. The New York City–born Holbrooke had a long and varied diplomatic career that, like Anthony Lake's, had begun in the US embassy in Saigon during the Kennedy administration and had included stints in the Johnson, Nixon, and Carter administrations. A polarizing figure within the administration, he possessed, even by Washington standards, an outsize ego as well as a weakness for doomsday scenarios when his advice wasn't followed. "Convinced he was engaged in historic work at all times, Holbrooke's pestering, hectoring, and sucking up made him a bit of a Washington cartoon," wrote journalist Mark Leibovich.[58] But the fifty-four-year-old diplomat also had a legion of admirers inspired by his courage and his combination of missionary zeal and hardheaded pragmatism. Injustice and human cruelty stirred him to rage; but he could also sit across from the negotiating table with war criminals for as long as it took.

Still, even with Holbrooke's pestering and hectoring, it was not until 1995 that a series of dramatic events ended two years of indecision and drift. In July, a Serbian offensive in the Muslim enclave of Srebrenica ended in what Holbrooke described as "the biggest single mass murder in Europe since World War II, while the outside world did nothing to stop the tragedy."[59] In August, three American negotiators died when their car plunged off a treacherous mountain pass in Bosnia. The twin tragedies steeled the resolve of the administration to redouble efforts to bring an end to the hostilities. By 1995, the situation on the ground was also improving. Although the Serbs remained on the offensive, they were now encountering resistance not only from the Muslims but also from the Croatians who had been holding back for fear of living under Muslim domination.

In a now-or-never moment, the United States convinced its NATO allies to launch air assaults on Serbian sites. The assaults, the largest in NATO's history, had the desired effect. Along with the Muslim-Croatian counteroffensive and multilateral economic sanctions, the airstrikes brought Milosevic to the negotiating table. The negotiations themselves, held at Wright-Patterson Air Force Base in Dayton, Ohio, were touch-and-go from the beginning. Holbrooke, who presided over the proceedings, had to contend not only with the representatives of the warring sides but also with deep divisions within American ranks. Successful implementation of any agreement would require the deployment of American troops as part of a NATO force. Colin Powell had long since stepped down as chairman of the Joint Chiefs of Staff. But his successor, John Shalikashvili, still feared being drawn into a Vietnam-like quagmire, as did just about everyone else. A bipartisan group of prominent senators, led by the upper house's senior member, Robert Byrd, urged Clinton to seek congressional approval before deploying troops to the Balkans. If approval were not forthcoming, the West Virginia senator insisted, the president should abide by the outcome. President Clinton and Vice President Gore suspected that when Pentagon officials testified before Congress they were subtly conveying their fears of troop deployment with a body language that read: "This is what we were told to say, but that's not what we really believe." Influential *New York Times* reporter Thomas Friedman didn't oppose sending troops if their purpose was to facilitate the safe exit from the region of French and British peacekeepers. After all France and Britain were historic allies. But if the purpose of sending troops was solely to save Bosnia, that was another matter. "I don't give two cents about Bosnia," Friedman wrote. "Not two cents. The people there have brought on their own troubles."[60] Then there was public opinion, which may not have been as immoveable as it seemed at the time, but still registered 70 percent opposition to troops in Bosnia. At one point, when the Dayton talks appeared close to collapse, some of the president's senior domestic advisers expressed relief that the president might be spared having to deploy troops during an election year. Summing up the ambivalent attitude of Clinton's top advisers, one of them told Holbrooke, "if Dayton failed, there would be a combination of relief and disappointment." If the talks succeeded, "there would be a combination of pride and apprehension."[61]

Against the odds, the talks ended on a high note with warring sides agreeing to a cease-fire and a complicated power-sharing agreement. To enforce the agreement, NATO stationed 60,000 troops, including 20,000 Americans, in the reconfigured nation. Congress rendered a split decision on the deployment of troops, with the Senate voting 69 to 30 in favor and the House voting 287 to 141 against. Although Bosnia was no crossing of the Rubicon to a consistent new policy for the post–Cold War era, it ended in unexpected political triumph for the president. As journalist John Harris observed, Clinton "prospered politically by defying public opinion." He looked like a leader.[62]

The Dayton Accords did little to quiet administration critics. Their near-unanimous complaint was that Clinton had failed to devise a credible replacement for containment. The title of an article by Henry Kissinger said it all: "At Sea in a New World." The administration's "basic problem," the former secretary of state wrote, "has been an inability to generate a conceptual framework and to manage the perplexities of the post-cold-war international order." "No ethical ballast, no strategic center, no convictions, no steadiness and a tendency to blame others," wrote president of the Council of Foreign Relations and former correspondent for the *New York Times* Leslie Gelb. Wrote the editors of the quarterly *Foreign Policy*, "It is the firm belief of the editors that the United States has yet to develop a foreign policy relevant to this post–Cold War world."[63]

Much of the criticism of Clinton's first-term policies derived from a distorted view of containment itself. Kennan's doctrine had never been the clear, bipartisan roadmap to victory Clinton's critics made it out to be. From the beginning, conservatives considered it tantamount to surrender. Why contain communism, they asked, when it should be overthrown? To critics on the left, containment neglected the Soviet Union's legitimate security concerns and was unnecessarily provocative. Kennan, believing Democratic and Republican administrations alike had distorted his ideas beyond all recognition, repudiated many of the actions taken under the name of containment, including the creation of NATO, massive arms buildups by the United States, and the wars in Korea and Vietnam.

With the passage of time, analysts viewed Clinton's early diplomacy more sympathetically than contemporaries did. Typical was the appraisal of historian James T. Patterson. "It is evident in retrospect that no Western leaders at that time had sure solutions for coping with the unfamiliar international scene that had so quickly replaced the bipolar world of the Cold War years," he wrote. "There were no obvious answers—only hard choices."[64]

Clinton understood that he was being held to a false standard. In one of his frequent discursive moods, he told Strobe Talbott that he "admired Franklin Roosevelt and Harry Truman for intuitively understanding what their world required of them" but believed "they got more credit than they deserved for knowing what they were doing when they were doing it." After reading biographies of Franklin and Eleanor Roosevelt by Doris Kearns Goodwin and Harry Truman by David McCullough, Clinton was convinced "that neither had grand strategies for how to exert American leadership against the global threats posed by Hitler and Stalin," but they did have "powerful instincts about what had to be done, and they just made it up as they went along." Clinton believed further that "strategic coherence . . . was largely imposed after the fact by scholars, memoirists and 'the chattering classes.'"[65]

But none of this, in Clinton's mind, obviated the need for a word or phrase that could convey a sense of purpose and direction. "You've still got to be able to crystallize complexity in a way people get it right away," he told aides. He was tired, he said, of always having to talk about the "post–Cold War era," a phrase he considered, in Talbott's words, "agnostic, provisional, backward-looking"—"an admission that while everyone knew what was finished, no one knew what had taken its place, to say nothing of what would or should come next." He did not want "his presidency to coincide with an age of uncertainty." With noticeable irritation, Clinton chastised his foreign policy advisers. "The operative problem of the moment," he said, "is that a bunch of smart people haven't been able to come up with a new slogan, and saying that there aren't any good slogans isn't a slogan either."[66] The search for the three-syllable word continued.

Hillary: "He arrived at Yale Law School looking more like a Viking than a Rhodes Scholar. . . . He had a vitality that seemed to shoot out of his pores." (Hillary Rodham Clinton, *Living History*, 52)

Bill: "She had thick dark blond hair and wore eyeglasses and no makeup, but she conveyed a sense of strength and self-possession I had rarely seen in anyone, man or woman." (Bill Clinton, *My Life*, 181; photo courtesy of William J. Clinton Presidential Library)

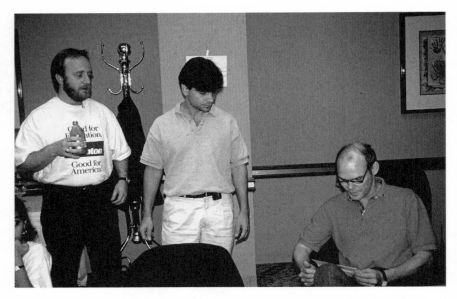

Political advisers Paul Bagala, George Stephanopoulos, and James Carville became fixtures in the "war room," the Little Rock–based command center of Clinton's 1992 campaign. (Courtesy of William J. Clinton Presidential Library)

Following the 1992 Democratic Convention, Clinton and Gore embarked on a series of bus tours that evoked memories of the famous "whistle stop" train trips of bygone campaigns. (Courtesy of William J. Clinton Presidential Library)

Of the three presidential debates in 1992, it was the second, "town-hall" style debate, held in Richmond, Virginia, that produced the most talked-about moments. (Courtesy of William J. Clinton Presidential Library)

As the president outlines his first budget proposal before a joint session of Congress, Federal Reserve Chairman Alan Greenspan chats with Hillary Clinton. Greenspan's presence was widely viewed as an endorsement of Clinton's deficit reduction plan. The president's mother looks on from the second row. (Courtesy of William J. Clinton Presidential Library)

Late-night conversation about foreign policy with former President Richard Nixon at the White House, March 1993. Despite striking differences in personality and style, the two presidents had much in common. (Courtesy of William J. Clinton Presidential Library)

Clinton bucked members of his own party to gain passage of the North American Free Trade Agreement (NAFTA). Attending the signing ceremony were, from left to right, President Gerald Ford, House Speaker Thomas Foley, Senate Majority Leader George Mitchell, President Jimmy Carter, Minority Leader Robert Dole, President George H. W. Bush, House Minority Leader Robert Michael, and Vice President Gore (December 8, 1993). (Courtesy of William J. Clinton Presidential Library)

Clinton utilized the new media to communicate with the public more than any previous president. Here he is interviewed by CNN's Larry King. (Clinton cut short the interview when he learned that his lifelong friend Vince Foster had committed suicide.) (Courtesy of William J. Clinton Presidential Library)

Hillary Clinton briefs House Republicans on health-care reform (Minority Leader Robert Michael [R-IL], right, Newt Gingrich [R-GA], left). (Courtesy of William J. Clinton Presidential Library)

Sharing a laugh with Senators Alan Simpson (R-WY) and Robert Byrd (D-WV).
With his encyclopedic knowledge of parliamentary procedure and unwavering
dedication to the Senate as an institution, Byrd (on right) shaped the timing
and content of much of Clinton's early agenda. (Courtesy of William J. Clinton
Presidential Library)

Arriving at the Capitol to address Congress on health-care reform (September
22, 1993). His speech, one of the best received of his presidency, temporarily
revived but ultimately could not save the reform effort. (Courtesy of William J.
Clinton Presidential Library)

Former President Jimmy Carter played significant but not always welcome roles in resolving crises in Haiti, North Korea, and elsewhere. (Courtesy of William J. Clinton Presidential Library)

At the funeral of President Nixon (April 1994), the Clintons, with George and Barbara Bush, Ronald and Nancy Reagan, Jimmy and Rosalynn Carter, and Gerald and Betty Ford. As a group, the presidents from Ford though Clinton presided over a transformative era that recalled the late nineteenth century. (Courtesy of William J. Clinton Presidential Library)

In August 1995, the Bosnian crisis took a tragic turn when a vehicle carrying three American diplomats sent to the region to help resolve the crisis plunged off a mountain road killing all aboard. Following memorial services at Fort Meyer, Virginia, Clinton confers with military and diplomatic advisors, including (seated clockwise from the president) National Security Advisor Antony Lake, Lt. General Wesley Clark, Chief of Staff Leon Panetta, Secretary of State Warren Christopher, CIA Director John Deutch, Assistant Secretary of State Richard Holbrooke, Defense Secretary William Perry, UN Ambassador Madeleine Albright, and Joint Chiefs of Staff Chairman General John Shalikashvili. (Courtesy of William J. Clinton Presidential Library)

Clinton's relationship with Russian President Boris Yeltsin helped shape the post–Cold War era. Here, at the ancestral home of Franklin D. Roosevelt in Hyde Park, New York, Yeltsin breaks up Clinton by telling reporters, "You are a disaster." Some pundits had predicted that the informal summit would end in disaster. "Be sure you get the right attribution there," Clinton added (October 23, 1995). (Courtesy of William J. Clinton Presidential Library)

Following the GOP takeover of Congress in 1994, the Clintons once again solicited advice from controversial political operative Richard "Dick" Morris. (Courtesy of William J. Clinton Presidential Library)

Negotiating an end to the government shutdown (December 1995), the president and vice president confer with GOP leaders Robert Dole (left) and Newt Gingrich (right). The shutdown, which most blamed on the Republicans, was a key factor in Clinton's political recovery. (Courtesy of William J. Clinton Presidential Library)

Signing the controversial welfare reform bill into law in August 1996. (Courtesy of William J. Clinton Presidential Library)

The Clintons walk back to the White House after the second inaugural address (January 1997). (Courtesy of William J. Clinton Presidential Library)

With the vice president and economic advisers (left to right), Lawrence Summers, Leon Panetta, Laura Tyson, and Robert Rubin. (Courtesy of William J. Clinton Presidential Library)

Moments after the House of Representatives approved two articles of impeachment, Clinton rallies supporters on the White House lawn (December 1998). (Courtesy of William J. Clinton Presidential Library)

Signing into law the Financial Services Modernization Act of 1999 (the Gramm-Leach-Bliley Act), which repealed New Deal–era regulations on the banking industry. Although later controversial, at the time the measure enjoyed overwhelming bipartisan support in Congress. Participants in the signing ceremony included chief sponsors Senator Phil Gramm (R-TX) and Representatives James Leach (R-IA) and Thomas Bliley (R-VA) as well as Treasury Secretary Lawrence Summers, Fed Chair Alan Greenspan, and Senators Paul Sarbanes (D-MD), Christopher Dodd, (D-CT), and John Edwards (D-NC). (Courtesy of William J. Clinton Presidential Library)

Hoping for a diplomatic breakthrough before leaving office, Clinton confers at Camp David with Israeli Prime Minister Ehud Barak and Palestinian leader Yasser Arafat. (Courtesy of William J. Clinton Presidential Library)

Hillary Clinton being sworn in as US senator from New York in January 2001. (Courtesy of William J. Clinton Presidential Library)

The Clintons left the White House much as they had entered it: engulfed in controversy. (Courtesy of William J. Clinton Presidential Library)

6

Rebound, 1995–1996

Those close to President Clinton had long since become accustomed to his volcanic temper. Suddenly his face would redden, and he would rant and rave. Years later Strobe Talbott could still remember one outburst: "God damn it, I'm the President. I'm tired of you people pushing me around, and you in particular." It rarely lasted long. An hour later there'd be "a big hug," followed by "I'm sorry."[1] In the weeks after the 1994 election, however, Clinton seemed different. There were no angry eruptions. No primal screams. In fact, there wasn't much of anything. This most outgoing of persons seemed strangely withdrawn.

Appearances were deceiving. Even as the Republicans were savoring their victory and Democrats contemplating life in the political wilderness, Clinton was plotting a surprising comeback. And what a comeback it was. In 1996 he became the first Democrat since Franklin Roosevelt to win a second term in the White House. The reversal of fortune was stunning and wholly unexpected, due in almost equal parts to Republican missteps and to his own deft moves to reassert himself as a "New Democrat." It was accomplished by appropriating traditional Republican issues: fiscal austerity and welfare reform.

Clinton's comeback became the stuff of political legend, joining Harry Truman's against-the-odds election in 1948 as a source of inspiration for presidents who lagged in the polls. As for whether Clinton's feat was accompanied by good and wise policy—that remained subject to debate.

Following the GOP takeover of Congress, Clinton looked for guidance from almost any quarter. At Hillary Clinton's suggestion, he began meeting at Camp David with self-help advocates like Stephen Covey, author of *The Seven Habits of Highly Effective People*, and late-night infomercial star Tony Robbins, who had written *Awake the Power Within: How to Take Immediate Control of Your Mental, Emotional, Physical and Financial Destiny.*[2] But the key figure during this period of wrenching self-examination was political operative Richard "Dick" Morris, whose on-again-off-again relationship with the president stretched back to the mid-seventies when Clinton first ran for office. The son of a New York City real estate lawyer and a cousin of infamous Joseph McCarthy henchman Roy Cohn, Morris advised members of both parties, although by the mid-nineties he was working almost exclusively for Republicans. Most of Clinton's aides despised the flamboyant, self-promoting, but brilliant Morris, whom they considered unprincipled and utterly untrustworthy. "Morris is without a moral center," said Harold Ickes. "He could advise Hitler or he could advise Mother Teresa—on the same night." "Half of Dick Morris's ideas are truly brilliant and half of them could get us all thrown into jail," recalled press secretary Michael McCurry. Clinton's "figuring out which were good ideas, and using them, was the whole art of the Clinton-Morris relationship." Morris was so disliked by Clinton's inner circle that for several months after secretly reentering the president's life, he showed up on White House logs under the pseudonym "Charlie," after the heard-but-unseen character in the popular television program *Charlie's Angels.*[3]

Some urged Clinton to go on the attack, as President Truman had done after the GOP captured Congress in 1946. Dick Morris disagreed. Instead of attacking Congress, the president should assume a conciliatory stance, pledging to work with the Republicans on issues of common interest. He also advised Clinton to endorse deficit reduction, welfare reform, and other popular planks in the GOP's "Contract with America," but repackage them as his own. Morris called his strategy "triangulation," by which he meant the president should stand apart from, and above, both parties, picking and choosing ideas from whatever the source.[4] In truth, triangulation not only reinforced Clinton's own instincts but was a fancy word for the "third way" that had been the cornerstone of his presidential campaign. Within the White House, New Democrats felt newly empowered. "I suddenly started getting invitations to political and strategic meetings from which I and others like me had been systematically excluded during the first eighteen months," recalled William Galston. It was "just a day and night transformation," he said.[5]

Even before the GOP takeover of Congress, Clinton sought to steady the ship by shaking up the White House staff. In July 1994, Office of Management and Budget (OMB) director and longtime member of Congress Leon Panetta replaced Mack McLarty as White House chief of staff. Upon assuming the job, Panetta confirmed what everyone already suspected: "There was very little organization that was in place. . . . There was really no chain of command. There was no organization chart that you could point to." "Man, I really am in deep shit now!" Panetta recalled thinking.[6] Things changed, and changed quickly. The new chief of staff put in place "a real organization chart as to who is responsible to who, and who supervises who"—a chart similar to the one he had helped set up when he had served in the army in the sixties. There was still no keeping the president on schedule, but at least White House meetings now started and ended on time and had fixed agendas. And there were fewer leaks to the press. The new chief of staff also restructured the president's decision-making process. When members of the administration sharply disagreed among themselves, Panetta would herd the key players into his office and let them air their differences. His aim was not necessarily to achieve consensus but to have opposing sides sharpen their arguments before presenting them to the president for a decision.[7]

Next to go was Press Secretary Dee Dee Myers. Panetta had sought her immediate ouster, but she won a six-month reprieve after a tearful meeting with the president. Myers had been with Clinton since the tumultuous New Hampshire Primary but had never gained entry into the "Boys' Club," as she described the inner circle. Too often she found herself fielding questions from the press without having been fully briefed. Her replacement was Michael McCurry, Warren Christopher's thirty-four-year-old spokesman at the State Department. McCurry never cracked the president's inner circle either, but he didn't want to. There were times, he said, when it was best not to know what was going on. But he had more access to the president than Myers had had and was better able to provide reporters with accurate information. *Washington Post* media critic Howard Kurtz described him as a "spinmeister extraordinaire," adept at "deflecting questions with practiced ease, sugar-coating the ugly messes into which the Clintons seemed repeatedly to stumble." Even so, his "considerable charm and quick wit" won him the respect of reporters, and Clinton's relationship with the media benefited as a result.[8]

Newt Gingrich, meanwhile, was centralizing power in the Speaker's office to an extent not seen since progressive insurgents had rebelled against autocratic Speaker "Uncle Joe" Cannon during the first decade of the twentieth century. Democrats had been strengthening the office since the 1970s, but it was Gingrich who completed the process. The new Speaker viewed himself as a transformative figure—"the most serious, systematic revolutionary of modern times," he told one audience. His self-proclaimed goals were to make elective officials more accountable to the public, require individuals to take responsibility for their own welfare, restrain the hand of government, and create new opportunities for citizens to pursue their own destinies. Republican control of the House, he said, "would be the first decisive step back to create a century of freedom for the entire human race."[9] Even more than Clinton, Gingrich was a polarizing figure. Detractors believed him to be a cynical opportunist, a modern-day Joe McCarthy who was willing to destroy faith in government to advance his own career. Some veteran Republicans had nothing but disdain for Gingrich, with one calling him "an acid-throwing, bomb-throwing nut."[10] But even they couldn't argue with success. In 1989, Gingrich had almost single-handedly brought down Democratic Speaker Jim Wright, and now he was more responsible than any single person for the GOP takeover of Congress. "Newt is King of the world," labor secretary Robert Reich noted sardonically in his journal. "The news was all Newt, all the time," recalled the editor of the *Washington Post*. At the end of his first 100 days as Speaker, the television networks gave him an unprecedented opportunity to address the nation. *Time Magazine* named him "Man of the Year," and a *Newsweek* cover story declared that it had only taken the Speaker three months to alter "the basic course run by government for the past 60 years."[11] No wonder that Clinton, even while mapping the road back, felt it necessary to assert his relevance.

Gingrich was riding high. But he now found himself in the unaccustomed position of having to craft policy rather than criticize it. The freshmen class in the House had run on a promise to cut taxes, increase military spending, downsize government, and balance the budget. How to achieve this feat? Purge the system of waste, fraud, and inefficiency. Republican newcomers learned during early budget briefings it wouldn't be that easy. Some calls were obvious, such as defunding the National Endowment for the Arts, the National Endowment for the Humanities, the Corporation for Public Broadcasting, and Clinton's volunteer program, AmeriCorps. The Departments of Commerce, Education, and Energy were convenient targets as was the Earned Income Tax Credit ("Poor people aren't our constituents," one new member told a reporter). But when all the savings were added up, they didn't come close to balancing the budget. Republicans were "stunned" to learn that farm subsidies, student loans, job training, veterans programs, Head Start, Meals on Wheels, and Medicare would also have to go under the knife. "There was a noticeable increase in the number of visitors to the bar after the budget presentation," wrote journalist Linda Killian who chronicled the "Republican Revolution."[12] After much gnashing of teeth, the House formulated a budget proposal balancing the budget in six years. Perhaps the most controversial provision reduced projected increases in Medicare by $270 billion. Corporate subsidies and tax breaks remained largely untouched.

In the midst of Republican bill drafting, a tragic incident—and Clinton's response to it—provided the first small hint that he might be regaining his footing. On April 19, 1995, terrorists bombed the Murrah Federal Building in Oklahoma City, killing 168 people, including 19 children. Owing to the climate of the times, most people initially assumed that the perpetrators were foreign, probably Middle Eastern in origin. It turned out they were white, native-born, antigovernment extremists from rural Michigan. The tragedy allowed Clinton to express the outrage and sorrow of the nation. It also gave him an opportunity to subtly link the antigovernment sentiments of his critics to the climate of hatred that had inspired the bombing. "You have lost too much, but you have not lost everything," Clinton told friends and family members of the victims at a memorial service in Oklahoma City. "And you have certainly not lost America, for we will stand with you for as many tomorrows as it takes." The next day, in Minneapolis, he deplored "the purveyors of hatred and division" and "promoters of paranoia" who used the airwaves to "spread hate" and "leave the impression . . . that violence is acceptable." He didn't name names or cite examples. He didn't have to. Others did it for him, singling out conservative talk show hosts Rush Limbaugh, G. Gordon Liddy, and others.[13] Liddy, who had gained fame as one of the Watergate burglars, was the most incendiary of the lot. Repeatedly warning listeners that the Clinton administration was out to confiscate their firearms, he urged gun owners to fight back: "If the Bureau of Alcohol, Tobacco and Firearms comes to disarm you and they are bearing arms, resist them with arms. Go for a head shot; they're going to be wearing bulletproof vests."[14] Commentator Carl Rowan pointed the finger at Newt Gingrich, Bob Dole, and other GOP leaders for "inflaming a bunch of nuts" like Liddy. Talk show hosts and their defenders indignantly denied that they had anything to do with the bombing and accused the president of exploiting the tragedy for political advantage.[15]

With his critics on the defensive, Clinton increasingly invoked the powers inherent in his office to act unilaterally. If Congress wouldn't advance his agenda, he would do it on his own. There ensued a flurry of executive orders, presidential directives, and White House proclamations. Clinton's big innovation was his deft appropriation of the authority of federal agencies to issue rules and regulations. Ironically, Ronald Reagan laid the foundation upon which Clinton built. Upon becoming president, Reagan barred federal agencies from issuing new rules and regulations before clearing them with the Office of Management and Budget, which reported directly to him. His purpose was to reduce the number of rules and regulations on business and industry. President George H. W. Bush retained Reagan's review requirement, as did Clinton. But Clinton turned the practice on its head. With increasing frequency after the 1994 election, he personally, and with much fanfare, ordered agencies to devise *new* rules and regulations, especially in the areas of education, health care, welfare, gun control, and the environment.[16] The issue of teenage smoking offers a case in point. On the morning of August 10, 1995, the president hosted a White House roundtable discussion on the subject. Three hours later he called a news conference to announce that he was taking action "to protect the young people of the United States from the awful dangers of tobacco." He was

ordering the FDA to develop rules requiring IDs for purchase of cigarettes and prohibiting billboards advertising cigarettes near schools and
playgrounds. Two days later, he devoted his weekly radio address to the
subject, and over the next twelve months, as the FDA drafted the new
regulations and invited public comment, as required by law, Clinton
touted the initiative every chance he had. When the regulations were
finally set to take effect, he staged a Rose Garden ceremony that had all
the trappings of a major bill signing. Guests included the vice president,
cabinet secretaries, members of Congress, former Surgeon General C.
Everett Koop, onetime Secretary of Health, Education, and Welfare Joseph A. Califano, Jr., and the widow of a tobacco lobbyist who had died
of lung cancer.[17] By his actions, recalled associate White House counsel
and future Supreme Court justice Elena Kagan, Clinton was sending "a
loud and lingering message: these were *his* agencies; *he* was responsible
for their actions; and *he* was due credit for their successes."[18] Not all of
Clinton's executive initiatives were successful. A federal appeals court
blocked his attempt to mend fences with organized labor by prohibiting businesses from hiring replacements for striking workers. And none
of his executive actions was as far-reaching as Jefferson's annexation of
the Louisiana Territory, Lincoln's Emancipation Proclamation, or Truman's desegregation of the armed forces. Even so, in an era of divided
government and diminished presidential opportunity, Clinton's "go-it-
alone" approach forcefully answered the question the skeptical reporter
had put to him in the aftermath of the 1994 election: The president was
relevant.[19]

The flurry of executive initiatives was but a prelude to the drama that
played out in late 1995 and early 1996. As the fiscal year neared its close,
ending the government's statutory authority to spend money, the president and Congress were at loggerheads over the budget. With Gingrich
and his newly elected followers in the House leading the way, Republicans held fast to their plan to slash spending by $1.2 trillion and balance
the budget in six years. Clinton angered many congressional Democrats
and some members of his own staff by seeming to meet the GOP at
least part way. In June 1995, he announced his willingness to balance
the budget in ten years, to cut discretionary spending by 20 percent, and
reduce projected increases in Medicare, though by not nearly as much as

the Republicans. Congressional Democrats like Richard Gephardt and David Obey, believing the "draconian" cuts in the GOP budget would backfire on the party, were caught off guard by what they considered the president's arbitrary and wholly unnecessary concessions. "Most of us learned some time ago," Obey told a reporter, "if you don't like the president's position on an issue, you simply need to wait a few weeks." If the president continued down this path, Leon Panetta and Laura Tyson decided, they would consider resigning.[20]

Still, with time running out, Clinton and the GOP remained far apart. Without an agreement on the budget by November 13, the government would have to partially shut down, laying off hundreds of thousands of federal workers and ceasing all but essential operations. As the deadline approached, Republicans engaged in a high-stakes form of brinkmanship. They passed a resolution that would fund the government until a final budget could be agreed upon. But to the resolution they attached a provision requiring the government to balance the budget in six years. For good measure, they also attached provisions cutting funding for Medicare and other programs. It was now up to the president. He could sign the resolution and enshrine the GOP agenda into law; or he could wield his veto pen and shut down the federal government.

Although this was the most dramatic showdown between a president and Congress over the budget, it was not the first. Between 1976 and 1995, budget disputes had temporarily curtailed at least some government operations fifteen times, once for up to seventeen days. The same scenario played out every time: "Each side would try to get the other to blink. And when neither would do so, they would eventually blink in unison."[21] In the latest standoff, the Republicans were confident the president would blink first. Many Democrats, fearing the influence of Dick Morris, believed he would, too. To the surprise of Republicans and relief of Democrats, he vetoed the resolution.

The ensuing impasse twice shut down the government—for five days in November 1995 and twenty-one days between December and January. More annoyance than crisis, the shutdown closed national parks, museums, and historic sites, delayed the issuance of visas and passports, stalled construction on federal projects, and furloughed 600,000 government employees. Military personnel, air traffic controllers, law enforcement officials, postal employees, and others providing services deemed essential were unaffected. Just as both sides believed the other would blink first, so at first, both sides believed the public would blame the other for the shutdown. But from the beginning, the Republicans took the brunt of public criticism. Twice as many held them responsible as blamed the president. Indeed, combined with his Oklahoma City speech earlier in the year, the government shutdown was a decisive turning point in Clinton's political fortunes. His public approval ratings soared into the fifties and never significantly declined again, even during the toughest times ahead. The standoff probably also diminished Republican chances of winning the White House in 1996. Senate Majority Leader Bob Dole, the eventual GOP standard bearer, had been dragged by Gingrich into the confrontation against his better instincts. By January he decided he'd had enough. He intervened decisively to end the stalemate.

The media's penchant for elevating personality over policy had hurt Clinton during his first two years in office. That same tendency now worked in his favor. The more voters saw of Newt Gingrich the less they liked him. His apocalyptic rhetoric stirred his troops—sometimes to levels even beyond Gingrich's control—but grated on the wider public. He could also seem petulant. When he told reporters that the government shutdown might have been avoided if Clinton hadn't snubbed him aboard Air Force One on a trip to the funeral of Israeli Prime Minister Yitzhak Rabin, an editorial cartoonist depicted him as an overgrown baby in diapers. The image rubbed off on the Speaker's freshmen followers. Once seen as "principled newcomers," they were now being depicted as "stubborn children . . . threatening to grab the steering wheel and drive the car off the road if they couldn't have the radio turned to their favorite station."[22]

Clinton decisively won the battle for public opinion. But it may have been a pyrrhic victory: he had yielded a surprising amount of ground to the Republicans during the battle's course. During the 1992 campaign, for example, he had proposed, by one count, seventy-eight domestic initiatives with a price tag of nearly $112 billion. Three years later, he had agreed to cuts in excess of $525 billion. Moreover, he had acceded to the GOP's demand to balance the budget in seven years, a timetable he had denounced as reckless just months before. And, in his 1996 State of the Union message, he famously proclaimed, "The era of big government is over." "The man knew how to change his mind," said one commentator, adding, "I have no hesitation in concluding that no other Democratic President of the twentieth century would have even considered cuts of the magnitude that Clinton was willing to support during the Republican budget revolution of 1995–96." The commentator was Ron Haskins, a key Republican staff member on the House Committee on Ways and Means.[23] But Haskins was a rare voice among Republicans, most of whom, convinced they had been outmaneuvered by Clinton, were now more determined than ever to discredit the president by whatever means possible, including continued investigations into Whitewater and other alleged wrongdoings. Some even talked of impeachment. What neither Clinton's foes nor anyone else yet knew was that the standoff with Congress would play into subsequent efforts to remove Clinton from office. It was during this time of budgetary tribulations that he began his fateful relationship with White House intern Monica Lewinsky.

Following the budget standoff, two issues of far-reaching consequence dominated the legislative agenda: the restructuring of the hugely important telecommunications industry and reform of the welfare system. Practically everyone agreed that a comprehensive review of the government's relationship with the telecommunications industry was long overdue. Except for a few tweaks in the system during the 1970s and 1980s, the existing regulatory structure dated to 1934—long before cable or satellite television, cellular phones, or the Internet. Policy makers in 1996—conservatives and liberals alike—were intent upon dismantling stifling regulations and unleashing upon the industry the competitive forces of the marketplace. Vice President Gore, the administration's point man on reform, set the tone for the debate: "We seek open and free competition in which any company is free to offer any information good or service to any customer. Why is that important? Very simply. Because competition lowers prices, increases choices, improves quality, and creates jobs."[24] The stakes involved in reconfiguring an industry that already controlled one-sixth of the economy were huge. Fortunes would be made or lost by the decisions made in Washington. Cable television companies alone stood to gain between $3 and $5 billion per year from deregulation. Not surprisingly, more lobbyists descended on Washington than at any time since the health-care debate. Despite the high stakes for investors and consumers alike, the debate received scant media attention, perhaps because many of the issues—like market shares and frequency allocations—were highly technical in nature. Proposals to ban pornography on the Internet and require manufacturers to install "V-chips" on televisions so that parents could block out objectionable programming attracted attention. Otherwise the debate was relegated to the back pages of the business section.

To formulate the White House position, President Clinton appointed an internal task force headed by the vice president. The impulse to deregulate reached deep into the administration. "Our deliberations were frequently contentious," recalled task-force member Joseph Stiglitz of the CEA. "Fierce fights broke out between the advocates of complete deregulation—let the markets take care of everything—and those who sought to retain some role for government."[25] In the end, the administration sided with those who sought to retain some role for government, though not as large a role as Stiglitz and a few others wanted. The sixty-two-year-old Federal Communications Commission, which Gingrich Republicans wanted to abolish, would remain. The government would continue to limit the number of television and radio stations one company could own in a market. It would also ban pornography from the Internet, require V-chips, and ensure that schools and libraries had access to the Internet. Aside from these and a few other provisions, the administration sided more often with the deregulators than with the regulators. So, too, did overwhelming majorities in both houses of Congress. The Telecommunications Act of 1996 passed the House 414 to 16 and the Senate 91 to 5. The handful of dissenters included Senators John McCain (R-AZ), who wanted less regulation, and Paul Wellstone (D-MN), who wanted more. Consumers Union, though not opposed to deregulation, complained that the public had been shortchanged in the deliberations. But these were lone voices. With much fanfare, the president presided over the first-ever signing ceremony at the Library of Congress. Hailing the act as "revolutionary," he compared it to the Federal Highway Act of the 1950s and said it would "strengthen our economy, our society, our families, and our democracy." Consumers, he predicted, would reap "the benefits of lower prices, better quality and greater choices in their telephone and cable services, and they will continue to benefit from a diversity of voices and viewpoints in radio, television and print media."

At first Clinton's predictions seemed justified. Although the Supreme Court invalidated the ban on pornography, the telecom industry flourished, thousands of jobs were created, and consumers had more choices than ever. But even before Clinton left office things began to sour. The telecom boom gave way to a telecom bust. "When the dust settled," said Stiglitz, "America was left with a tremendous amount of excess network capacity, and a marketplace that in some areas was more concentrated than before." Ten years after the act's passage, public-interest groups like Common Cause and Consumers Union, as if to say "we told you so," reported that deregulation "failed to serve the public and did not deliver on its promise of more competition, more diversity, lower prices, more jobs and a booming economy." Although conceding that the act would have been even worse without the White House intervention, Common Cause concluded that the media was more concentrated and less diverse than before and that consumers were paying 50 percent more for cable service and 20 percent more for phone costs.[26] Even administration insiders were critical in retrospect. "Deregulation of the telecom industry—that was a mistake," Laura Tyson stated flatly. Joseph Stiglitz had been wary from the start, but the results were even worse than he feared. The biggest mistake almost everyone had made, Stiglitz said, including himself, was to underestimate the "intensity of the drive for domination." Once companies gained a foothold in a market, they drove out the competition by whatever means necessary. The scenario Stiglitz described was reminiscent of the industrial wars of the late nineteenth century. Tellingly, President Clinton, except for praising the V-chip, barely mentioned the act in his memoirs.[27]

No issue was more central to Clinton's image as a New Democrat than his pledge to "end welfare as we know it." He was no newcomer to the issue. It had occupied his attention since his first days as governor. As chairman of the National Governors' Conference, he had successfully lobbied his colleagues to endorse, and Congress to pass, the Family Support Act of 1988, which encouraged the states to create job training programs to move people from welfare to work.[28] When asked why he supported welfare reform, Clinton always brought up Lillie Hardin, a woman from Pine Bluff, Arkansas, he had met when he was governor. She had just found a job, and Clinton asked her what the best thing was about being off welfare. She replied, "When my boy goes to school and they ask him, 'What does your mama do for a living?' he can give an answer."

Since the advent of polling in the 1930s, Americans have expressed ambiguous attitudes toward welfare, or "relief" as it was once called. In the depths of the Great Depression, 60 percent of respondents told pollsters the government was spending too much on relief and recovery measures. But 67 percent agreed that government had "a responsibility to pay the living expenses of needy people who are out of work." Not until decades later did welfare become a political liability for Democratic candidates. The turning point came in the 1960s. At the beginning of the decade, much of America "discovered" the existence of poverty amid unprecedented affluence, thanks in part to Socialist Michael Harrington, whose *The Other America* disclosed that 20 percent of the population was mired in poverty and yet remained invisible to all the rest.[29] Harrington's findings helped inspire the Kennedy and Johnson administrations' war on poverty, which initially enjoyed broad public support. But one part of the war on poverty eventually stigmatized the whole war itself. This was the dramatic expansion of a little-known provision of the Social Security Act of 1935: Aid to Dependent Children, renamed Aid to Families with Dependent Children (AFDC) in 1962. During the sixties, welfare proponents, led by the National Welfare Rights Movement, an offshoot of the black civil rights movement, argued that AFDC was not just a lifeline of last resort but a right to which all families at or below the poverty line were entitled. The result was a flurry of favorable court rulings and an explosion of the AFDC rolls—an eight-fold increase in big cities such as New York and Chicago. From then on, when people talked about welfare, it was AFDC they had in mind. That blacks, particularly single black women with children, constituted a disproportionate number of recipients added race to the mix. By the seventies and eighties, welfare recipients were no longer the invisible "other Americans" in Michael Harrington's stirring account but the all too visible targets of ridicule and scorn—the oft-repeated story about the Cadillac-driving, black "welfare queen" in Chicago being but one example.[30]

Few subjects were as fraught with misunderstanding and misinformation as welfare. Welfare payments, for example, constituted a far smaller portion of government spending—about 2 percent—than most people thought. More whites were on welfare than blacks (though not in proportion to their numbers in the population). And even when combined with other forms of aid such as food stamps and health-care assistance, AFDC afforded recipients a meager income that left most below the poverty line. Still, by Clinton's time welfare had become a millstone around the neck of almost every Democrat running for office.

By then, too, conservative critics of welfare, like George Gilder and Charles Murray, had begun to pursue a new line of attack. Instead of depicting recipients as slackers and cheats, they portrayed them as victims caught up in a cruel system that was making their lives worse. Welfare was consigning them and their children and their children's children to a hopeless cycle of poverty from which there was no escape. The most humane thing to do, these critics argued, was simply to scrap the system. The poor would be better off without it. In one of the most significant developments of the eighties, prominent liberals such as Vernon Jordan, Eleanor Holmes Norton, and Mario Cuomo began to argue that welfare was victimizing the very people it was meant to help.[31] The liberal view received its fullest expression in _Poor Support_, a study published in 1989, by David T. Ellwood, a professor of public policy at Harvard University. Ellwood did something that few other "experts" had done: He asked scores of welfare recipients, most of them single black mothers, how they felt about welfare. No one, he learned, hated welfare more than they did. They found it demeaning, demoralizing, and offering little chance for self-betterment. The system, Ellwood concluded, needed a drastic overhaul. Time limits should be imposed after which recipients would be required to find a job. But Ellwood's wasn't the sink-or-swim approach of Gilder, Murray, and others. When their payments stopped, poor people wouldn't be left to fend for themselves. The government would provide job training, health insurance, and child care. And if employment failed to open up in the private sector, the government would provide public service jobs as well. The key, Ellwood stressed, was to make sure that people were financially better off working than on welfare. Most people, who had an exaggerated notion of the costs of welfare in the first place, doubtless assumed that scrapping the system would save huge amounts of money. But not in Ellwood's scheme. Initially, at least, it would cost more to get people off than to keep them on welfare.[32]

Of the welfare reforms being discussed, Ellwood's appealed to candidate Clinton. It meshed nicely with his talk about people accepting responsibility for their actions but also getting a helping hand when they needed it. Moreover, like managed competition in the health-care field, it embodied his "third way" approach. It would allow him to achieve liberal goals—in this case lifting people out of poverty—by conservative means—overhauling an unpopular welfare system. (It was probably no coincidence that Ellwood's physician father was a prominent advocate of managed competition in the health-care field.) So it was that candidate Clinton announced that he had "a plan to end welfare as we know it—to break the cycle of welfare dependence." The government, he said, would "provide education, job training and child care, but then those that are able must go to work, either in the private sector or in public service."[33] Clinton's plan was notably short on details, especially regarding the costs of the promised education, job training, child care, and public service jobs. A few skeptics considered it an opportunistic bid for white middle-class and working-class votes. But on the whole, it was one of Clinton's most popular issues, with polls showing that 90 percent of the public supported such a plan.[34] Academic specialists were particularly encouraged. Better to have a Democrat overhaul welfare than a Republican. And among Democrats, few were better versed on the subject than Clinton.[35]

To formulate a welfare bill, Clinton created a task force headed by David Ellwood; Ellwood's Harvard colleague and scholarly collaborator, Mary Jo Bane; and speechwriter and aide Bruce Reed, who had coined the phrase "end welfare as we know it." The politics of welfare reform probably mattered more to Reed than to Ellwood and Bane. Growing up on the West Coast, he was dismayed when his political hero, the distinguished liberal senator Frank Church of Idaho, had been swept away by the Reagan tidal wave of 1980. From then on Reed believed that Democrats had to move to the center to avoid Church's fate. Overhauling the welfare system was a necessary first step. Despite the attention welfare reform received during the campaign, it took a backseat to deficit reduction, NAFTA, and health care during Clinton's first year in office. Not until the summer of 1994, when health care was in its death throes, did the task force complete its work and Clinton unveil a plan. Although budgetary constraints forced some scaling back, the essence of Ellwood's original plan remained intact: recipients would be eligible for cash payments for two years but then would have to get a job, even if they were single mothers with small children. But the government would live up to its side of the bargain by providing job training, child care, and a public service job if necessary. The government would also come down hard on fathers who failed to pay child support. The plan went nowhere. Clinton was preoccupied with other issues, and members of Congress, who had been largely excluded from the drafting process, had little stake in it.[36]

Then came the 1994 election. Of no mind to allow Clinton to co-opt one of their signature issues, victorious Republicans made welfare reform a priority. Even before the election, legislators such as Representatives Clay Shaw (R-FL), perhaps the most knowledgeable member of Congress on the subject on either side of the aisle, and Rick Santorum (R-PA) had been crafting a proposal.[37] Now the GOP turned to the task in earnest. Sharp disagreements split Republican ranks. Some wanted to deny payments to unwed mothers, while others favored a more generous approach. After much back-and-forth, first within the House and then between the House and Senate, a bill took shape. The GOP plan essentially turned welfare over to the states, replacing AFDC with annual block grants to the states. Welfare recipients would be limited to five years of assistance in a lifetime and would be required to get a job no latter than two years after first collecting payments. Immigrants, including legal immigrants, would be ineligible for welfare. Funding for Medicaid and food stamps would also be cut.[38]

Clinton vetoed the first two versions of the bill, saying that they went too far, especially by cutting Medicaid. In June 1996 Republicans prepared yet another version that addressed some, though not all, of Clinton's objections. The bill passed with bipartisan majorities in both houses of Congress. Bob Dole, Newt Gingrich, and other high-ranking Republicans privately hoped for a presidential veto. That way they could accuse Clinton of abandoning his popular campaign pledge to "end welfare as we know it." Other Republicans pointed out, however, that even if he signed the bill, Clinton would find himself in a tough spot, because many of his supporters would accuse him of abandoning the poor. Either way, GOP leaders reasoned, they would come out ahead.

There ensued within the administration the most impassioned debate of the Clinton presidency. Many, if not most, of Clinton's advisers urged a veto. Health and Human Service Secretary Donna Shalala presented the president with a study predicting that the bill would throw 60,000 more children into poverty. Chief of staff Leon Panetta, the son of Italian immigrants, was incensed at what he considered the bill's mean-spirited ban on assistance to legal immigrants. Clinton's economic team, including Robert Rubin and Laura Tyson, opposed the bill on humanitarian and economic grounds. AFDC, Tyson argued, acted as a kind of early warning system, detecting economic downturns in their early stages and automatically initiating corrective action with increased welfare outlays.[39] Without AFDC, the economy would suffer. David Ellwood, who had gone back to Harvard, pleaded for a veto. "No bill that is likely to push more than a million additional children into poverty—many in working families," Ellwood wrote in the *New York Times*, "is real reform." Shalala later recalled that she and others were not opposed to welfare reform per se. After all, she had already approved dozens of waivers allowing states to toughen eligibility requirements for welfare beyond those required by federal law. She just thought that Clinton should hold out for more concessions. Republicans had yielded ground after the first two vetoes. One more might do the trick. "But Clinton always cuts his deals a little earlier than I would and it was his right," she said.[40] Among those urging a presidential signature were task-force member Bruce Reed, Vice President Gore, and Mickey Kantor, who argued that this might be Clinton's last chance to overhaul a bad welfare system. The bill's flaws, they counseled, could be remedied with follow-up legislation. Political considerations figured prominently in the deliberations. "If you sign this bill and don't screw up the rest of the campaign," Dick Morris told Clinton, "I think you'll win [the election] by twelve to seventeen points." The Democrats might even retake Congress. Scrap a racially tinged welfare system, Morris added, citing his own polling, and relations between blacks and whites would improve. Feeling the pressure, Clinton lashed out at Morris, accusing him of skewing his poll results with loaded questions. "Did you ever ask if they want me to sign or veto a bill that would let three-year-old children starve, go hungry in the street, because their mother was cut off? You didn't ask that, did you? You didn't want to know the answer, did you?" Clinton went on: "Did you ask if they wanted a father who waits his turn, waits for years to come here, comes here, works hard, is always employed, and suddenly gets hit by a truck. Did you ask if they wanted me to cut off benefits to his six-month-old baby now that he can't work? Did you ask that? I'll bet you didn't."[41] Before reaching a big decision, Clinton was in the habit of rehearsing the arguments, pro and con. He was so good at it—better than the advocates themselves—that aides often didn't know what side he was going to come down on.

Clinton signed the bill. Three members of the administration resigned in protest, including task-force cochair Mary Jo Bane. "I don't want to sound apocalyptic," Daniel Patrick Moynihan told a reporter, "but the effects on New York City could be something approaching an Apocalypse." The New York senator predicted that terminating AFDC would swell the ranks of the homeless and force a third of a million children to spend their nights sleeping on New York City's heating grates.[42] Peter Edelman, one of those resigning in protest, was certain there would be "more malnutrition and more crime, increased infant mortality, and increased drug and alcohol abuse. There will be increased violence and abuse against children and women."[43] During the signing ceremony, protestors assembled outside the White House and shouted "shame, shame, shame." New York City activist Al Sharpton called for protesters to march on the upcoming Democratic National Convention, and New York Representative Charles Rangel (D-NY) said the bill was the worst piece of legislation since Reconstruction. Recalling Clinton's campaign pledge to be an advocate for children, he called the signing "a cruel decision based on the rawest kind of short-term political expediency."[44] Clinton, for his part, predicted that welfare would no longer be an incendiary political issue. Upon signing the cumbersomely titled Personal Responsibility and Work Opportunity Reconciliation Act (PRWORA), he declared: "The two parties cannot attack each other over it. Politicians cannot attack poor people over it."[45] Clinton may have sounded confident. But he wasn't. He privately admitted that he didn't know what would happen once welfare reform took effect.[46] Nor did anyone else. It was the biggest gamble of the Clinton presidency.

What did happen? It's safe to say that the results were mixed. The dire warnings of opponents did not materialize. Homeless children did not pile up on the grates of New York City. But neither did welfare reform

fulfill the extravagant hopes of advocates like the editors o:
Street Journal, who hailed it as "the greatest advance for Amei
since the rise of capitalism."[47] Because the fate of welfare recipients was
now in the hands of the states, their experiences varied widely. Those
in Wisconsin, Maryland, and Massachusetts fared better than those in
Louisiana and South Carolina. Thanks to a strong economy in the late
nineties and to Clinton's expansion of the Earned Income Tax Credit,
poverty declined steadily during the decade, especially among African
Americans. By 1999, welfare applications had declined by 60 percent,
even exceeding the expectations of PRWORA's most enthusiastic supporters. And true to his promise Clinton later persuaded Congress to
rescind the ban on aid to immigrants. "The results are much better than
I expected," said David Ellwood four years after the bill passed.[48] Like
Ellwood, Johns Hopkins University sociologist Andrew J. Cherlin, a
prominent expert on the impact of public policy on family life, originally predicted disaster. When that didn't happen, he set out to find out
why. "What surprised me most, as I have studied low-income families
under PRWORA," Cherlin reported, "is how Americans seem to de-
rive a sense of dignity and self-worth from paid work, even when the
pay is low." Welfare recipients "were eager to trade welfare for work
and . . . many who made the transition spoke positively of increased self-
esteem, decreased depressive symptoms, and greater independence."[49]
On the tenth anniversary of signing welfare reform into law, Bill Clinton
hailed the results: welfare rolls shrunk from 12.2 million to 4.5 million,
caseloads down by 54 percent, 60 percent of mothers who left welfare
now gainfully employed. "The last 10 years have shown that we did in
fact end welfare as we knew it, creating a new beginning for millions of
Americans."[50]

Not everyone agreed. Demographers pointed out that because those
most likely to be on welfare—women between the ages of eighteen and
twenty-eight—were declining relative to their numbers in the population, welfare rolls would have shrunk even without PRWORA. An-
ecdotal evidence suggested that some who could have qualified for
assistance declined to apply not because they'd found jobs but because
they had to surmount too many bureaucratic hurdles to sign up. To critics like Peter Edelman the numbers game was beside the point. It was

the principle that mattered. With welfare reform, the federal government had broken its commitment to protect the most vulnerable of American citizens.[51]

The true test of reform, everyone agreed, would come not during good times when jobs were plentiful but during bad times when they were scarce. But even the most serious economic downturn since the Great Depression, which began in 2008, brought no end to the standoff between critics and supporters of welfare reform. By 2011, the poverty rate had climbed to its highest level since 1993. The US Census Bureau reported that the poverty rate rose especially fast among those who had been the principal targets of welfare reform: single mothers and their offspring. Three years into the downturn, 40 percent of them were living in poverty—the highest percentage since 1997. Some analysts attributed that fact to welfare reform. Their eligibility for welfare had run out, but with unemployment over 9 percent, so had their job prospects.[52] "By almost any measure," freelance journalist Jake Blumgart concluded in the liberal *American Prospect*, welfare reform "has failed to cushion the neediest through recessions." Not so responded Brookings Institution scholar Ron Haskins, who as a GOP staffer in the nineties had helped craft the reform act. Marshaling his own impressive set of facts, Haskins argued that welfare reform, acting in tandem with other safety-net measures, had saved some 20 million people from falling into poverty during hard times. Fifteen years out, the debate continued, with no end in sight.[53]

Even as he signed welfare reform into law on the eve of the Democratic National Convention, Clinton was shrewdly moving to mitigate the threat on his left flank. He gained passage of a bipartisan bill sponsored by Senators Edward Kennedy and Nancy Kassebaum (R-KS) that barred insurance companies from denying coverage to persons when they changed jobs and safeguarded the confidentiality of patient information. Although falling far short of the comprehensive reform Clinton had originally sought, Kennedy-Kassebaum was a major achievement. Clinton also ended a nearly two-decade-long impasse when Congress increased the minimum wage.[54] When Democrats assembled in Chicago in August to renominate Clinton, he could claim more substantial legislative successes during a presidential election year than any president since Lyndon Johnson in the aftermath of the Kennedy assassination.

As for the campaign itself, it was over almost before it began. In the immediate aftermath of the 1994 election, when Republicans were riding high and Clinton was at his most vulnerable, he, Morris, and others had crafted a four-pronged reelection plan that was now, in the aftermath of welfare reform, in full deployment. The first component kept the president in the public eye with his never-ending array of poll-tested, values-laden initiatives, some of which reporter John Harris noted "did not seem quite worthy of Presidential attention." One day, for instance, Clinton summoned leaders of neighborhood watch groups to the White House to announce that he had persuaded the cell phone industry to donate phones and free air time to watch groups across the country. "This is a good day for the country," he said. "We're taking another step toward a safer future for our children, our families, and our communities." Another day he announced that he was ordering the Secretary of Education to send out to every school district—all 16,000 of them—a manual touting the benefits of school uniforms.[55] Some of Clinton's actions were purely defensive—and opportunistic—such as his signing of the Defense of Marriage Act (DOMA), which defined marriage as a union between a man and a woman and absolved states from having to recognize same-sex marriages in other states. He had previously denounced the measure as "gay baiting" but signed it to quell the still-simmering controversy over gays in the military. For Clinton, a bill signing, no matter how minor the content, was usually a big event, with cameras, speeches, and plenty of pens to hand out to those gathered around his desk. This time it was different. Clinton affixed his signature to the measure, which had passed both houses with veto-proof majorities, without fanfare at 12:50 a.m. on a Saturday. Opponents of the Defense of Marriage Act had nowhere else to turn; they knew it and so did Clinton. His deeds didn't match his words, but he had spoken more frequently and more eloquently about gay rights than any previous president. And many Republicans, not content with DOMA, wanted a constitutional amendment defining marriage as between a man and a woman. Describing the president as "eternally, infernally disappointing," playwright Tony Kushner said he intended "to follow the polls closely, just like the president always does, and if there is any possibility of Dole winning, I will vote for Dick Morris, I mean Bill Clinton." Polls subsequently showed that most gay voters, like Kushner, voted for Clinton.[56]

Some of the president's election-year actions were more positive, especially those he was able to take by bypassing Congress and invoking the executive authority of his office. So, for example, he strengthened government regulation of the meat-packing industry, limited the ability of tobacco companies to pitch their products to adolescents, and put nearly 2 million acres of scenic federal land off limits to mining. All in all, concluded reporter John Harris, Clinton's initiatives were "the most comprehensive melding of politics and domestic policy ever in the White House."[57] Clinton was hardly the first president to meld policy and politics. But he probably took the process to a higher, more systematic level than any of his predecessors, including the most recent master of the art, Ronald Reagan.

Clinton's poll-tested initiatives formed one part of his reelection strategy. Early deployment of television advertisements and prodigious fundraising were two others. Long before the parties convened to nominate their candidates, the Democrats were flooding key states with television spots. Although the spots were unambiguous in their depictions of the administration and its foes, the Supreme Court ruled that such ads did not violate limitations on campaign expenditures as long as they didn't endorse or oppose a candidate by name. Ironically, the Clinton ads resembled the "Harry and Louise" ads foes of health-care reform had run against him. Dick Morris later described Clinton as "the day-to-day operational director of our TV ad campaign. He worked over every script, watched every ad, ordered changes in every visual presentation and decided which ads would run when and where."[58] In Press Secretary Michael McCurry's view, the ad blitz was "the central story of the 1996 campaign." It "put Dole in a box" he never got out of, and, because the ads ran in local markets and not nationally, neither Republicans nor the press realized what was happening until it was too late. The advertising barrage, launched earlier than ever before in a presidential campaign, was bold but also risky. Had the race tightened in the homestretch, the Clinton campaign would have found itself fending off last-minute attacks with dangerously depleted resources.[59] But that didn't happen, and from then on candidates would try to get the jump on their opponents by employing Clinton's early-and-often media strategy. Clinton's media campaign was innovative in another respect. As two political scientists noted, "Clinton was the first candidate to realize the value of targeting TV ads to the most important markets rather than carpet bombing the nation with ads, wasting money in states that were overwhelmingly Democratic or Republican and therefore unswayable by adversity."[60] Before it was over, the Clinton campaign raised electioneering to new heights of sophistication. Focus groups underwent personality and consumer preference tests, from which the campaign learned that voters who played tennis and watched the popular television drama *ER* were more likely to vote Republican, while those who watched basketball and public television were in the Democratic corner. Because of Clinton's weak political base, a strong showing among independent or swing voters was critical. "We figured out who those [swing] voters were, everything from their sports, vacations, and lifestyles," recalled pollster Mark Penn. He and his associates then divided swing voters into four personality groups and nine other categories, ranging from "social liberals" to balanced-budgeters, to "young social conservatives." Exactly what use the campaign made of the television preferences of voters was apparently a trade secret, but from then on future campaigns would follow suit.[61]

To pay for his campaign, Clinton probably raised more money than any previous Democratic candidate. *The Wall Street Journal* might denounce him on its editorial pages; Rotary Club speakers might dismiss him as just another "tax and spend" Democrat; and billionaire publisher Richard Mellon Scaife might pour millions into a scurrilous campaign to defame both Bill and Hillary Clinton. But in the upper reaches of business and finance, where the big money resided, the president was earning a reputation as a reliable custodian of the nation's economy. Donors involved in overseas trade, computers and telecommunications, and the television and film industry were particularly generous with their contributions. Although Clinton was his own best fundraiser, he was aided in the process by Commerce Secretary Ronald H. Brown, who, before his death early in 1996, forged productive relationships with business and financial communities, and by reelection campaign cochairman Terry McAuliffe. The continued presence of Robert Rubin in the administration and the outwardly amicable relationship between the administration and Federal Reserve Board Chairman Alan Greenspan also reassured business and finance that their contributions would not go to waste. Some of Clinton's fund-raising practices raised eyebrows. It was later disclosed that dozens of potential donors were invited to off-the-record dinners and coffees at the White House while some got to spend a night in the Lincoln bedroom, accompany the president on Air Force One, or sit in the presidential box at the Kennedy Center. Before the campaign was even over, Clinton was forced to return illegal contributions from several foreign nationals. But Republican efforts to capitalize on these and other misdeeds proved ineffective, in large part because they, too, were raising unprecedented sums of so-called soft money not subject to campaign spending laws.[62]

Clinton's ability to tout his economic stewardship not only filled campaign coffers but was also the fourth and most effective component of his reelection strategy. And indeed, Clinton could boast a significant economic upturn since 1992: unemployment down to 5.4 percent from a high of 7.5; 11 million new jobs created, 3 million more than promised; and the largest decline in poverty in twenty years, from 15.1 percent to 13.8.[63] Skeptics, including some within the administration, noted that workers were being laid off at a higher rate than in the 1980s. And while many of them were being rehired, their new jobs paid less and had fewer benefits than their old jobs. Recalled a staff member with the CEA in 1995 and 1996: "We did not want to confront the idea that job insecurity had increased during Clinton's first term. That would be bad election-year strategy."[64] A draft of the CEA's 1996 report to the president contained a graph projecting a slight increase in the unemployment rate the following year. The word promptly came down from the office of Gene B. Sperling, deputy director of the president's National Economic Council, that the graph had to go. It was okay to discuss future unemployment trends in the text, but no pictures. "We don't want anything going up that's bad, and nothing going down that's good," a CEA staffer remembered a Sperling aide saying. The offending graph was excluded from the final report.[65]

Skeptics might also have noted that most of the policies the administration was crediting for the economic upturn—-deficit reduction, NAFTA and other trade agreements, and deregulation of the telecommunications industry—had not been in effect long enough to have made

President has little impact on economy. Common theme

a difference one way or the other. "The administration," economist James K. Galbraith noted, "benefited from an ordinary cyclical rebound not of its own making, abetted by low interest rates between 1991 and 1993." Galbraith added that the economy was performing well "not because the government did anything, but because people thought the government did something."[66]

As in 1992, Clinton benefited from the weakness of his opponents. As though performing on cue, the GOP played into his hands time and time again. Newt Gingrich continued to serve as a useful foil, and the Republican candidate, seventy-four-year-old Senate veteran Bob Dole, was simply outmatched from the beginning. By wide margins, voters believed that Clinton cared more about them than the "dour and saturnine" Dole.[67] As the campaign wound to a close, the senator tried to make an issue out of Clinton's ethical and moral lapses. "Where's the outrage?" he complained. It wasn't that the public had any illusions about Clinton being a paragon of virtue. Whitewater, Travelgate, the death of Vince Foster—all had taken a toll on Clinton's reputation, as had continuing rumors of marital infidelity. One poll showed that 56 percent of the public did not believe he had "high personal moral and ethical standards." Fifty-two percent did not believe he was "honest and trustworthy." By even larger margins, however, Americans did believe he had their best interests at heart.[68] At one campaign stop, Dole asked a rhetorical question of parents in the crowd: If, God forbid, something should happen to them, which candidate would they want to look after their children? An enterprising newspaper promptly put the question to a national audience. The results: 54 percent picked Clinton, 28 percent, Dole.

Poor planning and poor logistics also plagued the Dole campaign. In Jacksonville, Florida, the candidate's advance team had arranged for him to speak in an empty parking lot adjacent to a Hooters restaurant. As Dole began his speech on family values, he was perfectly framed from above by a line of loosely clad waitresses leaning over a railing to catch a glimpse of the Republican candidate.

The only surprise on election day was Clinton's smaller-than-expected margin of victory. Although he handily defeated Dole and H. Ross Perot, who ran for a second time but was not the force he had been four years earlier, Clinton fell just short of 50 percent, far below the 10 to 12 percent margin Dick Morris had predicted if Clinton were to sign welfare reform. Nor were the Democrats able to regain control of Congress. Probably because the outcome was never in doubt, voter turnout was the lowest in a presidential election since 1924.

Still, everyone agreed that the election was a remarkable personal victory for the president, who seemed almost certainly fated to one term just two years earlier. There was less agreement about the outcome's deeper meaning and what it portended for the future. Even Clinton's supporters were not sure. For backers of the centrist Democratic Leadership Conference (DLC), the meaning of the election was clear: Clinton won because he returned to the center after an unfortunate move to the left in pursuit of health-care reform. Or, as Morris cohort and Clinton pollster Mark Penn, put it, "Clinton won the election because on every issue that the Republicans hoped to dominate—balancing the budget, welfare, crime, immigration, and taxes—Clinton staked out a strong centrist position."[69] And these centrist positions, so the argument went, earned him the support of key groups that had been flirting with the Republicans, groups such as political independents, married families with children, and middle-class suburbanites. Blue-collar industrial workers had once formed the backbone of FDR's New Deal coalition. The core of Clinton's New Democratic coalition, Penn said, might well be "wired workers" who "use computers, have more flexibility in deciding how to do their jobs and often work in unstructured settings and as part of teams." Wired workers were optimistic, self-reliant, opposed to "race and gender preferences" in education, tired of the "ideological ax-grinding of the left-right debate" and in favor of "a smaller, non-bureaucratic form of government activism that equips people to help themselves." Old Democrats disagreed. Clinton pollster Stanley Greenberg, who was fired after the 1994 election, argued that Clinton owed reelection to his defense of Medicaid, Medicare, Social Security, and other traditional Democratic programs. The president secured a lock on the election not when he moved to the right to accommodate the GOP but when he forced the GOP to back down from a plan to gut entitlement programs. And the key voting blocs were not up-and-coming suburbanites but women and middle-class and working-class voters. Not surprisingly, based on their reading of the election, both sides offered strikingly different advice to the president about his second-term agenda. DLC supporters did propose some progressive measures such as weaning corporations from government subsidies and increasing investments in education. But the DLC also urged Clinton to outflank the GOP by restructuring Medicare, Medicaid, and Social Security. For Greenberg, fiddling with entitlements was just about the worst thing he could do: "Bad policy and bad politics." If anything, voters wanted more security, including health-care reform, in an uncertain and fast-changing world— not less. Both sides marshaled poll results and voter surveys in support of their recommendations. Even among fervent supporters, Clinton's vaunted Third Way remained contested territory.[70]

In the immediate aftermath of the election, Clinton was offering few clues about his future intentions. He seemed relieved enough to be getting a second chance. But even before he could chart a new course, a crisis, largely of his own making, was to bring his second term to a standstill.

Siege and Survival, 1997–1999

"One of the most extraordinary phenomena of our day, a phenomena which social historians in the future will very likely record with perplexity if not with astonishment," wrote one reporter, "is a consuming personal hatred" of the president and, "to an almost equal degree," of the first lady.[1] Actually the reporter was writing in 1936, and he was referring to Franklin and Eleanor Roosevelt. But his comments could just as easily have been written about Bill and Hillary Clinton. There were differences, of course. Hatred of the Roosevelts was more or less confined to the boardrooms and country clubs of the rich and wellborn, and it was more than offset by the adoration of their legions of admirers. Clinton-hating had a broader base. "Like horse-racing," a writer quipped, it was "one of those national pastimes that unite the elite and the lumpen."[2] But what made extreme enmity of the Clintons more perplexing—and this could be said of some of the ardent support they received as well—was its disproportionality to their actions.

How to explain the reaction that greeted Hillary Clinton during her trip to Seattle in 1994 to promote health-care reform? Her Secret Service detail had never seen anything like it. The crowds were so threatening, agents insisted she put on a bulletproof vest. They'd seen angry crowds before, but not for a first lady. As she was leaving the scene, hundreds of protestors menacingly surrounded her limousine.

It turned out that the protest wasn't as spontaneous as it first appeared. For weeks conservative radio hosts had been encouraging listeners to show up and tell the first lady what they thought about her. It turned out, too, that Newt Gingrich's office in Washington had helped recruit protestors as had the innocuous-sounding Citizens for a Sound Economy, which was being bankrolled by reclusive Pittsburgh billionaire Richard Mellon Scaife. Described in a *Washington Post* profile as "the most generous donor to conservative causes in American history," Scaife would spend $200 million dollars in an array of anti-Clinton ventures.[3]

But even a well-oiled orchestrated effort could not account for the furious reaction of the protestors. "What I could see from the car was a crowd of men who seemed to be in their twenties and thirties," Hillary Clinton recalled. "I'll never forget the look in their eyes and their twisted mouths as they screamed at me while the agents pushed them away." The Secret Service made several arrests and confiscated two guns and a knife.[4]

So what was behind it? In Hillary's case, *Time*'s Margaret Carlson summed up the dilemma: "Hillary, who personifies many of the advances made by a cutting-edge generation of women, finds herself held up against what is probably the most tradition-bound and antiquated model of American womanhood: the institution of the first lady."[5] Then there was the raw nerve the Clintons touched by supporting abortion rights, affirmative action, gays in the military, and gender equality. The president's infidelities also upset many. Still, most of their views resided safely in the political mainstream. Indeed, Clinton's economic and fiscal views made him one of the most conservative Democrats to occupy the White House in the twentieth century. Historian Arthur M. Schlesinger, Jr., once called Jimmy Carter—and he meant it as no compliment—the most conservative Democrat since Grover Cleveland. Clinton probably had as great, or greater, a claim on that distinction as Carter. Here after all was a president who hailed the end of big government; who was more pro-business than pro-labor; who wore his religion on his sleeve; who approved drastic cuts in welfare; and who supported the death penalty (even, as in the case of Ricky Ray Rector, for brain-damaged inmates). Before he became president, Clinton supported the Gulf War, and, after gaining his footing in the White House, showed himself more willing than many of his Republican critics to deploy American forces abroad.

When confronted with the president's stands on the issues, critics simply dismissed them as cynical attempts to win votes. Welfare reform? An insurance policy to guarantee reelection (a view, it might be noted, shared by more than a few Clinton supporters). Balanced budget? Forced on him by House Republicans. And so on down the list. True enmity toward the Clintons rested on the unshakable conviction that they were thoroughly disreputable characters who would do anything—anything—to get what they wanted. As evidence, if any were needed, detractors pointed to all the alleged scandals. First was Whitewater, short-hand for an allegedly fraudulent real estate deal involving the Clintons when they lived in Arkansas. Next came the "gates," to evoke memories of the most famous political scandal of all time: Travelgate (alleging that Hillary Clinton had fired seven employees from the White House Travel Office to make room for cronies); Filegate (accusing the first lady of hiding incriminating documents from the authorities); and Troopergate (charging the president with having bribed Arkansas state troopers to keeping quiet about Bill's gubernatorial dalliances). Throughout his two terms, several congressional committees, a succession of special prosecutors, and an army of investigative journalists looked into all of the allegations of wrongdoing without once turning up proof of criminal activity by the Clintons.[6]

The closest anyone came to unearthing a scandal of far-reaching importance involved the 1996 campaign. Early in 1997, Senate and House Republicans launched separate investigations into allegedly illegal practices by the Clinton reelection campaign—practices Newt Gingrich predicted would prove "bigger than Watergate." There was a story there, a big and important one. It involved the blatant disregard of campaign finance and disclosure requirements and the expenditures of unprecedented amounts of unregulated "soft money." Because both parties were culpable, the Republicans shut down the investigations when the trail began to lead to their doors.[7]

Confirmed Clinton-haters went in for fare more sensational than campaign finance irregularities. No tale, it seemed, was too farfetched. Vincent W. Foster, Jr., was a lifelong friend of Bill Clinton's, and a friend and former law partner of Hillary Clinton is at the Rose Law Firm in Little Rock. When Clinton became president, Foster reluctantly agreed to leave his lucrative practice and serve as deputy White House counsel. In the early evening of July 30, 1994, Foster's body was found at Fort Marcy Park in Northern Virginia, about a twenty-minute drive from the White House. All signs pointed to suicide. The forty-eight-year-old

Foster, the father of three, was known to have been fighting depression, and he was finding the pressures of public life too difficult to bear. Several editorials in the *Wall Street Journal* had singled him out for failing to furnish a photograph for an article on the influx of Arkansans into the government. Foster's mood darkened when he imagined friends and family back home reading the respected *Journal* and thinking that he had probably succumbed to the temptations of power and fame. "I was not meant for the job or the spotlight of public life in Washington," he wrote on a scrap of paper discovered after his death. "Here ruining people is considered sport." Despite multiple investigations confirming the original verdict of suicide, rumors quickly spread—and persisted long thereafter—that one or both of the Clintons had ordered a hit on their own friend lest he tell investigators what he knew about Whitewater and other scandals. A variation on the story had Hillary and Foster engaged in a long-standing affair. Rush Limbaugh helped put in circulation the rumor that "Vince Foster was murdered in an apartment owned by Hillary Clinton" before his body was removed to Fort Marcy Park.[8]

History is replete with conspiracy theories, some even involving the White House. In the 1930s, there were those who believed that Franklin Roosevelt ordered the assassination of arch-critic Louisiana Senator Huey Long and that Eleanor was inciting black maids in the South to rise up against their white mistresses. In 1991, director Oliver Stone's popular feature film, *JFK*, suggested that Vice President Lyndon Johnson (and dozens of others) may have been behind the Kennedy assassination. Television evangelist Jerry Falwell, whose endorsement had been sought and received by Presidents Reagan and Bush and whose followers numbered in the millions, promoted two videos, *Circle of Power* and *The Clinton Chronicles*, that tied Clinton not only to Foster but to dozens of others who had met their end in plane crashes, car accidents, and under other "mysterious" circumstances. (A separate report put the body count at fifty-six.) The common connection were the Clintons. *The Clinton Chronicles* sold 150,000 copies (at a "suggested" donation price of $40, plus $3 for handling). Evangelist Pat Robertson, host of the daily television program *The 500 Club*, also raised doubts about the official explanation of Foster's death.[9] Indiana Congressman Dan Burton, after visiting the scene of the "alleged suicide" and conducting ballistics tests in his own backyard, took to the floor of the House to tell colleagues that Foster's death could not have been suicide. Although Burton had a reputation for eccentricity, he was no fringe figure but chairman of the influential House Government Reform and Oversight Committee.

The Clintons could no more refute the most outrageous charges against them than disprove the existence of the Loch Ness Monster. But some troubles they brought on themselves, or at least made worse. Whitewater is a case in point. As overblown as it became, it did raise legitimate questions in the beginning. The bare facts were these: Clinton had been governor of a state that regulated savings and loan institutions; the Clintons had entered into a private business deal with the owner of a savings and loan; and the owner of the savings and loan appeared to have borne more than his fair share of the costs of the land deal with the Clintons. Did the owner get something in return? Favored treatment for his savings and loan perhaps? The answer turned out to be no on both counts; but there was nothing wrong with asking questions in the first place. The same was true of the "gates"—Travel-, File-, and Trooper-. But the Clintons' dismissal of questions—by turns cavalier, angry, and resentful—raised suspicions even among those who were predisposed in their favor. Their default setting was the overly aggressive, rapid-response, attack-the-attacker mode honed in the heat of two presidential campaigns. Their long delay in releasing old financial records that might have shed light on accusations added more damage. Hillary Clinton was especially resistant, insisting that disclosure would only feed demands for more disclosure until there would be nothing left of their privacy. When she finally relented, it made her initial reluctance look less like a matter of principle than an effort to avoid embarrassment. Their Arkansas tax returns revealed, for example, that one year she made a profit of $100,000 on an initial investment of $1,000 in cattle futures. The transaction, though legal, was, as the *Wall Street Journal* gleefully pointed out, ironic for a self-described tribune of the middle-class and member of an administration that had come to power promising "to reform the sins of the high-flying 1980s."[10] Of their reluctance to cooperate with investigators, the *New York Times* editorialized that from its first days the administration had "shown a reckless tendency to put the president's desire for a question-free existence ahead of the independence of law enforcement and regulatory officials."[11]

Several tiers below the haters and conspiracy theorists stood those who brought to mind the old nursery rhyme: "I do not like thee Dr. Fell. / The reason why I cannot tell. / But this I know, and know full well. / I do not like thee Dr. Fell." Harvard scholar Henry Louis Gates, who interviewed scores of Clinton critics for an article entitled "Hating Hillary," was struck by the inability of critics to articulate a coherent complaint about the first lady. "In the course of a single conversation," he wrote, "I have been assured that Hillary is cunning and manipulative but also crass, clueless, and stunningly impolitic; that she is a hopelessly woolly-headed do-gooder and, at heart, a hardball litigator; that she is a base opportunist *and* a zealot convinced that God is on her side." For some, like former Reagan and Bush speechwriter Peggy Noonan, it was Hillary's "air of apple-cheeked certitude," for others a belief that the first lady had a heart for humanity in the abstract but none for real people.[12] The Dr. Fell school included many members of the social and political establishment in the nation's capital, some of whom apparently resented the fact that the Clintons hadn't been properly deferential. Some, Henry Louis Gates found, looked upon the president as the members of a private country club might look upon the golf pro. They might like him. They might even invite him to their table for a drink or for dinner. But he would never be one of them, and shouldn't try. In a saying familiar to almost all southerners of a certain age, Bill Clinton was "getting above his raising."

For some defenders, hostility to the Clintons was a reaction to the sixties and its legacies. The first couple, said feminist leader Gloria Steinem, were "presenting, at a very high, visible level, a new paradigm of a male-female relationship. And that is very much resented." Clinton campaign strategist Mandy Grunwald believed that some women felt threatened by Hillary's decision to be more than the subordinate helpmate to her husband. "Hillary forces them to ask questions about themselves and the choices they've made that they don't necessarily want to ask." But the suggestion that sexism had anything to do with their feelings made critics all the angrier. "That's nonsense, that's old, it's not true, and it no longer applies," retorted Peggy Noonan. "And for her to suggest that her problems stem from the fact that there are many Americans that just can't stand a strong woman is infuriating to people, because she's hiding behind charges of 'You are a sexist,' and they think she is trying to divert attention from the real problem, which is who she is and what she's doing."[13] It was left to one of Clinton's oldest friends and greatest admirers to admit that not all of the anger and animosity the Clintons inspired was irrational. "There is something in most clichés that is true," said Strobe Talbott, "or has enough legitimacy to explain how they get to be clichés. 'Slick Willy' was not entirely a fabrication of his detractors—it was a dimension of his persona and his affect."[14]

The Clintons reacted very differently to the hostility they engendered. In the company of friends and aides, the president would go red in the face at the unfairness of it all. "No President has ever been treated like I've been treated," he would shout.[15] Hillary seemed more hurt than angry. With outsiders, she would try to make light of it: "I apparently remind some people of their mother-in-law or their boss, or something."[16] To her close friend, Diane Blair, a political science professor at the University of Arkansas, she expressed defiance. Recounted Blair after one conversation, "She has about come to the conclusion that no matter what she does [it] is going to piss off some people, so [she] will just continue to be herself and let everybody else make whatever adjustments they have to." "I'm a proud woman," Blair remembered Hillary as saying. "I'm not stupid; I know I should do more to suck up to the press, I know it confuses people when I change my hairdos. I know I should pretend not to have any opinions—but I'm just not going to. I'm used to winning and I intend to win on my own terms." She added: "I know how to compromise. I have compromised, I gave up my name, got contact lenses, but I'm not going to try to pretend to be somebody that I'm not." But close observers believed that behind the defiant façade, Hillary was deeply wounded. "I don't know whether she was seeing a doctor or not," said Clinton adviser David Gergen of her mental state.[17]

After the defeat of health care and the 1994 election, the first lady began to retreat into a more traditional role. "My first responsibility, I think" she told one interviewer, "is to do whatever my husband would want me to do that he thinks would be helpful to him. . . . I mean, whatever it takes to kind of be there for him, I think is the most important thing I have to do."[18]

The Clintons had legions of fans, too, although their intensity ran several degrees cooler than the intensity of Clinton foes. Of the president's attributes, his storied ability to empathize with others most endeared

him to supporters. Time and time again, respondents told t
that Clinton better understood ordinary people and their pro
did his opponents. When an AIDS activist accused Clinto
ing the epidemic during a campaign appearance in 1992, Clinton angrily
shot back: "I feel your pain, I feel your pain, but if you want to attack
me personally you're no better than Jerry Brown and all the rest of the
people, who say whatever sounds good at the moment."[19] Taken out
of context, softened in tone, and endlessly repeated, "I feel your pain"
became the emblematic Clinton statement. Readers of journalist Joe
Klein's political novel *Primary Colors* instantly recognized the fictional
Governor Jack Stanton as a Clinton stand-in. In one scene, after hearing
a hard-luck story from someone he's met for the first time, Stanton's
"face was beet red, his blue eyes glistening and tears were rolling down
his cheeks." Another scene has Stanton "in heavy listening mode, the
most aggressive listening the world has ever known: aerobic listening. It
is an intense, disconcerting phenomenon—as if he were hearing quicker
than you can get the words out, as if he were sucking the information out
of you." Close observers were drawn to a line in a memoir by Clinton's
mother about herself and her two sons: "If there are one hundred people
in a room and ninety-nine of them love us and one doesn't, we'll spend
all night trying to figure out why that one hasn't been enlightened."[20]

Just about everyone who ever met Clinton, however briefly, said the
same thing. For that moment, they were the center of his attention. On
a Saturday morning during his last year in the White House, Clinton
and his large entourage paid an unannounced visit to an independent
bookstore in San Jose, California. It was a raucous scene, with patrons,
Secret Service agents, and reporters shouting questions and jostling for
position. But for twenty minutes, recalled the shop owner, "it was like
I was alone with the president, walking up and down the aisles, taking books off the shelves, talking about authors and their works. And I
wasn't talking with the president of the United States but with a smart,
knowledgeable fellow booklover."[21]

Then there was the fabled charm—not the suffocating, overbearing
charm of a Lyndon Johnson, but one low-key and disarming. Novelist
Alice McDermott remembered attending an afternoon party with her
ten-year-old daughter to which the Clintons were invited. The Monica
Lewinsky scandal was in the news. McDermott and her friends were

furious at Clinton for his betrayal of Hillary. They resolved to give him the cold shoulder even if he was the president. Upon arriving, Clinton almost immediately spotted McDermott's daughter awkwardly standing alone while the adults all around her talked with one another. He went over to her, knelt down on one knee, and engaged her in conversation. Nobody but the president had paid the slightest attention to her, McDermott recalled, shaking her head and smiling as if to say, "You just couldn't stay mad at the guy." When Clinton announced his intention to sign the Republican welfare bill in 1996, historian Arthur Schlesinger, "infuriated and depressed," "resolved to stop defending Clinton in the future." His resolve lasted less than a month. Invited to attend a large celebration in honor of the president's fiftieth birthday, Schlesinger heard himself singled out for praise in the president's opening remarks. Later, when he started to introduce his son Robert to the president, Clinton interrupted: "I remember Robert. He represented your family at the Roosevelt dinner." Then Clinton made flattering reference to the historian's theory about recurrent cycles in American political history. Clinton's "talk of the Schlesinger cycles, his personal magnetism and his official power worked their insidious charm," Schlesinger wrote in his personal journal. "I am almost prepared to start defending Clinton again." During the impeachment crisis, Schlesinger would be one of the president's most prominent defenders.[22] Years after he had resigned from the administration in protest of welfare reform, Peter Edelman ran into Clinton at a memorial service. The president held his hand and said, "I'm so glad to see you. How are you doing? How's Marian? How's Josh? How's Jonah? How's Ezra?" *He's doing it to me*, Edelman remembered thinking to himself. Even Clinton's foes found themselves falling under his spell. "I've got a problem. I get in those meetings and as a person I like the president," Newt Gingrich told a reporter. "I melt when I'm around him. After I get out, I need two hours to detoxify. My people are nervous about me going in there because of the way I deal with this."[23] Clinton also had a gift for projecting his empathetic charm to the unseen millions on the other side of the television camera. For a moment at least, viewers could feel as though he were talking personally to them.

Roger Altman, who served for two years as deputy Treasury secretary, believed the first lady forged a stronger bond with her staff than the president did with his. "She inspires fierce loyalty and he doesn't."

When people came to work for Hillary, they stayed. Not so with the president. Altman attributed the difference "to the fact that she does not look at the world as . . . solely and only political. She wears her heart on her sleeve much more than he does."[24]

President Clinton's relationship with one group of supporters, African Americans, attracted special attention, especially after famed African American novelist Toni Morrison, in 1998, embraced Clinton as "the first black President." He was not always viewed so favorably. During the 1992 campaign, many blacks viewed him warily. This was because of his identification with the centrist Democratic Leadership Council and his efforts to distance himself from civil rights leader Jesse Jackson, even to the point of seeming to pick fights with Jackson. He supported the death penalty despite mounting evidence of its discriminatory application. The 82 percent of the black vote that Clinton garnered that year was the lowest percentage earned by any Democratic candidate since passage of the Voting Rights Act, in 1965.[25]

Once in office, Clinton's cabinet appointments, coupled with his close relationship with civil rights icon Vernon Jordan, momentarily raised black hopes. But doubts quickly resurfaced in the wake of his bungled appointment of Lani Guinier to head the Justice Department's Civil Rights Division. "Oh here we go again," a black journalist recalled thinking. "Another white boy in office who is talking the talk, but definitely not walking the walk." By the spring of 1993, Clinton's approval rating among blacks had fallen thirty points.[26]

As the 1996 election approached, Clinton began to make up for lost ground. His high-profile reaffirmation of affirmative action—"mend it, don't break it"—helped, as did his support for expanding the Earned Income Tax Credit, which lifted millions of black Americans out of poverty. But then came welfare reform, and in the election his support among African Americans dropped two percentage points from 1992.[27]

The turning point in relations between Clinton and African Americans initially had less to do with Clinton than with his enemies. Having failed to defeat Clinton at the polls in 1996, foes began to talk about impeachment. "He had the right enemies," recalled columnist Betty Baye. "I think African Americans looked at his enemies and saw the same crew that's been beating up on us." Following the election, blacks began to take another look at Clinton and to see commonalities between their story and his. "After all," wrote Toni Morrison in her famous essay, "Clinton displays almost every trope of blackness: single-parent household, born poor, working-class, saxophone-playing, McDonald's-and-junk-food-loving boy from Arkansas." But what most resonated was the treatment of Clinton by his enemies. Their message to Clinton, wrote Morrison, was clear: "No matter how smart you are, how hard you work, how much coin you earn for us, we will put you in your place or put you out of the place you have somehow, albeit with our permission, achieved. You will be fired from your job, sent away in disgrace, and—who knows?—maybe sentenced and jailed to boot. In short, unless you do as we say (i.e., assimilate at once), your expletives belong to us."[28] Comedian Chris Rock concurred. "I view Clinton as the first black President," he told an interviewer. "He's the most scrutinized man in history, just as a black person would be. . . . He spends a hundred-dollar bill, they hold it up to the light."[29]

Critics, black and white, bristled at Morrison and Rock's equating the treatment of Clinton with black persecution at the hands of whites. But they couldn't deny the bond between the president and African Americans, which, though a marriage of convenience before 1996, had grown immeasurably stronger thereafter, as attacks on the president continued to mount. Blacks started appreciating things about Clinton that had been there all along, like his enthusiastic, and totally unaffected, embrace of black culture. "That boy blew saxophone," said Joseph Lowry, one-time president of the Southern Christian Leadership Conference. "He wasn't no Chew Berry or Sonny Hodges. . . . But a saxophone is about as black an instrument as you can get." Or as columnist Deborah Mathis put it: "He was not only a white man who came to our church, but he was also one who clapped with the downbeat. He enjoyed our music, knew a lot of songs, and had some black hipness about him." Appreciated, too, was Clinton's celebration of the civil rights movement as a victory for whites as well as blacks. Many took notice that unlike the stereotypical white racist who claims that "some of his best friends were black," Clinton actually had a black best friend, Vernon Jordan. Mickey Kantor liked to illustrate the president's color-blind relationship with Jordan by telling about the time, in 1996, when the president asked Kantor, Leon Panetta, and Erskine Bowles to oversee the transition process from the first term to the second. In addition to the three of them, Clinton said, "we should get Vernon, Vernon will be the fourth." Then the president "looks and says, 'You know, God, we ought to have somebody from the black community.'" Not until his advisors burst out laughing did the president realize what he'd said.[30]

It was perhaps a telling comment about the state of race relations in the last decade of the twentieth century that African Americans seemed most impressed simply by how comfortable Clinton was in their presence. "Bill Clinton is probably the most comfortable Caucasian around black people that most of us have ever seen," said lawyer Johnnie Cochran, who gained fame as O. J. Simpson's defense lawyer. "Someone told me he must have been breast-fed by a black woman because he's so comfortable around us," said reporter April Woodward.[31]

Anti-Clinton fervor came to a head during the impeachment crisis that imperiled his presidency and dominated much of his second term. The tangled origins of the crisis stretched back to Clinton's first years in the White House, if not earlier. In January 1994, under intense pressure from critics, Clinton agreed to the appointment of an independent counsel to investigate Whitewater, the various "gates," and the circumstances surrounding the death of Vince Foster. A legacy of Watergate, the independent counsel, also known as the special prosecutor, had become something of an institution. It was an institution no president wanted but no president could do without, at least not without appearing to be hiding something. Clinton's White House counsel, Bernard Nussbaum, who had served as counsel to the House Judiciary Committee that recommended the impeachment of Richard Nixon, warned Clinton that the appointment of a special prosecutor would be asking for trouble. Not that Clinton had done anything wrong, Nussbaum said, it was just in the nature of the institution. "This will last as long as you're President and beyond. They'll be investigating things years from now that we haven't even dreamed about today. . . . They will chase your family. They'll chase you." But the pressure from Clinton's other advisers, from the press, and from prominent members of his own party was too hard to resist. During the president's first trip to Eastern Europe, all reporters seemed interested in were the alleged scandals. "The press is on me," he complained to aides. "I'm in the Ukraine. I can't have a press conference about foreign policy without somebody asking me about Whitewater. . . . This is terrible what's happening."[32]

Clinton's first special prosecutor, respected Republican jurist Robert Fiske, issued a preliminary report that, while not uncritical of the Clintons, cited no evidence of illegal activity on their part—a finding that convinced the president's foes that Fiske hadn't dug deeply enough. Meanwhile, with Fiske's statutory authority about to expire, Clinton yielded to political realities and extended the statutory life of the independent counsel. He did so fully expecting Fiske to quickly wrap up his investigation and issue to the Clintons a clean bill of health. But Clinton had no sooner reauthorized Fiske's position than events took an unexpected turn. It so happened that a three-member judicial panel in Washington had final say on who could or couldn't serve as independent counsel. Perhaps sharing the suspicion of Clinton's critics that Fiske hadn't been thorough enough, panel members replaced him with a new counsel, Kenneth Starr, who, though a conservative Republican, had a judicial background above reproach.

During the next two years, Starr and his deputies retraced all of his predecessor's steps—over Whitewater, Travelgate, Filegate, Troopergate, and Vince Foster; and while they uncovered wrongdoing by several Clinton associates, they found no definitive evidence of wrongdoing by the Clintons. According to one thoughtful student of the investigation, law professor and writer Ken Gormley, up to this point "Starr was not the diabolical Clinton-slayer that some (including Bill Clinton) would later make him out to be." Instead he was "deliberate and cautious . . . following closely in the footsteps of his predecessor Fiske."[33] Then, in 1997, following Clinton's reelection, Starr's investigation took its fateful turn. Tipped off by an informer, Starr began to look into allegations that Clinton had lied under oath while testifying in a civil suit filed by Paula Jones, an Arkansas woman who had accused Clinton of having sexually harassed her when he was governor and she was a state employee. During the course of the questioning, the lawyers for Paula Jones, also acting on a tip, asked Clinton if he had had a sexual relationship with a twenty-four-year-old White House intern named Monica Lewinsky. Clinton denied the allegation. Predictably, word of the allegation and of the president's denial soon leaked out, eventually finding its way to an obscure Internet website operated by Matthew Drudge. Clinton once again denied the charge, this time publicly. "I did not have sex with that woman," he said, stabbing his finger at the camera as he spoke.

But when Starr summoned Clinton to testify before a federal grand jury, Clinton altered his story. He still denied having sex with Lewinsky but now conceded that they had engaged in an "inappropriate relationship." The worst was still to come. Unbeknownst to the president, Monica Lewinsky, under pressure from the staff of the independent counsel, provided explicit details of her intimate relationship with the president. She also turned over to Starr's office a blue dress stained with semen that DNA tests later confirmed to be the president's.

In September 1998, Starr delivered to the House of Representatives a 354-page report detailing eleven actions of the president that, in Starr's words, "may constitute grounds for impeachment." The most serious charges were that Clinton had lied under oath and that he had obstructed justice by encouraging others to lie under oath. In addition to this, Starr supplied the House with thirty-six boxes of transcripts and other evidence collected over the previous four years. Two days later the House voted overwhelmingly to make Starr's report public. The last time a comparable document had been released to the public had been during the Nixon administration, and reporters and interested citizens had lined up for hours outside the Government Printing Office to get the first copies. In the Internet age, the Starr Report was available within minutes of its release to anyone with access to an online computer.

It was an instant sensation. In explicit detail the report recounted an on-again, off-again relationship between the president and the intern that lasted sixteen months and that included ten sexual encounters in rooms adjacent to the Oval Office and fifteen instances of "telephone sex." Within an hour, wrote one reporter, "the nation began history's first simultaneous reaction to smut. In coffee shops and exercise gyms, at soccer practices and cybercafés, Americans expressed exasperation, amusement, sorrow and anger as they scanned the voluminous text, stunned by its explicit recitations of the president's alleged sexual behavior."[34] Before reporting on the scandal, television stations advised viewers they might want to remove children from the room. *Newsweek*

predicted readers would want to "throw up" after reading about the
sexual acts detailed in the Starr Report, while Fox News tantalizingly
referred to those same acts as "unusual."[35]

Even before the release of the Starr Report, some prominent Democrats, including Senators Joseph Lieberman, Daniel Moynihan, and Bob
Kerrey, had denounced Clinton's actions as immoral and the president
"as deserving of rebuke."[36] Upon reading the report, senior House
Democrat David Obey told a colleague, "We have to get rid of this guy.
He will destroy the Democratic Party for a generation."[37] Within days,
some thirty newspapers, from Philadelphia to Atlanta to Seattle, called
upon the president to resign.[38] Longtime Clinton friends and aides were
furious. "For the love of God," Joe Purvis, a lifelong Clinton friend, recalled thinking, "if the son of a bitch was so stupid to do something like
that, he deserves what he gets."[39] Health and Human Service Secretary
Donna Shalala, a former university chancellor, likened what the president had done to a college professor "hitting" on a student. "It was the
young person thing," she recalled. "I've fired tenured professors over
this, and it was just unacceptable." And she told him so at a cabinet
meeting. "Everyone was being a bit of an apologist for him in the room
and I just blew up."[40]

The Starr Report led to much handwringing among politicians and
pundits about the moral climate of the nation. How could parents raise
their children to know right from wrong when the president was setting
such a bad example? "I approach this as a mother," said ABC commentator Cokie Roberts. "We have a right to say to this President, 'What
you have done is an example to our children that's a disgrace.'"[41]

More surprises awaited, but none bigger than the fact that the public
didn't react the way most pundits expected. Clinton continued to come
under blistering attack. But gradually attention shifted from president to
prosecutor (with help from the White House, it should be added). The
sheer volume of salacious material, including repetitive accounts of oral
sex and masturbation, struck many as either sickly obsessive or proof
that the independent counsel was out to destroy and humiliate Clinton.
"You don't have to show the severed head of a victim to show that the
victim died, and you don't have to show all these graphic details about
sex to show that sex took place," said Lawrence Fox, former chair to the
American Bar Association's ethics committee.[42] The public seemed to

agree. Following the release of the Starr Report, Clinton's job approval rating held steady at 60 percent. As the off-year elections in November approached, House Speaker Gingrich predicted a Republican landslide. Instead the GOP lost five seats in the House. Gingrich, who had directed his colleagues to make Clinton the issue in their campaigns, was forced by his colleagues to relinquish the speakership. Soon thereafter he left the House altogether.

The election returns, coupled with Clinton's poll numbers, confounded his critics. "Where's the outrage?" they said in unison, echoing Bob Dole's lament during the 1996 campaign. That the public wasn't "rising up in righteous indignation," said one commentator, "casts shame on the entire country."[43] James Dobson, head of the conservative Focus on the Family, declared that "our greatest problem is not in the Oval Office—it is with the people of this land."[44] It was as if the public had become "an unindicted co-conspirator," writer Joan Didion tellingly observed.

The reason the country wasn't rising up in righteous indignation and demanding Clinton's ouster from office didn't mean that people condoned the president's behavior. Far from it. His personal approval ratings—as opposed to his job performance rating—plummeted. Rather the absence of fresh outrage stemmed from the fact that in a sense the public had long since taken Clinton's measure. "Nothing that is now known about the forty-second President of the United States, in other words, was not known before the New Hampshire primary in 1992," wrote Joan Didion after the release of the Starr Report. Then, even as candidate Clinton was denying an affair with Gennifer Flowers, voters concluded that faithfulness to his wedding vows was probably the least of Clinton's virtues. But they had also concluded that he possessed other virtues useful in a president. They had agreed with the editors of the *Peoria Journal-Star* who, during the 1992 campaign, declared that with all the problems confronting the country, there was just one thing to say about Clinton's alleged marital infidelity: "So what? And that's all." When the Lewinsky scandal broke, the answer, for most people, stayed the same.[45]

Nor was it surprising that the details of the president's sex life, as chronicled in graphic detail by Starr, failed to elicit the mass, stomach-churning revulsion predicted by pundits and hoped for by Clinton's foes. As any number of studies demonstrated—studies going back to the Kinsey reports of the late forties and early fifties—Clinton and Lewinsky broke no new ground. Their activities were fairly commonplace as such things go, and after a while the tedium induced by reading about them was only relieved by the occasional riveting detail, such as the famously multitasking president taking phone calls from members of Congress while simultaneously carrying on with Lewinsky.

Rather than being chastened by Clinton's poll numbers or the outcome of the congressional elections, the president's Republican critics stepped up their assault. On December 12, 1998, the House Judiciary Committee, chaired by Illinois Republican Henry Hyde, approved four articles of impeachment, the most serious of which charged the president with perjury and obstruction of justice. Rejecting a sternly worded censure motion proposed by several Democrats, the full House, voting primarily along party lines, adopted two articles of impeachment, thus making Clinton only the second president in history to have to stand trial in the Senate. The first, Andrew Johnson, had been spared conviction by a single vote in proceedings dominated by the volatile and partisan politics of Reconstruction. Richard Nixon avoided almost certain impeachment and conviction by resigning the presidency in August 1974.

The House's action prompted the inevitable comparisons between the only two modern presidents to face the threat of impeachment. Superficially, they seemed like Janus-faced opposites—one outgoing and gregarious, the other introverted and awkward, a loner "whose choice of politics as a career was the most mysterious thing about him," as columnist Mary McGrory once described Nixon. Ideologically they were mirror images of one another, too: Nixon was more liberal than his base, Clinton more conservative than his. Even their misdeeds fell on different ends of the spectrum. McGrory again: Clinton's were "sordid," Nixon's "sinister." Yet the similarities between the two men were striking, if not startling, which helps account for the fascination each held for the other. Both hailed "from modest backgrounds, helped neither by blood nor money."[46] They viewed themselves as conspicuous players on the historical stage. They stirred more hatred than love and wallowed in petulance and self-pity. Their self-destructive streaks forever threatened to turn triumph into travail. For detractors, often journalists whom they held in complete disdain, Nixon would always be "Tricky Dick," Clinton "Slick Willy."

Following impeachment, a line from the eulogy Clinton delivered at Nixon's funeral took on new meaning: "Let us say, may the day of judging President Nixon on anything less than his entire life and career come to a close."

In truth, many Democrats, even those professing loyalty to the president, would not have shed a tear if Clinton had followed Nixon's example and left office on his own. Vice President Gore would have been a perfectly acceptable alternative to the chaotic debate about to get under way. And Democratic chances of holding the White House would seem to have been enhanced by giving Gore a two-year head start. Clinton would not hear of it. He let everyone know he would fight to the end. Years later he told an interviewer that memory of how his enemies had tried to blame him and Hillary for the death of Vince Foster also stiffened his resolve. "My country doesn't belong in the hands of people who think like this," he said. "This is not human. . . . This is way beyond the pale if people think that kind of behavior is legitimate." He compared Starr's pursuit to "a Stalinist show trial."[47]

Impeachment brought out in Clinton a disciplined focus and steely determination aides had not seen before. As the Senate debated his fate, he dealt firmly with crises in Iraq and the Middle East even at the risk of playing into the hands of critics who accused him of trying to distract the public from the impeachment inquiry. In a coincidence so bizarre it was almost laughable, one of the most provocative movies of 1998, *Wag the Dog*, came out just weeks before the Clinton-Lewinsky scandal broke. A brilliant satire, *Wag the Dog* told the story of a president who jeopardizes his reelection by fondling an underage visitor to the Oval Office. A crafty aide comes to the rescue by arranging for a fake war to be staged in Albania, a war that allows the president to win back public support by assuming the heroic mantle of commander in chief. The film put Clinton into a classic damned-if-you-do, damned-if-you-don't situation, for it had barely left theatres when Clinton's military high command unanimously recommended that he order bombing strikes, first against Sudan for allegedly developing chemical weapons, then against Iraq for its refusal to cooperate with weapons inspectors. If he refused to act, he would look weak; if he acted, he would look like a crass opportunist. With little hesitation, Clinton authorized the strikes. "This President is shameless in what he would do to stay in office," said a Florida congresswoman. "He will use our military and he will use our foreign policy to remain President." Several prominent Republicans tried to drum up support for an additional article of impeachment condemning the action.[48] But as in the movie, and to the consternation of Republicans, this episode ended happily for the president, with public opinion approving the air strikes.

As the impeachment drama unfolded in the Senate, one other factor, although little appreciated at the time, was working to Clinton's advantage. This was an almost cult-like devotion to the presidency itself, and it formed a kind of protective shield around Clinton. Following the GOP takeover of Congress in 1994, Clinton had felt compelled to assure the press that the president was still "relevant." He need not have worried. Franklin Roosevelt had made the presidency, of the branches of government, first among equals. But Godfrey Hodgson, the journalist and historian, dated the cult of the presidency to the 1950s and early 1960s, when liberals and conservatives alike made it an article of faith that a strong and active president was vital to the progress and security of the nation. That first wave of presidential exultation had produced scores of books from commercial and academic presses chronicling and extolling the rise of the modern presidency. Concerns about an "imperial presidency" during Vietnam and Watergate tamped down enthusiasm for an activist chief executive—but only momentarily.[49] For it was during Clinton's tenure that the presidency moved to a hallowed place at or near the center of American culture. "We live under an elective monarch," wrote political scientist Walter Dean Burnham. "Even in jaded late-twentieth century America the presidency as office has a regal aspect, including a touch of 'the divinity that doth hedge a king.'" "More than that," Burnham added, "Presidents are called on to be in a sense high priests of American civil religion; most visible in inaugural ceremonies, the liturgical function extends far beyond that."[50] Presidential politics also became something approaching the country's favorite form of entertainment. Between 1993 and 2000, more than fifty-five books about Clinton or his predecessors made the *New York Times* bestseller list for nonfiction, an unprecedented number for a comparable span of time. Purporting to go "Inside the Clinton White House" or "Behind the Oval Office" or "Inside the Complex Marriage of Bill and Hillary," many went heavy on process, personality, and character and light on policy; and this held true not only for books about the Clintons but also for books about their predecessors. Bestselling works of fiction also appeared, including Joe Klein's thinly veiled account of Clinton's 1992 campaign, *Primary Colors*, which was a kind of updated version of Robert Penn Warren's classic, *All the King's Men*.[51]

Hollywood fed the public's appetite for all-things-presidential with an unprecedented spate of movies featuring fictional chief executives. In some, like *Absolute Power, Murder at 1600, Executive Power*, and the aforementioned *Wag the Dog*, the president was a scoundrel. In others, like *Air Force One* and *Independence Day*, he was an action hero doing battle with hijackers in one and invaders from outer space in the other.[52] In the best of them, *Primary Colors*, based on the Joe Klein novel, the Clinton stand-in, played by John Travolta, was a richly complex combination of good and bad, invested, as one critic noted, "with a tragic human grandeur."[53] Late in the Clinton administration, the presidency made its way into the long-running television series *The West Wing*, for which several former Clinton advisers served as consultants. In 1997, just as the Monica Lewinsky scandal was about to break, a cable channel documentary, *Bill Clinton: Rock 'n' Roll President*, narrated by singer Carly Simon, whom the Clintons had befriended during their vacations on Martha's Vineyard, celebrated Clinton's love of music.[54]

Long before impeachment, Clinton jokes had become a staple of late-night comics. It was by no means certain that Clinton was harmed by the almost nightly attention. In fact, during the impeachment crisis, he may even have reaped considerable benefits. The sheer repetition of Clinton jokes—over 1,000 Clinton jokes on late-night television during the first nine months of 1998 alone, according to an institute that studied such things—probably helped trivialize the scandal. At the very time impeachment supporters were accusing the president of a grave breach of the public trust, humorists Jay Leno and David Letterman were boiling the whole thing down to a simple sex scandal. "Watergate wasn't funny," said one media observer. "It was serious." But the Clinton-Lewinsky scandal: "It's the joke on the boss that we all like, and we're really enjoying this." "Oh, the sex and chubby girls and all the power—what's better than that?" said Jay Leno during an interview on *Meet the Press* about the state of political humor in the United States. "If this thing gets any more sleazy, President Clinton's approval rating could shoot up to 100%," said Letterman.[55] It didn't hurt Clinton either that comics took particular delight in pointing out that some of his most outspoken critics, such as House leaders Henry Hyde and Robert Livingston and later Newt Gingrich, were themselves revealed to have had adulterous relationships.

There was no better example of the cult of the presidency than the emergence during the nineties of a new species of historian—the presidential historian, who helped transform all of American political history into presidential history. Historians, biographers, and political scientists had been writing about presidents for ages. But they would have been reluctant to describe themselves as presidential historians for fear of looking like "court historians" who serve the crown and not the craft. The presidential historian was largely a media creation, most probably dating to the early nineties, when public television's *MacNeil-Lehrer News Hour* began to showcase Michael Beschloss and Doris Kearns Goodwin on its nightly newscast and to introduce them as "Presidential historians." Princeton historian Sean Wilentz described the presidential historian as a "hitherto unknown scholarly species whose chief function is to offer television viewers anodyne tidbits of historical trivia that seem pertinent to current political events, and to look and sound remarkable when doing so."[56]

Wilentz might be critical of presidential historians, but he had a typically expansive view of the presidency itself. During the impeachment crisis, he rallied his professional colleagues across the country in defense of the president. With eminent historians Arthur Schlesinger and C. Vann Woodward, Wilentz drafted a statement to which over 400 scholars affixed their names. "Although we do not condone President Clinton's private behavior or his subsequent attempts to deceive," the statement read, "the current charges against him depart from what the Framers saw as grounds for impeachment." The theory underlying the impeachment drive, it asserted, was "unprecedented in our history," a threat to the Constitution, and if allowed to prevail would "leave the Presidency permanently disfigured and diminished, at the mercy as never before of the caprices of any Congress. The Presidency, historically the center of leadership during our great national ordeals, will be crippled in meeting the inevitable challenges of the future." Testifying before the House Judiciary Committee, Wilentz warned members that anyone voting for impeachment risked "going down in history with zealots and fanatics." "If you decide to do this," he said, "you will have done far more to subvert respect for the framers, for representative government, and for the rule of law than any crime that has been alleged against President Clinton, and your reputations will be darkened for as long as there are Americans who can tell the difference between the rule of law and the rule of politics." More than 400 law professors added their voices to those of the historians.[57] (Conservative scholars, such as Gary L. McDowell and Forrest McDonald, while stopping short of explicitly recommending impeachment, testified that some of the president's alleged misdeeds, including perjury, constituted "high crimes and misdemeanors" as the Framers of the Constitution understood them.)[58]

The upshot of all this obsessive focus on the presidency—even if the current occupant could be treated with derision from time to time—was to strengthen Clinton's hold on the office during the perilous impeachment crisis. His foes faced a problem akin to that Franklin Roosevelt had faced when he tried to pack the Supreme Court. Long a symbol of national unity, the court had become a sacred cow in the American political system.[59] Something like it had happened to the presidency by the nineties.

The chances of two-thirds of the Senate voting to convict Clinton were probably always pretty remote. But Clinton himself put any remaining doubts to rest during his State of the Union address in January 1999. Taking the podium just hours after the Senate recessed its trial for the day, he delivered a tour de force, his most masterful political performance since the health-care speech before the same body in 1993. Supremely in command, Clinton held forth for more than an hour. Not once did he directly refer to impeachment, though of course his listeners could think of little else. Clinton was by turns gracious to his foes, humorous, and substantive. Not once did he display the bitterness he felt toward many of the legislators sitting before him. It helped that he had good news to report: a booming economy, unemployment at a forty-year low, the welfare rolls the smallest in thirty years, wages growing at twice the rate of inflation. On top of everything else, the budget was in the black for the first time in years. A closer look behind the numbers might have revealed a less glowing picture. The distribution of wealth, for example, continued to be a problem. Still, by almost any other measure, things were looking good. As Clinton's speechwriter observed, for Republican onlookers, whose glum demeanor contrasted with the president's buoyant optimism, the address was like having a "root canal."[60]

Clinton also packed the address with substantive recommendations, such as dedicating most of the accumulating budget surplus to shoring up Social Security and Medicare. In a bow to those who wanted to privatize Social Security, Clinton proposed creating Universal Savings Accounts (USA), which would allow citizens to invest some of their earnings as they saw fit. Revisiting his agenda as governor, he proposed that the government should both require public school teachers to take competency tests and deny federal aid to schools that promoted students from grade to grade regardless of academic performance.

Response to the speech was not long in coming. "From a public relations standpoint, he's won," said televangelist Pat Robertson, who once had been in the vanguard of those trying to implicate the Clintons in the death of Vince Foster. Concluded Robertson: "They might as well dismiss the impeachment hearings and get on with something else, because it's over as far as I'm concerned."[61]

Clinton had won the public relations battle, but serious questions remained. Any fair reading of the evidence demonstrated that Clinton had at least misled, if not outright lied to, a federal grand jury. More troubling, even to Clinton's defenders, was the evidence that Clinton had coached his personal secretary, Betty Currie, to provide false information to investigators, which was an obstruction of justice. Curiously, the most damaging evidence against the president, and the evidence that most worried his attorneys, didn't even make it into the House's articles of impeachment. That was Clinton's sworn testimony in the Paula Jones civil suit that not only did he not have sex with Lewinsky but that he could not recall ever even being alone with her.

In the end, the case against Clinton came down to a single question:

By lying to, or at least misleading, a grand jury under oath did Clinton commit *the high crimes and misdemeanors* required by the Constitution for impeachment? His defenders argued that the founders had intended high crimes and misdemeanors to pertain to actions committed in an official capacity as president, not to personal failings. Opponents argued that Clinton had violated his sworn constitutional obligation to "see that the laws are faithfully executed." In the end, a majority of senators, as well as most historians and constitutional scholars, believed that Clinton's actions lacked the public component required by the founding fathers for removal from office. On February 12, 1999, the Senate acquitted Clinton on both articles of impeachment. On the charge of perjury, 45 Democrats and 10 Republicans voted not guilty. On the charge of obstruction of justice, the senators split 50–50, far short of the two-thirds required by the constitution to convict.

The outcome did little to soothe partisan feelings. For the rest of his days in office—and long after—Clinton believed that he had been the victim of an unjust crusade to destroy him by any means possible. He compared his impeachment supporters to religious zealots who believed God had "ordained them to crush the infidels." And if they had to ignore the facts and the rules of evidence, and the rule of law, then so be it. As for Kenneth Starr, he was "their errand boy. And he danced to their tune, just as hard as he could dance." Clinton's foes were just as convinced that he was in the wrong. Jackie Bennett, a high-ranking member of Starr's staff, later expressed the sentiments of many when he described Clinton as "the most corrupt political figure . . . we've ever had."[62]

Nor were Clinton's legal troubles over. He had vanquished Kenneth Starr and congressional Republicans, but Starr's successor as independent counsel, Robert Ray, continued where Starr had left off. The drama did not end until Clinton's last day in office when, as a condition of avoiding probable indictment after he left office, he admitted that he had lied under oath during the Paula Jones civil suit. He also agreed to pay a stiff financial penalty and not to contest the decision of the Arkansas Bar to strip him of his license to practice law.

Clinton survived impeachment, but not without sustaining casualties. None was probably closer to his heart than his ambitious, though widely underestimated, initiative on race. He set the stage for the initiative during his second inaugural address. "The divide of race has been America's constant curse," he said. "And each new wave of immigrants gives new targets to old prejudices. . . . These forces have nearly destroyed our Nation in the past. They plague us still." But if Americans could overcome the "dark impulses" of the soul and celebrate rather than scorn their diversity they would reap great benefits in the new twenty-first century. When Clinton talked about race, which he did with increasing frequency after 1996, commentators, especially white commentators, didn't know quite what to make of it. Most ignored it. "A string of bland banalities," wrote *Washington Post* media critic Tom Shales of the Inaugural Address. "In many ways, it sounded like a stump speech rather than an inaugural address," was the verdict of NBC's Tim Russert. No quotable lines, complained writer Jeff Greenfield, who had once written speeches for Robert Kennedy.[63] A few knew better. They knew that when Clinton talked about race, his words could be taken at face value.[64]

Clinton wanted to improve race relations. But how? Should he establish an independent commission like the famous Kerner Commission Lyndon Johnson established in the wake of the race riots that swept the nation in the sixties? Or should he initiate a national conversation on race, perhaps by holding a series of town hall meetings to be followed by a report to the nation? And in either case, should he limit the focus to race relations or expand it to include other victims of discrimination such as women, persons with disabilities, and gays and lesbians? After conferring with nearly two dozen civil rights and other leaders, Clinton's chief of staff, Erskine Bowles, and deputy chief of staff, Sylvia Mathews, outlined for the president the pros and cons of the various approaches. The chief drawback to a Kerner-like commission, they concluded, would be its independence from the White House: "Depending on the membership of the commission, it could give control over large aspects of your domestic agenda—involving, for example, welfare, education, and criminal justice—to an outside body that may or may not agree with your priorities or accept the constraints of your budget. Of course, you could reject all or part of the commission's eventual recommendations, but that could present a difficult situation." Appointing members to the commission could also be tricky. "Does Jesse Jackson have a place on the Commission? Colin Powell? How wide or narrow should be the spectrum of ideologies represented?" Nor, Clinton's aides noted, would a commission necessarily "take full advantage of your unique talent on the issue. You have the unprecedented ability to talk about race in a way that the American people respond to and to construct your *own* agenda for racial reconciliation."[65] In the end, Clinton chose the town hall option. So as not to go off in too many directions at the same time, he decided to limit the focus of the initiative primarily, though not exclusively, to race relations.

Clinton unveiled his race initiative during a commencement address at the University of California, San Diego, in June 1997. That he chose to make the announcement in California was no accident. It was there in 1992 that sixty persons died when riots erupted after the acquittal of four white policemen who had been videotaped beating black motorist Rodney King; and there in 1995 that a predominantly black jury had acquitted black football star O. J. Simpson on charges he had murdered his white wife and her friend; and there in 1996 that voters had amended the state's constitution to ban the use of affirmative action in public employment and public education. It was time, Clinton told graduates, to have a dialogue on race. "We have talked at each other and about each other for a long time. It's high time we all begin talking with each other." To that end, he said he was appointing a seven-member advisory committee "to help educate Americans about the facts surrounding issues of race, . . . to recruit and encourage leadership at all levels to help breach racial divisions, and to recommend how to implement concrete solutions to our problems." To head the committee, Clinton chose the eminent African American historian John Hope Franklin. A mixed reaction greeted the president's announcement. "Some felt that it was high time that the leaders in the United States took the initiative in calling for the nation to confront the race problem," recalled Franklin.[66] The most common reaction, however, was a collective "ho-hum." "It's all in keeping with time-honored Washington tradition," wrote *Washington Post* reporter Peter Carlson. "Presidents appoint boards, which hold hearings, write reports and make recommendations. Sometimes, the reports are actually read. Occasionally, the recommendations are even implemented, although that is not considered essential to the process."[67]

Determined to prove the skeptics wrong, the committee initiated what it called "a great and unprecedented conversation about race." During the next fifteen months, the committee initiated over 1,000 meetings during which participants exchanged views on race. Some meetings featured corporate and religious leaders. Most brought together "small groups of friends, neighbors, and coworkers." President Clinton presided over three televised forums. In April 1998, the committee helped organize a week's worth of race-related discussions at six hundred colleges and universities. In its final report, issued in September 1998, the committee noted that although life had gotten better for minorities, "persistent barriers to their full inclusion in American society remain." Its most important conclusion—unsurprising but no less significant— was that Americans held racial views so different "that an outsider could easily believe that whites and most minorities and people of color see the world through different lenses." Most whites thought prejudice was largely a thing of the past and that further investigation into it, much less action, was "unwarranted and inappropriate." Members of racial and ethnic minorities thought prejudice was an ever-present reality in their lives. Unless common ground could be found, the Franklin committee argued, it would be difficult to "improve race relations, eliminate disparities, and create equal opportunities in all areas of American life." And the best way to find common ground was to continue the interracial dialogue the Franklin committee had begun, through, among other things, the establishment of a permanent President's Council for One America.[68]

Like the president's initial announcement of the race initiative, the committee's report received a tepid response. Some civil rights advocates complained that the committee came up short. "There are not a lot of bold, new or exciting recommendations in the report," wrote a leading official of a Hispanic advocacy group. "Wishy-washy," said black columnist Clarence Page. Conservatives took the committee to task for ducking frank discussions of affirmative action and the destabilizing role of out-of-wedlock-births among minorities. Many dismissed the whole effort as a waste of time.[69]

Issued seven days after the Starr Report, the committee's report and the committee itself were soon forgotten. Lamented John Hope Franklin, "That the color line had damned the country for centuries, that national initiatives to confront the problem had been all too rare, and that the board was in fact encouraging the very conversation it was charged with, could not compete with a media more interested in digging up whatever it could to fan interest in events so obviously ephemeral in comparison."[70] More formidable as an obstacle to continuing the dialogue was the fact that, as the Franklin board itself had discovered, a majority of white Americans believed there was nothing to talk about. The problem of race had already been solved. Preoccupied with impeachment and morally compromised, Clinton was in no position to convince them otherwise.

8

The "New" Economy, 1998–2000

No economist wants to be remembered as a modern-day Irving Fischer, the eminent Yale professor who on the eve of the Great Stock Market Crash of 1929 proclaimed that "stock prices have reached what looks like a permanently high plateau."[1]

And yet the eminent economists who served in the Clinton administration had a hard time containing their enthusiasm as they surveyed the financial state of the nation during the president's final years in office. "Over the last 8 years," the members of the Council of Economic Advisers wrote in their final report to Congress, "the American economy has transformed itself so radically that many believe we have witnessed the creation of a New Economy." Lest anyone doubt that they included themselves in the ranks of the believers, they promised that their report would be replete with "evidence of fundamental and unanticipated changes in economic trends."[2] They hastened to add that these fundamental and unanticipated changes were almost entirely positive. Federal Reserve Chairman Alan Greenspan—whom one journalist described as resembling a "mountain rescue dog . . . with sad brown eyes, a big, bulbous nose, and a long, narrow mouth, the corners of which are often turned down, giving him a mournful cast"—believed it was his duty to dampen enthusiasm lest things get out of control. By the late nineties, even he was hailing the birth of a new economy.[3]

And why not? President Clinton had not been exaggerating when he boasted about the rosy state of the economy in his State of the Union address in January 1999—the address that essentially ended the drive to oust him from office. What's more, it was so unexpected. Not even a rookie speechwriter in Clinton's 1992 campaign would dared to have promised the longest peacetime economic expansion in the nation's history, the lowest unemployment numbers since the 1950s, or fat budget surpluses. The last was the biggest surprise. In 1992, the federal government was running an annual deficit of $290 billion, or 4 percent of the Gross Domestic Product (GDP). That same year, the Congressional Budget Office projected annual deficits of about $400 billion by the turn of the century. As it turned out, by 1999, the budget was in the black for the first time since the sixties and was running the largest surplus as a percentage of the GDP since the Truman presidency.[4]

In the 1970s, the confluence of high prices, high interest rates, *and* high unemployment defied the conventional wisdom. The economy wasn't supposed to act that way. High prices and high interest rates usually signified a big demand for goods and services, and that meant there should have been plenty of work for all. For want of a better term, pundits labeled the baffling phenomenon "stagflation." In the nineties, developments proved just as baffling, though pleasantly so. The economy was growing at an annual rate of 4 percent; unemployment, including unemployment among minority groups, was the lowest in a generation; and wages were increasing (though not at the same rate) for all income groups. Yet—and here was the puzzle—inflation and interest rates were lower and more stable than one would have expected in a well-stoked economy. "Everybody is a little bit mystified, in a pleasant way, about exactly why things are so good, how it is happening, and how long it can last," said Alice Rivlin, who had served in both congressional and White House budget offices. Added former CEA and Federal Reserve Board member Alan Blinder: "Growth has been a lot faster than anyone expected."[5]

Everyone agreed that the explosion of information technology was a large part of the story. Between 1992 and 2001, the telecommunications industry generated two-thirds of all new jobs and one-third of new investments.[6] The Internet had been under development for decades, but it was during the nineties that it came into its own—in much the same way radio in the thirties and television in the fifties came into their own. According to government estimates, between 1995 and 1998, the Internet alone accounted for a third of the nation's economic growth. It not only spurred a demand for computers in homes, schools, and businesses but also may have increased worker productivity. Indeed, it was the impact of information technology on productivity that struck many observers, including Alan Greenspan, as the defining characteristic of the new economy.[7] An office worker equipped with an online computer could now perform tasks in an hour that once had taken weeks or even months.

But where did the Clinton administration figure into all of this? How much credit could it legitimately claim for the impressive performance of the economy? The president and his advisers did not claim all the credit but did argue that they had set in motion the events that had produced the current happy state of affairs, events the CEA called "the virtuous cycle."[8] In the administration's telling, the pivotal moment came even before Clinton took office, when the president-elect decided to make deficit reduction his number-one priority—over health care, welfare reform, and all the investment initiatives he had promised during the campaign. After a tough fight and with no support from the Republicans, Congress adopted the president's deficit-reducing budget, with its combination of spending restraints and tax increases on the wealthy. That in turn, according to the official version, convinced the financial community that the administration could be trusted to rein in spending and keep inflation in check. The markets responded accordingly by lowering long-term interest rates. As a kind of bonus for good behavior, the administration was rewarded with an unexpected decline in short-term interest rates, which combined with the long-term rate decline, spurred a robust round of investment and consumption that gained strength as the decade wore on. In addition to fiscal restraint, the Clintonites cited two other administration initiatives that contributed to the virtuous cycle: investments in education and in scientific research and development and the expansion of foreign trade through NAFTA and its successors. Ever mindful of Yale's Irving Fischer, who spent the rest of his long life living down his pre-crash observation, Clinton and his advisers tried to avoid sounding a false note of optimism. Still, there was no mistaking their confidence that they had attained, if not an economic Golden Mean, then at least a near-perfect balance between government intervention and government restraint—a balance that avoided the government excesses of the sixties and the free-enterprise excesses of the eighties, a balance that could sustain "the virtuous cycle" indefinitely into the future. "No other financial system has combined so effectively the integrity of high-quality regulation with the absence of excessive state interference," boasted the Treasury Department's Lawrence Summers.[9]

Not everyone was willing to credit the administration with the central role it claimed for itself. Republicans and conservative economists like Martin Feldstein argued that the country was belatedly reaping the benefits of Reaganomics and of the austerity measures forced upon Clinton by the Republican Congress.[10] Others accorded the star role to Fed chairman Alan Greenspan, who, despite his hangdog demeanor and Delphic pronouncements, enjoyed almost cult-like adulation because of his supposedly masterful management of the nation's monetary policy. His appearances on Capitol Hill, a journalist wrote, were "often less like congressional hearings than like regal audiences." Journalist Bob Woodward wrote a book about him entitled *The Maestro*, and conservative Senator Phil Gramm (R-TX) called him "the most successful central banker in the history of the United States."[11] If Clinton deserved credit at all, said Greenspan's admirers, it was for following the Fed chair's advice and then getting out of the way. Getting out of the way wasn't always easy. Every time the Fed raised interest rates, Clinton became incensed, believing that Greenspan had double-crossed him. The president's economic advisers tried to calm him down, telling him that picking a fight with the Fed, as his predecessor had done, was a losing proposition. Clinton heeded their advice. "To his everlasting credit," recalled Alan Blinder, "he never made a peep publically that he was angry at the Fed, or in any way hinted that he was trying to jawbone the Fed."[12]

Even Clinton's supporters conceded that a run of good luck contributed to the nation's economic fortunes. Oil prices, which had helped undo the presidency of the last Democrat in the White House, remained stable; the costs of medical care rose more slowly than expected; and even periodic financial jolts abroad—in Mexico, Asia, and Russia—caused only momentary disruptions to the international economy. Then, too, it became clear in retrospect that the worst of the recession was over before Clinton ever set foot in the oval office. Moreover, as administration economists Alan Blinder and Janet Yellen later noted, "three of the foundation stones for what was to became the Fabulous Decade had already been put in place." They were "tighter fiscal policy, looser monetary policy, and industrial restricting that made American business 'leaner and meaner.'"[13] If Bush had been reelected in 1992, conceded Laura

Tyson and Joseph Stiglitz, the economy would have performed well. Insofar as information technology was responsible for the economic boom of the nineties, Clinton did give the green light to the deregulation of the telecommunications industry, and he, along with Vice President Gore, steadfastly promoted the goal of universal access to computers and the Internet. Still, the computer and the World Wide Web weren't the invention of young entrepreneurs like Bill Gates and Steve Jobs working out of their garages. As journalist Haynes Johnson and others pointed out, those inventions had deep taproots in the administrations of Franklin Roosevelt and Harry Truman, when the federal government, particularly during World War II and the Cold War, financed and organized almost all of the scientific and technological research that led to the telecommunications revolution of the nineties. The Internet, for example, grew out of Pentagon-supported research on ways to decentralize communications in the event of a nuclear war. The Clinton administration's contributions, whose dollar amounts were the equivalent of that of the Reagan and Bush administrations, would not have had time to materially shape the economy during Clinton's time in the White House. In the 1990s, the United States was reaping the benefits of nearly a half-century of investments.[14]

By the late nineties, the administration's economic policy apparatus was functioning like a well-oiled machine. The late-night cram sessions, replete with pizza deliveries, were a thing of the past.

Clinton's chief structural contribution to the formulation of economic policy was the National Economic Council (NEC), which served as a kind of clearinghouse for the gathering and analysis of economic recommendations from federal departments and bureaus. Robert Rubin was the NEC's founding chair, followed by Laura Tyson and Gene Sperling. The goal of the NEC, largely achieved by the late nineties, was to serve as an honest broker, fully and fairly presenting to the president recommendations originating in the myriad departments and agencies of the executive branch. Sperling's goal was to be so evenhanded in presenting these recommendations that the president wouldn't know until the last page where the NEC itself stood on the matter.

The NEC also served a valuable political function. As long as department and agency heads remained confident their proposals were getting a fair hearing, they were less likely to jump the chain of command by trying to buttonhole the president after cabinet meetings or at White House receptions, or, worse yet, leaking their views to the press. Before leaving the administration at the end of Clinton's first term, Robert Reich, who had often found himself on the short end of White House decisions, tried funneling information to the president through Hillary Clinton. When that didn't work, he just went public. One time, without first submitting his proposal to the NEC, Reich published an op-ed piece in the *New York Times* proposing a major new initiative. Corporations providing their workers with fair wages and benefits, he said, should be rewarded with lower taxes—or maybe no taxes at all. Clinton's economists quickly decided that Reich's proposal might sound good on paper but would be costly and probably impossible to put into practice. When Clinton declined to endorse Reich's proposal, it looked as though discord and disarray had reappeared in the administration. It made the president appear more sympathetic to corporations than to their employees.[15] In 1993, Bob Woodward, whose book had depicted a chaotic budget process, seemingly had a free run of the White House. By the late nineties, thanks in part to the NEC, the administration was talking with one voice and that voice was the president's.

Not that the NEC had risen above bureaucratic strife. It clashed frequently—but quietly—with the National Security Council, which jealously clung to information in areas of overlapping jurisdiction. The NEC did not exactly clash with the CEA; but it did eventually outshine the fifty-year-old council to the point some members of Congress tried to cut off the CEA's funding. Moreover, by Clinton's last years in office, the NEC had acquired a reputation among up-and-coming economists as "the" place to work in the administration.[16]

Structural innovations like the NEC mattered. But personalities mattered more. And among Clinton's economic advisers, some were more equal than others. Despite opposition to her appointment from professional colleagues like economist and pundit Paul Krugman, Laura Tyson quickly gained the ear of the president. It was she who helped talk Clinton out of backing Robert Reich's "corporate responsibility" initiative. And it was Tyson who may have prevented a rebellion among congressional Democrats by convincing Clinton not to endorse the Republican-backed balanced budget amendment to the Constitution. Tyson was married to Hollywood screenwriter Eric Tarloff, whose credits included episodes of television's *M*A*S*H* and *All in the Family* and who later wrote an insightful novel, *Face-Time*, about the seductive power of the presidency. In 1997, Tyson left the administration and returned with her husband to California.

Of Clinton's economic advisers, two towered in influence above all others: Robert Rubin, who served as chair of the CEA before succeeding Lloyd Bentsen as secretary of the treasury; and Lawrence Summers, deputy secretary of the treasury and Rubin's eventual successor as secretary. Rubin swiftly earned the trust of the president because of his even temperament, unpretentious style, progressive views on race and poverty, and knack for explaining the ins and outs of high finance without either oversimplifying or employing the impenetrable jargon of an economics profession that had come to resemble a branch of higher mathematics. That he was unafraid to disagree with the president, as he did on welfare reform, added to his credibility in the president's eyes. And when the bond markets reacted just as Rubin assured Clinton they would if he pursued deficit reduction in 1993, Rubin's stature soared. He was also transformed from the "mumbly, almost shy" personage he was in the beginning to an articulate, self-assured spokesman for the administration.[17] During the 1920s, admirers of the ultraconservative Andrew Mellon, who served in the Harding, Coolidge, and Hoover administrations, called him the greatest secretary of the treasury since Alexander Hamilton. There had been some notable treasury secretaries between Mellon and Rubin, including James Baker, who served during the second half of the Reagan administration and who became known for his superior political and diplomatic skills. But no secretary in the modern era exerted more influence on economic policy than Rubin.

Long before he succeeded Rubin as secretary, Rubin's understudy, Lawrence Summers, held sway not only over his area of academic expertise—international trade—but also over other areas. A staffer at the CEA once sketched a mock organizational chart of the treasury department. It showed the secretary occupying the top spot—and Summers all the others. The chart was not far off the mark. Although little known outside of the administration, the brash, suffer-no-fools Summers became a powerhouse within. For Rubin, the climb to the top came when the markets reacted to deficit reduction as he predicted they would. Summers's arrival at the pinnacle happened during the high-stakes Mexican loan crisis in 1995, a crisis the deputy secretary brought to the president's attention. When things turned out better than anyone could have expected, Summers's standing, like Rubin's, was assured. By the late nineties, Summers was the administration's chief operative on foreign economic matters.

Practically every profile of Summers contained obligatory references to two of his most pronounced characteristics: excessive self-esteem and dishevelment. "Larry Summers is to humility what Madonna is to chastity," wrote Paul Gigot of the *Wall Street Journal* with reference to the sexually provocative popular entertainer of the time. Summers, another journalist noted, was known "for his lack of social graces and his indifference to social convention, such as whether his socks matched and the shirt tail was tucked in." He was "a slob," recalled a former Harvard colleague. In time, and under Rubin's tutelage, Summers smoothed out some of the rough edges in his manner if not always in his appearance.[18]

By the late nineties, the secretary and his deputy were operating as a team. "The combination of Bob's feel for the markets and Larry's economic analysis makes them an incredibly effective pair,"—"a dynamic duo"—said NEC director Gene Sperling. Each considered himself a pragmatist with a social conscience, "a market oriented progressive," as Summers put it. Together they reinforced Clinton's centrist instincts by urging deficit reduction, expressing skepticism of new spending initiatives, and favoring a wide berth for market forces. They had their detractors, to be sure. But as long as the economy flourished, it was hard to argue with success. In 1999, when Rubin announced his intention to return to Wall Street (which some critics felt he had never left), the stock market lost forty points. When Summers was announced as his replacement, the market rebounded.[19]

Through it all the president remained a quick study, absorbing reams of facts and figures and getting right to the heart of complicated matters. During and after impeachment, however, he involved himself less often in day-to-day economic matters unless they involved the issues he cared most deeply about, such as affordable housing for minorities and low-income groups. But as often as not he increasingly deferred to his economic advisers, especially his "dynamic duo." Once he had met almost weekly with the CEA and the NEC; now he preferred to read their reports. At times, Clinton's economic leadership resembled Franklin Roosevelt's war leadership during the late stages of World War II. The course was set, able commanders were in place, and the machinery of state was grinding toward its inevitable conclusion.

Not that every issue had been resolved. Most pressing was the question of what to do with the unexpectedly large budget surplus. For the first time in decades, government revenues were outpacing expenditures. Clinton's first budget had contributed to the happy situation, as had the steadfast opposition of Republicans to major new spending initiatives. On the revenue side, economic growth increased incomes, and with them the taxes people paid. Paradoxically, the one conspicuous weakness in the overwhelmingly bright economic picture helped boost revenues. Although the incomes of all Americans were increasing, they were not increasing at the same rate. The wealthiest Americans were reaping the largest share of benefits of the economic boom, with the result that the gap between rich and poor, which had narrowed between the 1940s and the 1970s, had once again continued to increase. But because of the progressive nature of the tax code, upper-income groups were helping to fill government coffers.

But what to do with the surplus? Should some or all of it be invested in the type of projects Clinton had campaigned on in 1992 but that had been dropped in favor of deficit reduction? (Before he left the administration, Robert Reich, for one, argued for belatedly making good on the campaign pledges.) Or should surplus monies be used to shore up Medicare, Medicaid, and Social Security in anticipation of the aging of the baby boomers? And what of the demands of Republicans and some conservative Democrats to dispose of the surplus by slashing taxes?

An entrenched Republican opposition ruled out the investment option. Clinton and his advisers also ruled out major tax cuts, which, to their minds, would have squandered a major resource. As for entitlements, before impeachment, Clinton and Gingrich did hold preliminary discussions about reform, with Clinton open to slowing the growth of Medicare and Medicaid in exchange for Republican support for tax increases. Erskine Bowles, Clinton's third chief of staff, had decided to step down from his position and return to his home in North Carolina. But he was so confident an agreement was within reach that he delayed his departure to help broker a deal. Years later, he insisted that the president and the Speaker were serious about an agreement, even though both knew they would have to drag their respective congressional delegations kicking and screaming to the negotiating table.[20] Impeachment, however, ended any prospects of a deal. The atmosphere was toxic, and Clinton was in no position to bring his partisan backers to the table. Having asked them to stand by him during the trial, he could not now ask them to risk their careers by supporting cuts in entitlement programs.[21]

So that left Social Security, which faced a serious though not dire situation. By the nineties, analysts were projecting long-term imbalances in the system. The convergence of rising life expectancy and declining fertility rates translated into fewer working Americans paying into the system to support more and more retirees. The ratio was already three workers for every retiree. In another fifty years, the ratio would be two to one. In 1993, Clinton had appointed a panel of experts to recommend steps to shore up the sixty-year-old system. A divided panel offered a number of options, including increasing Social Security taxes, trimming benefits, raising the retirement age, and allowing the government to invest social security reserves in the stock market rather than in safer, but less lucrative, treasury bonds. The panel's most conservative member recommended cutting guaranteed benefits by half and allowing employees to save for retirement in whatever ways they thought best. A prominent non–panel member, Peter G. Peterson, an investment banker who had served as secretary of commerce in the Nixon administration, proposed pegging benefits to income, with the wealthiest retirees receiving 85 percent less than currently.[22]

In his discussions with Newt Gingrich before impeachment, Clinton may have given the Speaker the impression he was willing to consider—in addition to Medicare and Medicaid reforms—allowing employees to divert to private accounts a percentage of their earnings earmarked for Social Security. Or so Gingrich later claimed. But when impeachment ended the possibility of a bipartisan overhaul of entitlements, Clinton settled upon a more modest—and less politically risky—reform package, one put together by Lawrence Summers and Gene Sperling. In final form, the president proposed devoting 62 percent of the annual budget surplus to shore up Social Security; 15 percent to shore up Medicare; and

12 percent to "individual savings accounts" that would allow employees to invest in semiprivate accounts over and above what they were paying in Social Security taxes. Clinton's most controversial proposal was to invest 2 percent of the Social Security Trust Fund in the stock market rather than in treasury bonds. Both Robert Rubin and Alan Greenspan opposed this proposal not only because stocks were riskier than bonds but also because the government, with its vast holdings, could have a disproportionate impact on market activities. In the end, Clinton's proposals fell flat. All was not lost, however: the president was at least able to forestall Republican efforts to dispose of the surplus by reducing taxes.[23]

The administration's support for deregulating the nation's banking system received a far more receptive audience on Capitol Hill. By the late nineties, the movement to repeal, or at least drastically overhaul, the Glass-Steagall Act, a New Deal landmark that separated commercial and investment banking, had acquired unstoppable momentum. Even if Clinton had been inclined to block repeal he almost certainly would have failed. But neither he nor his advisers were so inclined. Believing a new economy was in the offing, they were looking for even more ways to release, in a controlled way, the creative energies of the private sector. Deregulation of telecommunications was done. Banking was next.

Adopted in 1933, Glass-Steagall was the legislative response to an explosive investigation into the role of banks and banking in causing the stock market crash and ensuing Depression. Conducted by the US Senate Committee on Banking and Currency, under the leadership of committee counsel Ferdinand Pecora, the probe exposed an array of shady, though perfectly legal, practices by some of the nation's leading financial institutions, including the fabled House of Morgan. Under Pecora's relentless questioning, august bankers such as J. P. Morgan, Jr., found themselves in the unaccustomed position of having to account for their actions in a public forum. As historian William E. Leuchtenburg described it: "On the witness stand, Morgan appeared to have been resurrected from some Dickensian countinghouse—he called one of his clerks a 'clark'—but as Pecora jabbed his stubby finger at him, while Morgan fondled the heavy gold chain across his paunch, he seemed less the awesome figure of Broad and Wall, more like a Main Street banker with his eye on the main chance."[24] The committee's hearings convinced most observers that the stock market crash, the devastating run on the banks, and the Depression itself owed much to the ability of a charlatan like J. P. Morgan to squander the hard-earned savings of bank depositors in the stock market. The Glass-Steagall Act, named after Senator Carter Glass, of Virginia, and Representative Henry B. Steagall, of Alabama, created two categories of banks where there had been one: commercial banks, which would be allowed to accept deposits and make loans but not buy and sell stocks and bonds, and investment banks, which would be allowed to buy and sell stocks and bonds but not accept deposits or make ordinary loans. Moreover, the federal government would insure deposits in commercial banks against losses, but not losses resulting from the speculative activities of investment banks. Thereafter, J. P. Morgan and Company was a commercial bank; Morgan Stanley was spun off as an investment bank. In 1956, during the Eisenhower administration, and with its support, the Bank Holding Company Act prohibited banks from selling insurance.

By the 1970s, a revolt was brewing. Large commercial banks were complaining that Glass-Steagall had outlived its usefulness. The financial climate of the country was changing, they said, but antiquated New Deal strictures were preventing banks from changing with it. Big corporations, for example, could now meet their short-term needs for seasonal funding by going to the commercial paper market rather than to commercial banks. Small-time customers, once the bread and butter of the banking industry, were increasingly putting their money into mutual funds, which commercial banks were prohibited from underwriting. With the advent of globalization, American banks were also finding themselves at a disadvantage vis-à-vis foreign competitors in Europe and Asia, who faced no such restrictions as those imposed by the Depression reforms.[25] From the end of World War II to the nineties, the share of financial assets held by commercial banks declined from 60 percent to 25 percent.

Though unsettled and restless, the financial community was at first far from united on a course of action. Big banks like J. P. Morgan wanted outright repeal of Glass-Steagall so they could offer customers a full range of services. Small banks, however, feared having to compete with the huge conglomerates that would surely form if commercial and investment banks were allowed to combine their activities. Many insurance companies had a similar fear. Investment banks were split down the middle: many wanted to expand their activities; others liked things the way they were.

Deregulation, meanwhile, was acquiring a momentum of its own. In 1983, the Federal Reserve Board allowed Bank of America, a commercial bank, to purchase Charles Schwab, an investment bank. The only stipulation was that the two institutions had to keep their funds separate. In the 1990s, the Fed, now led by Alan Greenspan, who had become a convert to the cause of repealing Glass-Steagall while serving on the board of J. P. Morgan, permitted commercial banks to sell stocks and bonds as long as the resulting business did not exceed 10 percent (later raised to 25 percent) of their revenue. In 1995, when the Supreme Court sanctioned these and other actions, repeal of Glass-Steagall seemed a mere formality.[26]

Two other developments hastened the onset of deregulation. One was a sustained assault on the historical and intellectual foundations of Glass-Steagall. For over a half-century the conventional wisdom held that the intermingling of investment and commercial banking had almost singlehandedly brought down the financial system and that erecting a wall between the two activities was the only rational solution. But now a number of scholars, upon reexamining the legislative proceedings that brought about reform, cast doubt about the historical accuracy of received wisdom. It turned out, these scholars argued, that the framers of Glass-Steagall had relied more on assertion than evidence. They ignored the fact that banks trading in securities had a lower failure rate than banks that stayed out of the stock market. Legislators, it seemed, had been eager to find a scapegoat for the nation's economic collapse, and bankers, smug and defiant as they were, provided easy targets. The bankers, feeling unfairly put upon, gave up the fight, perhaps fearing continued intransigence might lead to a worse fate, such as nationalization of the financial system.[27]

By the mid-nineties, after much internal wrangling and arm-twisting, previously warring components of the financial industry resolved their differences and coalesced around a bill sponsored by a trio of Republicans: Senator Phil Gramm, of Texas, and Representatives James Leach of Iowa and Thomas J. Bliley, of Virginia. Republicans may have led the repeal effort, but Democrats were not far behind. As early as the mid-eighties, Wisconsin's maverick Democrat, William Proxmire, who had earned a PhD in economics from Princeton, called for repeal, thus opening the doors for liberals to follow suit.[28]

As the debate in Congress got under way, supporters of repeal reprised the arguments they had made during the telecommunications debate: consumers would be the primary beneficiaries. Deregulation would spur competition among banks, offering customers more choices, lower prices, and the convenience of one-stop-shopping for financial services. An administration spokesperson projected $8 billion in annual savings for consumers. And then there were dire consequences should repeal fail. Said Democratic Senator Charles Schumer of New York: "We could find London or Frankfurt or years down the road Shanghai becoming the financial capital of the world." "There are many reasons for the bill," Schumer added, "but first and foremost is to ensure that U.S. financial firms remain competitive."[29]

A small band of mostly liberal holdouts, led by Massachusetts Democrat Ed Markey in the House and Minnesota Democrat Paul Wellstone in the Senate, opposed passage of Gramm-Leach-Bliley. Wellstone, a member of a nearly extinct group of middle-western progressives of the old school, warned that deregulation would "aggregate a trend toward economic concentration that endangers not only our economy, but also our democracy." Repeal of Glass-Steagall, he argued, would make "it easier for banks, security firms, and insurance companies to merge into gigantic new conglomerates that would dominate the U.S. financial industry and the U.S. economy." Administration economists boasted of the "virtuous cycle." Wellstone warned of the "vicious cycle." Were these conglomerates to fail, they could bring down the whole economy—a concern proponents like Democratic Senator Bob Kerrey, of Nebraska, dismissed as "dramatically overblown." Maybe so, Wellstone conceded, but wouldn't the federal government, regarding these new enterprises as "too big to fail," prop them up at the expense of taxpayers, as happened with the savings-and-loan crisis in the late eighties? What little government oversight remained in the bill, Wellstone argued, was so dispersed among government agencies that financial institutions would largely be free to do what they wanted. Critics like Wellstone and Markey also perceived in deregulation a threat to privacy. If commercial banks, investment banks, and insurance companies could combine their activities, they could also combine all the personal information they each had on customers, including medical histories, financial status, and purchasing preferences. This last concern struck a sympathetic chord with conservatives, such as *New York Times* columnist William Safire, who said they didn't welcome the intrusion of big companies into their private affairs any more than the intrusion of big government.[30]

President Clinton's chief contribution to bank reform was to insist that a newly restructured financial industry continue to abide by the provisions of the Community Reinvestment Act (CRA), a measure passed during the Carter administration that required the federal government to rate banks on their willingness to make loans, especially housing loans, to minorities and lower-income groups. Senator Gramm was intent upon eliminating the requirement. Clinton, however, believed CRA compliance was a critical tool in combating racial discrimination in housing. In 1992, an influential study sponsored by the Federal Reserve Bank of Boston found that blacks and Hispanics in the Boston area were 60 percent more likely to be turned down for housing loans than whites with comparable incomes and credit histories.[31] Too many Americans were being denied their piece of the American Dream, Clinton said. That had to change. Addressing himself in 1995 to young working couples just starting out, he said that by the time their children were ready to start first grade, they should be able to own their own homes. "All of our country will reap enormous benefits if we achieve this goal."[32] To combat discrimination, and to increase homeownership generally, Clinton and his secretaries of Housing and Urban Development, Henry Cisneros and Andrew Cuomo, leaned heavily on lenders, including the government-sponsored agencies, Fannie Mae and Freddie Mac, to increase their loans to minorities and other disadvantaged groups. They also strictly enforced the Community Reinvestment Act when banks sought to merge with other banks or open new branches. These efforts bore impressive results. Between 1993 and 1999, home mortgages to blacks increased by 58 percent, to Hispanics by 62 percent, and to persons with low and moderate incomes by 38 percent. Small businesses in less affluent communities also found it easier to secure loans.[33] Clinton insisted the CRA remain in operation or he would veto the entire deregulation bill. When Gramm finally relented, the Gramm-Leach-Bliley

Financial Services Modernization Act passed overwhelmingly, 362 to 57 in the House, 90 to 8 in the Senate.[34]

Upon signing the measure into law, Clinton said that Glass-Steagall was "no longer appropriate to the economy in which we live. It worked pretty well for the industrial economy, which was highly organized, much more centralized, and much more nationalized than the one in which we operate today."[35] The president's CEA assured the public that the measure maintained "appropriate safeguards" while allowing "consolidation in the financial sector that will result in efficiency gains and provide new services for consumers."[36]

Perhaps the most striking thing about bank reform was the disproportionality between its importance and the public attention it received. It had been under almost constant consideration for nearly two decades. Along with health-care and telecommunications reform, it was the most heavily lobbied issue of the era, with industry representatives taking up permanent residence on Capitol Hill and showering members of the key committees with millions of dollars in campaign contributions. In contrast to the deliberations that led to Glass-Steagall, the debate that led to its repeal was largely confined to the back pages or business sections of most newspapers. Neither passage of Gramm-Leach-Bliley nor the president's signing statement got more than twenty seconds on the evening newscasts. Not surprisingly, a poll conducted shortly after the bill became law disclosed that most Americans had never even heard about it.[37] President Clinton was himself partly responsible for the news blackout. At no time did he try to explain in everyday language the workings of the modern banking system and what reform would mean to the average person as, say, Franklin Roosevelt did in his famous fireside chats.

Like bank reform, the administration's antitrust policy offered an example of the third way in action, of its effort to chart a path between too much government and too little. "The goal of Clinton antitrust," recalled Robert Pitofsky, chairman of the Federal Trade Commission during the Clinton years, "was . . . to find a sustainable middle ground between the over-enforcement of the 1960s and the under-enforcement of the 1980s."[38]

Whether deliberate or not, the administration approached antitrust the way Theodore Roosevelt had at the beginning of the century. Few historical reputations are as misleading as Theodore Roosevelt's as trust-buster. For one thing, he believed there was no turning back the clock. Big business was here to stay. Yet he also believed big business could confer many benefits on the American public, including efficiencies of production and lower prices. Still, corporate America could not do whatever it wanted. It must learn to act in the national interest. So Roosevelt brought to heel several of the nation's biggest corporations, including John D. Rockefeller's Standard Oil Company. But having warned businessmen of what awaited them if they did not practice self-restraint, he backed off, authorizing far fewer antitrust suits than his conservative successor, William Howard Taft.

So it was with the Clinton administration, with the exception that Clinton, unlike Roosevelt, rarely involved himself personally in the actions of the antitrust division of his Justice Department. Under the leadership of a hard-driving Joel Klein, Clinton's second assistant attorney general for antitrust, the government filed high-profile suits against computer giant Microsoft—the Standard Oil of the 1990s—and also computer-chip maker Intel and American Airlines. Even so, having made its presence felt, especially in the emerging computer industry, the administration also made it clear that like Teddy Roosevelt it was no enemy of bigness, per se. The Microsoft suit may have dominated the headlines, noted Stephen Labaton, chief economic reporter for the *New York Times*, but the administration was more likely to be remembered "as encouraging the largest number of business mergers—and in some industries the greatest concentration of economic power—in many years." Although Clinton's Justice Department filed more antitrust suits than the Reagan and Bush administrations, it approved 51 percent more corporate mergers, valued at nearly $10 trillion, than its two Republican predecessors combined.[39]

One outspoken member of the administration believed that the administration's effort to find a third way was erring too much on the side of deregulation. She was Brooksley E. Born, and her views ultimately led to an extraordinary showdown with Clinton's most influential economic advisers.

In 1996, Born became head of the Commodity Futures Trading Commission (CFTC), a federal agency created during the Ford administration primarily to oversee the agricultural markets in futures and options. By the time Born assumed her post, the agency, though little-known outside agricultural and government circles, was fighting for its life. Lawmakers from both parties were trying to strip it of much of its authority. Illustrative of the depth of antiregulatory fervor in the nineties, the chief sponsors of the legislation to downsize Born's agency included Richard Lugar, a moderate Republican senator from Indiana, and two liberal Democratic senators, Patrick Leahy of Vermont and Tom Harkin of Iowa.

Born had no intention of presiding over the demise of her agency. Moreover, she resolved not only to preserve her agency's current regulatory authority but also to expand its reach into the complex, little-understood, but increasingly important market in financial derivatives. The CFTC was already regulating two types of derivatives in the agricultural field: futures, in which one party would agree to buy a commodity, say wheat or corn, at a fixed price and at a fixed date in the future; and options, which gave one party the option, but not the obligation, to buy a commodity at a fixed price and time. Derivatives had existed for centuries, and for good reason. They introduced a degree of stability into the field of commercial agriculture, allowing buyers and sellers of derivatives to plan for the future. They were also a potentially lucrative investment in their own right. By the 1990s, derivatives had long since become more complicated. They now involved transactions not only in commodities like corn and wheat but also in financial entities such as stocks, bonds, interest rates, and currencies (foreign and domestic). One of the most important inventions of the nineties was a new type of derivative called a credit-default swap (CDS), which, at its most basic level, was a high-level insurance policy in which one party charged a premium and in exchange agreed to cover possible losses the other parties might incur with their investments. But that was only the start. Modern derivatives, one writer later noted, were "likely to involve a mix of options, futures, currencies, and debt, structured and priced in ways which are the closest extant thing to rocket science."[40] And it almost required the economic equivalent of a rocket scientist to understand them.

Modern derivatives were not only enormously complex but also largely unregulated. The prevailing assumption was that persons buying and selling derivatives were likely to be wealthy and savvy enough that they didn't need some federal agency looking over their shoulders. Should they slip up from time to time, the market would set them right. Or as Lawrence Summers put it: "The parties to these kinds of contract are largely sophisticated financial institutions that would appear to be eminently capable of protecting themselves from fraud and counter-party insolvencies."[41]

No one was talking about banning derivatives. It was recognized that they often served useful purposes. They helped institutions and individuals better manage risk. Even credit-default swaps, though much disparaged years later, probably helped thousands, perhaps millions, of deserving families to become homeowners. But with the value of derivatives now running into the trillions of dollars, a few persons, including several legislators, suggested that it might be time to regulate them. After all, despite deregulation, banks were still required to keep a certain percentage of their assets in cash and to abide by other rules set up by the Federal Deposit Insurance Corporation. Even Wall Street, the symbol of the free market system, had to abide by any number of regulations governing the buying and selling of stocks. So why not regulate, or at least establish guidelines for, the market in derivatives, some asked. In the early nineties, legislators from both parties, including Republican James Leach, who would soon be leading the fight for bank deregulation, and Democrats Donald W. Riegle, Henry Gonzalez, and Edward Markey called for regulation of derivatives. Nothing came of their efforts.[42]

Then Brooksley Born, at age fifty-seven, came into the picture. Upon taking over at CFTC, she raised the possibility of bringing financial derivatives under the purview of her agency. After all, modern derivatives might be mind-numbingly complicated, but they operated on the same basic principles as futures and options over which her agency already had jurisdiction. At least it was worth considering, she suggested.

The reaction was immediate and intense. Along with Robert Rubin, Alan Greenspan, and Securities and Exchange Commission Chairman Arthur Levitt, Jr., Born was a member of the president's Working Group on Financial Markets. The Working Group had been established in the late eighties, in the aftermath of the savings-and-loan collapse, as a kind of war room for dealing with financial crises. At the Group's April 1998 meeting, Born's colleagues took turns warning her she was treading dangerous ground. Regulating derivatives was a very bad idea. Even raising the possibility of regulation could create uncertainty and disrupt financial markets. Persisting would only succeed in driving the derivatives trade overseas, where financial conditions were more hospitable. "You're not going to do anything, right?" Robert Rubin asked Born after everyone had spoken. Lawrence Summers, though not a member of the Working Group, also weighed in, telling Born he'd been inundated with angry calls from industry representatives.[43]

This was not the first time Born had encountered resistance to her ideas. A native of San Francisco, she had been steered away from medical school by a college vocational counselor who thought nursing a more appropriate field of study for a woman. She enrolled instead in the Stanford University School of Law, where she edited the law review and finished at the top of her class—both firsts for a woman on the Palo Alto campus. She was also the first woman anywhere in the country to edit a major law journal. Despite her stellar performance, the university committee in charge of recommending students for US Supreme Court clerkships passed over Born in favor of two men with academic records inferior to hers. Born eventually made partner in a prestigious law firm in Washington, DC, from which vantage point she championed the cause of women in the legal profession. In 1992 she made the short list for attorney general in the Clinton administration, but "the call never came." In 1996, she received what was widely regarded as a consolation prize when Clinton nominated her to head the Commodity Futures Trading Commission. A Republican senator temporarily blocked her confirmation because she was friends with Hillary Clinton and might therefore be reluctant to investigate her success in the cattle futures market fifteen years earlier.[44]

As an admiring newspaper profile later noted, Born "had grown used to being the only woman in the room. She didn't like to be pushed around." Still, nothing had prepared her for the reaction to her derivatives initiative. Opposition from the financial lobby was to be expected. But not from her colleagues in the administration. Born dug in. "Once she took a position, she would defend that position and go down fighting," a senior staff member of her agency recalled. "When someone pushed her, she was inclined to stand there and push back."[45]

Robert Rubin, Arthur Levitt, and Alan Greenspan now went to extraordinary lengths to stop Born in her tracks. They called upon Congress to pass legislation prohibiting Born's agency from regulating derivatives until the president's Working Group, on which she was outnumbered, had studied the matter. Alan Greenspan was known for his ability to obfuscate. But not this time. "Regulation of derivatives transactions that are privately negotiated by professionals is unnecessary," he told a congressional committee. "Regulation that serves no useful purpose hinders the efficiency of markets to enlarge standards of living."[46] Rubin and Levitt added that even if Born wanted to regulate derivatives, her agency had no statutory authority to do so. Bureaucratic infighting was hardly new. But to have three government agencies—Treasury, the Securities and Exchange Commission, and the Fed—join forces to block another agency was rare, if not unprecedented. Ironically, Rubin later conceded that he, too, harbored concerns about derivatives and especially about the lack of any minimum margin requirements for their purchase. Indeed, he said he'd been concerned about derivatives since his days at Goldman Sachs, before he joined the Clinton administration. But he didn't like the way Born was forging ahead. "I do think it was a deterrent to moving forward," he recalled. "I thought it was counterproductive. If you want to move forward . . . you engage with parties in a constructive way." Born's approach was too "strident."[47]

In the summer of 1998, in the midst of the standoff between Born and Rubin and company, a dramatic event suddenly cast Born's concerns in a new light. It was the near-collapse of Long-Term Capital Management, a highly touted hedge fund that traded heavily in the kinds of derivatives Born was concerned about. Hedge funds were risky, but potentially lucrative, forms of investment that among other things involved the nearly simultaneous buying and selling of undervalued and overvalued securities and derivatives—then predicting which were which. Because of the risks involved, hedge funds were open only to small groups of wealthy individuals and institutions. Like derivatives, they were exempt from regulation—and for the same reason. If you were worth $5 million (the minimum net worth to invest in a hedge fund), you probably knew what you were getting into. You were capable of assessing the risks. And if something did go wrong, you could absorb the loss. The prevailing view on Wall Street (and in much of Washington, DC) was that the relationship between investors and their hedge funds or derivative traders was like the relationship between consenting adults. As long as no one else got hurt, what happened between them was their business alone. Certainly it was not the business of the US government.

Hedge funds dated to the late forties but only became popular among the wealthy and well-connected in the nineties. By that time they numbered in the hundreds and accounted for a third of all investment funds.[48] No hedge fund offered more promise than Long-Term Capital Management. In just one year, the Greenwich, Connecticut–based firm rewarded investors with annual returns in excess of 40 percent. Other years were almost as good. But the chief attraction of this particular hedge fund was its decidedly unconventional staff of traders. One journalist described them as "nerdy-looking men" with ill-fitting ties and hair that "cascaded around their ears," another as "physically unintimidating, their bodies merely life-support systems for their brains, which were in turn extensions of their computers."[49] Many of the "young professors," as they were called, had PhDs in math from MIT; two had taught at Ivy League colleges; and one had been vice-chairman of the Federal Reserve Board. Two board members were Nobel Laureates in economics. Obviously a brainy bunch, they had supposedly used the newest technology to crack the secrets of the market. "Instead of playing hunches, traders at Long-Term Capital used computers to discover temporary pricing anomalies between similar securities," explained economic writer John Cassidy. Within a few years the fund had attracted an A-list of investors, including top executives at Wall Street giants like Merrill Lynch, Bear Stearns, and Paine Webber. These executives, wealthy and successful all, might not themselves understand the complex computer models the Long-Term Capital traders were using, but they were confident the young professors did. If there was any doubt, one need only look at the firm's annual performance record.[50]

Long-Term Capital performed spectacularly well until the summer of 1998. Then disaster struck. During a brief, but severe, world financial crisis precipitated by a Russian loan default, Long-Term Capital lost $4 billion in six weeks. Suddenly it teetered on the brink of collapse. Some experts, including high-ranking officials at the Federal Reserve, feared that because of its high-profile investors and creditors, it could capsize the nation's entire financial structure. To forestall the worst, the head of the Federal Reserve Bank in New York City, with the approval of Fed Chair Alan Greenspan, convened a meeting of the Wall Street executives that had extended credit to Long-Term Capital. The next day, sixteen firms—including Goldman Sachs, Merrill Lynch, J. P. Morgan, and Morgan Stanley—pumped nearly $4 billion into the listing firm to keep it afloat.[51]

Disaster was averted, but the episode would seem to have undermined the rationale for exempting hedge funds and derivatives from regulation. A more market-savvy group than the men who had eagerly lined up to invest in Long-Term Capital or extend it credit could scarcely be imagined. Investing is what they did for a living. They were enormously successful at it. Yet, to a person they had failed to ask the most basic questions before lavishing their resources on the firm, like what was the firm's debt situation and the extent of its trading in derivatives as opposed to stocks and bonds. They were awestruck by the "young professors" and their track record. Nor was Long-Term Capital required to open its books. When it did as part of the rescue effort, many of its investors and creditors were shocked by what they found. They were "astonished to discover," a journalist noted, "that its leverage ratio was close to thirty to one, and that its derivatives exposures totaled about $1.4 trillion."[52]

The firm's downfall also demonstrated that the fallout from a deal gone bad wasn't necessarily confined to the parties directly involved. As Brooksley Born explained to a congressional committee in her "I-told-you-so moment": "Many of us have interests in the corporations, mutual funds, pension funds, insurance companies, municipalities and other entities trading in these instruments." Defending the Fed's action in helping to facilitate the bailout of Long-Term Capital, Alan Greenspan said, in his measured way, that if the firm had been allowed to go bankrupt, "substantial damage could have been inflicted on many market participants . . . and could have potentially impaired the economies of many nations, including our own."[53]

For a time the demise of the country's most celebrated hedge fund prompted intense anxiety and calls for reform. "We need improved financial oversight," one former Wall Street insider told a reporter. "We need a process that will clearly state what capital standards are required, what reporting requirements ought to be imposed, what the trading and accounting standards should be for all major markets and all major institutions. At the moment we don't have any of these."[54] On the other hand, key Republican legislators complained that the Federal Reserve Board had exceeded its authority by convening the meeting of Wall Street brokerages that agreed to underwrite Long-Term Capital's losses.

Following the firm's collapse, the president's Working Group on Financial Markets, the group that had given Brooksley Born a hard time, launched its own investigation. In April 1999, Robert Rubin reported the group's findings to the president. What had happened was this, he wrote: "Our market-based economy relies on market participants to provide discipline, but market discipline can break down. In the case of Long-Term Capital, none of its investors, creditors, or counterparties provided an effective check on its overall activities. In addition, market history indicates that even painful lessons recede from memory with time." The problems exposed by the hedge fund's collapse, Rubin wrote, were not confined to hedge funds. "Other financial institutions, including some banks and securities firms, are larger, and generally more highly leveraged, than hedge funds." The remedy? Government needed to do its part, Rubin said, such as requiring the disclosure to the public of "more frequent and meaningful information on hedge funds." But the main burden for dealing with the problem remained with the private sector—with those "investors, creditors, and counterparties" who had let down their guard. This wouldn't be enough for some people, Rubin predicted. They'd call for direct government regulation of hedge funds, "or other measures to expand the regulatory net with the aim of constraining leverage." But not the Working Group. Concluded Rubin: "We do not believe that such measures would be realistic in the current political and regulatory climate."[55] A year later, Rubin's successor as Treasury secretary, Lawrence Summers, underscored the point. "Let me be clear," he said, "it is the private sector, not the public sector, that is in the best position to provide effective supervision. Market discipline is the first line of defense in maintaining the integrity of our financial system." Long-Term Capital had been a "wake up call." Now the private sector needed to step up to the challenge.[56] Of the Working Group's report, Nobel Laureate Merton Miller said: "This was a nothing burger if ever there was one. Be careful. Set standards. Sure, we know all that. I haven't seen one serious suggestion for legislative change."[57]

In June, when her term expired, Brooksley Born quietly left the administration and was replaced by someone more in line with the views of her critics. Although she said later that President Clinton had offered to reappoint her, reports at the time suggested that she had been eased out of her position and that she had so alienated her colleagues that few even bothered to return her telephone calls. A trio of journalists described her farewell party: "Although it was customary at the agency for others to organize an outgoing chairman's going-away bash, she personally sprang for an ice cream cart in the commission's beige-carpeted auditorium. On a June afternoon, employees listened to subdued, carefully worded farewells while serving themselves sundaes."[58] A decade later, after the fiscal collapse of 2008, Born would be hailed as a heroine, a modern-day Horatius at the bridge, fighting alone for a righteous cause.[59]

In the summer of 2000, Congress began consideration of the Commodity Futures Modernization Act, a bill ostensibly intended to bring legal clarity to the trade in derivatives, particularly derivatives known as credit-default swaps (CDS). Were CDSs options or futures, and therefore subject to federal regulation, as Brooksley Born had argued? Or were they a unique financial product beyond the reach of Born's old agency, as Robert Rubin, Alan Greenspan, and Arthur Levitt had insisted? The bill sought to incorporate the Rubin-Greenspan-Levitt position. CDSs were not options or futures and were therefore not subject to regulation. Testifying in favor of the bill, Lawrence Summers enumerated the economic benefits of derivatives. By helping financial institutions "hedge their risks more efficiently," derivatives lowered the costs consumers had to pay for mortgages, insurance premiums, and other financial services. "By allowing for the transfer of unwanted risk," derivatives also promoted "more efficient allocation of capital across the economy, increasing productivity." Failure to act, Summers warned, not only risked denying the US economy the full benefit of derivatives but also hamstringing American businessmen and financiers in their efforts to compete in the global economy.[60] In October, the House passed the bill by a vote of 377 to 4. It then went to the Senate, where it encountered opposition from Texas Senator Phil Gramm, who wanted assurances that CDSs were beyond the reach not only of Born's agency but also of any agency, including the Securities and Exchange Commission. After two months of negotiations between Gramm and Summers, Gramm got most of what he wanted. In December, the bill was attached as a rider to an omnibus spending bill. With the administration's blessings, the spending bill, and with it the Commodity Futures Modernization Act (CFMA), overwhelmingly passed both houses of Congress. In one of his last official actions as president, Clinton signed it into law.

At the time, the CFMA attracted little public attention. Aside from a few trade publications and industry newsletters, no mainstream newspaper assigned a reporter to the measure. Not the *New York Times* or the *Washington Post* or even the *Wall Street Journal.*

Only later did the act stir controversy. In 2001, when the mammoth energy company, Enron, collapsed in bankruptcy and scandal, investigators pointed to an obscure provision of the CFMA, the so-called Enron loophole, that excluded from federal regulation the very kind of energy derivatives that had led to Enron's demise. During and after the economic meltdown of 2008, many held the unregulated market in derivatives at least partly to blame. Suddenly the enactment of the CFMA appeared in sinister light: Free-market zealots like Phil Gramm, aided and abetted by Clinton's economic advisers, had put one over on an unsuspecting Congress and an uninformed public. "It was an especially tense time in Washington," wrote one reporter. The president and Congress were "locked in a budget showdown," and the Supreme Court had just handed down its decision on *Bush v. Gore.* "It was," the reporter continued, "the perfect moment for a wily senator to game the system. As Congress and the White House were hurriedly hammering out a $384-billion omnibus spending bill, Gramm slipped in a 262-page measure called the Commodity Futures Modernization Act. It passed with few, if any, legislators even reading it."[61]

The real story of how the bill became a law was less dramatic, though no less important. Rather than being put over on an unsuspecting Congress in the dead of night, the bill had been under consideration for the better part of a year. Its sponsors included Republican conservatives like Gramm but also Democratic liberals like Tom Harkin of Iowa. At one time or another, six committees—four in the House and two in the Senate—held hearings on it. The problem was, as the writer John Lanchester later explained it: "Legislators had next to no idea what derivatives were or how they worked; there was something lulling and seductive about the idea that the banks should be allowed to police themselves, thanks to self-regulation and, of course, 'market discipline.'"[62] President Clinton and his economic advisers had a better understanding of derivatives and how they worked. But perhaps beguiled by the wonders of the New Economy, even they were lulled into a state of neoliberal complacency.

9

Last Chance: Clinton and the World, 1998–2000

President Clinton could hardly believe it. In December 1996, shortly after he was reelected, the *New York Times* published a poll of prominent historians and political scientists ranking the presidents from great to failure. He ranked in the "average" category, sandwiched between Benjamin Harrison and Martin Van Buren but also grouped with the likes of William Howard Taft, Chester A. Arthur, and George H. W. Bush. Clinton understood that greatness was reserved for Lincoln and Roosevelt, who had surmounted grave threats to the nation's existence, and for Washington, whose every action set a precedent for his successors. But what about "near great," a tier occupied by Jefferson, Polk, Theodore Roosevelt, and Truman?

Not long after the rankings appeared, a participant in the poll, historian and biographer Doris Kearns Goodwin, found herself seated next to Clinton at a White House dinner. The president was almost inconsolable. How could he be ranked so low? Goodwin tried to make light of the poll. An avid Boston Red Sox fan, she told Clinton she would change her vote if he could prevent an impending player's strike that threatened to wipe out the upcoming baseball season. The president remained bitterly disappointed.[1]

During his final years in office, even as he struggled through impeachment and its inglorious aftermath, a series of international crises in the Balkans, Iraq, and elsewhere unexpectedly offered Clinton a last chance to burnish his historical reputation. He even had a chance, or so he believed, to bring peace to the Middle East, a goal that had eluded all of his predecessors since the creation of Israel. It was ironic. Clinton came into office fixated on domestic affairs. He left preoccupied with foreign affairs.

Clinton began his second term with a new foreign policy team in place. For the most part, it acted more forcibly and with greater cohesion than the first term players. The key figure was National Security Adviser Samuel R. "Sandy" Berger, who replaced Anthony Lake. Born and raised in a small town in New York State and educated at Cornell and Harvard, Berger had known Clinton since their joint service on the McGovern campaign in 1972. He commanded the president's complete trust. Thomas A. Bailey, a distinguished US diplomatic historian, once said that formulating foreign policy in a democracy was more difficult than in any other system because of the importance of public opinion and politics. Berger's usefulness to Clinton stemmed in no small part from the fact that he instinctively understood the truism of Bailey's observation. Although no grand strategist, Berger cultivated useful relationships with leaders of both parties in a bitterly divided Congress, and he worked closely with the secretaries of state and defense, the director of the CIA, and the other relevant members of the administration. Especially during the impeachment crisis, when Clinton's attention to foreign policy was sporadic, the national security adviser helped maintain a sense of needed stability.

Second in importance was Madeleine Albright, who had left her position as ambassador to the United Nations to serve as secretary of state, the first woman to do so. Born in Prague, Albright was the daughter of a Czechoslovakian diplomat who had twice fled his native country, first to escape the Nazis, then the Communists. She grew up in Prague, London, and Denver, Colorado, where her father, after gaining political asylum, taught political science. For most Clintonites, Vietnam was the formative international experience of their lives. For Madeleine Albright it was the Munich Conference and the events that led to World War II. Like Sandy Berger, she understood the importance of domestic politics, and she worked hard to cultivate congressional support for the administration's positions, even managing to hold at bay the ultraconservative chairman of the Senate committee on foreign relations, Jesse Helms (R-NC). In contrast to her cautious predecessor William Christopher, Albright was the most outspoken advocate within the administration for an interventionist foreign policy. Once, while still at the UN, she had berated the chair of the Joint Chiefs, Colin Powell, for his reluctance to deploy American forces in the Balkans. "What are you saving this superb military for, Colin, if we can't use it?"[2] For much of her tenure, influential commentators depicted Albright as a big talker who promised more than the administration was willing or able to deliver. Shortly after assuming office, Albright, who had been raised Catholic, learned from a journalist who had probed into her family's history that she was Jewish and that some of her relatives had perished in the Holocaust—facts her parents had concealed from her. When she expressed surprise at the findings, some scoffed, saying she must have known but had denied her own heritage to advance her career.

President Clinton admired Albright for her deep convictions. She also got under his skin. He sometimes considered her a grandstander who too often played to the cameras. "She'll screw me every time," he complained on one occasion when he suspected her of trying to upstage him.[3] As she herself conceded in her memoir, when she was making a pitch to the president and his inner circle for some initiative or another, she could see the eyes rolling. "There goes Madeleine again," they were thinking. Still, by force of personality and conviction, Albright kept her department from being marginalized, as it had been for much of the twentieth century. She could not match Berger's closeness to the president. No one could. But she more than held her own with the national security adviser. It is unlikely that the United States would have played as prominent a role in the Balkans and perhaps elsewhere without Albright's insistent advocacy.

As for the rest of the foreign policy team, Vice President Gore continued to wield influence, more often than not by aligning himself with Albright in advocating forceful action. Then there was the able backfield of Dennis Ross, who headed the Middle East desk at the State Department; former Senator George Mitchell, whom Clinton asked to help broker a peace in Northern Ireland; Richard Holbrooke, who left the administration after the Dayton Accords but was summoned back into action to help deal with recurring crises in the Balkans; and the hard-driving Richard A. Clarke, who was transforming himself into the government's chief terrorism expert.

For Clinton, foreign affairs increasingly provided escape from his

domestic woes, just as they had for Richard Nixon during his impeachment crisis. During one of their late-night sessions early in 1998, Taylor Branch was surprised that "what preoccupied Clinton was neither
domestic politics nor special prosecutors" but the president's "knotted
concentrations overseas." In the course of their conversation, Clinton
conducted a world tour, discussing the current state of affairs in Northern
Ireland, South Korea, Indonesia, Iran, Iraq, and Syria. Uppermost in his
mind was the Israeli-Palestinian conflict, which, Branch noted, brought
him "near despair."[4] Clinton brought to foreign policy a highly personal
component. Like Lyndon Johnson, he looked upon foreign leaders first
and foremost as fellow politicians who, like himself, had to negotiate
the cross-currents of domestic politics. "Clinton was extraordinarily
successful in establishing personal relationships with foreign leaders,
just as he is with just about anybody," remembered Anthony Lake. "I
mean it is phenomenal. . . . There would be schmooze, schmooze, kiss,
kiss, common language of democracy, isn't being a leader difficult." The
drawback to the president's approach, according to Lake, was that he
would sometimes be reluctant to raise tough issues with foreign leaders,
like differences over trade or human rights. The role of "bad cop" the
president would relegate to the vice president, the secretary of state, or
his national security adviser. Clinton was the Will Rogers of the Oval
Office, Lake concluded. "He never met a leader he didn't like."[5]

The leaders with whom he forged the closest relationships were
Boris Yeltsin of Russia, Tony Blair of Great Britain, Helmut Kohl of
Germany, Ernesto Zedillo of Mexico, Antonio Guterres of Portugal,
and Nelson Mandela of South Africa. The leader he most admired was
Yitzhak Rabin of Israel, who was assassinated in 1995 and at whose
funeral Clinton delivered a memorable address.[6] Perhaps the leader he
most enjoyed spending an evening with was Helmut Kohl. When the
German Chancellor came to town, they would go to a restaurant better
known for the quantity of the food than its quality. "Watching them in
their pig-out contests was one of the revolting experiences of my life,"
recalled Lake.[7] Saddam Hussein, Slobodan Milosevic, and later Osama
bin Laden headed his list of villains. Clinton was not naïve, but again,
like Lyndon Johnson, he believed he could bend all but the most intran-
sigent foreign leader to his will once he located their common thread of
experience.

Clinton's engagement in foreign affairs stood in marked contrast to that of his fellow citizens. Perhaps not since the late 1920s or early 1930s had the American public been as disengaged from international developments as they were in the late nineties. In 1998, the Chicago Council of Foreign Affairs conducted a poll asking respondents to identify the biggest international problems facing the United States. The most common response was "don't know."[8] During the thirties, public detachment was born of absorption with economic hardship. In the nineties, it stemmed from a booming economy, coupled with an abundance of domestic attractions, including the impeachment drama.

In trying to engage the United States abroad Clinton had to overcome not only public reticence but also the reluctance of the Pentagon and the Joint Chiefs to deploy American military forces. As far as Clinton's military chiefs were concerned, the Powell doctrine remained operative. Intervention, when necessary, must be pursued with overwhelming force, clear objectives, and a well-marked exit strategy. In other words: No more Vietnams. The military also continued to regard Clinton with icy disdain, and their estimation of his secretary of defense during the second term, William Cohen, the former Republican senator from Maine, wasn't much better.

No knowledgeable observer could have been surprised that the first international crisis Clinton faced during the second term bore the familiar face of Slobodan Milosevic. Clinton had last encountered the Serbian leader in December 1995 at the formal signing to the Dayton Accords. Milosevic, Clinton recalled, "was intelligent, articulate, and cordial" but also "paranoid" and with "the coldest look in his eyes" he had ever seen. "After spending time with him," Clinton concluded, "I was no longer surprised by his support of the murderous outrages in Bosnia, and I had the feeling that I would be at odds with him again before long."[9] The Dayton Accords had more or less resolved the conflict between Serbs and Bosnians. By 1998, however, a long-simmering feud between ethnic Albanians and Serbs in the Serbian province of Kosovo had erupted into open warfare. Following Dayton, Milosevic had increasingly pressured Albanians to leave Kosovo, where they constituted 90 percent of the population. A reign of terror ensued. Albanians by the thousands fled for their lives. The situation took a dire turn when it was revealed that a

Serbian assault on the small village of Racak claimed the lives of forty-five civilians, including women, children, and elderly men.

When diplomacy proved of no avail, Clinton sought to convince other NATO members to resume the airstrikes that had brought Milosevic to the peace table in Dayton. From the standpoint of international law and world opinion, however, Kosovo entailed far greater complexities than Bosnia. Unlike Bosnia, it was not a sovereign nation being attacked from the outside; it was a province of Serbia, legitimately under the control of Milosevic and his forces. Essentially the United States was calling upon itself and its NATO allies to intervene in a civil war. In addition, as the legendary birthplace of Serbian independence, Kosovo was more symbolically important to the Serbs than Bosnia ever had been. Due in part to the relentless efforts of Madeleine Albright, NATO members did, however, agree to airstrikes, largely on humanitarian grounds but also out of concern that the flood of Albanian refugees would unsettle the entire region.[10]

In his address to the nation, Clinton said the United States and its allies must heed the lessons of history. Twice in the twentieth century, they had failed to act before it was too late. The results: two world wars and the Holocaust. "What if someone had listened to Winston Churchill and stood up to Adolph Hitler earlier?" he asked. "How many lives might have been saved? And how many American lives might have been saved?" Lest anyone fear another Vietnam, Clinton assured Americans he had no intention of introducing ground troops into combat.

Within the White House, opinion was sharply divided on the advisability of the air campaign. Recalled National Security Adviser Sandy Berger: "We had a 78-day bombing campaign in Kosovo, which nobody except Bill Clinton, Sandy Berger, Madeleine Albright, Bill Cohen, and our spouses believed would work."[11]

Outside the administration, reaction was a mirror image of reactions to Vietnam in its late stages. Liberals supported intervention in Kosovo, conservatives opposed it. As one columnist noted, "The core support for the war comes from doves with long records of opposition to America's Cold War interventions. . . . From Paul Wellstone to Maxine Waters, virtually every congressional liberal has gone on record to say the threat posed by Milosevic requires a U.S. military response." House Democratic whip David Bonior (D-MI) had risen within his party's ranks principally because of his opposition to Reagan's intervention in Central America in the eighties. Now he was willing to go even further than Clinton. "If it takes more than air power, so be it. Including ground troops."[12] On the other hand, Henry Kissinger, an architect of the war in Vietnam, decried intervention in Kosovo as "an unprecedented extension of NATO authority; an extraordinary assertion of international law; and a dangerous precedent for America."[13]

Even historians who supported the airstrikes took exception to Clinton's historical analogies. "To draw a link with the outbreak of two world wars is a great oversimplification of history," said Yale historian John Lewis Gaddis. The invocation of the Holocaust offended many. Wrote political scientist Stephen Cohen, the comparison "wantonly debases the historical reality and memory of the Holocaust; Milosevic's reign of terror has turned most Kosovars into refugees fleeing toward sanctuaries; Hitler gave Europe's Jews no exit and turned them into ash."[14]

In the beginning, critics of the bombing strikes appeared prophetic. Instead of backing down as he had in Bosnia, Milosevic stepped up his assault. Indeed, the deadliest part of the war for the Kosovars came after, not before, NATO intervention. Within weeks, thousands had been killed or forced to flee. Before long over half of Kosovo's 1.8 million people were dead, missing, or in exile. The low point of the air campaign came when NATO planes, relying on outdated maps supplied by the CIA, mistakenly bombed the Chinese embassy in Belgrade, killing three diplomats and provoking a diplomatic crisis between the United States and China. Backers of the war now began to have cold feet. But Clinton held firm, reassuring doubters he was doing the right thing. "The prospect of failure was very real," reporter John Harris later wrote, and "so was the poise with which Clinton confronted the prospect and resolved to avoid it."[15] As the war dragged on, Britain's Tony Blair, Madeleine Albright, and NATO commander and fellow Arkansan Wesley Clark told the president he had no choice but to commit ground forces. After anguished consideration, Clinton authorized the mobilization of 100,000 American troops. It was a move eerily reminiscent of Lyndon Johnson's fateful decision to deploy the first combat troops to Vietnam in 1965.

Then, just when events appeared to be spinning out of control, fate intervened. Milosevic relented. Russia, not Clinton's resolve, appears to have been the decisive factor. Russia had angrily opposed the NATO airstrikes at first. NATO, after all, had been formed in 1949 for the sole purpose of containing the Soviet Union. But now, with the Cold War over, Clinton was not only maintaining the military alliance but expanding it to include Poland and other former Soviet satellites. Under Clinton, NATO had even engaged in combat for the first time in its history. If the alliance could intervene in the Balkans, the Russians worried, what would stop it from intervening in Chechnya or other states deemed essential to national security? The Russians weren't alone in the disdain for NATO. George Kennan, after all, had characterized Clinton's expansion of the alliance as "a tragic mistake" and "the beginning of a new cold war."[16]

In the end Russian Premier Boris Yeltsin reasoned that the future of his country rested more with the United States than with Slobodan Milosevic. Once Yeltsin let the Serbian leader know he could no longer rely on Russian support, Milosevic agreed to settle. For Yeltsin's critically important intervention, Clinton could claim at least some of the credit, for, despite the NATO provocations, he had worked hard at maintaining ties with the erratic Russian leader. Once, on a visit to Washington, the Secret Service found Yeltsin, naked and drunk in the middle of the night, trying to hail a cab to take him to a pizza parlor. When asked by his friend Taylor Branch what happened next, Clinton said, "Well, he got his pizza."[17]

Kosovo faded from public memory before most Americans had learned to locate it on the map. Its most tangible legacy was the accretion of war-making power it bestowed upon the presidency. Before the war began, Clinton asked Congress to pass resolutions supporting intervention. The Senate complied but the House, on a tie vote, declined. Clinton was hardly the first president to go to war without congressional approval. Indeed, American forces had gone into battle nearly 200 times without a declaration of war or a resolution of congressional support. But Clinton was the first president who failed to comply with the War Powers Act, which Congress had passed in 1974 in a desperate attempt to rein in "the imperial presidency." According to the act, the president could initiate military action without congressional authorization; but unless the United States had been directly attacked, he was required to seek statutory authorization from Congress within sixty days. In Kosovo, sixty days came and went but Clinton sought no authorization. Seventeen members of Congress took the president to court but federal judges threw out the challenge.[18] In truth, presidents had become so intent upon violating the spirit of the War Powers Resolution that Clinton's action (or inaction) was more in the nature of a mercy killing than a mortal blow to a vital legislative statute. Still, the episode took on special importance because the president who undermined the War Powers Act had come of age believing the chief executive had too much power to make war. President Clinton helped legitimize the autonomous war-making power of the presidency in much the same way President Eisenhower helped legitimize the legislative legacies of Franklin Roosevelt and the New Deal.

Clinton not only bequeathed to his successors more robust war-making powers but also a blueprint for dealing with Saddam Hussein's Iraq. Following the Gulf War, the Iraqi leader had agreed to allow the United Nations to inspect facilities that had the capacity to produce so-called weapons of mass destruction—biological, chemical, and nuclear weapons. By Clinton's second term, however, Saddam was blocking access to suspected production sites. At first the Clinton administration responded in measured tones, saying it would do everything possible to resolve the problem diplomatically. When Saddam continued to defy the inspectors, the administration began to prepare the public for the possibility of military intervention. On November 15, 1997, Clinton told a gathering of Democrats in Sacramento that one of the biggest threats the country would face now and in the future was the spread of "chemical and biological weapons and maybe small-scale nuclear weapons." Even small amounts of a nuclear cake "put in a bomb"—Clinton held up his forefinger and thumb—"would do ten times as much damage as the Oklahoma City bomb did." The world had to combat "the organized forces of destruction" that would spread weapons of mass destruction. That, he said, was "fundamentally what is at stake in the stand off we're having in Iraq today."[19] The next morning on ABC's *This Week*, Defense Secretary Cohen placed on the table a five-pound sack of sugar and asked viewers to imagine it contained anthrax, which Iraq was known to have produced during the Gulf War. If spread over a city the size of Washington, Cohen said, it would kill half of the population. Cohen next held up a thimble: if it contained VX, a nerve agent also suspected in Iraq's arsenal, one drop "will kill you within a few minutes." At a Pentagon briefing ten days later, Cohen said that the United Nations believed Saddam Hussein may have in his possession "as much as 200 tons of VX, and this would, of course, be theoretically enough to kill every man, woman and child on the face of the earth." If anyone doubted the Iraqi leader's capacity for evil, Madeleine Albright told an audience at Tennessee State University, that perhaps not since Hitler had the world seen "somebody who is quite as evil as Saddam Hussein." If the world didn't stand firm against him, Clinton said, Saddam "will conclude that he can go right on and do more to rebuild an arsenal of devastating destruction. And some day, some way, I guarantee you he'll use his arsenal."[20] And so it went.

In October 1998, Congress passed, and President Clinton signed, the Iraq Liberation Act, declaring it to be "the policy of the United States to support efforts to remove the regime headed by Saddam Hussein from power in Iraq and to promote the emergence of a democratic government to replace that regime." The vote in the House was 360 to 38 and unanimous in the Senate. The act authorized the president to equip opponents of Saddam's regime with up to $97 million worth of weapons and military training.

Two months later, when Saddam once again blocked weapons inspectors, the United States launched massive airstrikes on Iraq. Over four nights, American ships, submarines, and planes pummeled Iraq with missiles and bombs. In advance of the aerial attacks, President Clinton said that "Saddam Hussein must not be allowed to threaten his neighbors or the world with nuclear arms, poison gas, or biological weapons." Other nations might possess weapons of mass destruction, he explained, but only Saddam Hussein had used them not only against other nations but also against his own people. Unless stopped, he would "use these terrible weapons again." Echoing arguments made by the Johnson and Nixon administrations during Vietnam, Clinton argued that the failure to hold Saddam accountable for his actions would damage the credibility of the United States and encourage mischief in other parts of the world.[21]

In 1947, Senator Arthur Vandenberg reputedly told President Truman that the only way Congress would approve the president's request for military and economic aid for the anti-Communist regimes in

Greece and Turkey was to "scare the hell out of the American people." As with their depiction of Milosevic as a modern-day Hitler, it was hard to know if Clinton administration officials believed Saddam posed as grave a threat to the world as they said he did. Or, believing in the necessity of containing Saddam, did they reason as Vandenberg did that only by exaggerating the threat could a distracted public and a skeptical Congress be persuaded to do the right thing?

As it turned out, the administration had no concrete evidence that Saddam Hussein's arsenal contained weapons of mass destruction. It was not for want of trying. In addition to aerial and satellite surveillance, the United States listened in on the telephone calls of top Iraqi officials. CIA operatives worked hand-in-glove with the UN weapons inspectors. Still no hard evidence ever materialized. In 1995, a high-ranking Iraqi defector claimed that Saddam had ordered the destruction of weapons of mass destruction in 1991. "The whole topic of Iraq's WMD was riddled with propaganda, poisoned by misinformation and unsubstantiated assertions, and it had spun entirely out of control," wrote journalist Richard Sale years later.[22]

Sale was right, but he was also writing with the full advantage of hindsight. Up against it was Saddam Hussein's highly suspicious behavior at the time. If he had nothing to hide, why resist inspections? And why was he willing to endure devastating airstrikes and an international trade boycott that was crippling Iraq's economy?

The aerial attacks of December 1998 left Saddam weakened but still very much in power. It would be a mistake to draw a straight line between Clinton's Iraqi policies and the invasion of Iraq in 2003 under his successor's administration. During his remaining years in office, Clinton limited expenditures under the Iraq Liberation Act to nonlethal assistance, and even that didn't add up to much. The administration wanted Saddam gone. It was just having trouble finding Iraqis it considered reliable replacements. A lot of history was still to play out. Yet, anyone who paid even the slightest attention to events during Clinton's last years could be easily forgiven for believing that Iraq possessed weapons of mass destruction, that Saddam Hussein posed a threat not only to the Middle East but to the United States, and that the world would be better off if he were somehow deposed or removed from power. Moreover, those who supported the deployment of American forces in Iraq in 2003, including President George W. Bush, frequently cited the Iraq Liberation Act in their war briefs.

Clinton had no sooner come to office than he had to address a problem to which he had given little attention: terrorist attacks in the United States and abroad. Five days after the inauguration, a young Pakistani citizen killed two CIA employees and wounded three others as they were driving to work at CIA headquarters in Langley, Virginia. One month later, a car bomb exploded in the parking garage of the World Trade Center in New York City killing ten and wounding a thousand. Oklahoma City occurred in 1995 but so, too, did a car bombing in Riyadh, Saudi Arabia, that killed American military personnel, and a foiled plot to blow up a dozen commercial airliners over the Pacific. So it went until October 2000, just months before Clinton left office, when explosives ripped a huge hole in the USS *Cole*, an American destroyer docked for refueling in Aden, Yemen. Seventeen American sailors were killed, thirty wounded.

Despite the increasing frequency of attacks, terrorism drifted in and out of the public's consciousness, never occupying a central position for very long. Although 235 Americans died at the hands of terrorists during the Clinton years, most attacks occurred on foreign soil, in places like Kenya, Tanzania, and Yemen. As a result, "Americans were still much more likely to die from bee stings than from terrorist strikes" observed journalist Steve Coll.[23]

The Clinton administration committed its share of sins. Unresponsiveness to terrorism was not among them. It responded forcefully to terrorist attacks, at least within the context of the times. When possible, perpetrators were tracked down, arrested, and put on trial. When foreign countries were believed to be responsible, reprisals were meted out. Upon learning that Iraq had tried to assassinate former President Bush during his visit to Kuwait, Clinton ordered missile strikes on Iraqi intelligence headquarters in Baghdad. During his two terms, Clinton more than doubled funding for the government's antiterrorist activities.

By the late nineties, he had become particularly concerned about the possibility of a chemical or biological attack on the United States, which accounts in part for the alarms he sounded about Saddam Hussein and weapons of mass destruction. In 1995 members of a religious cult released a deadly nerve gas in a Tokyo subway, causing Clinton and others in the administration to worry that a similar incident could happen in the United States. He became even more alarmed in 1998 after reading Richard Preston's *The Cobra Event*, a novel about a mad scientist who infects New Yorkers with a deadly genetically engineered virus that spreads as fast as the common cold. When medical experts told the president that such an attack was possible, he brought them in to conduct seminars for cabinet members and to conduct war games to assess the readiness of the government to respond to a crisis. At his direction, the administration made plans to stockpile antidotes and vaccines in case the worst happened.[24]

Extraordinary rendition was one of the most controversial practices the George W. Bush administration employed after 9/11 to track down suspected terrorists. For all practical purposes, it originated in the Clinton administration. It allowed US officials to bypass extraditions procedures by apprehending suspected terrorists on foreign soil and either bringing them to the United States for trial or sending them to other countries for interrogation and incarceration. The Clinton administration did not invent extraordinary rendition. But previous administrations had employed it only three times. In 1993, when Richard Clarke first asked Clinton to authorize the practice, the president seemed skeptical. White House counsel Lloyd Cutler strongly opposed rendition on the grounds that it violated international law, and Clinton seemed to agree. But then Vice President Gore weighed in. "That's a no-brainer," Richard Clarke remembered Gore telling the president. "Of course it's a violation of international law, that's why it's a covert action. The guy is a terrorist. Go grab his ass." From then on, recalled Clarke, Clinton never refused a rendition request, and by the mid-nineties the practice had become "routine."[25]

Frequent destinations for suspects included Jordan, Syria, and especially Egypt. It worked this way: the CIA would capture a suspected terrorist and turn him over to, say, the Mukhabarat, Egypt's secret police. The system operated with the efficiency of a dry cleaner offering same-day service. In the morning the CIA would drop off a suspect and a list of questions for Egyptian interrogators to ask. By evening, it could pick up its answers. US law required the CIA to get assurances from Egypt and other "host" countries that detainees would not be tortured. But as reporter Jane Mayer wrote in an authoritative account of extraordinary rendition, "even during the Clinton Administration, this obligation appears to have been little more than a sham." One CIA official, who supported rendition as an absolute necessity, later admitted that pledges not to torture "weren't worth a bucket of warm spit."[26] One suspect later claimed that Egyptian interrogators applied electric prods to his genitals, hung him by his limbs, and confined him to a cell with dirty water up to his knees. Some detainees were executed, the fate of others never known.[27]

Almost everything Clinton did in response to terrorist attacks, to the extent it became public, was criticized as being either too much or too little. Some critics dismissed the airstrikes on Baghdad in 1993 as an all-too-obvious way of showing he was no draft-dodging holdover from the sixties. Some Bush supporters, by contrast, considered those same airstrikes inadequate punishment for the attempt on the life of the former president. When Clinton wanted to prepare for a Cobra-like virus being loosened on the public, normally defense-minded Republicans complained about the costs, while others said the money would be better spent on traditional weapons systems. Those who shared the president's concern about the dangers of chemical and biological warfare deplored his preparedness plans as woefully inadequate. The administration wanted to require the manufacturers of explosives to include in their products chemical markers—taggants. That way authorities could trace detonated explosives back to their sellers. It got nowhere. Recalled Sandy Berger: "A coalition of civil libertarians on the left and 'Don't interfere with my guns' on the right came together to kill the proposal." A proposal to adapt government-authorized wiretapping to the cell phone age met a similar fate.[28] And so it went.

Clinton first heard Osama bin Laden's name shortly after becoming president. But except for the basic facts—Saudi-born, Islamic fundamentalist, member of a wealthy engineering family—bin Laden remained a shadowy figure, appearing only sporadically in Clinton's daily intelligence briefings. By 1995, still sketchy reports had him possibly bankrolling terrorist activities from the Balkans to the Philippines. Not until 1996 did bin Laden come more sharply into focus as not only the financier of a far-flung terrorist network but also its mastermind. Even then, administration officials like CIA Director George Tenet viewed him primarily, as journalist Steve Coll put it, as "a blowhard, a dangerous and wealthy egomaniac, and a financier of other radicals" but also someone exiled to Afghanistan, an unlikely staging area for world domination.[29] Moreover, intelligence estimates linking bin Laden to specific terrorist acts almost always carried with them a high probability of error.

Bin Laden's worldview also made it hard for the Clinton administration to fully comprehend the danger he posed. His grievances against the United States were apparently rooted in the military presence it had maintained in Saudi Arabia since the Gulf War. For nonbelievers to occupy Islam's most sacred lands was, for bin Laden, tantamount to an American declaration of war "on Allah, His Prophet, and Muslims." In response, every Muslim not only had the right but also the obligation "to kill and fight Americans and their allies, whether civilians or military."[30] This absolutist view—"the conviction that he was in possession of the absolute truth and therefore free to play God by killing innocent people," as Clinton put it—was simply hard for him and most Americans to fathom. It wasn't that he had too rosy a view of human nature. He'd grown up in the American South after all and had seen the depths of depravity tapped by violent opponents of the civil rights movement. But this was the sickness of racism at work. Bin Laden's appeal was harder to fathom. Even at the height of the Cold War, the Soviet Union and the People's Republic of China had been open to negotiation and coexistence. Bin Laden was something different. The only comparisons Clinton could think of were villains out of James Bond movies like Dr. No or Hugo Drax: incredibly wealthy, stateless figures bent on holding the world hostage to their will.[31]

By 1997, the CIA had created within its counterterrorism center a small unit devoted exclusively to keeping tabs on bin Laden. The members of this unit gathered every bit of information they could about the al Qaeda leader. They pored over everything they could find by and about him, and they tried to keep track of his whereabouts. The more they learned about him, the more convinced they became—almost to the point of obsession—that he posed a mortal threat to the United States. By 1998, they had devised the first of what would be many plans to capture or kill bin Laden. The plan called for a group of CIA-trained

Afghans to launch a middle-of-the-night raid on an isolated compound bin Laden was known to frequent. Once abducted, the al Qaeda leader would be turned over to the CIA and sent to the United States for prosecution. To the consternation of the plan's designers, it never made its way to the president's desk. CIA Director Tenet and other top officials rated its chances of success at no more than 40 percent. Richard Clarke, who wanted to get bin Laden as much as anybody, thought the plan hair-brained. The invading force, he believed, was likely to get cut down before ever reaching the compound. And if somehow it did manage to get in, dozens of women and children who were known to be living in the compound were likely to get caught in the crossfire.[32]

In August 1998, following the bombing of the American embassies in Tanzania and Kenya, intelligence sources reported that al Qaeda leaders, possibly including bin Laden, were planning to meet at a training camp in Afghanistan. At Clinton's order, naval vessels, stationed off the coast, bombarded the site with seventy-five cruise missiles. Twenty-one people were killed. Bin Laden was not among them. Simultaneous with the attack, US missiles leveled a factory in Sudan thought to be producing chemical and biological weapons for bin Laden's forces. The strikes were costly failures. The Sudan factory may or may not have been owned by bin Laden, as it turned out. What it did turn out to be, however, as Clinton critic Christopher Hitchens pointed out, was a desperately poor country's "chief source of medicines and pesticides."[33] As for bin Laden, the failure to kill him boosted his image around the Islamic world. Here after all was the world's most powerful nation, possessed of the world's most sophisticated weaponry, being out-maneuvered by a figure most people had never before heard of. The missile strikes, wrote journalist Steve Coll, were bin Laden's "biggest publicity payoff to date."[34]

During ensuing months, CIA operatives claimed to have bin Laden in their sights a half-dozen or more times. No further kill or capture orders were authorized. The president came close at times to issuing the go-ahead, but always backed away, sometimes at the last moment. One time, intelligence reports placed bin Laden at a hunting camp in eastern Afghanistan. The problem was that if present he was possibly in the company of members of the royal family of the United Arab Emirates, an unsavory regime but also an ally of the United States. Other times the president worried that an attack, even a successful one, would claim the lives of innocent people and create a backlash of sympathy for bin Laden. "I could just imagine the news report: U.S. bombs Kandahar, hundreds of women and children killed; Bin Laden press conference to follow."[35] From experience, Clinton also had reason to be skeptical of the accuracy of intelligence reports. The Somali disaster of the first term had been Clinton's Bay of Pigs. It taught him, as the earlier disaster had taught President Kennedy, that the intelligence community was hardly infallible. More recent events had reinforced Clinton's caution. It was during the war in Kosovo after all that faulty intelligence had led to the disastrous bombing of the Chinese Embassy in Belgrade.

9/11 prompted a rash of finger pointing. The members of the special bin Laden unit led the way. The unit's first head, Michael Scheuer, accused all of the higher-ups in the Clinton administration, including Richard Clarke, CIA Director Tenet, and the president himself of not having taken bin Laden seriously enough. Viewing him alternatively as a madman or master criminal, they failed to understand the depth of his religious convictions as well as the specific grievances against the United States that earned bin Laden an increasingly large and passionate following.[36] Thusly underestimating him and the threat he posed, they didn't seize the opportunities they had to eliminate him. Bin Laden "should have been a dead man," one CIA operative told the commission that investigated 9/11.[37] Finger pointing wasn't confined to the bin Laden unit. At the White House, Richard Clarke held the CIA and the Pentagon responsible. After the embassy bombings in 1998, he said, Clinton pulled his military and intelligence chiefs aside and told them in no uncertain terms what he wanted done. "Listen," Clarke remembered the president saying, "retaliation for these attacks is all well and good, but we gotta get rid of these guys once and for all. You understand what I'm telling you?"[38] But Clinton's chiefs didn't follow through. Nor did the president. Clinton, Clarke later told a reporter, had an "odd combination of complacency and deference to the subordinates who were supposed to be deferential to him. Clinton would make requests, and just assume these were being done, or that people around him knew best."[39]

CIA Director Tenet pointed fingers at those both below and above. The opportunities to capture or kill bin Laden were never as great as the operatives in the bin Laden unit believed, Tenet argued. There was the low, 40 percent chance their first "snatch" plan would meet with success.

There was the slightly better 50 or 60 percent probability of pinpointing bin Laden's whereabouts long enough for cruise missiles to hit him. But the possibilities of something going wrong—killing innocent civilians, leveling a mosque, inflaming anti-American sentiments in the Islamic world—these odds were always as great or greater than the chances of pulling off a mission without a hitch. The real problem was the lack of support from the top. "The fact is," Tenet wrote in his memoir, "that by the mid- to late 1990s American intelligence was in Chapter 11, and neither Congress nor the executive branch did much about it." The CIA's budget had been slashed by 10 percent, its workforce by 25 percent. Morale had hit rock bottom. Then, too, Tenet said, he received uncertain guidance from the administration. Clarke remembered the president telling the director "we gotta get rid of these guys once and for all." Tenet's recollection was that the president constrained plans for getting bin Laden by ordering that he be captured alive. "It was understood that in the context of such an operation, Bin Laden would resist and might be killed in the ensuing battle. But the context was almost always to attempt to capture him first." According to Tenet, no less a figure than Attorney General Janet Reno told him "she would view an attempt simply to kill Bin Laden as illegal."[40]

But the second-guessing was almost all with the advantage of hindsight. As hard as it would be for a post-9/11 generation to believe, the simple fact was that in the late nineties, in the minds of Clinton and almost everyone else, other issues crowded out the looming threat of bin Laden and al Qaeda. If the bin Laden trackers at the CIA and Richard Clarke at the White House spent most of their waking hours thinking about bin Laden, the president, while worrying about the al Qaeda leader, too, also had to concern himself with ongoing crises in the Balkans, Iraq, Russia, and North Korea. To Clinton's mind, the greatest threat to world peace during his administration was the sudden eruption of a long-simmering dispute between Pakistan and India. In 1998, India caught the United States by surprise by conducting a nuclear test. Despite urgent pleas from US officials, Pakistan soon followed with a test of its own. In 1999, the two nations, now armed with nuclear weapons, came close to all-out war over the disputed Himalayan Kingdom of Kashmir. A Pakistani incursion into Indian-occupied territory sparked what became known as the Kargil War. It was, Clinton confided to Taylor Branch, the most serious crisis of his presidency. He was reminded of how an assassination in the Balkans had escalated into global war in 1914 and of how close the Cuban Missile Crisis had come to spiraling out of control. Resolving the crisis would be the diplomatic equivalent of defusing an intricately wired time bomb. "If they called tonight, and said I could end this thing by flying over there, I would have no choice but to jump on a plane," Clinton said. "There is no greater responsibility for me than to reduce conflicts that threaten nuclear war, and this one certainly does."[41] In the end, Clinton helped talk Pakistan's prime minister, Nawaz Sharif, away from the edge. On July 4, 1999, the two leaders met at Blair House in Washington, DC. This was not one of those "schmooze schmooze, kiss kiss" meetings Anthony Lake had talked about. "Do you recognize what even one nuclear bomb would mean?" Clinton asked Sharif. "It would be a catastrophe," the prime minister replied. If he did not relent, Clinton warned, the United States "would blame Pakistan for starting a war that could end in nuclear disaster."[42] There would be other consequences as well. Reluctantly Sharif ordered his troops to withdraw, bringing the crisis, at least for the moment, to an end. "Avoiding Armageddon" was how the administration's South East Asia expert, Bruce O. Riedel, described the episode. The point here is that administration insiders knew that combating al Qaeda was important. But at the time, there were a score of other threats that seemed more important.

True, as some critics pointed out, Clinton might have done more to alert the public to the danger posed by bin Laden. He might, for example, have put him on the same level with Saddam Hussein and Slobodan Milosevic. But in so doing he might have made bin Laden an even greater magnet than he already was for those with grievances, real and imagined, against the United States.

Clinton was not alone in seeming to minimize bin Laden. Between the late nineties and 9/11 virtually all appraisals of Clinton's foreign policy, many of which were critical, scarcely mentioned bin Laden or al Qaeda. David Halberstam, for example, omitted the subject entirely in *War in a Time of Peace*, which he intended to be a sequel to his celebrated book on Vietnam, *The Best and the Brightest*. The same lack of interest flavored the numerous journalistic overviews that appeared as Clinton was about to leave office. The truth is, 9/11 made Osama bin Laden. It defined him.

During his final months in office, the quest for peace in the Middle East dominated Clinton's attention. An easing of tensions between Israelis and Palestinians was a worthy goal in itself of course. But Clinton believed it would also weaken the appeal of bin Laden and al Qaeda, for whom the status quo was a powerful recruiting tool. And if Clinton could broker an agreement that had eluded all of his predecessors since the creation of Israel, he might still have a chance to reach the second tier of presidents.

During the course of the Clinton presidency the peace process had veered between hope and disappointment. Perhaps the one bright spot during Clinton's first year in office was the famous handshake he choreographed on the White House lawn between Israeli Premier Yitzhak Rabin and Palestine Liberation Organization leader Yasser Arafat. But soon thereafter, the momentum petered out and hope faded. The assassination of Rabin in 1995 by a young Israeli opposed to any concessions to the Palestinians, coupled with the ascension to power of Benjamin "Bibi" Netanyahu, threw the peace process into chaos. A member of the hard-line Likud party, Netanyahu was ill inclined to resume where Rabin had left off. Moreover, from the beginning he successfully resisted President Clinton's charms. Of the Israeli leader, Clinton privately complained, "he thinks he is the superpower and we are here to do whatever he requires."[43]

Still, Clinton had reason for optimism. The resolution of conflicts in Bosnia and Kosovo cast doubt on the "ancient ghosts" theory that some conflicts were so deeply rooted in history as to defy resolution. By the late nineties progress was also being made to resolve the seemingly endless conflict between Protestants and Catholics in Northern Ireland, thanks in part to the efforts of Clinton and his special envoy to Northern Ireland, former senator George Mitchell. So Clinton had reason to believe that revisiting the Middle East might yield positive results. In October 1998, with the State Department taking the lead, the administration sequestered Netanyahu and Arafat at the Wye River Plantation on the Chesapeake Bay in Maryland. For nine days Clinton commuted between Washington and the secluded estate, working first with one delegation, then with the other. Clinton was at his best. "I mean, he doesn't stop," said Netanyahu. "He has this ability to maintain this tireless pace and to nudge and prod and suggest and use a nimble and flexible mind."[44] But as in the past, hopes for a breakthrough were short-lived.

It was not Clinton, however, but Netanyahu's successor as Israeli prime minister, Ehud Barak, who initiated the last peace effort before Clinton left office. Both Clinton and his State Department advisers were initially skeptical that any good could come of it; they worried that another failed summit could deal a greater blow to the peace process than no summit at all. Moreover, Yasser Arafat insisted that the time was not right. Nevertheless, when Barak persisted, Clinton convinced himself that he just might be able to pull it off. In July 2000, he summoned the Israeli and Palestinian leaders to Camp David, where President Carter had overseen the historic agreement between Egypt and Israel. By the time the conference began, Clinton calculated the chances of success as better than fifty-fifty.[45] Clinton played an even larger role than he had at the Wye Plantation, impressing even the most skeptical participants with his determination to broker an agreement. The Palestinians were particularly impressed by Clinton's skill at "breaking barriers." Their reaction to him was reminiscent of the reaction, a quarter century earlier, of black law students at the University of Arkansas to the bushy-haired, white professor who unselfconsciously pulled up a chair and asked if he could join them in the cafeteria. During mealtimes at Camp David, Clinton would serve himself from the buffet table and then sit down with delegates from one side or the other. Recalled a Palestinian participant: "He would easily initiate conversation, moving from an enthusiastic discussion of the implications of genetic mapping, to analyzing his wife's chances for winning the Senate race in New York, to a trip to the Balkans and his impression of the people there, and so on."[46] Clinton moved just as effortlessly from dinner-table conversation to intense debates over the issues that most divided the delegates. One night he presided over a session with two Israelis and two Palestinians that lasted from eleven o'clock to five in the morning.

There came a moment in the talks when the Palestinians thought Clinton just might be able to pull it off. As one member of their delegation explained, they came to view Clinton as "a person who could listen and understand. Perhaps because they suffered, and still suffer, from the total pro-Israeli bias of the US peace team, they were betting on—or had convinced themselves of—Clinton's objectivity."[47] But the mood of optimism quickly dissipated. The summit, dubbed Camp David II, ended with no agreement.

Clinton persisted, and during the next six months his negotiating team, led by Dennis Ross, shuttled between the two sides in an effort to find common ground. In December and early January, just weeks before leaving office, Clinton made one last effort. Summoning Barak and Arafat to the White House Cabinet Room, he verbally outlined the "parameters" of a final settlement. The parameters would create a demilitarized Palestinian state covering Gaza and some 95 percent of the West Bank and with a capital in East Jerusalem. Other items dealt with security matters, compensation for refugees displaced by the Arab-Israeli War of 1948, and divided sovereignty over Arab, Jewish, and Christian sectors of Jerusalem. A settlement along these lines, Clinton believed, not only embodied unprecedented concessions on the part of Israel but also offered the best chance for peace since the creation of the Israeli state. "Never before," wrote Dennis Ross, "had the United States put a comprehensive set of proposals on the table designed to end the conflict between Israelis and Palestinians—or at least shrink the differences on all the core issues to a point where a final deal could be hammered out quickly."[48]

What happened next was—and remains—a matter of dispute. According to Clinton, Dennis Ross, Madeleine Albright, and other US officials, the response to the president's overture was unequivocal: Ehud Barak said yes and Yasser Arafat said no. "Arafat's rejection of my proposal after Barak accepted it was an error of historic proportions," Clinton wrote in his memoir.[49] "Sadly," said Sandy Berger, "the Palestinians did not have a Nelson Mandela at the moment in history when they needed somebody who could pivot from being a revolutionary and the leader of a movement to being a statesman and the leader of a country. Arafat was simply not capable of doing that."[50]

Palestinian participants countered, more out of sadness than criticism, that President Clinton had not been the honest broker he had presented himself to be. Some members of Clinton's own negotiating team took issue with accounts casting Arafat in the role of spoiler. Said Robert Malley, the president's special assistant for Arab-Israeli affairs, these accounts grossly oversimplified complex events. "They ignored history, the dynamics of the negotiations, and the relationships among the three parties [Israel, the Palestinians, the United States]." For one thing, Malley argued, the Palestinian leader didn't outright reject a final settlement because none existed. Neither Clinton nor Barak had committed the "parameters" to paper. They remained "a moving target of ideas" and "a work in progress." Moreover, if Arafat seemed wary of committing himself to an agreement, it was because Barak had failed to implement earlier agreements leading up to Camp David. What assurance was there he would follow through on a pledge to establish a Palestinian state? And even if he did try to follow through, it was by no means certain he could muster enough support in Israel to bring it off. Malley's account brought sharp rejoinders from Ross and others who had been on the scene. Camp David was beginning to remind some of *Rashomon*, the classic Japanese film in which all the participants remember the same event differently. Years later, Aaron David Miller, another member of Clinton's negotiating team, may have come closest to the truth when he argued that a permanent settlement was probably never a realistic possibility: too little time remained in Clinton's term to bridge the enormous gap between the Israelis and the Palestinians. "In an effort to produce a quick Presidential legacy," Clinton had overreached.[51]

Camp David had put many of Clinton's attributes on display: his keen intelligence, sophisticated grasp of detail, unmatched ability to connect personally with people, tenacious persistence, and noble desire to bring peace to a long-troubled region. The summit underscored the fact there was much more to Clinton's foreign policy than he was given credit (or blame) for at the time, including NAFTA, NATO expansion, nuclear arms reductions, peacekeeping in Bosnia and Kosovo, and the Iraq Liberation Act. Still, a defeat was a defeat. Camp David, Clinton told Strobe Talbott, was the most disappointing and frustrating experience of his presidency. "You don't get points for trying in this game. You get points for delivering, and we came up short. This one goes down in the loss column: it's that simple."[52]

The elections of 2000 did little to quell Clinton's disappointment. Hillary's victory in the New York senate race provided solace, of course. But the presidential election was a disaster. Clinton believed the Supreme Court decision awarding the disputed election to George W. Bush was a travesty. It belonged in the company of Dred Scott, *Plessy v. Ferguson*, the World War II case sanctioning the internment of Japanese

Americans, and other infamous decisions. Worse, it should never have gotten to the Supreme Court. If Gore had run a decent campaign, Clinton believed, the outcome never would have come down to a few thousand disputed ballots in Florida. When the House impeached Clinton in December 1998, Gore, although appalled by revelations about Clinton's relationship with Monica Lewinsky, declared that Clinton would "be regarded in the history books as one of our greatest presidents."[53] Gore spent most of his campaign trying to live down the comment. Clinton's personal behavior, he said repeatedly, was reprehensible. "I felt what the president did, especially as a parent, was inexcusable." At one campaign event the Clintons and Gores were scheduled to appear at a reception together. At the last minute, Gore's wife, Tipper, refused. "No, I'm not doing it," she told an aide. "I'm not going out there with that man." Up to a point, Clinton could understand the vice president's desire, exaggerated as it might be, to establish his own identity. What he couldn't understand was Gore's reluctance to embrace the accomplishments of their administration. After the Supreme Court decision, Clinton and Gore had their first substantive conversation in over a year. As one reporter later noted, Gore had a lot to get off his chest. "For more than an hour, in uncommonly blunt language, Gore forcefully told Clinton that his sex scandal and low personal approval ratings were the major impediment keeping him from the presidency." Then it was Clinton's turn. "Soon, anger rising, he pushed back. It was Gore's failure to run on the administration's record that hobbled his ambitions."[54]

Still, both men knew that nothing changed the fact that the Republicans now occupied the White House. For Clinton that meant that the task of burnishing his legacies rested in his own hands—and Hillary's.

EPILOGUE:
THE THIRD TERM

The Clintons left the White House much as they had entered it eight years earlier: engulfed in controversy. Two hours before his term expired, President Clinton issued 140 pardons, bringing to 459 the total number he had issued during his presidency. This in itself was not unusual. All but two presidents had invoked their constitutional powers to grant pardons and commute sentences, and many had done it far more often than Clinton. He did raise eyebrows by pardoning his half-brother Roger Clinton, Jr., who had served time for cocaine possession; his and Hillary's business partner in the failed Whitewater land deal, Susan McDougall; his secretary of housing and urban development, Henry Cisneros; and a few others with connections to the White House.[1] Also drawing attention were grants of clemency to kidnapped newspaper heiress Patty Hearst and to Susan Rosenberg, both of whom had been convicted of crimes during the Vietnam Era. But it was his pardon of billionaire financier Marc Rich that ignited a firestorm of protest. Twenty years earlier, Rich had fled the country and renounced his citizenship after being charged with tax fraud, racketeering, trading with the enemy, and other crimes. Rich's ex-wife Denise, a generous donor to Democratic causes and a friend of the Clintons, had personally urged the president to issue the pardon, as had Marc Rich's lawyer, a former legal counsel to the president. Others, including Israeli Prime Minister Ehud Barak, citing Rich's subsequent philanthropic enterprises, had weighed in on Rich's behalf as well, and Clinton insisted there were extenuating circumstances. Still, it smacked of an inside job, a quid-pro-quo, especially when it came out that Denise Rich had contributed to the campaigns of both Clintons, had donated seven thousand dollars' worth of furniture to the White House, and had pledged nearly a half million dollars to the building of Clinton's presidential library. "A shocking abuse of Presidential power," editorialized the *New York Times.* A sign of Clinton's "hopelessly cracked ethical barometer," wrote the editors of *USA Today.* "Outrageous," said former Clinton aide George Stephanopoulos.[2] Added Democratic Senator Joseph Biden: Clinton must have been "brain dead." There were immediate calls for congressional investigations, and the Justice Department opened a preliminary inquiry. Some members of Congress threatened impeachment. Could you even impeach an ex-president? Theoretically yes, said Republican Senator Arlen Specter, chair of the Judiciary Committee. It wouldn't necessarily take that long, he speculated, and if convicted, Clinton could be stripped of his pension and the other perquisites routinely accorded former presidents.[3]

In the midst of the Marc Rich controversy, the *Washington Post* and other publications reported that the Clintons were walking away with nearly two hundred thousand dollars' worth of gifts given to the White House during their stay, including artwork, china, furniture, and rugs. Donors included Hollywood celebrities like actor Jack Nicholson, director Steven Spielberg, and Spielberg's actress-wife, Kate Capshaw. Some of the gift-givers, believing the Clintons had been forced to run up legal bills defending themselves against bogus charges, intended for them to keep the gifts. Others did not. Hillary Clinton was even rumored to have opened a gift registry in a swank department store so that friends could help the Clintons furnish their new homes in Chappaqua, New York, and Washington, DC. The rumors turned out to be false. To settle the matter, the Clintons returned some of the gifts and paid for others.[4]

Then there were the complaints from Bush administration officials that departing Clinton staffers had left obscene messages on White House answering machines, glued desk drawers shut, scrawled anti-Bush graffiti on bathroom walls, and pried the "W" off computer keyboards ("W" was George W. Bush's nickname). The Government Accounting Office set the costs from "damage, theft, vandalism and pranks" to between $13,000 and $14,000.[5]

Clinton defenders insisted that the double standard was once again in play. Playing pranks on the incoming administration, though perhaps adolescent, was part of the game. When they entered the White House, Clinton staffers had found "Draft Dodger" signs posted on the walls. And as for gifts, what about Dwight Eisenhower's wealthy friends building him a cottage on the grounds of the Augusta National Golf Course in Georgia and stocking his Gettysburg farm with prize livestock? Or the friends of Ronald and Nancy Reagan buying them a $2.5 million ranch house in Bel Air, California? But the damage was done, and no amount of rationalizing could undo it. "In their revolving-door exit," wrote columnist Maureen Dowd, "the Clintons seemed more like grifters than public servants." At the peak of the impeachment proceedings, Clinton's approval rating stood at 60 percent. Months after he left office, it had fallen to 39 percent.[6]

The Clintons experienced personal travails as well. They were hardly "dead broke" when they left office as Hillary Clinton later put it. They had after all just bought two homes, and both Clintons were set to earn millions for writing their memoirs. On the other hand, Clinton had run up $12 million in legal fees defending himself in the Paula Jones and other lawsuits. Because the Arkansas Supreme Court had suspended his license to practice law for five years, he would be unable to make any money from lawyering. And given their clumsy departure from the White House, it was not immediately clear that either Clinton would be a big draw on the lucrative lecture circuit. Clinton also began having serious health problems. In September 2004, after becoming short of breath, he checked into New York Presbyterian Hospital, where he had a quadruple heart bypass. A subsequent buildup of fluid and scar tissue in his chest cavity necessitated another major operation six months later. About the only good news for the Clintons were the rave reviews Hillary Clinton was drawing for her new role as US senator from New York.

Bill Clinton spent a lot of time during his first years out of office replaying his presidency. "I loved being President," he told a reporter. "I'd have done it again if there hadn't been term limits, until the people threw me out." If he'd had only six months more, he said, he was convinced he could have gotten Yasser Arafat to agree to a Mideast deal. And he regretted that before he left office the FBI and CIA had not been able to confirm that Osama bin Laden had been responsible for the attack on the USS *Cole*. "Then we could have launched an attack on Afghanistan earlier. I don't know if it would have prevented 9/11, but it certainly would have complicated it."[7]

Others were looking back, too. Some blamed him for 9/11, saying he should have pulled the trigger when he had bin Laden in his sights. The bipartisan 9/11 Commission concluded that there was plenty of blame to go around. On the one hand, the commission reported, "Policymakers in the Clinton administration, including the president and his national security adviser, told us that the president's intent regarding covert action against bin Laden was clear: he wanted him dead. This intent was never well communicated or understood within the CIA." On the other hand, commission members were struck with "the narrow and unimaginative menu of options for action" offered by military and intelligence agencies to both President Clinton and President Bush.[8]

Clinton's economic stewardship was also coming under critical scrutiny. Columbia University economist Joseph E. Stiglitz served on Clinton's Council of Economic Advisors from 1993 to 1995, as its chair from 1995 to 1997, and as chief economist at the World Bank from 1997 to 2000. In 2001 he was corecipient of the Nobel Prize in economics for work he had done two decades earlier. During the Clinton administration, Stiglitz had maintained a low profile. After he left Washington, however, he let loose with a series of articles, books, and interviews critical of economic policy during "the roaring nineties." "Americans should face up to the fact," he wrote, that the boom of the Clinton years planted "some of the seeds of destruction, seeds which would not yield their noxious fruits for several years." He added: "We were too swept up by the deregulatory, pro-business mantra." Stiglitz had good things to say about the Clinton years as well, and he was unsparing in his criticism of George W. Bush. It was not surprising that his barbed comments about the administration of which he had been a part received the most attention.[9]

Clinton, meanwhile, was dismissing criticism with the flick of his wrist. By 2005, the ill will he and Hillary had engendered leaving office was finally dissipating. Both had written bestselling memoirs, the Clinton Presidential Library had opened in Little Rock, and Hillary was now being touted as a likely presidential candidate. The ex-president was an international celebrity, able to attract an admiring crowd almost anywhere he went. A reporter accompanying him on an unannounced visit to Stone Town, Zanzibar, described the scene: "Startled residents begin to follow him by the hundreds, choking off the town's coral alleyways; merchants line the narrow sidewalks beckoning him into their shops." Between 2001 and 2005 he visited sixty-seven foreign countries, and almost everywhere it was the same. Perhaps only the Pope and Nelson Mandela were bigger draws.[10]

Now for the first time he was looking ahead more than behind. "I can count on one hand the number of times I've woken up and said, 'Gosh, I wish I were still President,'" he said. "I just don't do it anymore." Any doubts about his drawing power on the lecture circuit were long since resolved. By 2005, he was delivering three or four speeches a month and earning between $150,000 and $250,000 for each. A decade later he was commanding $500,000 per speech. He was offered cameo appearances in movies but turned them down. For the first time in his life he was making lots of money, and he was unapologetic about it. "I've got to pay our bills," he said.[11]

Jimmy Carter had set a new standard for post-presidential philanthropy. Clinton followed in his footsteps. His most ambitious undertaking was the formation of the Clinton Foundation and its offshoots, the Clinton Global Initiative (CGI) and the Clinton Health Access Initiative. The foundation unleashed Clinton's fabled fundraising prowess, now unfettered by legal restrictions on political contributions. In a little over a decade, Clinton raised nearly $1.5 billion dollars from the likes of billionaires in India, Ukraine, Nigeria, and the Middle East; the governments of Saudi Arabia, Kuwait, Qatar, and Norway; and foundations like those run by Bill and Melinda Gates and Wal-Mart. Unlike traditional charities, the Clinton Foundation played the role of facilitator, bringing groups and individuals together to address problems such as climate change, economic development, global health, and the conditions faced by women and girls. The foundation's showcase event, at which Clinton was the undisputed star, was the annual meeting of the Clinton Global Initiative, where attendees pledged to do something specific to improve the world, with the understanding that the CGI would track their progress. The foundation's biggest success was the deal it brokered between the pharmaceutical industry and poor countries in Africa, Asia, and Latin America that were being ravaged by HIV/AIDs. In exchange for a large volume of orders, manufacturers agreed to lower the costs of antiretroviral drugs that previously had been prohibitively expensive.[12] The Clinton Foundation's emphasis on market-based solutions, partnerships between government and industry, and volunteerism conformed to Clinton's "third way" philosophy. Whether he knew it or not, it also brought to mind Herbert Hoover's famous pre-presidential enterprise, the Belgian Relief Program during World War I, which distributed aid to war-torn Europe.

Toward his successor, Clinton showed restraint. His criticisms were guarded and rarely personal. He obviously liked Bush, and the two shared a love of politics for its own sake. At President Bush's request,

Clinton accompanied the elder Bush on several humanitarian missions, during which the onetime foes struck up a friendly relationship. Upon returning from the site of a devastating East Asian tsunami, the elder Bush wrote: "I thought I knew him; but until this trip I did not really know him." True, Clinton had to express himself on every subject and he simply could not be punctual. But he was considerate and engaging. "You cannot get mad at the guy."[13]

The run-up to the Iraq War in late 2002 and early 2003 momentarily pushed Clinton into the spotlight. He was, of course, on record warning that Saddam Hussein possessed chemical and biological weapons and calling for his ouster. And the Iraq Liberation Act of 1998, which made regime change a matter of US policy and which Clinton had signed into law, was cited again and again by advocates for decisive action in Iraq. But in the fall of 2002, when President Bush requested congressional authorization to use force if Saddam Hussein refused to disarm, Clinton urged caution. He still had no doubt about the existence of weapons of mass destruction but argued Saddam was more likely to use them if he knew the US was coming to get him. He also warned that an attack, no matter how carefully planned, would likely claim civilian casualties and create support for Saddam. Better, he said, to postpone action in Iraq until Osama bin Laden was caught and al Qaeda defeated. "Saddam Hussein didn't kill 3,100 people on September 11. Osama bin Laden did, and as far as we know, he's still alive."[14] But as the Bush administration, now joined by British Prime Minister Tony Blair, sought support to deliver an ultimatum to Saddam—"disarm or be forced to disarm"—Clinton assumed a more militant stance. Hillary Clinton supported a Senate resolution authorizing the president to use force if diplomacy failed, a resolution Bill Clinton later said he, too, would have supported if he had been a member of Congress. In February 2003, he called Saddam "a murderer, a liar and a thug" who would "have to disarm" to avoid war. Bush, he said, "was doing the right thing now."[15]

Clinton's shifting pronouncements were followed closely in the United States, especially by nervous Democratic lawmakers looking for positioning guidance from the master. After all, nobody wanted to risk handing the president a blank check, as Congress did in 1964 when it passed the Gulf of Tonkin Resolution giving Lyndon Johnson a free hand in Vietnam; but neither did most legislators want to appear weak by seemingly kowtowing to Saddam Hussein.

Clinton's views were also being tracked in Great Britain, where an embattled Prime Minister Tony Blair, whose rise to power was modeled on Clinton's "third way," was under fire for hewing too closely to the Bush administration line that Saddam Hussein must be held to account, even if it required a first strike. In March 2003, Blair sought parliamentary approval to deploy military forces in Iraq. To help persuade skeptics in his own Labour Party, Blair enlisted Bill Clinton, who was still widely admired in Great Britain. Six months earlier, at a Labour party conference in Blackpool, England, Clinton had brought the audience to its feet with his "coded jibes" at the Bush administration's gung-ho rush to war in Iraq. "Americans can't elect him President again," journalist Jonathan Freedland wrote. "But if Bill Clinton ever wants to head the British Labour Party, they would have him in a heartbeat."[16] Now, however, Clinton's goal was to muster support for Blair's call to war. Blair, Clinton wrote in an opinion piece in *The Guardian* newspaper, had done everything he could to avoid war but also hold Saddam Hussein's feet to the fire. But to no avail. Saddam continued to be defiant, France and Russia vowed to veto any UN Security Council resolution that would sanction the use of force, and Blair was backed into a corner and had to make the best of it. Clinton stopped just short of calling for a joint US-British strike against Iraq. Still, he left no doubt of where he stood. "Now in another difficult spot," he concluded, "Blair will have to do what he believes to be right. I trust him to do that and hope the British people will too." What Blair believed to be right was to employ "all means possible" to disarm Saddam Hussein. Blair requested and received parliamentary authority to do just that. Two days later Great Britain joined the United States in attacking Iraq.[17]

Like most Americans, Clinton believed the United States would make short order of Saddam Hussein—a week or two would be all that it would take, he predicted. When the war stretched on for months and then years, he, like many Democrats, including his wife, began to distance himself from the war. Asked by a reporter in 2005 if he, like Bush, would have gone to war, Clinton neither denied nor confirmed the possibility.[18] Later that year, however, he called the invasion "a big mistake" and by 2007 was saying that he had opposed the war "from the beginning."[19]

Clinton's next foray into national politics was far more damaging to his reputation than an ambiguous call on Iraq. In 2008, Hillary Clinton made her long-expected run for the Democratic presidential nomination. The Clintons sought to reprise their "two-for-the-price-of-one" campaign of 1992, only with their roles reversed. Senator Clinton opened as the prohibitive favorite. Illinois Senator Barack Obama unexpectedly emerged as her chief rival, ensuring that the outcome would be historic—either the first African American or the first woman to win the presidential nomination of a major party. Obama had first gained notoriety for his electrifying keynote address at the Democratic National Convention in 2004. It was one of the few times in his life that Bill Clinton, who also spoke to the convention, found himself upstaged. Even so, four years later Obama remained a relative newcomer to national politics and was given little chance to win the nomination. "The Clintons," Obama biographer David Remnick later noted, "had a vast network of operatives and fundraisers at their disposal—a machine developed over decades—while Obama had nothing like it."[20] Clinton pollster Mark Penn reassured the Clintons that Obama appealed primarily to the "brie and cheese set" that "drives fund-raising and elite press but does not drive the vote."[21] Bill Clinton brushed Obama off with the wave of his hand. "When is the last time we elected a President based on one year of service in the Senate before he started running?" Bill Clinton asked television interviewer Charlie Rose.[22] He was even more dismissive in private. "A few years ago, this guy would have been carrying our bags," he reputedly told Senator Ted Kennedy.[23] As Obama overtook and then surpassed Hillary Clinton in the delegate count, the campaign turned acrimonious. Obama, for his part, had a knack for getting under Bill Clinton's skin. Clinton wore with pride the appellation as America's "first black President." Obama was unimpressed. "Ronald Reagan changed the trajectory of America in a way that, you know, Richard Nixon did not, and in a way that Bill Clinton did not," Obama said.[24] Clinton struck back during the South Carolina primary. With Obama headed toward victory, Clinton reminded reporters that Jesse Jackson had twice won the South Carolina primary but had gone on to lose the nomination. Some interpreted Clinton's remarks as a subtle suggestion that Obama, like Jackson, owed his victory to bloc voting among blacks rather than to broad support among the electorate. As for Obama's anti–Iraq War credentials, Clinton dismissed them as "the biggest fairy tale I've ever heard."[25] Clinton's attacks earned sharp rebukes from prominent Democrats who, hitting close to his core, accused him of "playing the race card." "We're witnessing a smear campaign," said Robert Reich, who called Clinton attacks on Obama "ill-tempered and ill-founded." Edward Kennedy and Caroline Kennedy Schlossberg, the brother and the daughter of Clinton's hero, made their displeasure known by endorsing Barack Obama.[26] Clinton had his defenders. Princeton historian Sean Wilentz, who had rallied his professional colleagues to oppose impeachment, argued that it was Obama and the national press corps, not the Clintons, who were playing the race card. To characterize the Clintons as race-baiters, he wrote, was "the most outrageous deployment of racial politics since the Willie Horton ad campaign in 1988 and the most insidious since Ronald Reagan kicked off his 1980 campaign in Philadelphia, Mississippi, praising states' rights." But even Clinton's admirers were concluding that he was hurting both his wife and himself. Employing one of the affectionate nicknames by which Clinton was known, Arkansas columnist and longtime defender Gene Lyons wrote: "Somebody needs to put the Big Dog back on the porch. His attacks on Obama are unbecoming in a former president; people are tired of the Clinton melodrama; and the bigger he looms, the smaller Hillary looks."[27]

It got worse. In the July 2008 issue of *Vanity Fair* magazine, Todd Purdum, who had covered the Clinton White House for the *New York Times*, published a scathingly critical article about Clinton entitled "The Comeback Id." "Old friends and longtime aides," Purdum wrote, "are wringing their hands over Bill Clinton's post-White House escapades, from the dubious (and secretive) business associations to the media blowups that have bruised his wife's campaign, to the private-jetting around with a skirt-chasing, scandal-tinged posse." Purdum highlighted Clinton's relationship with "bachelor buddy, fund-raiser, and business partner," supermarket magnate Ron Burkle, whose private plane, on which Clinton sometimes travelled, was dubbed by Burkle's aides as "Air Fuck One."[28] That Purdum was married to Clinton's former press secretary, Dee Dee Myers, made the explosive innuendoes all the more credible. Clinton erupted in anger. He called Purdum "sleazy," "dishonest," "slimy," and a "scumbag," and the article "part of the national media's attempt to nail Hillary for Obama." "It's just the most biased press coverage in history," he added. "It's another way of helping Obama." Clinton also accused Obama of getting other people "to slime" Hillary by calling her a white racist.[29]

Less volatile, but harmful nonetheless, were insinuations that the Clintons must be hiding something by refusing to fully disclose the names of donors to the Clinton Presidential Library or to the Clinton Foundation. Critics also accused the Clintons of dragging their feet in granting public access to the library's voluminous collection of presidential papers for fear of disclosing material that might harm Hillary's candidacy—although professional scholars pointed out that delay in granting access stemmed less from foot dragging than from a restrictive executive order issued by the Bush administration in 2003 (and not rescinded until Obama became president in 2009).[30] By the summer of 2008, Bill Clinton's favorability rating had once again dropped, from 63 percent to 50 percent. Within the Hillary Clinton campaign, some blamed the ex-president for his wife's defeat. "Bill Clinton is like nuclear energy," Obama advisor David Axelrod said later. "If you use it properly, it can be enormously helpful and proactive. If you misuse it, it can be catastrophic."[31]

Despite the ill will engendered by the primary campaign, Barack Obama, having bested Hillary Clinton for the nomination and John McCain for the presidency, appointed a large number of Clintonites to key positions in his administration. Hillary Clinton as secretary of state headed the list, but Clinton administration veterans also included Lawrence Summers as national economic adviser, Timothy Geithner as treasury secretary, Peter Orszag as director of the Office of Management and Budget, Rahm Emanuel as chief of staff, and Eric Holder as attorney general. By one count, of the Obama appointees requiring Senate confirmation during his first term, 40 percent had served under Clinton. Their presence insured a large degree of continuity between the two presidencies, especially in economic policy. Style was a different matter. Asked to compare the two presidents as administrators, persons who served under both rated Obama higher. "They marvel at Obama's discipline and roll their eyes as they remember Clinton's agonizing before making decisions," wrote a reporter. "They admire Obama's cool as they recall Clinton's 'purple rages' at his staff behind closed doors."[32]

Even Clinton's harshest critics had to admit that he never stayed down for long. Not after his defeat for reelection as governor in 1980; his embarrassing nomination speech for Michael Dukakis in 1988; or the sex, draft, and dope controversies during the 1992 presidential campaign. Nor after the GOP takeover of Congress in 1994, the subsequent impeachment crisis, or his disastrous exit from the White House. Journalist Anna Quindlen once said that Clinton had "come to resemble one of those inflatable children's toys with sand weighting the bottom. You knock him down and he pops back up."[33] Indeed, the example of personal resiliency may be Clinton's most durable legacy. What historian Garry Wills wrote of Richard Nixon upon his death was equally true of Bill Clinton: "He rose again, eerily, from each stumble or knockout, apparently unkillable. He raised undiscourageability to heroic scale."[34]

Before long, he was once again on the ascent, his approval ratings rising as President Obama's were in decline. Now in his sixties, with a hearing aid and a slight, late-in-the-day tremor in his left hand, he looked "older than the boy President who dominated American politics in the 1990s," wrote reporter Peter Baker, but remained "more robust than most men his age and full of intellectual energy." With the help of a vegan diet he shed twenty pounds.

While forcefully defending his record from critics on the right and the left, he began to reconcile with some of his fiercest foes from the nineties, including media mogul Rupert Murdoch, whose holdings included the fortress of anti-Clinton broadcasting, Fox News; and billionaire Richard Mellon Scaife, who had bankrolled what Hillary Clinton once called "the vast rightwing conspiracy." Journalist Christopher Ruddy had once accused the Clintons of complicity in the deaths of Vince Foster and Commerce Secretary Ron Brown. Now they were lunching together like old friends. Clinton was less forgiving of old friends like Ted Kennedy and his energy secretary and UN ambassador Bill Richardson, who had supported Obama over Hillary. Conservatives waxed nostalgic about the nineties. "We miss you Bubba," wrote David Boaz, executive vice president of the libertarian Cato Institute, describing the Clinton presidency as "a sort of Golden Age." By 2012, former foes, including those who had supported impeachment, were practically falling over themselves to embrace Clinton and rewriting the history of the nineties in the process. It was also their way of using Clinton as a foil to attack Obama. "He was just a heck of a lot better President than Barack Obama," said Clinton nemesis New Gingrich, who had led the impeachment drive.[35] According to the Gallup poll, 69 percent of the public viewed him favorably. A *Newsweek* poll ranked Clinton and Ronald Reagan the two greatest presidents of the twentieth century.[36]

Clinton doubtless took particular relish in the role he played in the 2012 presidential race. Hopelessly stalemated with Congress, presiding over a sluggish economic recovery, and tied in the polls with GOP presidential candidate Mitt Romney, President Obama asked Clinton to nominate him for a second term. This was not the first time an ex-president had spoken at a national convention. It was the first time an ex-president had delivered a nominating speech. Some of Obama's aides worried that Clinton might overshadow the president either by making the speech all about himself or by setting the oratorical bar too high. Clinton did steal the show but not in a way that hurt Obama. By almost all accounts, in his riveting, 48-minute speech, he made a more compelling case for the president's reelection than the president had made for himself. "I wish to God as a Republican we had someone on our side who had the ability to do that," said one GOP adviser. "We don't."[37] It was an Obama partisan who made the most telling observation. "We don't need Clinton the man. We need Clinton the myth."[38] That's what they got.

Clinton was even better at touting his own accomplishments. Following Obama's reelection, Hillary Clinton stepped down as secretary of state and began to lay the groundwork for a second run at the presidency. Against that backdrop, President Clinton, in the spring of 2014, delivered a masterful defense of his—and by extension, his wife's—economic policies. The occasion was a two-hour, fact-filled lecture, replete with tables and graphs, at his alma mater, Georgetown University. There was no disputing the numbers that flashed up on the screen beside the podium: 30 million jobs created during his presidency; median income up 17 percent; unemployment and inflation down; 7.7 million persons lifted out of poverty (as compared to 77,000 during the Reagan administration, Clinton was quick to note); and three consecutive budget surpluses to round out the nineties. Skeptics, Clinton noted, liked to say, "Oh, Clinton was lucky, he caught the tech boom." Or "Clinton was lucky, he came out of a recession." Luck had nothing to do with it, he insisted. The economic record of the nineties was the result of setting goals and then, within an ever-shifting political environment, carefully designing and executing policies to achieve those goals. By 2014, perhaps the most pressing economic issue was income inequality, with a concentration of wealth at the top perhaps not seen since the first Gilded Age. Because of their support for financial deregulation and closeness to Wall Street, the Clintons could take credit—or blame—for that, too. In his Georgetown talk, Clinton struck back at detractors even on that point, claiming he had a far better record combatting inequality than his predecessors going back to the sixties or his successors.[39] Neither then nor later did Clinton persuade all of the skeptics. During her second presidential campaign, Hillary distanced herself from some of the economic and social policies of the 1990s. Still, even her husband's detractors had to agree: there was no more formidable defender of the Clinton presidency than Clinton himself. A half-dozen or more of Clinton's predecessors—including John Quincy Adams, Teddy Roosevelt, William Howard Taft, and Jimmy Carter—had as consequential postpresidential careers as Clinton. Yet with the possible exception of Roosevelt, none had as commanding a presence as Clinton. As long as he was there to defend it, his legacy was secure.

NOTES

INTRODUCTION: BILL CLINTON AND THE NEW GILDED AGE

1. Mark Twain, *The Gilded Age* (New York: Oxford University Press, 1996). Twain and Warner may also have been invoking Shakespeare's use of "gild" in *King John*: "to gild refined gold, to paint the lily . . . is wasteful and ridiculous excess."
2. Michael Norman, "Raconteur Conducts Tour Along Millionaires' Row," *New York Times*, July 11, 1983; "Newport: Carriage Fashion," *New York Times*, August 24, 1986.
3. Kevin P. Phillips, "A Capital Offense; Reagan's America," *New York Times Magazine*, June 17, 1990.
4. Richard Hofstadter, *The American Political Tradition and the Men Who Made It* (New York: Knopf, 1948), 164.
5. E. J. Dionne, Jr., "End of Reform," *Washington Post*, February 19, 2002.
6. Jackson Lears, "Teddy Roosevelt, Not-So-Great Reformer," *New Republic*, March 14, 2014.
7. James Fallows, "A Talk with Bill Clinton," *Atlantic*, October 1996, http://www.theatlantic.com/magazine/archive/1996/10/a-talk-with-bill-clinton/305066/.
8. Ibid.
9. James L. Roark et al., *The American Promise, Volume II: Since 1865: A History of the United States* (New York: Macmillan, 2012), 590.
10. Stephen Labaton, "Despite a Tough Stance or Two, White House Is Still Consolidation Friendly," *New York Times*, November 8, 1999.
11. David E. Sanger, "Seismic Shift in the Parties Reflects View on Business," *New York Times*, September 24, 1995.
12. Kenneth T. Walsh, "Learning from Big Jumbo," *U.S. News & World Report*, January 26, 1998, 33.
13. Todd S. Purdum, "Striking Strengths and Shortcomings: A Flawed Leader in an Ambivalent Age," *New York Times*, December 24, 2000.
14. Unless otherwise noted, all presidential quotations are from The American Presidency Project (americanpresidency.org).
15. Margaret Sullivan, "Lodestars in a Murky Media World," *New York Times*, March 9, 2014.

CHAPTER 1. MAKING OF A PRESIDENT, 1946–1992

1. David Maraniss, *First in His Class: A Biography of Bill Clinton* (New York: Simon & Schuster, 1995), 24–29; Bill Clinton, *My Life* (New York: Knopf, 2004), 4–5.
2. Virginia Kelley, *Leading with My Heart* (New York: Simon & Schuster, 1994), 79–81, 157.
3. Clinton, *My Life*, 12.
4. Ibid., 17.
5. Kelley, *Leading with My Heart*, 134.
6. Quoted in ibid., 170.

7. Clinton, *My Life*, 46; Nigel Hamilton quoted in Program Transcript, "Clinton," *The American Experience: Clinton*, PBS, 2012: http://www.pbs.org/wgbh/ameri canexperience/features/transcript/clinton-transcript/.

8. Maraniss, *First in His Class*, 36; Peter Applebome, "Bill Clinton's Uncertain Journey," *New York Times*, March 8, 1992.

9. Maraniss, *First in His Class*, 56.

10. Ibid., 130–142.

11. Ibid., 50–121.

12. Strobe Talbott Interview, February 25, 2010, 13, William J. Clinton Presidential History Project, Miller Center, University of Virginia (hereafter referred to as Miller Center).

13. Maraniss, *First in His Class*, 149–205.

14. Quoted in Noam Scheiber, "Crimson Tide," *New Republic*, February 4, 2009, 15.

15. Maraniss, *First in His Class*, 233–234.

16. Ibid., 265–286.

17. Important treatments of Democratic factionalism and the role of race include Dan T. Carter, *George Wallace, Richard Nixon, and the Transformation of American Politics* (Waco, TX: Markham Press Fund, 1992); Rick Perlstein, *Before the Storm: Barry Goldwater and the Unmaking of the American Consensus* (New York: Hill and Wang, 2001); Allen J. Matusow, *The Unraveling of America: A History of Liberalism in the 1960s* (Athens: University of Georgia Press, 2009).

18. Andrew Levison, *The Working-Class Majority* (New York: Coward, McCann & Geoghegan, 1974); Jefferson Cowie, *Stayin' Alive: The 1970s and the Last Days of the Working Class* (New York: New Press, 2010), 75–124.

19. See, for example, Carl Bernstein, *A Woman in Charge: The Life of Hillary Rodham Clinton* (New York: Knopf, 2007), 38–60; Chafe, *Bill and Hillary*, 33–46.

20. Hillary Rodham Clinton, *Living History* (New York: Simon & Schuster, 2003), 11.

21. Bernstein, *A Woman in Charge*, 38–60; "The Class of 69," *Life*, June 20, 1969, 28–31. One of the other students featured was Ira Magaziner, at Brown, who would be Hillary Clinton's collaborator in health-care reform in the Clinton White House.

22. Maraniss, *First in His Class*, 292.

23. Quoted in Maraniss, *First in His Class*, 313.

24. Virginia Kelley, *Leading with My Heart*, 219.

25. Roy Reed, "Clinton Country," *New York Times*, September 6, 1992.

26. Maraniss, *First in His Class*, 338.

27. Wright quoted in David Maraniss, *First in His Class*, 397.

28. Ibid., 352–357; Dick Morris, *Behind the Oval Office: Winning the Presidency in the Nineties* (New York: Random House, 1997), 44–50.

29. William Galston Interview, April 22–23, 2004, 31, Miller Center.

30. Sidney Blumenthal, *The Clinton Wars* (New York: Farrar, Straus and Giroux, 2003), 33.

31. Meredith L. Oakley, *On the Make: The Rise of Bill Clinton* (Washington, DC: Regnery Publishing, 1994), 135.

32. Clinton, *My Life*, 303.

33. Ibid., 126, 215, 233.

34. Maraniss, *First in His Class*, 358–359.
35. Max Brantley, quoted in Michael Takiff, *A Complicated Man: The Life of Bill Clinton as Told by Those Who Know Him* (New Haven, CT, and London: Yale University Press), 46.
36. Martin Walker, *The President We Deserve: Bill Clinton, His Rise, Falls, and Comebacks* (New York: Crown Publishers, 1996), 85.
37. Pryor quoted in Takiff, *A Complicated Man*, 35.
38. Clinton, *My Life*, 76.
39. David Maraniss, *First in His Class*, 88–89, 239.
40. Ibid., 376–386.
41. Clinton, *My Life*, 287.
42. Maraniss, *First in His Class*, 399.
43. Walker, *The President We Deserve*, 96.
44. Clinton, *My Life*, 306.
45. Hanes Walton, Jr., *Reelection: William Jefferson Clinton as a Native-Son Presidential Candidate* (New York: Columbia University Press, 2000), 64.
46. Charles Flynn Allen, "Governor William Jefferson Clinton: A Biography with a Special Focus on His Educational Contributions" (Ph.D. diss., University of Mississippi, 1991).
47. Clinton, *My Life*, 320–329.
48. David Osborne, *Laboratories of Democracy* (Boston: Harvard Business School Press, 1990), 83–110. The other governors Osborne singled out were Michael Dukakis of Massachusetts, Mario Cuomo of New York, Richard Thornburgh of Pennsylvania, James Blanchard of Michigan, and Bruce Babbitt of Arizona. Clinton wrote the book's foreword.
49. David Maraniss and Michael Weisskopf, "In Arkansas, the Game Is Chicken," *Washington Post*, March 22, 1992.
50. Quoted in Walker, *The President We Deserve*, 100–101.
51. Clinton, *My Life*, 322.
52. Ibid., 334.
53. Maraniss, *First in His Class*, 440–441.
54. Quoted in Takiff, *A Complicated Man*, 91.
55. Maraniss, *First in His Class*, 444–447.
56. The fullest and best account of the DLC, and Clinton's role in it, is Kenneth S. Baer's *Reinventing Democrats: The Politics of Liberalism from Reagan to Clinton* (Lawrence: University Press of Kansas, 2000).
57. Baer, *Reinventing Democrats*, 35, 127.
58. William Galston and Elaine Ciulla Kamarck, "The Politics of Evasion: Democrats and the Presidency" (Washington, DC: Progressive Policy Institute, 1989), available at www.ppionline.org.
59. "The New Orleans Declaration," DLC (http://www.dlc.org/ndol_ci360e.html ?kaid=86&subid=194&contentid=878).
60. Joe Klein, *The Natural: The Misunderstood Presidency of Bill Clinton* (New York: Doubleday, 2002).
61. Arthur M. Schlesinger, Jr., "For Democrats Me-Too Reaganism Will Spell Disaster," *New York Times*, July 6, 1986.
62. Baer, *Reinventing Democrats*, 184.

63. Ellen Debenport, "Democrats Need a Message," *St. Petersburg Times*, May 13, 1991; David Broder, "The DLC at Six," *Washington Post*, May 12, 1991.

64. Quoted in Baer, *Reinventing Democrats*, 163.

65. Ibid.

66. Klein, *The Natural*, 28.

67. Baer, *Reinventing Democrats*, 164–65.

68. Ibid., 177–181.

69. Ibid.

70. Klein, *The Natural*, 38; Al From Interview, April 27, 2006, 42, Miller Center.

71. Broder, "The DLC at Six."

72. Jack W. Germond and Jules Witcover, *Mad as Hell: Revolt at the Ballot Box, 1992* (New York: Warner Books, 1993), 99–100.

73. Peter Louis Goldman et al., *Quest for the Presidency, 1992* (College Station: Texas A&M University Press, 1994), 48–72.

74. Richard Cohen, "A 'Natural' but . . . ," *Washington Post*, February 18, 1992.

75. Goldman et al., *Quest for the Presidency, 1992*, 89–125.

76. Kroft quoted in Takiff, *A Complicated Man*, 111.

77. Joe Klein, "Cain Game: Why Sexual-Harassment Allegations Won't Sink Herman's Campaign," *Time*, November 1, 2011.

78. Meyers quoted in Takiff, *A Complicated Man*, 126; Memo to Clinton from Stan Greenberg, James Carville, and Frank Greer, April 23, 1992, cited in Goldman, *Quest for the Presidency*, 657–664.

79. Takiff, *A Complicated Man*, 117.

80. David R. Obey, *Raising Hell for Justice: The Washington Battles of a Heartland Progressive* (Madison: University of Wisconsin Press, 2007), 283–284.

81. Goldman, *Quest for the Presidency, 1992*, 126–193.

82. Begala quoted in Takiff, *A Complicated Man*, 129.

83. Memorandum, Mandy Grunwald and Frank Greer to "Clinton Campaign," April 27, 1992, reprinted in *Quest for the Presidency*, 665–666.

84. Elizabeth Kolbert, "The 1992 Campaign," *New York Times*, June 5, 1992; Walter Shapiro, "Clinton Plays All Cool," *Time*, June 15, 1992.

85. Goldman, *Quest for the Presidency*, 416.

86. "The 1992 Campaign: On the Trail; Poll Gives Perot a Clear Lead," *New York Times*, June 11, 1992. The Gallup poll had Perot at 39 percent, Bush at 31, and Clinton at 25. No third party candidate had ever led the race since the beginning of polling.

87. Bruce Reed Interview, February 19–20, 2004, 7–8, 27, Miller Center.

88. Goldman, *Quest for the Presidency*, 276–293, 483–489.

89. Ibid., 398–410. Germond and Witcover, *Mad as Hell*, 403–416.

90. Germond and Witcover, *Mad as Hell*, 416–434, 496, 500, 503.

91. Ibid., 424–425.

92. Michael (Mickey) Kantor Interview, June 28, 2002, 25, Miller Center; Goldman, *Quest for the Presidency*, 573.

93. William L. O'Neill, *A Bubble in Time: America during the Interwar Years, 1989–2001* (Chicago: Ivan R. Dee, 2009), 111.

94. Stanley B. Greenberg, *Dispatches from the War Room: In the Trenches with Five Extraordinary Leaders* (New York: Thomas Dunne Books/St. Martin's Press, 2009), 410–414.

95. Tim Hibbitts, "The Man Who Supposedly Cost George H. W. Bush the Presidency," The Polling Report, January 30, 2012.

96. Steven A. Holmes, "The 1992 Elections: Disappointment," *New York Times,* November 5, 1992. But see also Dean Lacy and Barry C. Burden, "The Vote-Stealing and Turnout Effects of Ross Perot in the 1992 U.S. Presidential Election," *American Journal of Political Science* 43 (January 1999): 233–255.

97. George Stephanopoulos, *All Too Human: A Political Education* (Boston: Little, Brown, 1999), 86.

98. Roper Center, "How Groups Voted," 1980, 1984, 1988, 1992: http://www.ropercenter.uconn.edu/polls/us-elections/how-groups-voted/; Germond and Witcover, "What Happened in 'Home of Reagan Democrats,'" *Baltimore Sun,* November 30, 1992.

99. Goldman, *Quest for the Presidency,* 537.

100. Gerald M. Pomper, *The Election of 1992* (Chatham, NJ: Chatham House, 1993), 153.

CHAPTER 2. TAKING OFFICE, 1993

1. Robert B. Reich, *The Work of Nations: Preparing Ourselves for the 21st-Century Capitalism* (New York: Knopf, 1991), 171–224.

2. William Hyland, *Clinton's World: Remaking American Foreign Policy* (Westport, CT: Praeger, 1999), 197.

3. Francis Fukuyama, *The End of History and the Last Man* (New York: Free Press, 2006); Samuel P. Huntington, *The Clash of Civilizations and the Remaking of the World Order* (New York: Simon & Schuster, 1996).

4. Quoted in Steven E Schier, *The Postmodern Presidency: Bill Clinton's Legacy in U.S. Politics* (Pittsburgh: University of Pittsburgh Press, 2000), 99.

5. Donald A. Ritchie, *Reporting from Washington: The History of the Washington Press Corps* (New York: Oxford University Press, 2005), 270–302.

6. Arthur M. Schlesinger, Jr., *The Disuniting of America: Reflections on a Multicultural Society* (New York: W. W. Norton, 1991), 20.

7. James T. Patterson, *Restless Giant: The United States from Watergate to Bush v. Gore* (New York: Oxford University Press, 2005), 255.

8. E. J. Dionne, *Why Americans Hate Politics* (New York: Simon & Schuster, 1992).

9. Barbara Sinclair, *Party Wars: Polarization and the Politics of National Policy Making* (Norman: University of Oklahoma Press, 2006).

10. Reich, *The Work of Nations,* 17.

11. Alicia Munnell, interview with author, August 4, 2010.

12. Robert B. Reich, *Locked in the Cabinet* (New York: Vintage Books, 1998), 78.

13. Reich, *The Work of Nations,* 3, 112–113, 254–255.

14. Reich, *Locked in the Cabinet,* 180.

15. Bates Medal Citation, AEA website.

16. David Plotz, "Larry Summers," *Slate,* June 29, 2001; Noam Scheiber, "Free Larry Summers," *New Republic,* April 1, 2009.

17. Executive Order 12835—Establishment of the National Economic Council, January 25, 1993.

18. Robert Rubin, *In an Uncertain World: Tough Choices from Wall Street to Washington* (New York: Random House), 55–56.

19. Ibid.
20. Ibid.
21. Memorandum, Robert E. Rubin to the President, January 15, 1996, Cabinet Memos—SOTU Memos, OA/Box 14457, Michael Waldman, Speechwriting, William J. Clinton Library (hereafter referred to as Clinton Library).
22. Hobart Rowen, "Squabbling Economists," *Washington Post*, January 14, 1993; Mark Memmott, "Economist Weathers Firestorm of Criticism," *USA Today*, January 27, 1993.
23. Laura Tyson, interview with author, November 10, 2010.
24. Tyson interview with author; "Commanding Heights," PBS interview with Tyson, http://www.pbs.org/wgbh/commandingheights/shared/minitext/int_lauratyson.html.
25. Alan Blinder Interview, June 27, 2003, 35–37, Miller Center, University of Virginia, William J. Clinton Oral History Project (hereafter cited as Miller Center).
26. Lani Guinier, *Lift Every Voice: Turning a Civil Rights Setback into a New Vision of Social Justice* (New York: Simon & Schuster, 2003), 25.
27. Guinier, *Lift Every Voice*, 28.
28. David Plotke, "Racial Politics and the Clinton-Guinier Episode," *Dissent* (Spring 1995), 232.
29. Clint Bolick, "Clinton's Quota Queens," *Wall Street Journal*, April 30, 1999.
30. Anthony Lewis, "The Case of Lani Guinier," *New York Review of Books*, August 13, 1998; Guinier, *Lift Every Voice*, ix, 50.
31. "Withdraw Guinier," *New Republic*, June 14, 1993, 7.
32. Quoted in Michael Isikoff, "White House Affirms Support of Guinier," *Washington Post*, May 28, 1993.
33. Memo, Bill Galston to President Clinton, "Nomination of Lani Guinier," June 1, 1993, Clinton Library.
34. Taylor Branch, *The Clinton Tapes: Wrestling History with the President* (London and New York: Simon & Schuster, 2009), 69–70.
35. Michael Takiff, *A Complicated Man: The Life of Bill Clinton as Told by Those Who Know Him* (New Haven, CT, and London: Yale University Press), 162.
36. Guinier, *Lift Every Voice*, 49–50.
37. Branch, *The Clinton Tapes*, 69–70.
38. "William J. Clinton: Remarks on the Withdrawal of the Nomination of Lani Guinier to be an Assistant Attorney General and an Exchange with Reporters."
39. Guinier, *Lift Every Voice*, 25.
40. Michael Tackell and William Gaines, "Mack McLarty, Clinton's Alter Ego," *Chicago Tribune*, December 19, 1993.
41. Thomas F. "Mack" McLarty Interview, November 16, 1999, "Clinton Administration Transition Interviews," http://www.archives.gov/presidential-libraries/research/transition-interviews/pdf/mclarty.pdf.
42. Tackell and Gaines, "Mack McLarty, Clinton's Alter Ego."
43. Alan Blinder Interview, 35–37.
44. Leon Panetta Interview, May 4, 2000, "Clinton Administration Transition Interviews," http://www.archives.gov/presidential-libraries/research/transition-interviews/pdf/panetta.pdf; Alice Rivlin Interview, December 13, 2002, 31, Miller Center; William Galston Interview, April 22–23, 2004, 41, 46, Miller Center.

45. Tyson interview with author; William Galston Interview, 70; Leon Panetta and Jim Newton, *Worthy Fights: A Memoir of Leadership in War and Peace* (New York: Penguin Press, 2014), 105.

46. Robert Murphy, interview with author, August 1, 2010.

47. McLarty Interview, "Clinton Administration Transition Interviews."

48. Samuel Berger Interview, March 24–25, 2005, Anthony Lake Interview, May 21, 2002, Miller Center.

49. Murphy interview with author.

50. Richard N. Haass, "Bill Clinton's Adhocracy," *New York Times Magazine*, May 29, 1994; Steven Pearlstein, "Managing the March of Change," *Washington Post*, January 31, 1993; Peters quoted in Jennifer Wells, "Under Cover," *Globe and Mail* (Canada), January 29, 1993. See also Jack H. Watson, Jr., "The Clinton White House," *Presidential Studies Quarterly* 23 (July 1, 1993): 429–435.

51. Anthony J. Bennett, *The American President's Cabinet* (New York: St. Martin's Press, 1996).

52. Reich, *Locked in the Cabinet*, 111.

53. Ibid., 153.

54. Joe Klein, *The Natural: The Misunderstood Presidency of Bill Clinton* (New York: Doubleday, 2002), 59; George Stephanopoulos, *All Too Human: A Political Education* (Boston: Little, Brown, 1999), 135.

55. Maureen Dowd, "On Washington," *New York Times Magazine*, June 19, 1994; Stanley B. Greenberg, *Dispatches from the War Room: In the Trenches with Five Extraordinary Leaders* (New York: Thomas Dunne Books/St. Martin's Press, 2009), 78.

56. Carl Bernstein, *A Woman in Charge: The Life of Hillary Rodham Clinton* (New York: Knopf, 2007), 277–283.

57. Sidney Blumenthal, "The Education of a President," *New Yorker*, January 24, 1994, 36.

58. Bernstein, *A Woman in Charge,* 277–283.

59. Ibid.

60. Dowd, "On Washington."

61. Bill Clinton, *My Life* (New York: Knopf, 2004), 481.

62. Rubin, *In an Uncertain World,* 134; Tyson interview with author; Stimson quoted in James MacGregor Burns, *Roosevelt: The Soldier of Freedom* (New York, Harcourt Brace Jovanovich, 1970), 351.

63. Jeffrey H. Birnbaum, *Madhouse: The Private Turmoil of Working for the President* (New York: Times Books, 1996), 178–180.

64. Tyson and Munnell interviews with author.

65. Betty Currie Interview, May 11–12, 2006, 68–71, Miller Center; Donna Shalala Interview, May 15, 2007, 45, Miller Center; and Joan N. Baggett Interview, February 10–11, 2005, 62, Miller Center.

66. Kenneth T. Walsh, *Feeding the Beast: The White House versus the Press* (New York: Random House, 1996), 127–205.

67. Branch, *The Clinton Tapes*, 411.

68. Interview, Michael McCurry, White House Interview Program, March 27, 2000.

CHAPTER 3. "ON THE EDGE," 1993

1. Elizabeth Drew, *On the Edge: The Clinton Presidency* (New York: Simon & Schuster, 1994), 15.
2. *Time*, June 7, 1993; *Newsweek*, June 7, 1993.
3. Bill Clinton and Al Gore, *Putting People First: How We Can All Change America* (New York: Times Books, 1992), 3–32.
4. Recalled Princeton economist Alan Blinder, who contributed to *Putting People First* and later served on the Council of Economic Advisors: "By the standard of political documents, that had very high integrity, but the standard is low. . . . If you grade that on the curve, it was an A in terms of economics. If you grade it on an absolute standard, it was probably a C." Alan Blinder Interview, June 27, 2003, 12, Miller Center, University of Virginia, William J. Clinton Oral History Project (hereafter cited as Miller Center).
5. Clinton and Gore, *Putting People First*, 3–32; Bennett Harrison, "Where Private Investment Fails," *American Prospect*, Fall 1992; Elizabeth Whitney, "For America's Future: Investment Economics?" *St. Petersburg Times*, November 20, 1988; *PR Newswire*, October 6, 1988.
6. Alan Greenspan, *The Age of Turbulence: Adventures in a New World* (New York: Penguin, 2007), 160.
7. The role of Fed Chair Alan Greenspan is disputed. Bob Woodward's famous account of the early years of the Clinton administration, *The Agenda: Inside the Clinton White House* (New York: Pocket Books, 1994), accorded Greenspan a pivotal role in persuading Clinton to prioritize deficit reduction. Members of Clinton's economic team, such as Laura Tyson, Alice Rivlin, and Alan Blinder, believed Greenspan's role was exaggerated. Alan Blinder Interview; Alice Rivlin Interview, December 13, 2002, Miller Center; Laura Tyson, interview with author, November 10, 2010.
8. Woodward, *The Agenda*, 84.
9. Alan Blinder Interview, 20.
10. Tyson interview with author; William Galston Interview, April 22–23, 2004, 27, Miller Center.
11. Drew, *On the Edge*, 124.
12. Leon Panetta and Jim Newton, *Worthy Fights: A Memoir of Leadership in War and Peace* (New York: Penguin Press, 2014), 111.
13. Iwan Morgan, "A New Democrat's New Economics," in Mark J. White, ed., *The Presidency of Bill Clinton: The Legacy of a New Domestic and Foreign Policy* (London: I. B. Tauris, 2012), 65–91; Alan Blinder Interview; Panetta and Newton, *Worthy Fights*, 111–115.
14. For a cogent description and critique of the EITC, see Marjorie E. Kornhauser, "Cognitive Theory and the Delivery of Welfare Benefits," *Loyola University Chicago Law Journal* 40 (January 2009): 253–296. See also Jonathan Barry Forman, "Earned Income Credit," in *The Encyclopedia of Taxation and Tax Policy*, Joseph J. Cordes, Robert D. Ebel, and Jane G. Gravelle, eds. (Urban Institute Press, 1999), 91–93.
15. Dawn Erlandson, "The BTU Tax Experience: What Happened and Why It Happened," *Pace Environmental Law Review* 12 (Fall 1994): 173–184.
16. Brinkley, *The End of Reform: New Deal Liberalism in Recession and War* (New York: Alfred A. Knopf, 1995).

17. Quoted in Arthur M. Schlesinger, Jr., "The Great Carter Mystery," *New Republic*, April 12, 1980, 21.

18. Iwan Morgan, "Jimmy Carter, Bill Clinton, and the New Democratic Economics," *Historical Journal* 47 (December 2004): 1015–1039.

19. Seymour Melman, "Jimmy Hoover?" *New York Times*, February 7, 1979; Schlesinger, "The Great Carter Mystery," 21.

20. Morgan, "Jimmy Carter, Bill Clinton, and the New Democratic Economics" 1015.

21. Joe [Bouchard] to Bob [Bell], March 27 [1993], Gays in the Military file, OA/Box 3154, National Security Council, Clinton Library. In his note, Bouchard refers to the naval officer as McVeigh. A correction appended to the note says he is referring to Meinhold.

22. Samuel Berger Interview, March 24–25, 2005, Miller Center; *Congressional Record*, 103rd Congress (1993), Senate, February 4, p. S1221.

23. George Stephanopoulos, *All Too Human: A Political Education* (Boston: Little, Brown, 1999), 128.

24. Bill Clinton, *My Life* (New York: Knopf, 2004), 520.

25. Panetta and Newton, *Worthy Fights*, 115.

26. Erlandson, "The Btu Tax Experience."

27. Michael Wines, *New York Times*, "Congress's Twists and Turns Reshape Bill on Energy Tax," *New York Times*, June 2, 1993.

28. Erlandson, "The Btu Tax Experience." It is revealing that in his memoir, Clinton gave Vice President Gore the credit (or blame) for proposing the Btu tax in the first place. See Clinton, *My Life*, 461.

29. Sidney Blumenthal, "The Education of a President," *New Yorker*, January 24, 1994, 38.

30. Quoted in Charles Brain Interview, March 22–23, 2004, 41, Miller Center.

31. Mickey Kantor Interview, June 28, 2002, 35–36, Miller Center.

32. Ibid., 27.

33. For an insightful analysis of the budget battle, see M. Stephen Weatherford and Lorraine M. McDonnell, "Clinton and the Economy: The Paradox of Policy Success and Political Mishap," *Political Science Quarterly* 111 (October 1996): 403–436.

34. According to Leon Panetta, as the final vote neared, Senator Kerrey was absent from the floor. A call to his office revealed that he had gone to a movie. An angry Panetta dispatched aides to local theatres, eventually finding the Nebraska senator and hauling him back to the Senate floor where he cast his bill-saving yes vote. Panetta and Newton, *Worthy Fights*, 119–120.

35. Woodward, *The Agenda*.

36. Because NAFTA retained many restrictions (and created others involving copyrights and intellectual property), it would be more accurate to call NAFTA a "freer trade" agreement.

37. Between June and December 1993, Clinton spoke extensively in support of NAFTA. His comments are accessible at http://www.presidency.ucsb.edu/ws/index.php.

38. Reich, *Locked in the Cabinet* (New York: Vintage Books, 1998), 137.

39. Eric M. Uslaner, "Let the Chits Fall Where They May? Executive and Constituency Influences on Congressional Voting on NAFTA," *Legislative Studies Quarterly* 23, no. 3 (August 1, 1998): 347–371.

40. Ernest Hollings Interview, 20, 2012, George J. Mitchell Oral History Project, Bowdoin College Library, Brunswick, Maine.
41. "What We've Learned from Nafta—Room for Debate," *New York Times*, http://www.nytimes.com/roomfordebate/2013/11/24/what-weve-learned-from-nafta. The parameters of the debate are well outlined in Gary Clyde Hufbauer, *NAFTA Revisited: Achievements and Challenges* (Washington, DC: Institute for International Economics, 2005). See also Louis Uchitelle, *The Disposable American: Layoffs and Their Consequences* (New York: Knopf, 2006), 174–176, 261–262. Some critics argued that Clinton's trade policies were not free enough—that administration-negotiated agreements retained too many high tariffs protecting politically connected businesses and industries. See, for example, Jeffrey A. Frankel and Peter R. Orszag, eds., *American Economic Policy in the 1990s* (Cambridge, MA: MIT Press, 2002). On the ambivalence of the public, see the compendium of poll results in "AEI Studies in Public Opinion: Polls on NAFTA and Free Trade," American Enterprise Institute, http://www.aei.org/files/2008/06/26/20031203_nafta2.pdf.
42. Frankel and Orszag, *American Economic Policy in the 1990s.*
43. Memorandum, Thomas Hubbard to the Secretary, "Commerce Secretary Brown's Trip to China," September 2, 1994, National Security Archive (http://nsarchive.gwu.edu/).
44. Warren Christopher Interview, April 15–16, 2002, 51–53, Miller Center; Warren Christopher, *Chances of a Lifetime: A Memoir* (New York: Scribner, 2001), 236–241.
45. Ronald Brownstein, "Clinton Drawing Visionary Blueprint of Global Economy," *Los Angeles Times*, December 5, 1994.
46. Santorum quoted in Mark O'Keefe, "Former Skeptics Warm to AmeriCorps," *St. Paul Pioneer Press*, December 23, 2001; Clinton, *Putting People First*, 87.

CHAPTER 4. DEFEAT, 1993–1994
1. Haynes Johnson and David S. Broder, *The System: The American Way of Politics at the Breaking Point* (Boston: Little, Brown, 1997), ix.
2. Council of Economic Advisors, 1994 Economic Report to the President, 131–136. http://www.presidency.ucsb.edu/economic_reports/1994.pdf. The best brief overview of previous reform efforts is Paul Starr, *The Social Transformation of American Medicine* (New York: Basic Books, 1982).
3. Avik Roy, "The Tortuous History of Conservatives and the Individual Mandate," *Forbes*, February 2 and February 7, 2012.
4. Theda Skocpol, *Boomerang: Clinton's Health Security Effort and the Turn against Government in US Politics* (New York: W.W. Norton, 1996), 25–30. Other issues figured into the outcome, but analysis of polling results made clear the pivotal role of health care. See, for example, Jane H. White, "Pennsylvania Voters Prove Healthcare Is an Important Issue," *Health Progress* (January-February 1992): 10–16. And almost all commentators attributed the outcome to Wofford's promise to fight for health-care reform.
5. The following account of the origins and course of the health-care debate draws heavily on three accounts that, though written soon after the fact, have not been superseded in coverage or analysis: Skocpol, *Boomerang*; Johnson and Broder,

The System; and Jacob S. Hacker, *The Road to Nowhere: The Genesis of President Clinton's Plan for Health Security* (Princeton, NJ: Princeton University Press, 1997).

6. David R. Obey, *Raising Hell for Justice: The Washington Battles of a Heartland Progressive* (Madison: University of Wisconsin Press, 2007).

7. Michael Schrage, "A Onetime Whiz Kid Transforms America's Healthcare Debate," *Washington Post*, December 3, 1993.

8. Alain Enthoven, "The History and Principles of Managed Competition," *Health Affairs* 12 (1993): 24–48; Schrage, "A Onetime Whiz Kid Transforms America's Healthcare Debate."

9. Enthoven, "The History and Principles of Managed Competition." Other lucid explanations of managed competition include Johnson and Broder, *The System*, 73.

10. Blair journal entry, February 23, 1993, FreeBeacon.com. http://www.scribd.com/doc/205858605/The-Clinton-Files.

11. Barbara Ehrenreich, "A Cure for the Wrong Disease," *Time*, March 29, 1993.

12. Johnson and Broder, *The System*, 12.

13. Patrick J. Maney, "The Forgotten New Deal Congress," in Julian E. Zelizer, ed., *The American Congress* (Boston: Houghton Mifflin, 2004): 446–471; Maney, "Political Reputation," in William D. Pederson, ed., *A Companion to Franklin D. Roosevelt* (Malden, MA: Wiley-Blackwell), 690–709.

14. Carville quoted in Hillary Rodham Clinton, *Living History* (New York: Simon & Schuster, 2003), 149.

15. Obey, *Raising Hell for Justice*, 289.

16. Kenneth S. Baer, *Reinventing Democrats: The Politics of Liberalism from Reagan to Clinton* (Lawrence: University Press of Kansas, 2000).

17. Memorandum, Jennings to Hillary Rodham Clinton, February 24, 1993, Domestic Policy Council, Chris Jennings Subject File, Clinton Library.

18. Adam Clymer, *Edward M. Kennedy: A Biography* (New York: Morrow, 1999), 525.

19. Laura Tyson, interview with author, November 10, 2010.

20. Maureen Dowd, "First Lady Takes Stage, Ending Era on the Hill," *New York Times*, September 29, 1993.

21. "Health Care Reform Overseer Big Believer in Revamping System," *Palm Beach Post*, March 28, 1993.

22. Jacob Weisberg, "Dies Ira," *New Republic*, January 24, 1994, 18–24.

23. John Solomon, "For Magaziner, Reform Is the Road to Paradise," *Newsweek*, September 20, 1993. See also Lee Bowman, "Ira Magaziner: The Man behind the Plan," *Dallas Morning News*, October 10, 1993.

24. Alan Blinder Interview, June 27, 2003, 58, Miller Center, University of Virginia, William J. Clinton Oral History Project (hereafter cited as Miller Center).

25. Magaziner quoted in Clinton, *Living History*, 144.

26. Weisberg, "Dies Ira."

27. Jennings to Magaziner, "Outline of Congressional Strategy for Health Reform," February 5, 1993, Health Care Task Force Papers, Box 3516, Clinton Library.

28. Memo, Chris Jennings and Steve Edelstein to HRC, "Meeting with Senators Leahy & Pryor," June 14, 1993; memo, Chris Jennings to HRC, "Current

Congressional Status & Suggested Upcoming Weeks," May 10, 1993, Health Care Task Force, Box 3681, Clinton Library.

29. Memos, Chris Jennings, "US Senators," "Targeting," Papers of Domestic Policy Council, Chris Jennings, Box 8991, Clinton Library.

30. Memo, Jennings to Steve R., April 9, 1993, Papers of Domestic Policy Council, Chris Jennings, Box 8991, Clinton Library.

31. Harold Ickes Interview; Bill Bradley Interview, July 17, 2009, George J. Mitchell Oral History Project, Bowdoin College Library, Brunswick, Maine (hereafter referred to as Mitchell Oral History Project).

32. Memos, Jennings to HRC, "Meeting with Chairman John Dingell," April 25, 1993; "Current Congressional Status," May 10, 1993, Health Care Task Force, Box 3681, Clinton Library; Jennings to HRC, "Senate Retreat," April 22, 1993, Health Care Task Force, Box 3533, Clinton Library.

33. John Breaux Interview, January 28, 2010; Richard Gephardt and Thomas J. O'Donnell, interview, March 17, 2010, Mitchell Oral History Project.

34. Alan Blinder Interview, 55–56.

35. William J. Clinton, "Address to a Joint Session of the Congress on Health Care Reform," September 22, 1993.

36. Strobe Talbott, *The Great Experiment: The Story of Ancient Empires, Modern States, and the Quest for a Global Nation* (New York: Simon & Schuster, 2008), 326.

37. Margaret M. Suntum to Gabrielle M. Bushman, transcript of speech preparation, January 22–23, 1996, email, WHO (Oklahoma Bombing), Box 500000, Clinton Library.

38. Anthony Lewis, "'This Is Our Journey': Can the Healthcare Plan Work?" *New York Times*, September 24, 1993; "Health Plan Gets Thumbs-up," *USA Today*, September 27, 1993.

39. Johnson and Broder, *The System*, 5.

40. http://www.gallup.com/poll/116584/Presidential-approval-ratings-bill-clinton.aspx.

41. Adam Clymer, "Captivates Lawmakers on 2 Major House Panels: Hillary Clinton Wins Raves on the Hill." *New York Times*, September 29, 1993; Ellen Goodman, "'The Hillary Chronicles': From Harridan to Heroine," *Oregonian* October 5, 1993; Maureen Dowd, "First Lady Takes Stage, Ending Era on the Hill." *New York Times*, September 29, 1993.

42. Johnson and Broder, *The System*, 205.

43. Ibid., 213.

44. "Economist Enthoven Criticizes Clinton Health Plan," *Houston Chronicle*, July 8, 1974. Later Enthoven described the bill as "an absolutely dreadful, unrealistic, grandiose, impractical scheme." Sherry Jacobson, "The Blame Game," *Dallas Morning News*, Oct. 2, 1994, 15; Roy, "The Tortuous History of Conservatives and the Individual Mandate."

45. Skocpol, *Boomerang*, 93–97, 161.

46. Godfrey Hodgson, *The Gentleman from New York: Daniel Patrick Moynihan: A Biography* (Boston: Houghton Mifflin, 2000), 354.

47. Roy, "The Tortuous History of Conservatives and the Individual Mandate."

48. Alan Blinder Interview, 58.

49. Gramm quoted in Johnson and Broder, *The System*, 363–365.

50. "William Kristol's 1993 Memo—Defeating President Clinton's Health Care Proposal," *Scribd*: http://www.scribd.com/doc/12926608/William-Kristols-1993-Memo-Defeating-President-Clintons-Health-Care-Proposal.

51. Johnson and Broder, *The System*.

52. Memo, Patrick J. Griffin, "Meeting with Senator Feinstein," August 3, 1994, Domestic Policy Council, Chris Jennings, Box 21536, Clinton Library.

53. Memo, Ira Magaziner to President, "Broder/Johnson Interview," July 14, 1995, WHORM-Subject File-General, FG001–07, Box 21793, Clinton Library.

54. Donna Shalala Interview, May 15, 2007, 12–13, 25, Miller Center.

55. Memo, Ira Magaziner to President, "Broder/Johnson Interview."

56. Various analyses of health care's defeat are summarized in Skocpol, *Boomerang*, 9–19; Hacker, *Road to Nowhere*; Carol S. Wiessert and William G. Weissert, *Governing Health: The Politics of Health Policy* (Baltimore, MD: Johns Hopkins University Press, 1996), 296–315; Mark E. Rushefsky and Kant Patel, *Politics, Power and Policy Making: The Case of Health Care Reform in the 1990s* (Armonk, NY: M. E. Sharpe, 1998), 243–253; Jacob Hacker, "Learning from Defeat? Political Analysis and the Failure of Health Care Reform in the United States," *British Journal of Political Science* 31 (January 2001): 61–94.

57. Johnson and Broder, *The System*, 209–210.

58. Bill Clinton, *My Life* (New York: Knopf, 2004), 601.

59. Hacker, "Learning from Defeat," 63.

60. Tyson interview with author; Reich, *Locked in the Cabinet*, 166; Donna Shalala Interview, 27.

61. Perhaps the chief objection of Clinton's Council of Economic Advisors was the claim of task-force leaders and the president that the reform plan would pay for itself. Alan Blinder Interview.

62. Hacker, *The Road to Nowhere* and "Learning from Defeat."

63. Even a quick look at the early history of Social Security is instructive. See, for example, Edwin E. Witte, *The Development of the Social Security Act* (Madison: University of Wisconsin Press, 1963); Roy Lubove, *The Struggle for Social Security, 1900–1935* (Cambridge, MA: Harvard University Press, 1968); Daniel Nelson, *Unemployment Insurance: The American Experience, 1915–1935* (Madison: University of Wisconsin Press, 1969); William Graebner, *A History of Retirement: The Meaning and Function of an American Institution, 1885–1978* (New Haven, CT: Yale University Press, 1980).

64. Johnson and Broder, *The System*, xiv.

65. Dan Balz, "The Whip Who Would Be Speaker," *Washington Post*, October 20, 1994; Jurek Martin, "Republicans Resort to Fire and Brimstone," *Financial Times* (London), August 24, 1992; Jeffrey A. Frank, "Washington Loves Newt," *Washington Post*, January 15, 1995; Frank Rich, "Ding, Dong, the Cultural Witch Hunt Is Dead," *New York Times*, February 24, 2002; Ann Devroy and Tom Kenworthy, "GOP Aide Quits over Foley Memo: Bush Says Attack on House Speaker Is 'Disgusting,'" *Washington Post*, June 8, 1989.

66. Thomas E. Mann and Norman J. Ornstein, *It's Even Worse Than It Looks: How the American Constitutional System Collided with the New Politics of Extremism* (New York: Basic Books), 39.

67. Hendrik Hertzberg, "Cookie Monster," *New Yorker*, July 17, 1995; Gingrich quoted in "Spiro Agnew with Brains," *Newsweek*, November 27, 1994.
68. Linda Killian, *The Freshmen: What Happened to the Republican Revolution?* (Boulder, CO: Westview Press, 1998), 6.
69. John B. Judis, "Here's Why the Democrats Got Crushed—And Why 2016 Won't Be a Cakewalk," *The New Republic*, November 5, 2014.
70. Everett Carll Ladd, "The 1994 Congressional Elections: The Postindustrial Realignment Continues," *Political Science Quarterly* 110 (April 1, 1995): 1–23. See also Alfred J. Tuchfarber et al., "The Republican Tidal Wave of 1994: Testing Hypotheses about Realignment, Restructuring, and Rebellion," *PS: Political Science and Politics* 28 (December 1995): 689–696; Charles S. Bullock III, Donna R. Hoffman, and Ronald Keith Gaddie, "The Consolidation of the White Southern Congressional Vote," *Political Research Quarterly* 58 (June 1, 2005): 231–243.
71. Johnson and Broder, *The System*, 552.
72. Walter Dean Burnham, "Realignment Lives: The 1994 Earthquake and Its Implications," in Colin Campbell and Bert A. Rockman, eds., *The Clinton Presidency: First Appraisals* (Chatham, NJ: Chatham House Publishers, 1996), 363.
73. Ladd, "The 1994 Congressional Elections," 3.
74. Michael Matza, "For 4 Hectic Days, It's 'Newt' Hampshire," *Philadelphia Inquirer*, June 11, 1995.
75. The President's News Conference, April 18, 1995.
76. Warren Christopher Interview, April 15–16, 2002, 80, Miller Center.

CHAPTER 5. IN SEARCH OF THREE SYLLABLES:
FOREIGN POLICY, 1993–1996

1. Kennan and Clinton quoted in Strobe Talbott, *The Russia Hand: A Memoir of Presidential Diplomacy* (New York: Random House, 2002), 133–134.
2. Patrick J. Buchanan, "Now That Red Is Dead, Come Home, America," *Washington Post*, September 8, 1991; Richard Gwyn, "Bush's 'New World Order' a Cynical Ruse," *Toronto Star*, April 14, 1991; John B. Judis, "George Bush, Meet Woodrow Wilson," *New York Times*, November 20, 1990; Talbott, *The Russia Hand*, 269–270.
3. Thomas L. Friedman, "The 1992 Campaign: Foreign Policy: Turning His Sights Overseas, Clinton Sees a Problem at 1600 Pennsylvania Avenue," *New York Times*, April 2, 1992.
4. Peter Grier, "Clinton Hits Bush on Foreign Policy, but Not Too Hard," *Christian Science Monitor*, April 3, 1992.
5. Jason DeParle, "The Man inside Bill Clinton's Foreign Policy," *New York Times Magazine*, August 20, 1995.
6. Ibid.; Matthew Cooper, "An Unlikely Tough Guy," *Newsweek*, February 24, 1997.
7. Anthony Lake Interview, May 21, 2002, Miller Center, University of Virginia, William J. Clinton Oral History Project (hereafter cited as Miller Center).
8. Cooper, "An Unlikely Tough Guy"; Laura Tyson, interview with author, November 10, 2010; Clinton quoted in Anthony Lake Interview, 32.
9. DeParle, "The Man inside Bill Clinton's Foreign Policy"; Cooper, "An Unlikely Tough Guy."

10. Quoted in John F. Harris, *The Survivor: Bill Clinton in the White House* (New York: Random House, 2005), 49.

11. Anthony Lake Interview, May 21, 2002, 15; Strobe Talbott, *The Great Experiment: The Story of Ancient Empires, Modern States, and the Quest for a Global Nation* (New York: Simon & Schuster, 2008), 281.

12. Talbott, *The Russia Hand*, 26.

13. Ibid., 94.

14. Ibid., 46; Samuel Berger Interview, March 24–25, 2005, Miller Center.

15. Talbott, *The Russia Hand*, 54, 5, 8.

16. Kennan quoted in ibid., 231.

17. Talbott, *The Russia Hand*, 186–187; Clinton quoted in ibid., 38, 186–187.

18. Robert S. Norris and Hans M. Kristensen, "Global Nuclear Weapons Inventories, 1945–2010," *Bulletin of the Atomic Scientists* 66 (July 1, 2010): 77–83; Talbott, *The Russia Hand*, 79.

19. Warren Christopher, *In the Stream of History: Shaping Foreign Policy for a New Era* (Stanford, CA: Stanford University Press, 1998), 25.

20. Anthony Lake, "From Containment to Enlargement," Speech at the John Hopkins University School of Advanced International Studies, Washington, DC, September 21, 1993, http://babel.hathitrust.org/cgi/pt?id=mdp.39015051567645;view=1up;seq=1.

21. Lake, "From Containment to Enlargement."

22. Elaine Sciolino, "New US Peace-Keeping Policy De-emphasizes Role of the U.N.," *New York Times*, May 6, 1994; Sciolino, "US Narrows Terms for Its Peace Keeper," *New York Times*, September 22, 1993; Ruth Marcus, "Bush Endorses Expansion of U.N. Peace-Keeping Role," *Washington Post*, September 22, 1992.

23. Douglas Brinkley, "Democratic Enlargement: The Clinton Doctrine," *Foreign Policy* 106 (Spring 1997): 119.

24. Anthony Lake Interview.

25. Samuel Berger Interview, 32.

26. Jonathan Moore, "Deciding Humanitarian Intervention," *Social Research* 74 (Spring 2007): 170–172.

27. Eric Schmitt, "US Set to Limit Role of Military in Peacekeeping," *New York Times*, January 29, 1994.

28. Harris, *The Survivor*, 51.

29. Presidential Decision Directive/NSC-25, May 3, 1994, Clinton Library http://clinton.presidentiallibraries.us/items/show/12749.

30. Sciolino, "New US Peacekeeping Policy De-emphasizes Role of the U.N."

31. Martin Walker, "Withdrawal Symptoms," *The Guardian* (London), May 7, 1994; Ann Devroy, "Clinton Signs New Guidelines for US Peacekeeping Operations," *Washington Post*, May 6, 1994.

32. Shmuley Boteach, "Bill Clinton: The First Rwandan President," *Jerusalem Post*, January 22, 2004, 15.

33. Elaine Sciolino, "For West, Rwanda Is not Worth the Political Candle," *New York Times*, April 15, 1994.

34. Anthony Lake Interview.

35. Warren Christopher Interview, April 15–16, 2002, 80, Miller Center, 23.

36. Holly J. Burkhalter, "The Question of Genocide: The Clinton Administration and Rwanda," *World Policy Journal* 11 (1994/1995): 44–54; Clinton quoted in Harris, *The Survivor*, 128.

37. Clinton, "William J. Clinton: Remarks to Genocide Survivors in Kigali, Rwanda," March 25, 1998.

38. Quoted in Bill Clinton, *My Life* (New York: Knopf, 2004), 591.

39. Anthony Lake Interview, 61; "Washington Was On Brink of War with North Korea 5 Years Ago," October 4, 1999, http://www.cnn.com/US/9910/04/korea.brink/.

40. Burton I. Kaufman, *The Post-Presidency from Washington to Clinton* (Lawrence: University Press of Kansas, 2012), 456.

41. "Showboater" quoted in Harris, *The Survivor*, 131; Carter quoted in Douglas Jehl, "Carter His Own Emissary, Outpaces White House," *New York Times*, June 20, 1994; Anthony Lake Interview, 62.

42. Harris, *The Survivor*, 128.

43. Ralph Pezzullo, *Plunging into Haiti: Clinton, Aristide, and the Defeat of Diplomacy* (Jackson: University Press of Mississippi, 2006); Samuel Berger Interview.

44. Philippe R. Girard, *Clinton in Haiti: The 1994 US Invasion of Haiti* (New York: Palgrave Macmillan, 2004), 168.

45. Ryan C. Hendrickson, *The Clinton Wars: The Constitution, Congress, and War Powers* (Nashville, TN: Vanderbilt University Press, 2002), 63; Girard, *Clinton in Haiti*, 62–66.

46. Clinton quoted in Taylor Branch, *The Clinton Tapes: Wrestling History with the President* (London and New York: Simon & Schuster, 2009), 186–187.

47. Clinton quoted in ibid., 192.

48. Ibid., 178.

49. Lugar quoted in Donald M. Rothberg, "Clinton's Toughest Critics on Haiti Unswayed by Speech," Associated Press, September 16, 1994.

50. Michael Kelly, "Letter from Washington: It All Co-depends," *New Yorker*, October 3, 1994, 80.

51. Anthony Lake and Warren Christopher Interviews; Strobe Talbott Interview, February 25, 2010, 6, Miller Center.

52. Amy Wilentz, "Aristide in Waiting," *New York Times Magazine*, November 5, 2000, 58.

53. Clinton, *My Life*, 509–513; Sidney Blumenthal, *The Clinton Wars* (New York: Farrar, Straus and Giroux, 2003), 61–64.

54. Richard C. Holbrooke, *To End a War* (New York: Random House, 1998), 41–42.

55. Blumenthal, *The Clinton Wars*, 62–63; Robert D. Kaplan, *Balkan Ghosts: A Journey through History* (New York: St. Martin's Press, 1993); Holbrooke, *To End a War*, 22.

56. Wiesel and Clinton quoted in Jason Dick, "Elie Wiesel's Scolding of Clinton Was Weather-Related," *Roll Call*, July 12, 2013.

57. Holbrooke, *To End a War*, 94.

58. Mark Leibovich, *This Town: Two Parties and a Funeral—Plus, Plenty of Valet Parking!—in America's Gilded Capital* (New York: Blue Rider Press, 2013), 225.

59. Holbrooke, *To End a War*, 69.

60. Thomas L. Friedman, "Foreign Affairs; Allies," *New York Times*, June 7, 1995.
61. Holbrooke, *To End a War*, 307.
62. Harris, *The Survivor*, 221.
63. Henry A. Kissinger, "At Sea in a New World," *Newsweek*, June 6, 1994; Leslie H. Gelb, "Can Clinton Deal with the World?" *Washington Post*, March 6, 1994; Editors, "The New Look of Foreign Policy," *Foreign Policy* 98 (Spring 1995): 4. An extended critique along these lines is William G. Hyland, *Clinton's World: Remaking American Foreign Policy* (Westport, CT: Praeger, 1999).
64. James T. Patterson, *Restless Giant: The United States from Watergate to Bush v. Gore* (New York: Oxford University Press, 2005), 341.
65. Clinton quoted in Talbott, *The Russia Hand*, 133, 444.
66. Ibid.

CHAPTER 6. REBOUND, 1995–1996

1. Strobe Talbott Interview, February 25, 2010, 12, William J. Clinton Presidential History Project, Miller Center, University of Virginia (hereafter referred to as Miller Center). The "you in particular" was not Talbott but Sandy Berger.
2. John F. Harris, *The Survivor: Bill Clinton in the White House* (New York: Random House, 2005), 156.
3. Ickes and McCurry quoted in Michael Takiff, *A Complicated Man: The Life of Bill Clinton as Told by Those Who Know Him* (New Haven, CT, and London: Yale University Press), 253.
4. Dick Morris, *Behind the Oval Office: Winning the Presidency in the Nineties* (New York: Random House, 1997), 79–105.
5. William Galston Interview, April 22–23, 2004, 72, Miller Center.
6. Leon Panetta Interview, May 4, 2000, White House Interview Program, Clinton Library; Leon Panetta and Jim Newton, *Worthy Fights: A Memoir of Leadership in War and Peace* (New York: Penguin Press, 2014), 137.
7. Ibid., 138–142, passim.
8. Michael McCurry Interview, March 27, 2000, White House Interview Program, Clinton Library; Howard Kurtz, *Spin Cycle: Inside the Clinton Propaganda Machine* (New York: Free Press, 1998), 14.
9. Steven M. Gillon, *The Pact: Bill Clinton, Newt Gingrich, and the Rivalry That Defined a Generation* (Oxford and New York: Oxford University Press, 2008), 126.
10. Quoted in Gillon, *The Pact*, 58.
11. Gillon, *The Pact*, 141; *Newsweek*, April 10, 1995.
12. Linda Killian, *The Freshmen: What Happened to the Republican Revolution?* (Boulder, CO: Westview Press, 1998), 103. My account of the GOP's budget process draws heavily on Killian.
13. Carol Goar, "Trash Talking," *Toronto Star*, April 30, 1995.
14. http://fair.org/take-action/action-alerts/did-msnbc-know-liddys-history/.
15. Goar, "Trash Talking."
16. Elena Kagan, "Presidential Administration," *Harvard Law Review* 114 (June 1, 2001): 2245–2385.
17. William J. Clinton: "Remarks Prior to a Roundtable Discussion on Teenage Smoking," August 10, 1995; "The President's News Conference," August 10,

1995; "The President's Radio Address," August 12, 1995; "Remarks Announcing the Final Rule To Protect Youth From Tobacco," August 23, 1996.

18. Kagan, "Presidential Administration," 2302.

19. For an assessment of executive actions, see Phillip J. Cooper, *By Order of the President: The Use and Abuse of Executive Direct Action* (Lawrence: University Press of Kansas, 2002); Kenneth R. Mayer, *With the Stroke of a Pen: Executive Orders and Presidential Power* (Princeton, NJ: Princeton University Press, 2001).

20. David R. Obey, *Raising Hell for Justice: The Washington Battles of a Heartland Progressive* (Madison: University of Wisconsin Press, 2007), 306; Panetta, *Worthy Fights*, 163–166.

21. David Rosenbaum, "House and Senate Act to Avert a Default," *New York Times*, November 10, 1995.

22. Linda Killian, *The Freshmen*, 185.

23. Ron Haskins, *Work over Welfare: The Inside Story of the 1996 Welfare Reform Law* (Washington, DC: Brookings Institution Press, 2006), 261–262.

24. Quoted in Dick W. Olufs III, *The Making of Telecommunications Policy* (Boulder, CO: Lynne Rienner, 1999), 87.

25. Joseph E. Stiglitz, *The Roaring Nineties: A New History of the World's Most Prosperous Decade* (New York: W. W. Norton, 2003), 96.

26. Common Cause, "The Fallout from the Telecommunications Act of 1996: Unintended Consequences and Lessons Learned," May 9, 2005, http://www.commoncause.org/research-reports/National_050905_Fallout_From_The_Telecommunications_Act_2.pdf; Consumers Union, "Lessons from 1996 Telecommunications Act: Deregulation before Meaningful Competition Spells Consumer Disaster," February 2000, https://consumersunion.org/wp-content/uploads/2013/03/lesson.pdf.

27. Laura Tyson, interview with author, November 10, 2010; Stiglitz, *The Roaring Nineties*, 100–101; Bill Clinton, *My Life* (New York: Knopf, 2004), 302, 309.

28. Jason DeParle, *American Dream: Three Women, Ten Kids, and a Nation's Drive to End Welfare* (New York: Penguin Books, 2005), 99–100.

29. Actually it was an article in *The New Yorker* magazine by Dwight MacDonald about Harrington's book that eventually brought the subject to public attention.

30. Key works on the history of welfare include Linda Gordon, *Pitied but Not Entitled: Single Mothers and the History of Welfare* (New York: Free Press, 1994); Michael B. Katz, *The Undeserving Poor: From the War on Poverty to the War on Welfare* (New York: Pantheon Books, 1989); Guida West, *The National Welfare Rights Movement: The Social Protest of Poor Women* (New York: Praeger, 1981); Jason DeParle, *American Dream*. For a fascinating profile of the person behind Reagan's "welfare queen," see Josh Levin, "The Real Story of Linda Taylor, America's Original Welfare Queen," *Slate Magazine*, December 19, 2013.

31. Marisa Chappell, *The War on Welfare: Family, Poverty, and Politics in Modern America* (Philadelphia: University of Pennsylvania Press, 2010).

32. David T. Ellwood, *Poor Support: Poverty In The American Family*, Reprint edition (New York: Basic Books, 1989); DeParle, *American Dream*, 107–108; DeParle, "Mugged by Reality: The Story of the Recent Welfare Revolution Is, in Many Respects, a Story of David Ellwood's Ideas," *New York Times Magazine*, December 8, 1996.

33. Clinton quoted in Richard L. Berke, "Clinton Getting People off Welfare," *New York Times*, September 10, 1992.
34. David T. Ellwood, "Welfare Reform as I Knew It: When Bad Things Happen to Good Policies," *American Prospect*, May 1, 1996.
35. DeParle, *American Dream*, 110.
36. Ibid., 105–122.
37. Haskins, *Work over Welfare*, 37–58.
38. The most detailed account of the ensuing debate is Haskins, *Work over Welfare*.
39. DeParle, *American Dream*, 138–154; Taylor Branch, *The Clinton Tapes: Wrestling History with the President* (London and New York: Simon & Schuster, 2009), 368–370; Robert Edward Rubin, *In an Uncertain World: Tough Choices from Wall Street to Washington* (New York: Random House, 2003), 200.
40. David T. Ellwood, "Welfare Reform in Name Only," *New York Times*, July 22, 1996; Donna Shalala Interview, May 15, 2007, 30, Miller Center. On the waivers granted by the administration, see DeParle, *American Dream*, 109; Haskins, *Work over Welfare*, 317.
41. Morris, *Behind the Oval Office*, 300–305.
42. Godfrey Hodgson, *The Gentleman from New York: Daniel Patrick Moynihan: A Biography* (Boston: Houghton Mifflin, 2000), 378.
43. Peter Edelman, "The Worst Thing Bill Clinton Has Done," *Atlantic Monthly* 279 (March 1997).
44. "Liberals Shun Clinton as He Signs Welfare Bill," *Akron Beacon Journal*, August 23, 1996.
45. Clinton, "Statement on Signing the Personal Responsibility and Work Opportunity Reconciliation Act of 1996," August 22, 1996.
46. Branch, *The Clinton Tapes*, 368–369.
47. *Wall Street Journal* quoted in DeParle, *American Dream*, 15.
48. Ellwood quoted in Joe Klein, *The Natural: The Misunderstood Presidency of Bill Clinton* (New York: Doubleday, 2002), 154.
49. Andrew J. Cherlin, "Can the Left Learn the Lessons of Welfare Reform?" *Contemporary Sociology* 37 (March 1, 2008): 101–104.
50. Bill Clinton, "How We Ended Welfare, Together," *New York Times*, August 22, 2006. Summarizing the scholarly literature a decade after its passage, two experts concluded that as of 2008: "Despite dire predictions, previous research has shown that program caseloads declined and employment increased, with no detectible increase in poverty or worsening of child well-being." Marianne P. Bitler and Hillary W. Hoynes, "The State of the Social Safety Net in the Post-Welfare Reform Era," Brookings Papers on Economic Activity (Fall 2010): 71.
51. Peter Edelman, *Searching for America's Heart: RFK and the Renewal of Hope* (Boston: Houghton Mifflin, 2001).
52. "Families Feel Sharp Edge of State Budget Cuts," *New York Times*, September 6, 2011; US Census Bureau, "Income, Poverty, and Health Insurance Coverage in the United States: 2010"; Jason DeParle and Sabrina Tavernise, "Poor Are Still Getting Poorer, but Downturn's Punch Varies, Census Data Show," *New York Times*, September 15, 2011.
53. Jake Blumgart, "Happy Birthday, Welfare Reform," *American Prospect*, August 19, 2011, http://prospect.org/article/happy-birthday-welfare-reform; Ron

Haskins, Vicky Albert, and Kimberly Howard, "The Responsiveness of the Temporary Assistance for Needy Families Program during the Great Recession," The Brookings Institution, http://www.brookings.edu/research/papers/2014/08/responsiveness-tanf-great-recessions-haskins; but see also Thomas Edsall, "Cutting the Poor out of Welfare," *New York Times*, June 18, 2014.

54. Harris, *The Survivor*, 240.

55. Ibid., 245; Clinton, "Remarks Announcing the Donation of Cellular Telephones to Neighborhood Watch Groups," July 16, 1996; "Memorandum on the Manual on School Uniforms," February 24, 1996.

56. Peter Baker, "Bill Clinton's Decision, and Regret, on Defense of Marriage Act," *New York Times*, March 25, 2013; Tony Kushner, "Holding Our Noses," *Advocate*, October 29, 1996. Years later Clinton said he regretted signing the Defense of Marriage Act. For a sympathetic account of Clinton's gay rights policies, see Kevan M. Yenerall, "The Clarion Call, the Muted Trumpet, the Lasting Impact: Gay Rights," in Mark J. White, ed., *The Presidency of Bill Clinton: The Legacy of a New Domestic and Foreign Policy* (London: I. B. Tauris, 2012), 120–157.

57. Harris, *The Survivor*, 245–246.

58. Morris, *Behind the Oval Office*, 144.

59. Michael McCurry Interview, White House Transition Interviews, March 27, 2000.

60. D. Hillygus, *The Persuadable Voter: Wedge Issues in Presidential Campaigns* (Princeton, NJ: Princeton University Press, 2009), 12–13.

61. Douglas B. Sosnik, *Applebee's America: How Successful Political, Business, and Religious Leaders Connect with the New American Community* (New York: Simon & Schuster, 2006), 11–27.

62. Ruth Marcus and Charles R. Babcock, "Money Machine: The System Cracks under the Weight of Cash Candidates," *Washington Post*, February 9, 1997.

63. Reports of the Council of Economic Advisors, 1996, 1997.

64. Quoted in Louis Uchitelle, *The Disposable American: Layoffs and Their Consequences* (New York: Knopf, 2006), 155.

65. Robert Murphy, interview with author, August 1, 2010. By this time Joseph Stiglitz had replaced Laura Tyson as CEA chair. Tyson was chair of the National Economic Council, and Gene Sperling was her deputy.

66. James K. Galbraith, "The Clinton Administration's Vision," *Challenge* 40 (July–August 1997): 45–57.

67. Gerald M. Pomper, *The Election of 1996: Reports and Interpretations* (Chatham, NJ: Chatham House Publishers, 1997), 14.

68. Harris, *The Survivor*, 241.

69. Quoted in "Controversy: Why Did Clinton Win?" *American Prospect*, March 1, 1997.

70. Will Marshall, "Controversy: Why Did Clinton Win?" *American Prospect*, December 19, 2001.

CHAPTER 7. SIEGE AND SURVIVAL, 1997–1999

1. Marquis Childs, "They Hate Roosevelt," *Harper's Magazine*, May 1936, 634.

2. Henry Louis Gates, "Hating Hillary," *New Yorker*, February 26, 1996, 116.

3. Robert G. Kaiser, "Money, Family Name Shaped Scaife," *Washington Post*, May 3, 1991.
4. Hillary Rodham Clinton, *Living History* (New York: Simon & Schuster, 2003), 246.
5. Margaret Carlson, "All Eyes on Hillary," *Time*, September 14, 1992.
6. Among the many accounts of the alleged scandals, the following provide concise summaries: Peter Baker, *The Breach: Inside the Impeachment and Trial of William Jefferson Clinton* (New York: Scribner, 2000); and Ken Gormley, *The Death of American Virtue: Clinton vs. Starr* (New York: Crown Publishers, 2010).
7. Jackie Koszczuk and Rebecca Carr, "Campaign Finance: GOP Fails to Transform Probe into 'Clinton's Watergate,'" *CQ Weekly*, November 1, 1997, 2656–2659. For a superior account of the financing of the 1996 campaigns see Ruth Marcus and Charles R. Babcock, "Money Machine: The Fund-Raising Frenzy of Campaign '96," a four-part series in the *Washington Post*, February 9–12.
8. Gormley, *The Death of American Virtue*, 108.
9. Joe Conason and Gene Lyons, *The Hunting of the President: The Ten-Year Campaign to Destroy Bill and Hillary Clinton* (New York: St. Martin's Press, 2000), 136–159.
10. Robert L. Bartley and Micah Morrison, eds., *Whitewater: From the Editorial Pages of the Wall Street Journal: Journal Briefing* (New York: Dow Jones & Company, 1994), 279.
11. "Not Criminal, Just Reprehensible," *New York Times*, July 1, 1994.
12. Quoted in Gates, "Hating Hillary," 118, 132.
13. Ibid., 119.
14. Strobe Talbott Interview, April 15–16, 101, William J. Clinton Presidential History Project, Miller Center, University of Virginia (hereafter referred to as Miller Center).
15. Carl Bernstein, *A Woman in Charge: The Life of Hillary Rodham Clinton* (New York: Knopf, 2007), 356.
16. Gates, "Hating Hillary," 116.
17. Diane Blair, Memo, Thanksgiving Day, 1996, University of Arkansas, http://www.scribd.com/doc/205858605/The-Clinton-Files; Gergen quoted in Bernstein, *A Woman in Charge*, 408.
18. Ibid., 419.
19. "Heckler Stirs Clinton Anger: Excerpts from the Exchange," *New York Times*, March 28, 1992.
20. Anonymous (Joe Klein), *Primary Colors: A Novel of Politics* (New York: Random House, 1996), 2, 8; Virginia Kelley, *Leading with My Heart* (New York: Simon & Schuster, 1994), 38–39.
21. Catherine Adkins, interview with author. Adkins was the owner of the Willow Glen Bookstore and is the author's sister-in-law.
22. Arthur M. Schlesinger, Jr., *Journals, 1952–2000* (New York: Penguin Press, 2007), 800–802, 834–840.
23. Peter Edelman Interview, May 24–25, 2004, 66, Miller Center; Gingrich quoted in David Maraniss, "Time to Bring Back Bill Clinton," *Washington Post*, January 23, 2012.

24. Roger Altman Interview, April 22, 2003, 67, Miller Center.
25. David A. Bositis, *Blacks and the 2004 Democratic National Convention* (Washington, DC: Joint Center for Political and Economic Studies), 9.
26. DeWayne Wickham, *Clinton and Black America* (New York: Ballantine, 2002), 60–61, 47–48.
27. Bositis, *Blacks and the 2004 Democratic National Convention*, 9.
28. Toni Morrison, "Talk of the Town: Comment," *New Yorker*, October 5, 1998, 31–32.
29. David Kamp, "The Color of Truth," *Vanity Fair*, August 1998, 167.
30. Michael (Mickey) Kantor Interview, June 28, 2002, 63–64, Miller Center.
31. Quoted in Wickham, *Clinton and Black Americans*, 30, 94, 96.
32. Bernard Nussbaum Interview, September 24, 2002, 33–40, Miller Center.
33. Gormley, *The Death of American Virtue*, 169.
34. Quoted in *Washington Post, The Starr Report* (New York: Public Affairs, 1998), xxxi.
35. Joan Didion, *Political Fictions* (New York: Alfred A. Knopf, 2001), 236.
36. Baker, *The Breach*, 433.
37. Quoted in Jeffrey Toobin, *A Vast Conspiracy* (New York: Random House, 1999), 331–332.
38. *The Starr Report*, xxxi.
39. Gormley, *The Death of American Virtue*, 414.
40. Shalala Interview, May 15, 2007, 30, Miller Center.
41. Quoted in Joan Didion, *Political Fictions*, 236.
42. *Washington Post, The Starr Report*, xxix.
43. Quoted in Didion, *Political Fictions*, 234.
44. Dobson quoted in Frank Rich, "Pig vs. Prig," *New York Times*, September 23, 1998.
45. Didion, *Political Fictions*, 216, 230.
46. Mary McGrory, "Nixon, Clinton and Common Sense," *Washington Post*, February 1, 1998; Rupert Cornwell, "Nixon Style Lives in White House," *The Independent* (London), April 28, 1994.
47. Gormley, *The Death of American Virtue*, 90, 249.
48. Melissa King, "Buying Time with Bombs," *Advertiser* (Adelaide, South Australia), December 18, 1998.
49. Godfrey Hodgson, *America in Our Time* (New York: Vintage Books, 1978), 99–110; Godfrey Hodgson, *All Things to All Men: The False Promise of the Modern American Presidency* (New York: Simon and Schuster, 1980).
50. Quoted in Pomper, *The Election of 1996*, 17.
51. This tabulation is based on a review of the *New York Times* bestseller lists.
52. For a history of film depictions of presidents, including Clinton, see Michael A. Genovese, "Celebrity in Chief," in Lori Cox Han and Diane J. Heith, eds., *In the Public Domain: Presidents and the Challenges of Public Leadership* (Albany: State University of New York Press, 2005), 13–27.
53. Frank Rich, "Pulp Nonfiction," *New York Times*, March 18, 1998.
54. James Bennet, "At 50, a Rock-and-Roll President Acts His Age in a Cable Special," *New York Times*, June 3, 1997.
55. Calvin Woodward, "The Slings and Arrows of Outrageous Jokes," Associated

Press, September 26, 1998; "Clinton-Lewinsky Story Sparks Late-nite Humor Frenzy," Cox News Service, February 11, 1998; Transcript, *Meet the Press*, April 30, 2000.

56. A Google Ngram search, which tracks the frequency of words and phrases in books, demonstrates the spike in the occurrence of "presidential historian" during the nineties. See also Sean Wilentz, "America Made Easy," *New Republic*, July 2, 2001, 38.

57. "Historians' Statement on Impeachment," *Washington Post*, October 28, 1998; Wilentz quoted in "Excerpts from What Witnesses Had to Say," *Boston Globe*, December 9, 1998, 32; "White House Trial Memorandum," *Washington Post*, January 13, 1999. (The author was one of the signers of the Historians' Statement.)

58. Hearing, Committee on the Judiciary, House of Representatives, 105 Congress, 2nd Sess., November 9, 1998, 28–31, 211–218.

59. William E. Leuchtenburg, *The Supreme Court Reborn: The Constitutional Revolution in the Age of Roosevelt* (New York: Oxford University Press, 1995), 132–162; Kyle Graham, "A Moment in the Times: Law Professors and the Court-Packing Plan," *Journal of Legal Education* 52 (March 1, 2002): 159.

60. Michael Waldman, *POTUS Speaks: Finding the Words That Defined the Clinton Presidency* (New York: Simon & Schuster, 2000), 260.

61. Richard L. Berke, "Robertson, Praising Speech, Sees Trial as Peril to G.O.P.," *New York Times*, January 21, 1999.

62. Quoted in Gormley, *The Death of American Virtue*, 151, 159.

63. Tom Shales, "The Networks, Jumping All over the Story," *Washington Post*, January 21, 1997.

64. Walter Shapiro, "On the Issue of Race, Clinton Has a Shot at Greatness," *USA Today*, January 21, 1997.

65. Memos, Sylvia Mathews and Maria Echaveste to the President, "RE: Reconciliation Outreach Efforts," May 21, 1997, Speechwriting, Michael Waldman, Box 14450; Erskine Bowles to the President, "RE: Action on Reconciliation," n.d., Speechwriting, Michael Waldman, Box 14451, Clinton Library.

66. John Hope Franklin, *Mirror to America: The Autobiography of John Hope Franklin* (New York: Farrar, Straus and Giroux, 2005).

67. Peter Carlson, "The Nitty-Gritty on Committees: Welcome to Official Washington, Where an Advisory Board Is as Good as a Solution," *Washington Post*, June 14, 1997.

68. President's Initiative on Race in the U.S., *One America in the 21st Century: Forging a New Future: The President's Initiative on Race* (Washington, DC: Advisory Board to the President's Initiative, 1998). The most detailed treatment of the Initiative is Lila Docken Bauman, "Talking toward One America: The President's Initiative on Race (1997–1998) in the Press and Local Community" (PhD diss., New York University, 2002).

69. Steven F. Lawson, "One America in the 21st Century," http://yalepress.yale.edu/yupbooks/book.asp?isbn=9780300116694; Clarence Page, "Race Report Mired in Middle Ground," *San Jose Mercury News*, September 22, 1998.

70. Franklin, *Mirror to America*, 359.

CHAPTER 8. THE "NEW" ECONOMY, 1998–2000

1. Quoted in John Kenneth Galbraith, *The Great Crash 1929* (Boston: Houghton Mifflin, 1955), 75.
2. *Annual Report of the Council of Economic Advisors*, December 29, 2000, 19 http://www.presidency.ucsb.edu/economic_reports/2001.pdf.
3. John Cassidy, "The Fountainhead," *New Yorker*, April 24, 2000, 162–175; Cassidy, "The Productivity Mirage," *New Yorker*, November 27, 2000, 106–118.
4. *Annual Report of the Council of Economic Advisors.*
5. John Cassidy, "The Experiment," *New Yorker*, May 24, 1999, 48–53.
6. Joseph E. Stiglitz, *The Roaring Nineties: A New History of the World's Most Prosperous Decade* (New York: W. W. Norton, 2003), 91–92.
7. Cassidy, "The Productivity Mirage"; Haynes Johnson, *The Best of Times: America in the Clinton Years* (New York: Harcourt, 2001), 19; Alan S. Blinder and Janet L. Yellen, *The Fabulous Decade: Macroeconomic Lessons from the 1990s* (New York: The Century Foundation Press, 2001), 62–63.
8. *Annual Report of the Council of Economic Advisors*, 3, 24.
9. "Remarks of Treasury Secretary Lawrence H. Summers to the Futures Industry Association," Boca Raton, Florida, March, 17, 2000, http://www.treasury.gov /press-center/press-releases/Pages/ls472.aspx.
10. Jeffrey Frankel and Peter Orszag, eds., *American Economic Policy in the 1990s* (Cambridge, MA: MIT Press, 2002), 124–125.
11. Cassidy, "The Fountainhead"; Bob Woodward, *Maestro: Greenspan's Fed and the American Boom* (New York: Simon & Schuster, 2000).
12. Alan Blinder Interview, June 27, 2003, 80, Miller Center, University of Virginia, William J. Clinton Oral History Project.
13. Blinder and Yellen, *The Fabulous Decade*, 4.
14. Johnson, *The Best of Times*, 1–106.
15. For an excellent account of the NEC and the process of economic policymaking during the Clinton administration, see "The Role of Institutions in the White House," in Frankel and Orszag, eds., *American Economic Policy*, 983–1049. Robert Reich, "How to Avoid These Layoffs," *New York Times*, January 4, 1996.
16. Frankel and Orszag, eds., *American Economic Policy.*
17. Jeffrey Birnbaum, *Madhouse: The Private Turmoil of Working for the President* (New York: Times Books, 1996), 139.
18. John Cassidy, "The Triumphalist," *New Yorker*, July 6, 1998.
19. Ibid.
20. Steven M. Gillon, *The Pact: Bill Clinton, Newt Gingrich, and the Rivalry That Defined a Generation* (Oxford and New York: Oxford University Press, 2008).
21. Ibid., 187–283.
22. Frankel and Orszag, eds., *American Economic Policy*, 80–119, 120–123; John Cassidy, "Spooking the Boomers," *New Yorker*, January 13, 1997, 30–35.
23. Frankel and Orszag, eds., *American Economic Policy*, 80–119.
24. William E. Leuchtenburg, *Franklin D. Roosevelt and the New Deal* (New York: Harper & Row, 1963), 59.
25. Jill M. Hendrickson, "The Long and Bumpy Road to Glass-Steagall Reform: A

Historical and Evolutionary Analysis of Banking Legislation," *American Journal of Economics and Sociology* 60, no. 4 (October 2001): 849–879.

26. Ibid.

27. As an example of an influential scholarly critique of Glass-Steagall, see George J. Benston, *The Separation of Commercial and Investment Banking: The Glass-Steagall Act Revisited and Reconsidered* (New York and Oxford: Oxford University Press, 1990). See also James R. Barth et al., "The Repeal of Glass-Steagall and the Advent of Broad Banking," *Journal of Economic Perspectives* 14 (Spring 2000): 191–204.

28. Kathleen Day, "Proxmire Bill Would Repeal Glass-Steagall," *Washington Post*, September 23, 1987.

29. Schumer quoted in Stephen Labaton, "Congress Passes Wide-Ranging Bill Easing Bank Laws," *New York Times*, November 5, 1999.

30. *Congressional Record* 106: 1, 1999, vol. 145, S13871–13874.

31. "The Clinton Administration's National Urban Policy Report" (Washington, DC: US Department of Housing and Urban Development), July 25, 1995; Alicia Munnell et al., "Mortgage Lending in Boston: Interpreting HMDA Data," Federal Reserve Bank of Boston, 1992. The lead author of the study, Alicia Munnell, served as assistant secretary of the treasury and as a member of the Council of Economic Advisors in the Clinton administration. It should be noted that these were not high-risk subprime mortgages. They wouldn't flood the market until the mortgage-backed securities industry et al. undercut the underwriting standards of the mortgage industry, including Fannie Mae and Freddie Mac.

32. Quoted in Helena Yeaman, "The Bipartisan Roots of the Financial Services Crisis," *Political Science Quarterly* 124 (December 2009): 684–685.

33. Draft memo, Robert Rubin et al. to the President, April 7, 1999, "Community Reinvestment Act Legislative Strategy," Policy Development, Lisa Green, Box 20587, Clinton Library.

34. *Congressional Record* 106:1, vol. 145, no. 154, S13871–13881; Stephen Labaton, "Congress Passes Wide-Ranging Bill Easing Bank Law," *New York Times*, November 5, 1999; Lebaton, "Deal on Bank Bill Was Helped Along by Midnight Talks," *New York Times*, October 24, 1999.

35. "Remarks on Signing the Gramm-Leach-Bliley Act," November 12, 1999.

36. *Annual Report of the Council of Economic Advisors.*

37. Vanderbilt Television Archives; "Paine Webber Index of Investor Optimism," November 1999, Roper Public Opinion Archives, University of Connecticut.

38. Frankel and Orszag, eds., *American Economic Policy*, 488.

39. Stephen Labaton, "U.S. versus Microsoft: The Policy Maker," *New York Times*, November 8, 1999.

40. John Lanchester, *I.O.U.: Why Everyone Owes Everyone and No One Can Pay* (New York: Simon & Schuster, 2010), 52.

41. Quoted in Lanchester, *I.O.U.*, 74.

42. Anthony Faiola, Ellen Nakashima, and Jill Drew, "What Went Wrong," *Washington Post*, October 15, 2008; Rick Schmitt, "Prophet and Loss," *Stanford Alumni Magazine* (March/April 2009).

43. Rubin quoted in Faiola, Nakashima, and Drew, "What Went Wrong."

44. Faiola, Nakashima, and Drew, "What Went Wrong."
45. Ibid.
46. Greenspan quoted in Deborah Solomon and Michael Schroeder, "How Refco Fell through Regulatory Cracks," *Wall Street Journal*, October 18, 2005.
47. Faiola, Nakashima, and Drew, "What Went Wrong."
48. Franklin R. Edwards, "Hedge Funds and the Collapse of Long-Term Capital Management," *Journal of Economic Perspectives* 13 (Spring 1999): 189–210.
49. Michael Lewis, "How the Eggheads Cracked," *New York Times Magazine*, January 24, 1999.
50. John Cassidy, "Time Bomb," *New Yorker*, July 5, 1999.
51. Edwards, "Hedge Funds and the Collapse of Long-Term Capital Management."
52. John Cassidy, *How Markets Fail* (New York: Farrar, Straus and Giroux, 2009), 230.
53. As quoted in Edwards, "Hedge Funds and the Collapse of Long-Term Capital Management," 201.
54. Cassidy, "Time Bomb," 32.
55. Memo, Rubin to the President, "Report of the President's Working Group on Financial Markets on Hedge Funds and Long-Term Capital Management," April 22, 1999, WHORM Subject File-General, F1, Box 21844, Clinton Library.
56. "Remarks of Treasury Secretary Lawrence H. Summers to the Futures Industry Association."
57. Miller quoted in Cassidy, "Time Bomb," 32.
58. Faiola, Nakashima, and Drew, "What Went Wrong."
59. Cheryl Strauss Einhorn, "CFTC Could Be Hurt by Infighting," *Financial Post*, May 17, 1999; Editorial, "Barack Wrote a Letter," *Wall Street Journal*, October 29, 2008; Rick Schmitt, "Prophet and Loss," *Stanford Alumni Magazine*.
60. US Congress, Senate Committee on Agriculture and Banking, *Hearing of the Commodity Futures Modernization Act to the Senate Agriculture and Banking Committee, June 21, 2000*, 106th Cong., 1st sess., (Washington, DC: GPO, 2000) (testimony of Lawrence H. Summers, Secretary, US Treasury).
61. David Corn, "Foreclosure Phil," *Mother Jones*, July/August 2008.
62. Lanchester, *I.O.U.*, 184.

CHAPTER 9. LAST CHANCE: CLINTON AND
THE WORLD, 1998–2000

1. "The Ultimate Approval Rating," *New York Times*, December 15, 1996. Doris Kearns Goodwin recalled her conversation with President Clinton during an appearance at Boston College on March 21, 2011.
2. Madeleine Albright, *Madame Secretary* (New York: Miramax Books, 2003), 230.
3. Quoted in John F. Harris, *The Survivor: Bill Clinton in the White House* (New York: Random House, 2005), 369.
4. Taylor Branch, *The Clinton Tapes: Wrestling History with the President* (London and New York: Simon & Schuster, 2009), 486–490.
5. Anthony Lake Interview, May 21, 2002, 44, Miller Center, University of Virginia, William J. Clinton Oral History Project (hereafter cited as Miller Center).
6. Branch, *The Clinton Tapes*, 486–490.
7. Anthony Lake Interview.

8. John Dumbrell, *Clinton's Foreign Policy: Between the Bushes, 1992–2000* (London and New York: Routledge/Taylor & Francis, 2009), 2.

9. Bill Clinton, "Ending the Bosnian War: The Personal Story of the President of the United States," Bosnia, Intelligence, and the Clinton Presidency, Conference Paper, October 1, 2013, Clinton Library.

10. David Halberstam, *War in a Time of Peace: Bush, Clinton, and the Generals* (New York: Scribner, 2001).

11. Samuel Berger Interview, March 24–25, 2005, 49, Miller Center.

12. Harold Meyerson, "Why Are We in (or Anyway, Over) Kosovo," *LA Weekly*, April 23, 1999.

13. Hearing Before the Committee on International Relations, House of Representatives, March 10th, 1999, 12–14.

14. Gaddis and Cohen quoted in George C. Herring, "Analogies at War: The United States, the Conflict in Kosovo, and the Uses of History," in Albrecht Schnabel and Ramesh Thakur, eds., *Kosovo and the Challenge of Humanitarian Intervention: Selective Indignation, Collective Action, and International Citizenship* (Tokyo, New York, Paris: United Nations University Press, 2000), 347–359. See also Ethan Bronner, "Conflict in the Balkans: The Scholars," *New York Times*, March 26, 1999.

15. Harris, *The Survivor*, 369.

16. Thomas L. Friedman, "Foreign Affairs; Now a Word from X," *New York Times*, May 2, 1998.

17. Harris, *The Survivor*, 374–375; Clinton quoted in Branch, *The Clinton Tapes*, 198.

18. Geoffrey S. Corn, "Clinton, Kosovo, and the Final Destruction of the War Powers Resolution," *William and Mary Law Review* 42 (2001): 1149–1190.

19. "Remarks at a Democratic National Committee Luncheon in Sacramento," November 15, 1997.

20. Cohen, Albright, and Clinton quoted in "The Clinton Administration's Public Case against Saddam Hussein," at the Project for the New American Century (http://www.newamericancentury.org/iraq-20040623.htm).

21. "Address to the Nation Announcing Military Strikes on Iraq," December 16, 1998.

22. Richard Sale, *Clinton's Secret Wars: The Evolution of a Commander in Chief* (New York St. Martin's Press, 2009), 240–275.

23. Steve Coll, *Ghost Wars: The Secret History of the CIA, Afghanistan, and Bin Laden, from the Soviet Invasion to September 10, 2001* (New York: Penguin Books, 2004), 253–254.

24. Richard A. Clarke, *Against All Enemies: Inside America's War on Terror* (New York: Free Press, 2004), 155–179; Judith Miller and William J. Broad, "Exercise Finds U.S. Unable to Handle Germ Threat," *New York Times*, April 26, 1998, and "Terrorist Use of Weapons of Mass Destruction," *New York Times*, January 21, 1999.

25. Clarke, *Against All Enemies*, 143.

26. Jane Mayer, *The Dark Side: The Inside Story of How the War on Terror Turned into a War on American Ideals* (New York and London: Doubleday, 2008), 111–115.

27. Ibid., 114.
28. Samuel Berger Interview, 69.
29. Coll, *Ghost Wars*, 366.
30. Quoted in ibid., 380.
31. Branch, *The Clinton Tapes*, 511.
32. George Tenet, *At the Center of the Storm: My Years at the CIA* (New York: Harper Collins, 2007), 113–115.
33. Christopher Hitchens, *No One Left to Lie To: The Triangulations of William Jefferson Clinton* (London and New York: Verso, 1999), 90–91.
34. Coll, *Ghost Wars*, 413.
35. Clinton quoted in Harris, *The Survivor*, 405.
36. Anonymous [Michael Scheuer], *Imperial Hubris* (Washington, DC: Brassey's, 2004).
37. *The 9/11 Commission Report: The Final Report of the National Commission on Terrorist Attacks upon the United States* (Washington, DC: U.S. Government Printing Office, 2004), 130–131; 140–141.
38. Clinton quoted in Clarke, *Against All Enemies*, 185.
39. Clarke quoted in Harris, *The Survivor*, 406.
40. Tenet, *At the Center of the Storm*, 14–17, 107–131.
41. Clinton quoted in Branch, *The Clinton Tapes*, 556.
42. Clinton and Sharif quoted in Bruce O. Riedel, *Avoiding Armageddon: America, India, and Pakistan to the Brink and Back* (Washington, DC: Brookings Institution Press, 2013), 133–134.
43. Quoted in Dumbrell, *Clinton's Foreign Policy*, 151.
44. Netanyahu quoted in ibid., 152.
45. Branch, *The Clinton Tapes*, 611–612.
46. Akram Hanieth, "The Camp David Papers," *Journal of Palestine Studies* 30 (Winter 2001): 75–97.
47. Ibid., 78.
48. Dennis Ross, *The Missing Peace: The Inside Story of the Fight for Middle East Peace* (New York: Farrar, Straus, and Giroux, 2004), 4.
49. Bill Clinton, *My Life* (New York: Knopf, 2004), 944–945.
50. Samuel Berger Interview, 93.
51. Robert Malley and Hussein Agha, "Camp David: The Tragedy of Errors," *New York Review of Books* 48 (August 9, 2001); Aaron David Miller, "The Long Dance: Searching for Arab-Israeli Peace," *Wilson Quarterly* 32 (Spring 2008): 38–44.
52. Strobe Talbott, *The Great Experiment: The Story of Ancient Empires, Modern States, and the Quest for a Global Nation* (New York: Simon & Schuster, 2008), 346.
53. David Von Drehle, "Yesterday Was Not a Chapter in a Washington Novel," *Washington Post*, December 20, 1998.
54. Harris, *The Survivor*, 386–387, 426.

EPILOGUE: THE THIRD TERM

1. "Clinton Issues 140 Pardons," *South Bend Tribune (Indiana)*, January 21, 2001.
2. Editorial, *New York Times*, January 24, 2001; "A Fitting End for Clinton," *USA Today*, January 22, 2001; Tom Topousis, "Furor over Clinton Pardon," *New York Post*, January 22, 2001.

3. "GOP Senator Hints at New Impeachment," *NY Daily News*, February 12, 2001.
4. Thomas B. Edsall, "Clintons Take Away $190,000 in Gifts; Hollywood Helped with Furnishings," *Washington Post*, January 21, 2001; "Clintons' Presents Solicited: Ex-staffer," *Daily News (New York)*, February 19, 2001; "New Lows in Diabolical Greed," *New York Post*, January 30, 2001; John F. Harris, "For the Clintons' Last Act, Reviews Don't Look Good," *Washington Post*, January 27, 2001.
5. Robert Pear, "White House Vandalized in Transition, G.A.O. Finds," *New York Times*, June 12, 2002.
6. "Bill's Very Bumpy Road from White House" *Daily News (New York)*, February 11, 2001; Maureen Dowd, "Liberties: Cats, Dogs and Grifters," *New York Times*, January 24, 2001.
7. Jennifer Senior, "Bill Clinton's Plan for World Domination," *New York Magazine*, July 22, 2005.
8. National Commission on Terrorist Attacks upon the United States, "The 9/11 Commission Report: Final Report of the National Commission on Terrorist Attacks upon the United States" (National Commission on Terrorist Attacks upon the United States, 2004), 133, 350.
9. Joseph E. Stiglitz, *The Roaring Nineties: A New History of the World's Most Prosperous Decade* (New York: W. W. Norton, 2003), 9, 14.
10. Senior, "Bill Clinton's Plan for World Domination."
11. Ibid; Michael Tomasky, "The Hillary in Our Future," *New York Review of Books*, June 25, 2015.
12. Peter Baker and Charlie Savage, "In Clinton List, a Veil Is Lifted on Foundation," *New York Times*, December 19, 2008; Peter Baker, "The Mellowing of William Jefferson Clinton," *New York Times Magazine*, May 31, 2009; "Help Change Lives across the Globe," *Clinton Foundation* (http://www.clintonfoundation.org/front); Philip Rucker, "Eclectic Bunch of Donors—Near, Far, Left, Even Right—Gave to Clinton Group," *Washington Post*, January 2, 2010; Joe Conason, "The Third Term," *Esquire* (December 2005), 190–195, 257–258. For a critical account of the foundation, see Alec MacGillis, "Scandal at Clinton Inc.," *New Republic*, September 22, 2013.
13. "George H. W. Bush on Bonding with Bill Clinton," http://politicalticker.blogs.cnn.com/2013/03/05/george-h-w-bush-on-bonding-with-bill-clinton/.
14. James Hardy, "Forget Saddam," *The Mirror*, September 7, 2002, 4, 5.
15. David Von Drehle, "Clinton Diverges from Bush on Iraq; Democrat Supports Relaxed Deadline," *Washington Post*, March 13, 2003.
16. Jonathan Freedland, "Clinton's Coded Jibes at Bush Gives Conference What It Wants to Hear," *The Guardian*, October 3, 2003, 5.
17. Bill Clinton, "Comment & Analysis: Trust Tony's Judgment," *The Guardian*, March 18, 2003; "'Not the Time to Falter': Blair: War Vote Passes: Things Could Still Go Wrong for British PM," *The Gazette (Montreal, Quebec)*.
18. Senior, "Bill Clinton's Plan for World Domination."
19. "Bill Clinton Says He Opposed Iraq War from Start," http://www.outsidethebeltway.com/bill_clinton_says_he_opposed_iraq_war_from_start/.
20. David Remnick, *The Bridge: The Life and Rise of Barack Obama* (New York: Knopf, 2009), 443.

21. Ibid., 481.
22. "Clinton an Odd Advocate to Stand up for President Obama," *Augusta Chronicle (Georgia)*, August 5, 2012.
23. Ryan Lizza, "Let's Be Friends," *New Yorker*, September 10, 2012, 40–49.
24. Baker, "The Mellowing of William Jefferson Clinton," 47.
25. Paul Harris, "International: 'Bill Effect' Threatens a Civil War: The Former President's Central Role in His Wife's Bid for the White House Has Taken an Ugly Twist," *The Observer (England)*, January 27, 2008; Sheldon Alberts, "Obama Trounces Clinton in South Carolina Primary; Clintons' 'Race Card' Efforts Backfire," *Calgary Herald (Alberta)*, January 27, 2008; Jenny McCartney, "Bill & Hillary: A Bad Dream Team," *Sunday Telegraph (London)*, January 27, 2008.
26. Baker, "The Mellowing of William Jefferson Clinton"; Conason, "The Third Term."
27. Sean Wilentz, "Race Man," *New Republic*, February 27, 2008; Gene Lyons, "Clinton Melodrama Becoming Tiresome in 2008," *York Dispatch (Pennsylvania)*, February 4, 2008.
28. Todd S. Purdum, "The Comeback Id," *Vanity Fair*, July 1, 2008.
29. Mayhill Fowler, "Bill Clinton: Purdum a 'Sleazy' 'Slimy' 'Scumbag,'" *Huffington Post*, June 10, 2008.
30. "Anna K. Nelson: Testimony on Presidential Records," http://hnn.us/article/36168; Anna K. Nelson, "At Last Bush's Restrictions on Presidential Records Are Lifted," http://hnn.us/article/60542; "Fact Checker—Is Hillary Responsible for the 'Library Lockdown'?" http://blog.washingtonpost.com/fact-checker/2007/11/is_hillary_responsible_for_the.html; "The Battle over the Clinton Papers." http://www.cbsnews.com/news/the-battle-over-the-clinton-papers/. There were more legitimate causes for complaint when the lifting of the order did not immediately lead to a rapid release of documents.
31. Philip Rucker, "Hillary Clinton Campaign Looks at Role of Former President," *Boston Globe*, May 17, 2015.
32. Baker, "The Mellowing of William Jefferson Clinton."
33. Anna Quindlen, "The State of the Union," *New York Times*, October 22, 1992, and Maureen Dowd, "A Popular President," *New York Times*, July 19, 2014.
34. Garry Wills, "Richard Nixon: Petty Schemes and Grand Designs," *New York Times*, April 24, 1994.
35. Richard Wolf, "The Clinton Gamble; Bill's Speech Tonight Could Lift President Obama—or Make Him Look Small in Comparison," *USA Today*, September 5, 2012.
36. Baker, "The Mellowing of William Jefferson Clinton"; Debra Saunders, "Debra Saunders: Leave It to President Bill to Be the Last Man Standing," *San Gabriel Valley Tribune (California)*, August 1, 2012; "Favorability: People in the News," Gallup Historical Trends http://www.gallup.com/poll/1618/favorability-people-news.aspx; Doug Schoen and Jessica Tarlov, "The Presidential Perception Gap," *Daily Beast*, September 24, 2012.
37. Robert Jackson, "Old Rogue Could Make Phone Book Interesting," *Evening Standard (London)*, September 6, 2012.
38. Maureen Dowd, "The Comeback Vegan," *New York Times*, September 5, 2012.
39. Amy Chozick, "Bill Clinton Defends a Legacy," *New York Times*, May 1, 2014.

What follows is an attempt to indicate the major primary and secondary sources consulted in the preparation of this study, to refer readers to important books and articles that contain additional information on particular topics, and to suggest areas in need of further study. For reasons discussed in the epilogue, the William J. Clinton Presidential Library in Little Rock, Arkansas, which houses some 64 million documents, has been slow to open many of its most important collections to the public. In the spring of 2014, the Library began posting online an estimated 30,000 documents that had been withheld ostensibly because they contained advice to the president or dealt with federal appointments. Still, despite their volume, there is reason to believe that the Clinton papers may not be as revealing as the papers of previous presidents. Because of the hyper-partisanship of the time, the penchant of congressional critics to invoke their subpoena powers, and the emergence of a newly intrusive media, the Clinton White House seems to have embraced Louisiana governor Earl Long's famous maxim: "Don't write anything you can phone. Don't phone anything you can talk. Don't talk anything you can whisper. Don't whisper anything you can nod. Don't nod anything you can wink." White House lawyers advised incoming members of the administration to think twice about anything they put down on paper or included in emails. "You don't write things down. You don't take notes," Clinton's National Security Adviser Samuel Berger told interviewers at the University of Virginia's Miller Center. Berger's colleague, Anthony Lake, agreed: "More and more officials are loath to put anything in writing . . . which is one of the sad costs for history." "You'll find a lot of memos, but I didn't keep notes," recalled Health and Human Services Secretary Donna Shalala. Joan Baggett, who headed the president's public affairs office, cautioned her staff not to put anything in writing they would be embarrassed to see on the front page of the *Washington Post* or *New York Times*. When the Clinton Library released tens of thousands of documents in 2014 and 2015, news organizations and political opponents eagerly scoured the contents. They found no bombshells and few surprises. Still, it is those memos Shalala mentioned that are of most interest to serious scholars, and they exist in abundance. For the purposes of this study, recently released memos dealing with health-care reform and economic policy were particularly helpful. I would also call attention to the papers of Clinton's speechwriters, including Michael Waldman, which shed light on how the administration grappled with the task of putting its accomplishments and goals into historical perspective.

Scholars will do well to follow the example of legendary journalist I. F. Stone, who understood that the most important and revealing information was most often not hidden away in an archive but within full view on the public record—in congressional hearings and debates, government reports, and the like. In the digital age, a daunting amount of material is easily accessible. For Clinton, there is no better starting point than the remarkable American Presidency Project at the University of California Santa Barbara (Americanpresidency.org), which contain all of Clinton's major addresses, proclamations, transcripts of press conferences and press briefings, presidential debates, assorted campaign documents, and the exceptionally useful annual reports of the Council of Economic Advisers. A searchable database facilitates the research process. The National Security Archive at George Washington University (http://nsarchive.gwu.edu/), though consulted sparingly in this study, is a key online source for an ever-increasing number of unclassified documents relating to foreign policy. Of particular interest were documents relating to the Clinton administration's efforts to balance human rights and foreign trade in dealing with China and other nations.

Because members of the administration were cautious about what they committed to writing, their recollections acquire even more importance than they otherwise might. Beginning with the Carter administration, scholars at the University of Virginia's Miller Center have conducted lengthy interviews with key members of every administration. Some 134 persons who either served in or closely observed the Clinton administration were interviewed. In November 2014, the center began releasing interview transcripts along with detailed timelines of key events. As of this writing, about half of the interviews have been released and may be accessed at: http://millercenter.org/president/clinton/oralhistory. The George J. Mitchell Oral History Project at Bowdoin College contains richly detailed interviews not only with Clinton's Senate leader and Northern Ireland negotiator George Mitchell but also with a dozen or more members of Congress including Senators William "Bill" Bradley, John Breaux, Dale Bumpers, Kent Conrad, David Durenberger, John "Jay" Rockefeller and Representative Richard Gephardt. The interviews shed much light on Clinton's relationship with Congress, especially during the debate over health-care reform. The interviews may be accessed at: http://digitalcommons.bowdoin.edu/mitchelloralhistory/#A. The Clinton Administration Transition Interviews (http://www.archives.gov/presidential-libraries/research/transition-interviews/clinton-administration.html), maintained by the National Archives, contain interviews with eight members of the administration including Chiefs of Staff Thomas F. (Mack) McLarty and Leon Panetta and Press Secretary Michael D. McCurry. Personal interviews in possession of the author with Council of Economic Advisers members Laura Tyson and Alicia Munnell and CEA staffer Robert Murphy also yielded valuable insights. Michael Takiff, *A Complicated Man: The Life of Bill Clinton as Told by Those Who Know Him* (New Haven, CT, and London: Yale University Press, 2010), is a rich collection of recollections by persons who knew and worked with Clinton throughout his life. The journals of Diane Blair, political science professor at the University of Arkansas and close friend of Hillary Clinton, contain many revealing accounts of conversations with the Clintons. Portions of the journal may be accessed at: http://www.scribd.com/doc/205858605/The-Clinton-Files.

The Clinton presidency has produced fewer memoirs than one might have expected by this time. This is probably because those who served in the administration are reluctant "to talk out of school" while the Clintons remain at, or near, the center of American political life. The first half of Bill Clinton's oddly underestimated autobiography, *My Life* (New York: Alfred A. Knopf, 2004), is both a revealing self-portrait and a handbook on the art of politics in the pre-Internet age. Though less revealing on his presidential years, it is a powerful reminder that history doesn't happen in categories—domestic affairs one year, foreign policy the next—but all at once. Even better in this regard is historian and longtime Clinton friend Taylor Branch's *The Clinton Tapes: Wrestling History with the President* (London and New York: Simon & Schuster, 2009), a summary of the late-night conversations Branch periodically taped with Clinton throughout his presidency. One eagerly awaits release of the original tapes. If Clinton had never become president his mother would never have written a memoir. That would have been a shame. Virginia Kelley, *Leading with My Heart* (New York: Simon & Schuster, 1994), is a fascinating, unvarnished self-portrait of a remarkable woman. It may be an "as told to" work, but it has the ring of authenticity. There are many accounts of Bill Clinton's early life but no better starting point than this.

The top tier of memoirs focusing on domestic affairs includes, roughly in order of usefulness: Sidney Blumenthal, *The Clinton Wars* (New York: Farrar, Straus and Giroux, 2003), a partisan but highly revealing and compellingly written account of how the world appeared from inside the White House; Robert B. Reich, *Locked in the Cabinet* (New York: Vintage Books, 1998), the observations of a cabinet member who became disillusioned with the administration's inability to better prepare the nation to participate in the new global economy; George Stephanopoulos, *All Too Human: A Political Education* (Boston: Little, Brown, 1999); Michael Waldman, *POTUS Speaks: Finding the Words That Defined the Clinton Presidency* (New York: Simon & Schuster, 2000), not only a thoughtful memoir by a speechwriter but also an intellectual history of sorts of the Clinton presidency. Warren Christopher, *Chances of a Lifetime: A Memoir* (New York: Scribner, 2001), is a useful and, like the man, discreet account of foreign policy but especially informative about Clinton's search for a vice presidential running mate and members of his cabinet. Two books by Clinton pollster Stanley B. Greenberg, *Middle Class Dreams: The Politics and Power of the New American Majority* (New York: Times Books, 1995) and the more reflective *Dispatches from the War Room: In the Trenches with Five Extraordinary Leaders* (New York: Thomas Dunne Books/St. Martin's Press, 2009), are also essential accounts, as is Hillary Rodham Clinton's understated *Living History* (New York: Simon & Schuster, 2003), which, if read closely, provides revealing details of administration policymaking. Lani Guinier describes her failed nomination to the Justice Department and her disappointment with the Clintons in *Lift Every Voice: Turning a Civil Rights Setback into a New Vision of Social Justice* (New York: Simon & Schuster, 1998).

Other useful memoirs include, on economic policy, Robert E. Rubin, *In an Uncertain World: Tough Choices from Wall Street to Washington* (New York: Random House, 2003); Federal Reserve Chairman Alan Greenspan's *The Age of Turbulence: Adventures in a New World* (New York: Penguin Press, 2007); and Leon Panetta and Jim Newton, *Worthy Fights: A Memoir of Leadership in War and Peace* (New York: Penguin Press, 2014); and, on politics and campaigns, Dick Morris, *Behind the Oval Office: Winning the Presidency in the Nineties* (New York: Random House, 1997). On the internal problems that beset the White House during the first term, see Webb Hubbell, *Friends in High Places: Our Journey from Little Rock to Washington, D.C.* (New York: William Morrow, 1997), which also describes the friendship between Hubbell, Vince Foster, and Hillary Clinton at the Rose Law Firm as well as the personal and financial entanglements that would shadow Hubbell and the Clintons to Washington; and David Gergen, *Eyewitness to Power: The Essence of Leadership* (New York: Simon & Schuster, 2000). Louis J. Freeh, *My FBI: Bringing Down the Mafia, Investigating Bill Clinton, and Fighting the War on Terror* (New York: St. Martin's Press, 2005), is an unflattering portrait of Clinton and especially critical of his attempts to thwart investigations into fund-raising efforts. Terry McAuliffe, *What a Party! My Life among Democrats: Presidents, Candidates, Donors, Activists, Alligators, and Other Wild Animals* (New York: Thomas Dunne Books/St. Martin's Press, 2007), is a superficial and unapologetic memoir by Clinton's prodigious fund-raiser but also a reminder about the increasing role of money in politics (its message evokes memories of Huey Long/Willie Stark: you can't do good without having power). Benjamin R. Barber, *The Truth of Power: Intellectual Affairs in the Clinton White House* (New York: W. W. Norton, 2001), is a revealing, if self-important, memoir about Clinton's attempt to consult and court intellectuals. Two works by historian and liberal activist Arthur M. Schlesinger, Jr., contain scattered but rich insights into the Clintons: *Journals, 1952–2000* (New York: Penguin Press, 2005) and *Letters of Arthur M. Schlesinger, Jr.* (New York: Random House, 2013). The Schlesinger materials are also interesting as an example of the scholar trying to influence the president, and vice versa.

Memoirs dealing primarily with foreign policy are dealt with elsewhere.

The best secondary work on Clinton's early life remains David Maraniss, *First in His Class: A Biography of Bill Clinton* (New York: Simon & Schuster, 1995), which is good overall, but especially helpful on Clinton's Georgetown/Oxford years and the ensuing draft controversy. The best biography of Hillary Rodham Clinton is Carl Bernstein, *A Woman in Charge: The Life of Hillary Rodham Clinton* (New York: Alfred A. Knopf, 2007). Bernstein's is also the best account of the Clintons' tumultuous personal life together in the White House. Hanes Walton, Jr., *Reelection: William Jefferson Clinton as a Native-Son Presidential Candidate* (New York: Columbia University Press, 2000), has useful voter analyses of Clinton's Arkansas campaigns (as well as his presidential campaigns). Soft, but with some insights, is Ernest Dumas, editor, *The Clintons of Arkansas: An Introduction by Those Who Know Them Best* (Fayetteville: University of Arkansas Press, 1993). Critical but useful accounts of Clinton's Arkansas career are John Brummett, *Highwire: From the Back Roads to the Beltway* (New York: Hyperion, 1994), and Meredith L. Oakley, *On the Make: The Rise of Bill Clinton* (Washington, DC: Regnery, 1994), which contains revealing anecdotes of Clinton on the stump. Martin Walker, *The President We Deserve: Bill Clinton, His Rise, Falls, and Comebacks* (New York: Crown Publishers, 1996), helps explain Clinton's appeal by showing how his early life exemplified the experiences and contradictions of America's post–World War II, baby-boom generation. A laudatory account of Clinton's governorship—an account that raised Clinton's national profile—is David Osborne's *Laboratories of Democracy* (Boston: Harvard Business School Press, 1990), 83–110.

The Clintons have also been the subjects of a number of more or less interchangeable biographies that, though not devoid of interest, delve heavily into amateur psychologizing and character analysis at the expense of policy. See, for example, Nigel Hamilton's massive, two-volume *Bill Clinton: An American Journey* (New York: Random House, 2003) and *Bill Clinton: Mastering the Presidency* (New York: Public Affairs, 2007); and Roger Morris, *Partners in Power: The Clintons and Their America* (New York: Henry Holt and Company, 1996). A recent, and more credible, addition to the genre is William H. Chafe, *Bill and Hillary: The Politics of the Personal* (New York: Farrar, Straus and Giroux, 2012).

For the political and historical context of Clinton's pre-presidential career, the following works are especially insightful: E. J. Dionne, *Why Americans Hate Politics* (New York: Simon & Schuster, 1992), a Clinton favorite; Thomas and Mary Edsall, *Chain Reaction: The Impact of Race, Rights, and Taxes on American Politics* (New York: W. W. Norton, 1992); Dan T. Carter, *The Politics of Rage: George Wallace, the Origins of the New Conservatism, and the Transformation of American Politics* (New York: Simon and Schuster, 1995); and *From George Wallace to Newt Gingrich: Race in the Conservative Counterrevolution, 1963–1994* (Baton Rouge: Louisiana State University Press, 1996). On the state of the modern Democratic Party, two works are indispensable: Steven M. Gillon, *The Democrats' Dilemma: Walter F. Mondale and the Legacy of Liberalism* (New York: Columbia University Press, 1992), and Kenneth Baer, *Reinventing Democrats: The Politics of Liberalism from Reagan to Clinton* (Lawrence: University Press of Kansas, 2000). Also important are David G. Lawrence, *The Collapse of the Democratic Presidential Majority: Realignment, Dealignment, and Electoral Change from Franklin Roosevelt to Bill Clinton* (Boulder, CO: Westview Press, 1996), and William G. Mayer, *The Divided Democrats: Ideological Unity, Party Reform, and Presidential Elections* (Boulder, CO: Westview Press, 1996). The impact of the modern media on politics is dealt with by Donald A. Ritchie, *Reporting from Washington: The History of the Washington Press Corps* (New York: Oxford University Press, 2005).

Two much-discussed books by future administration members helped shape Clinton's thinking on the transformation of the American economy: Robert B. Reich, *The Work of Nations: Preparing Ourselves for the 21st Century Capitalism* (New York: Knopf, 1991), and Ira C. Magaziner and Robert B. Reich, *Minding America's Business: The Decline and Rise of the American Economy* (New York: Harcourt Brace Jovanovich, 1982).

The best general account of the 1992 presidential campaign is Peter Goldman et al., *Quest for the Presidency, 1992* (College Station: Texas A&M University Press, 1994), which not only presents a lively narrative but also reprints revealing memoranda written by Clinton and Bush staffers. Also important are Gerald M. Pomper, *The Election of 1992* (Chatham, NJ: Chatham House, 1993); Charles O. Jones, "Campaigning to Govern: The Clinton Style," in Colin Campbell and Bert A. Rockman, editors, *The Clinton Presidency: First Appraisals* (New York: Chatham House, 1996); and Jack W. Germond and Jules Witcover, *Mad as Hell: Revolt at the Ballot Box, 1992* (New York: Warner Books, 1993). Bill Clinton and Albert Gore, *Putting People First: How We Can Change America* (New York: Times Books, 1992), is several cuts above the standard campaign document. The previously mentioned memoirs of Clinton aides also provide pertinent details, including George Stephanopoulos, *All Too Human,* and Stanley B. Greenberg, *Middle Class Dreams* and *Dispatches from the War Room.* See also Mary Matalin and James Carville, *All's Fair: Love, War, and Running for President* (New York: Random House, 1994). The riveting campaign documentary *The War Room,* directed by Chris Hegedus and D. A. Pennebaker, made celebrities of Clinton aides Carville and Stephanopoulos but also gives viewers an unrivaled "feel" for the 1992 campaign.

A number of works provide useful starting points for a study of the Clinton presidency. The best overview is *Washington Post* reporter John F. Harris's balanced

The Survivor: Bill Clinton in the White House (New York: Random House, 2005). Other general accounts include William C. Berman, *From the Center to the Edge: The Politics and Policies of the Clinton Presidency* (Lanham, MD: Rowman & Littlefield, 2001), which, though generally straightforward and balanced, is skeptical of Clinton's quest for a third way; "The Clinton Legacy," a superb five-part series in the *New York Times* (December 24–28, 2000); E. J. Dionne's retrospective in Gerald M. Pomper et al., *The Election of 2000: Reports and Interpretations* (New York: Chatham House, 2001); and Joe Klein, *The Natural: The Misunderstood Presidency of Bill Clinton* (New York: Doubleday, 2002), which argues that Clinton was a man of heroic talents in an unheroic time. "Clinton's Challenge," the preface to a new edition of Steven M. Gillon, *The Democrat's Dilemma: Walter F. Mondale and the Liberal Legacy* (New York: Columbia University Press, 1992), nicely situates Clinton in the modern Democratic Party and presents a shrewd analysis of the problems that defined Clinton's presidency, as does William C. Berman's wide-focus approach in *American's Right Turn: From Nixon to Clinton* (Baltimore MD: Johns Hopkins University Press, 1998). An excellent collection of scholarly papers is Steven E. Schier, *The Postmodern Presidency: Bill Clinton's Legacy in U.S. Politics* (Pittsburgh: University of Pittsburgh Press, 2000), which covers everything from Clinton's interaction with the institution of the presidency to the role of race and gender during the Clinton years. Todd G. Shields et al., *The Clinton Riddle: Perspectives on the Forty-second President* (Fayetteville: University of Arkansas Press, 2004), is an eclectic but useful collection of scholarly appraisals. Tevi Troy, *Intellectuals and the American Presidency: Philosophers, Jesters, or Technicians?* (Lanham, MD: Rowman & Littlefield, 2002), 171–186, contains a brief but suggestive account of Clinton's "brain trust," a subject eminently worth fuller development.

Thoughtful efforts to place the Clinton presidency in historical perspective include Sean Wilentz, *The Age of Reagan: A History 1974–2008* (New York: HarperCollins, 2008), which, though sympathetic to Clinton, emphasizes the political constraints that hindered bold action; Stephen Skowronek, *Presidential Leadership in Political Time: Reprise and Reappraisal* (Lawrence: University Press of Kansas, 2008), which provocatively groups Clinton with "preemptive" presidents; Leo P. Ribuffo, "From Carter to Clinton: The Latest Crisis of American Liberalism," *American Studies International* 35 (June 1997): 4–29; Fred I. Greenstein, *The Presidential Difference: Leadership Style from FDR to Barack Obama* (Princeton, NJ: Princeton University Press, 2009), 173–191; and Marc Landy and Sidney Milkis, *Presidential Greatness* (Lawrence: University Press of Kansas, 2000). Haynes Johnson, *The Best of Times: America in the Clinton Years* (New York: Harcourt, 2001), argues persuasively that the "best" of the nineties, especially the technological and scientific advances, owed much to farsighted government investments in research and development in the decades after World War II. The nineties generation, Johnson argues, bequeathed to future generations a much more ambiguous legacy. Other useful overviews of the Clinton years are James T. Patterson, *Restless Giant: The United States from Watergate to Bush v. Gore* (New York: Oxford University Press, 2005), and William L. O'Neill's acerbic *A Bubble in Time: America during the Interwar Years, 1989–2001* (Chicago: Ivan R. Dee, 2009).

The administration's relations with the press is the subject of Howard Kurtz's *Spin Cycle: Inside the Clinton Propaganda Machine* (New York: Free Press, 1998), which details, from a decidedly journalistic point of view, the administration's efforts to manipulate the media. See also Kenneth T. Walsh, *Feeding the Beast: The White House Versus the Press* (New York: Random House, 1996).

Scholars are still trying to come to grips with Clinton's "third way" or "vital center" approach, unsure if it was a thoughtful political ideology or a pragmatic political strategy (or both). Kenneth S. Baer's *Reinventing Democrats* is an important and sympathetic study of the third way's progenitor, the Democratic Leadership Council, and the DLC's impact on the Democratic Party and the Clinton presidency. James MacGregor Burns and Georgia J. Sorenson, *Dead Center: Clinton–Gore Leadership and the Perils of Moderation* (New York: Scribner, 1999), is highly critical of Clinton's centrist approach. It is additionally important because it suggests the value of viewing the presidency not as a one-man show but as a collaborative effort, involving, in this case, the president, first lady, and vice president. Jeff Faux, "Lost on the Third Way," *Dissent* 46 (Spring 1999): 67–76, takes a global—and critical—approach to the third way. Ted Halstead and Michael Lind, *The Radical Center: The Future of American Politics* (New York: Doubleday, 2001), though not really about Clinton, provides a thoughtful frame of reference for viewing his presidency.

Two general reference works of note are Peter B. Levy, *Encyclopedia of the Clinton Presidency* (Westport, CT: Greenwood Press, 2002), with 200 succinct entries on everything from partial birth abortion to Rwanda to Welfare Reform; and Shirley Anne Warshaw, *Presidential Profiles: The Clinton Years* (New York: Checkmark Books, 2005), which contains succinct biographical sketches of the major players during the Clinton years.

On Clinton's first term, journalistic "first drafts of history" include Elizabeth Drew, *On the Edge: The Clinton Presidency* (New York: Simon & Schuster, 1995) and *Showdown: The Struggle between the Gingrich Congress and the Clinton White House* (New York: Simon & Schuster, 1997); Bob Woodward's *The Agenda: Inside the Clinton White House* (New York: Pocket Books, 1994); and the previously mentioned John Harris, *The Survivor*. Jeffrey Birnbaum, *Madhouse: The Private Turmoil of Working for the President* (New York: Times Books, 1996), provides an anecdote-filled account of life in the White House through the eyes of six Clinton staff members. Birnbaum also has important things to say about gender relations in the White House.

On Clinton's relationship with Congress, Barbara Sinclair, *Party Wars: Polarization and the Politics of National Policy Making* (Norman: University of Oklahoma Press, 2006), and David Mayhew, *Divided We Govern: Party Control, Lawmaking and Investigation, 1946–1990* (New Haven: Yale University Press, 1991), provide essential background, while Charles O. Jones, *Clinton and Congress, 1993–1996* (Norman: University of Oklahoma Press, 1999), and Richard E. Cohen, *Changing Course in Washington: Clinton and the New Congress* (New York: MacMillan College Publishing, 1994), assess Clinton's legislative leadership during the first term. William W. Lammers and Michael A. Genovese, *The Presidency and Domestic Policy: Comparing Leadership Styles, FDR to Clinton* (Washington, DC: CQ Press, 2000), views Clinton's legislative leadership in historical perspective. The view from the Hill can be found in David R. Obey, *Raising Hell for Justice: The Washington Battles of a Heartland Progressive* (Madison: University of Wisconsin Press, 2007); Richard E. Cohen, *Rostenkowski: The Pursuit of Power and the End of the*

Old Politics (Chicago: Ivan R. Dee, 1999); and Godfrey Hodgson, *The Gentleman from New York: Daniel Patrick Moynihan: A Biography* (Boston: Houghton Mifflin, 2000), which probes the fraught relationship between president and powerful Senate leader.

The best starting point on economic policy is Jeffrey Frankel and Peter Orszag, editors, *American Economic Policy in the 1990s* (Cambridge, MA: MIT Press, 2002), a highly accessible work that covers nearly all economic issues—foreign and domestic—from monetary policy to information technology to health care. The book contains papers and comments from noted economists and academic experts, many of whom served in the Clinton administration. Despite a decidedly pro-Clinton stance, this book is indispensable. It also contains abundant references to other key sources. Also indispensable are the lucid reports of the Council of Economic Advisers, a treasure trove of economic information and analysis accessible to noneconomists, which can be accessed at the American Presidency Project. Indeed, the CEA reports constitute a kind of Economics 101 for general readers. The reports should be read alongside economist James K. Galbraith's incisive critiques in the economic journal *Challenge.* Written from the perspective of a Keynesian, he provides rich insight into "Clintonomics."

Experts, including those who served in the Clinton administration, sharply disagree on Clinton's economic record. Alan S. Blinder and Janet L. Yellen, in *The Fabulous Decade: Macroeconomic Lessons from the 1990s* (New York: The Century Foundation Press, 2001), persuasively argue for the defense. The most substantial—and persuasive—critique is Joseph E. Stiglitz, *The Roaring Nineties: A New History of the World's Most Prosperous Decade* (New York: W. W. Norton, 2003), which deplores the rush to deregulation, and *Globalization and its Discontents* (New York: W. W. Norton, 2003), which is equally hard on Clinton's international economic policies. For an illuminating discussion of how much Clinton owed to Jimmy Carter and how both of them departed from their Democratic predecessors, see two works by Iwan Morgan: "Jimmy Carter, Bill Clinton, and the New Democratic Economics," *Historical Journal* 47 (December 2004): 1015–1039, and "A New Democrat's New Economics," in Mark J. White, editor, *The Presidency of Bill Clinton: The Legacy of a New Domestic and Foreign Policy* (London: I. B. Tauris). Alan Brinkley, *The End of Reform: New Deal Liberalism in Recession and War* (New York: Knopf, 1995), though not discussing the Clinton record, offers a lens through which to view economic policy in the nineties.

On Clinton's relationship with Alan Greenspan and the Federal Reserve, see Bob Woodward, *Maestro: Greenspan's Fed and the American Boom* (New York: Simon & Schuster, 2000); Justin Martin, *Greenspan: The Man Behind Money* (Cambridge, MA: Perseus Publishing, 2000); and Greenspan's previously mentioned memoir. John Cassidy, "The Fountainhead," *New Yorker*, April 24, 2000, 162–175, is also excellent. Accounts of Greenspan's leadership of the Fed took a decidedly negative turn after 2000.

Few subjects remain as contentious as Clinton's trade policies, particularly NAFTA. The legislative history of the trade agreement is detailed in Maxwell A. Cameron and Brian W. Tomlin, *The Making of NAFTA: How the Deal was Done* (Ithaca, NY: Cornell University Press, 2000). Important critiques of Clinton's trade policies include Louis Uchitelle, *The Disposable American: Layoffs and Their*

Consequences (New York: Knopf, 2006). See also Thomas I. Palley, *Plenty of Nothing: The Downsizing of the American Dream and the Case for Structural Keynesianism* (Princeton, NJ: Princeton University Press, 1998); Eric Alterman, *Who Speaks for America?: Why Democracy Matters in Foreign Policy* (Ithaca, NY: Cornell University Press, 1998); Joseph Stiglitz, *Globalization and Its Discontents*; and William Greider, *One World, Ready or Not: The Manic Logic of Global Capitalism* (New York: Simon & Schuster, 1998). For examples of how the debate continued unabated well into the next century, see "What We've Learned from NAFTA—Room for Debate," *New York Times*, http://www.nytimes.com/roomfordebate/2013/11/24/what-weve-learned-from-nafta. The parameters of the debate are well outlined in Gary Clyde Hufbauer, *NAFTA Revisited: Achievements and Challenges* (Washington, DC: Institute for International Economics, 2005).

Clinton's deregulatory policies, though largely overshadowed at the time, may constitute his most consequential economic legacy. On banking deregulation, a succinct account is Jill M. Hendrickson, "The Long and Bumpy Road to Glass-Steagall Reform: A Historical and Evolutionary Analysis of Banking Legislation," *American Journal of Economics and Sociology* 60, no. 4 (October 2001): 849–879. Hendrickson suggests that by the nineties, repeal had acquired an almost unstoppable momentum. See also George J. Benston, *The Separation of Commercial and Investment Banking: The Glass-Steagall Act Revisited and Reconsidered* (New York and Oxford: Oxford University Press, 1990), an influential scholarly critique of Glass-Steagall itself. On the ominous collapse of the hedge fund Long-Term Capital Management, see John Cassidy's prescient "Time Bomb," *New Yorker*, July 5, 1999, 28–32. Cassidy, author of the "Annals of Finance" column in *The New Yorker*, was one of the decade's most perceptive and lucid economic commentators. Long-Term Capital Management is also the subject of Roger Lowenstein, *When Genius Failed: The Rise and Fall of Long-Term Capital Management* (New York: Random House, 2000), and Michael Lewis, "How the Eggheads Cracked," *New York Times Magazine*, January 24, 1999. Although dealing primarily with a later time period, John Lanchester, *I.O.U.: Why Everyone Owes Everyone and No One Can Pay* (New York: Simon & Schuster, 2010), offers a clear explanation of financial developments during the nineties, including the proliferation of credit default swaps, subprime mortgages, and other financial products. Helena Yeaman, "The Bipartisan Roots of the Financial Services Crisis," *Political Science Quarterly* 124 (December 2009): 681–696, argues that both parties during the nineties contributed to the financial crises of the next century.

On health-care reform, the key works include Jacob Hacker, *The Road to Nowhere: The Genesis of President Clinton's Plan for Health Care* (Princeton NJ: Princeton University Press, 1997); Theda Skocpol, *Boomerang: Clinton's Health Security Effort and the Turn against Government in US Politics* (New York: W. W. Norton, 1996); and Haynes Johnson and David S. Broder, *The System: The American Way of Politics at the Breaking Point* (Boston: Little, Brown, 1997), a superb work of reportage by two veteran journalists. See also Mark E. Rushefsky and Kant Patel, *Politics, Power and Policy Making: The Case of Health Care Reform in the 1990s* (Armonk, NY: M. E. Sharpe, 1998). Jacob Hacker's "Learning from Defeat? Political Analysis and the Failure of Health Care Reform in the United States," *British Journal of Political Science* 31 (January 2001): 61–94, discusses many of the misconceptions about the health-care effort. The best brief overview of previous reform efforts is Paul Starr, *The Social Transformation of American Medicine* (New York: Basic Books, 1982). Much needs to be done on this enormously complicated, but important subject. Yet to be tapped are the voluminous records of the Health Reform Task Force at the Clinton Library, which may constitute the single richest source of information about the health-care system in late-twentieth-century America.

The 1994 takeover of Congress that followed in the wake of the health-care debate has been the subject of much analysis, much of it exaggerating its long-term impact. A measured analysis is Everett Carll Ladd, "The 1994 Congressional Elections: The Postindustrial Realignment Continues," *Political Science Quarterly* 110 (April 1, 1995): 1–23. But see also Alfred J. Tuchfarber et al., "The Republican Tidal Wave of 1994: Testing Hypotheses about Realignment, Restructuring, and Rebellion," *PS: Political Science and Politics* 28 (December 1995): 689–696; Walter Dean Burnham, "Realignment Lives: The 1994 Earthquake and Its Implications," in Colin Campbell and Bert A Rockman, editors, *The Clinton Presidency: First Appraisals* (Chatham, NJ: Chatham House Publishers, 1996), 363–401; E. J. Dionne, *They Only Look Dead: Why Progressives Will Dominate the Next Political Era* (New York: Simon & Schuster, 1996); Philip A. Klinker, editor, *Midterm: The Elections of 1994 in Context* (Boulder, CO: Westview Press, 1996); and Douglas L. Koopman, *Hostile Takeover: The House Republican Party, 1980–1995* (Lanham, MD: Rowman & Littlefield, 1996).

On the relationship between Clinton, Newt Gingrich, and the Republican Congress, the best work is Steven M. Gillon, *The Pact: Bill Clinton, Newt Gingrich, and the Rivalry That Defined a Generation* (Oxford and New York: Oxford University Press, 2008). For all their public differences, Gillon persuasively argues, Clinton and Gingrich were kindred spirits. Linda Killian, *The Freshmen: What Happened to the Republican Revolution?* (Boulder, CO: Westview Press, 1998), is a richly detailed account of the efforts of Republicans elected in 1994 to put their ideas into policy. Elizabeth Drew, *Showdown* (New York: Simon & Schuster, 1996), also assesses the impact of the struggle between Clinton and the GOP Congress.

Welfare reform was second only to health care as the most controversial, complex, and divisive issue of Clinton's first term. Essential works on the evolution of the welfare system include Linda Gordon, *Pitied but Not Entitled: Single Mothers and the History of Welfare* (New York: Free Press, 1994); Michael B. Katz, *The Undeserving Poor: From the War on Poverty to the War on Welfare* (New York: Pantheon Books, 1989); Guida West, *The National Welfare Rights Movement: The Social Protest of Poor Women* (New York: Praeger, 1981). For an illuminating profile of the person behind Ronald Reagan's "welfare queen," see Josh Levin, "The Real Story of Linda Taylor, America's Original Welfare Queen," *Slate Magazine,* December 19, 2013. A masterful—and sympathetic—account of welfare reform is Ron Haskins, *Work over Welfare: The Inside Story of the 1996 Welfare Reform Law* (Washington, DC: Brookings Institution Press, 2006). It's an excellent, old-fashioned, how-a-bill-becomes-a-law account, of which there are few these days. Accounts critical of reform include Jason DeParle, *American Dream: Three Women, Ten Kids, and a Nation's Drive to End Welfare* (New York: Penguin Books, 2005), which also examines the Wisconsin experiment in welfare reform that helped inspire the national effort; Marisa Chappell, *The War on Welfare: Family, Poverty, and Politics in Modern America* (Philadelphia: University of Pennsylvania Press, 2010);

and Peter Edelman, *Searching for America's Heart: RFK and the Renewal of Hope* (Boston: Houghton Mifflin, 2001). Edelman resigned from the administration to protest Clinton's signing of the final reform bill, and his critique is scathing.

On the impact of welfare reform, no consensus has emerged. There are thoughtful, serious, empirically based assessments on both sides. Positive assessments include Bill Clinton, "How We Ended Welfare, Together," *New York Times*, August 22, 2006, and Haskins, *Work over Welfare*; Andrew J. Cherlin, "Can the Left Learn the Lessons of Welfare Reform?" *Contemporary Sociology* 37 (March 1, 2008): 101–104; and Ron Haskins, Vicky Albert, and Kimberly Howard, "The Responsiveness of the Temporary Assistance for Needy Families Program during the Great Recession," The Brookings Institution, http://www.brookings.edu/research/papers/2014/08 /responsiveness-tanf-great-recessions-haskins.

Marianne P. Bitler and Hillary W. Hoynes, "The State of the Social Safety Net in the Post-Welfare Reform Era," Brookings Papers on Economic Activity (Fall 2010): 71, summarizes the scholarly literature a decade after the passage of welfare reform and concludes, as of 2008, that "despite dire predictions, previous research has shown that program caseloads declined and employment increased, with no detectible increase in poverty or worsening of child well-being." Serious critical assessments include, in addition to Edelmen, "Families Feel Sharp Edge of State Budget Cuts," *New York Times*, September 6, 2011; US Census Bureau, "Income, Poverty, and Health Insurance Coverage in the United States: 2010"; Jason DeParle and Sabrina Tavernise, "Poor Are Still Getting Poorer, but Downturn's Punch Varies, Census Data Show," *New York Times*, September 15, 2011; Jake Blumgart, "Happy Birthday, Welfare Reform," *American Prospect*, August 19, 2011; and Thomas Edsall, "Cutting the Poor out of Welfare," *New York Times*, June 18, 2014.

Accounts of Clinton's stunning reelection campaign in 1996 include Evan Thomas, *Back from the Dead: How Clinton Survived the Republican Revolution* (New York: Atlantic Monthly Press, 1997); James W. Ceaser and Andrew E. Busch, *Losing to Win: The 1996 Elections and American Politics* (Lanham, MD: Rowman & Littlefield, 1997); and the always reliable Gerald M. Pomper, *The Election of 1996: Reports and Interpretations* (Chatham, NJ: Chatham House Publishers, 1997). The Clinton campaign's innovative tactics are described in Douglas B. Sosnik, *Applebee's America: How Successful Political, Business, and Religious Leaders Connect with the New American Community* (New York: Simon & Schuster, 2006), 11–27, and D. Hillygus, *The Persuadable Voter: Wedge Issues in Presidential Campaigns* (Princeton, NJ: Princeton University Press, 2009), 12–13. The use of wedge issues such as abortion, gay marriage, and immigration has become standard political strategy in contemporary presidential campaigns. Why do candidates use such divisive appeals? Who in the electorate is persuaded by these controversial issues? And what are the consequences for American democracy? In this provocative and engaging analysis of presidential campaigns, Sunshine Hillygus and Todd Shields identify the types of citizens responsive to campaign information, the reasons they are responsive, and the tactics candidates use to sway these pivotal voters. Even Clinton's supporters disagreed among themselves about why Clinton had prevailed, as demonstrated by the illuminating debate between New and Old Democrats in Will Marshall, "Controversy: Why Did Clinton Win?" *American Prospect*, December 19, 2001 (http:// prospect.org/article/controversy-why-did-clinton-win).

In 1996 and later, Clinton was able to go over the heads of a hostile Congress by employing the executive power and rule-making authority of the presidency. The seminal work on the subject is Elena Kagan, "Presidential Administration," *Harvard Law Review* 114 (June 1, 2001): 2245–2385. But see also William G. Howell, "Introduction: Unilateral Powers: A Brief Overview," *Presidential Studies Quarterly* 35 (Sept. 2005): 417–439; Phillip J. Cooper, *By Order of the President: The Use and Abuse of Executive Direct Action* (Lawrence: University Press of Kansas, 2002); and Kenneth R. Mayer, *With the Stroke of a Pen: Executive Orders and Presidential Power* (Princeton, NJ: Princeton University Press, 2001). For a sharp critique of Clinton's use of his power to pardon, especially in the case of Marc Rich, see Louis Fisher, "The Law: When Presidential Power Backfires: Clinton's Use of Clemency," *Presidential Studies Quarterly* 32 (Sept. 2002): 586–599.

To say that the Clintons were polarizing figures does not do justice to the passions they aroused. A sampling of the voluminous anti-Clinton literature would include Ann H. Coulter, *High Crimes and Misdemeanors: The Case against Bill Clinton* (Washington, DC: Regnery, 1998); Christopher Ruddy, *The Strange Death of Vincent Foster: An Investigation* (New York: Free Press, 1997); Dan E. Moldea, *A Washington Tragedy: How the Death of Vincent Foster Ignited a Political Firestorm* (Washington, DC: Regnery, 1998); anything by R. Emmett Tyrell, including *The Impeachment of William Jefferson Clinton: A Political Docu-Drama* (Washington, DC: Regnery, 1997); Ambrose Evans-Pritchard, *The Secret Life of Bill Clinton: The Unreported Stories* (Washington, DC: Regnery, 1997); David Brock, *The Seduction of Hillary Rodham* (New York: Free Press, 1996); Brock's "Trooper-Gate" articles in *The American Spectator*; Peggy Noonan, *The Case against Hillary Clinton* (New York: Regan Books / Harper-Collins, 2000); Barbara Olson, *Hell to Pay: The Untold Story of Hillary Rodham Clinton* (Washington, DC: Regnery, 1999); and *The Final Days: The Last, Desperate Abuses of Power by the Clinton White House* (Washington, DC: Regnery, 2001). The following also provide insight into the minds of the anti-Clintonites: Gail Sheehy, *Hillary's Choice* (New York: Random House, 1999); Jerry Oppenheimer, *State of a Union: Inside the Complex Marriage of Bill and Hillary Clinton* (New York: Harper Collins Publishers, 2000); and Joyce Milton, *The First Partner: Hillary Rodham Clinton* (New York: William Morrow, 1999).

Defenses of the Clintons include Joe Conason and Gene Lyons, *The Hunting of the President: The Ten-Year Campaign to Destroy Bill and Hillary Clinton* (New York: St. Martin's Press, 2001); Gene Lyons, *Fools for Scandal: How the Media Invented Whitewater* (New York: Franklin Square Press, 1996); the previously mentioned David Brock, who recants his past in *Blinded by the Right: Conscience of an Ex-conservative* (New York: Crown, 2001); Jeffrey Toobin, *A Vast Conspiracy: The Real Story of the Sex Scandal That Nearly Brought Down a President* (New York: Random House, 2000); and numerous selections in Susan K. Flinn, editor, *Speaking of Hillary: A Reader's Guide to the Most Controversial Woman in America* (Ashland, OR: White Cloud Press, 2000)—an excellent collection of pro and con pieces by the likes of Camille Paglia, Ellen Goodman, Anna Quindlen, Meg Greenfield, Doris Kearns Goodwin, Maureen Dowd, and many others. The standout essay may be Henry Louis Gates, "Hating Hillary." Works that demonstrate the insights to be gained by examining the images presidents project include John William Ward, *Andrew Jackson: Symbol for an Age* (New York: Oxford University Press, 1955); Garry

Wills, *Reagan's America: Innocents at Home* (Garden City, NY: Doubleday, 1987); and Merrill D. Peterson, *The Jefferson Image in the American Mind* (New York: Oxford University Press, 1960). Greil Marcus's provocative pieces on Clinton, collected in *Double Trouble: Bill Clinton and Elvis Presley in a Land of No Alternatives* (New York: Henry Holt, 2000), discuss how people were simultaneously attracted to and repelled by Clinton's identity as a poor white Southerner. He, like Elvis, was fine so long as "he didn't get above his raising." Marcus's essays also serve as a reminder of the importance of popular culture in understanding modern American politics.

Works that discuss Clinton's relationship with black Americans include Toni Morrison's famous "first black president" essay, "Talk of the Town: Comment," *New Yorker*, October 5, 1998, 31–32; DeWayne Wickham, *Bill Clinton and Black America* (New York: Ballantine, 2002); and Lani Guinier's previously mentioned memoir.

On impeachment, the key works are Peter Baker, *The Breach: Inside the Impeachment and Trial of William Jefferson Clinton* (New York: Scribner, 2000), the most concise overview; Richard Posner, *An Affair of State: The Investigation, Impeachment, and Trial of President Clinton* (Cambridge, MA: Harvard University Press, 1999), a critique of impeachment from a conservative perspective; Michael Isikoff, *Uncovering Clinton: A Reporter's Story* (New York: Crown Publishers, 1999); Susan Schmidt and Michael Weisskopf, *Truth at Any Cost: Ken Starr and the Unmaking of Bill Clinton* (New York: Harper Collins, 2000), which is sympathetic to Kenneth Starr and the Special Prosecutor's Office. In a class by itself is Ken Gormley, *The Death of American Virtue: Clinton vs. Starr* (New York: Crown Publishers, 2010), a Rashomon-like account that gives both sides, including Clinton and Starr, their say. Better than perhaps any other work, *The Death of American Virtue* documents the divide that led to political dysfunction. Other works of note include Joan Didion, *Political Fictions* (New York: Alfred A. Knopf, 2001); James B. Stewart, *Blood Sport: the President and His Adversaries* (New York: Simon & Schuster, 1996), a detailed account of the convoluted Whitewater affair that absolves the Clintons of criminality but not egregious errors in judgment; and Elizabeth Drew, *The Corruption of American Politics: What Went Wrong and Why* (Woodstock, NY: Overlook Press, 2000), which discusses a subject that probably deserves more attention than it got: alleged campaign finance scandals. *The Starr Report: The Findings of Independent Counsel Kenneth W. Starr on President Clinton and the Lewinsky Affair with Analysis by the Staff of the Washington Post* (New York: Public Affairs, 1998) is a useful version of Starr's X-Rated document.

The president's Initiative on Race, which was overshadowed by impeachment, is discussed in John Hope Franklin, *Mirror to America: The Autobiography of John Hope Franklin* (New York: Farrar, Straus and Giroux, 2005); Steven F. Lawson, "One America in the 21st Century," http://yalepress.yale.edu/yupbooks/book.asp?isbn=9780300116694; and Lila Docken Bauman, "Talking toward One America: The President's Initiative on Race (1997–1998) in the Press and Local Community" (PhD diss., New York University, 2002). Also overshadowed was the equally ambitious "National Conversation on American Pluralism and Identity," spearheaded by Clinton's appointee to head the National Endowment for the Humanities, Sheldon Hackney. Hackney described the project in *One America Indivisible: A National*

Conversation on American Pluralism and Identity (Washington, DC: National Endowment for the Humanities, 1997).

Even though foreign policy has not received the attention it deserved, it has produced some of the best writing there is on the Clinton presidency. Excellent introductions to the subject are "Clinton's Foreign Policy," *Foreign Policy* 121 (November-December, 2000): 18–29, and Stephen M. Walt, "Two Cheers for Clinton's Foreign Policy," *Foreign Affairs* 79 (March-April 2000): 63–79, both of which are balanced but generally sympathetic; and on the negative side, see William G. Hyland, *Clinton's World: Remaking American Foreign Policy* (Westport, CT: Praeger, 1999), which argues that Clinton blew a great opportunity at the beginning of his administration to fashion a new role for the United States in the world. Drawing on his own experiences, Strobe Talbott puts Clinton's foreign policy in broad historical perspective in *The Great Experiment: The Story of Ancient Empires, Modern States, and the Quest for a Global Nation* (New York: Simon & Schuster, 2008). Important overviews include David Halberstam, *War in a Time of Peace: Bush, Clinton, and the Generals* (New York: Scribner, 2001), with its colorful but critical portraits of the Clinton team and its discussion of how Vietnam continued to haunt policy makers; Richard Sale's crisply written, informative, and opinionated *Clinton's Secret Wars: The Evolution of a Commander in Chief* (New York: St. Martin's Press, 2009), which argues that after a dithering start Clinton gained his footing and became a bold and decisive commander in chief. Especially important is Samantha Power, *A Problem from Hell: America and the Age of Genocide* (New York: Basic Books, 2002). Powerfully argued, this is a book to be reckoned with. Critical of Clinton's failure to respond to the Rwandan crisis and his slowness to act in Kosovo, Power ties Clinton to a century of American neglect of genocide, including the Holocaust. But like those who argue that FDR should have done more to avert the Holocaust, Power maximizes hindsight and minimizes the political realities of the time. Ryan C. Hendrickson, *The Clinton Wars: The Constitution, Congress, and War Powers* (Nashville, TN: Vanderbilt University Press, 2002), documents the administration's accretion of war powers at the expense of Congress, as does Geoffrey S. Corn's detailed "Clinton, Kosovo, and the Final Destruction of the War Powers Resolution," *William and Mary Law Review* 42 (2001): 1149–1190. The lawsuit filed by members of Congress challenging President Clinton's war-making authority can be accessed at: http://lawofwar.org/campbell_v_Clinton.htm. Robert D. Kaplan's *Balkan Ghosts: A Journey through History* (New York: St. Martin's Press, 1993), is the book recommended to Clinton by Colin Powell that made the president wary of intervention in the Balkans.

The writings of administration members shed much light on the conduct of foreign policy and military affairs. Strobe Talbott, *The Russia Hand: A Memoir of Presidential Diplomacy* (New York: Random House, 2003), beyond its indispensable account of US-Russian relations, describes Clinton's efforts to articulate a compelling description of post–Cold War policy. Samuel R. Berger, "A Foreign Policy for the Global Age," *Foreign Affairs* 79 (November-December, 2000): 22–39, comes as close as anyone to articulating a "Clinton Doctrine." Warren Christopher, *In the Stream of History: Shaping Foreign Policy for a New Era* (Stanford, CA: Stanford University Press, 1998), is a neglected collection of speeches and commentaries by Clinton's first secretary of state, carefully laying out the rationale for administration policies during the first term. Christopher's successor, Madeleine Albright, *Madam Secretary* (New York: Miramax Books, 2003), does the same for the second term. Albright's candid recollections also shed light on internal divisions within the administration, as does Richard C. Holbrooke's riveting account of American intervention in Bosnia, *To End a War* (New York: Random House, 1998). See also Anthony Lake, *Six Nightmares* (Boston: Little, Brown, 2000), and on the administration's role in diffusing the dangerous conflict between India and Pakistan, Bruce O. Riedel, *Avoiding Armageddon: America, India, and Pakistan to the Brink and Back* (Washington, DC: Brookings Institution Press, 2013), especially 103–136.

9/11 necessarily focused attention on the Clinton administration's response to terrorism. Steve Coll, *Ghost Wars: The Secret History of the CIA, Afghanistan, and Bin Laden, from the Soviet Invasion to September 10, 2001* (New York: Penguin Books, 2004), is the essential starting point for an understanding of how the administration's response evolved as the nature of the threat came more into focus. Richard Sale, *Clinton's Secret Wars*, accords the administration high marks, arguing that Clinton acted more forcefully than was known at the time. Despite their retrospective finger-pointing, the memoirs of several administration members are important: Richard A. Clarke, *Against All Enemies: Inside America's War on Terror* (New York: Free Press, 2004); Michael Scheuer, *Osama bin Laden* (Oxford and New York: Oxford University Press, 2011); George Tenet, *At the Center of the Storm: My Years at the CIA* (New York: Harper Collins, 2007); and the previously mentioned Louis J. Freeh, *My FBI*. The public testimony of administration officials before the 9/11 Commission is recorded in *The 9/11 Commission Report: The Final Report of the National Commission on Terrorist Attacks upon the United States* (Washington, DC: U.S. Government Printing Office, 2004). Jane Mayer, *The Dark Side: The Inside Story of How the War on Terror Turned into a War on American Ideals* (New York and London: Doubleday, 2008), is an important study of extraordinary rendition that puts most of the blame on Clinton's successor.

For other aspects of diplomatic and military policy see, on Somalia, Mark Bowden, *Black Hawk Down: A Story of Modern War* (New York: Atlantic Monthly Press, 1999); on Haiti, Philippe R. Girard, *Clinton in Haiti: The 1994 US Invasion of Haiti* (New York: Palgrave Macmillan, 2004), and Ralph Pezzullo, *Plunging into Haiti: Clinton, Aristide, and the Defeat of Diplomacy* (Jackson: University Press of Mississippi, 2006); on the peace agreement in Northern Ireland, George J. Mitchell, *Making Peace* (New York: Knopf, 1999); on the Balkans, Robert Thomas, *The Politics of Serbia in the 1990s* (New York: Columbia University Press, 1999), Tim Judah, *Kosovo: War and Revenge* (New Haven: Yale University Press, 2000), Judah, *Kosovo: What Everyone Needs to Know* (Oxford and New York: Oxford University Press, 2008); and Wesley K. Clark, *Waging Modern War: Bosnia, Kosovo, and the Future of Combat* (New York: Public Affairs, 2001). A concise, even-handed treatment of almost all of the administration's diplomatic ventures is Warren John Dumbrell, *Clinton's Foreign Policy: Between the Bushes, 1992–2000* (London and New York: Routledge/Taylor & Francis, 2009).

On Camp David II and US Middle East policy in general, the memoirs of Bill Clinton and Madeleine Albright are important, but the indispensible work is Dennis Ross, *The Missing Peace: The Inside Story of the Fight for Middle East Peace* (New York: Farrar, Straus, and Giroux, 2004), a first-hand account by Clinton's chief Middle East envoy who had also served in the Carter, Reagan, and George H. W. Bush administrations. Ross, however, must be read alongside Robert Malley and Hussein Agha, "Camp David: The Tragedy of Errors," *New York Review of Books* 48 (August 9, 2001), which challenges the Clinton-Ross view that Yasser Arafat was primarily responsible for the failure of Camp David. See also in this regard, Aaron David Miller, "The Long Dance: Searching for Arab-Israeli Peace," *The Wilson Quarterly* 32 (Spring 2008): 38–44. A much-needed first-hand account of Camp David from the Palestinian perspective is Akram Hanieth, "The Camp David Papers," *Journal of Palestine Studies* 30 (Winter 2001): 75–97.

Useful scholarly treatments include William L. Cleveland and Martin Bunton, *A History of the Modern Middle East* (Boulder, CO: Westview Press, 2013), 464–480, a concise and balanced overview; William B. Quandt, "Clinton and the Arab-Israeli Conflict: The Limits of Incrementalism," *Journal of Palestine Studies* 30 (Winter 2001): 26–40; Jerome Slater, "What Went Wrong? The Collapse of the Israeli-Palestinian Peace Process," *Political Science Quarterly* 116 (Summer 2001): 171–199, which blames Israel for the Camp David impasse; and Myron J. Aronoff, "Camp David Rashomon: Contested Interpretations of the Israeli/Palestine Peace Process," *Political Science Quarterly* 124 (Spring 2009): 143–167, a thoughtful summary and analysis of the conflicting perspectives on Camp David.

On Clinton's post-presidential career, Burton I. Kaufman, in *The Post-Presidency from Washington to Clinton* (Lawrence: University Press of Kansas, 2012), provides a succinct account. Of the hundreds of profiles that have appeared since Clinton left office, several are particularly revealing: Jennifer Senior, "Bill Clinton's Plan for World Domination," *New York Magazine*, August 22, 2005; Peter Baker, "The Mellowing of William Jefferson Clinton," *New York Times Magazine*, May 31, 2009, 40–47, 80–82; and Simon Schama, "Bill Clinton Talks to Simon Schama," *Financial Times*, October 14, 2011. Peter Schweizer, *Clinton Cash: The Untold Story of How and Why Foreign Governments and Businesses Helped Make Bill And Hillary Rich* (New York: Harper, 2015), is a scathing account by a longtime critic of the Clinton Foundation and its foreign fund-raising activities.